Key Terms in Latino/a Cultural and Literary Studies

D1294287

Key Terms in Latino/a Cultural and Literary Studies

Paul Allatson

Blackwell
Publishing

© 2007 by Paul Allatson

BLACKWELL PUBLISHING
350 Main Street, Malden, MA 02148-5020, USA
9600 Garsington Road, Oxford OX4 2DQ, UK
550 Swanston Street, Carlton, Victoria 3053, Australia

The right of Paul Allatson to be identified as the Author of this Work has been asserted in accordance with the UK Copyright, Designs, and Patents Act 1988.

All rights reserved. No part of this publication may be reproduced, stored in a retrieval system, or transmitted, in any form or by any means, electronic, mechanical, photocopying, recording or otherwise, except as permitted by the UK Copyright, Designs, and Patents Act 1988, without the prior permission of the publisher.

First published 2007 by Blackwell Publishing Ltd

Library of Congress Cataloging-in-Publication Data

Allatson, Paul.
  Key terms in Latino/a cultural and literary studies / Paul Allatson.
    p. cm.
  Includes bibliographical references.
  ISBN-13: 978-1-4051-0250-6 (hbk. : alk. paper)
  ISBN-10: 1-4051-0250-0 (hbk. : alk. paper)
  ISBN-13: 978-1-4051-0251-3 (pbk. : alk. paper)
  ISBN-10: 1-4051-0251-9 (pbk. : alk. paper) 1. Hispanic Americans—Intellectual life—Dictionaries. 2. Hispanic Americans—Social life and customs—Dictionaries. 3. Hispanic Americans—Social conditions—Dictionaries. 4. Hispanic Americans—Study and teaching—Dictionaries. 5. American literature—Hispanic American authors—Study and teaching—Dictionaries. I. Title.

  E184.S75A795 2007
  973'.0468003—dc22

                                                    2006026267

A catalogue record for this title is available from the British Library.

Set in Bell Gothic 9.75/14
by NewGen Imaging Systems Pvt Ltd., Chennai, India

For further information on
Blackwell Publishing, visit our website:
www.blackwellpublishing.com

To my mother,
for teaching me to read
and abetting my curiosity about the world

Contents

xii *Contents*

Acknowledgments

Many people have responded kindly to and influenced the contents of this book and, by extension, my slant on its critical concerns and selection of material. Primary thanks go to Laura Gutiérrez, who was originally to collaborate on this project, and who did so much to support its genesis. Laura's inputs, and our discussions about Latino/a cultures, have meant that *Key Terms* is much richer than it otherwise would have been. I particularly want to acknowledge Laura's contributions to the following entries: **Adelita, Bato/a, Charco, Corrido, Mojado/a, Nuyorican Aesthetics, Pocho/a, Quinceañera, Ranchera, Rap and Hip-Hop, Rasquachismo, Rock en español, Salsa, Teatro Campesino,** and ***Telenovela.*** I am greatly indebted to the following people for their conversation, feedback, and friendship: Susana Chávez-Silverman, Andrea Connor, Trish Hill, and Alberto Sandoval-Sánchez. Thanks to Vek Lewis for his inputs. I could not have hoped for better support from the team at Blackwell: Jayne Fargnoli, Annie Lenth (in her time there), Ken Provencher, and the many other people involved in producing this book. Their faith in this project was unwavering, as was their patient understanding of the vicissitudes of personal and professional life. I received great sustenance from my colleagues at the Institute for International Studies (IIS), at the University of Technology Sydney. Jeffrey Browitt, Murray Pratt, and Maja Mikula, Marivic Wyndham, in particular, provided astute responses to specific entries, while my graduate student Mariana Rodríguez was a wonderful sounding board, for which I am grateful. I am also indebted to the students in my Contemporary Latino USA classes who (unwittingly) tested the usefulness of many of this book's entries. Finally, for nudging me at my desk as a prelude to our daily walks I must acknowledge my dog, Dougal. Throughout the evolution of this book he has been the best and most grounding of mates.

Introduction

In the most general of senses, Latino/a Studies designate studies of the USA's many communities with origins in the Hispanophone-dominant parts of the Americas, a heterogeneous conglomerate of peoples that is now the USA's largest collective minority. This broad ambit needs, nonetheless, to be qualified by the fact that Latino/a Studies are anchored historically in scholarship about, or emanating from, two communities: Chicano/as or Mexican Americans; and US-resident Puerto Ricans. As a consequence of that history, Latino/a Studies is a rapidly evolving comparative academic enterprise and a field with a long critical genealogy in distinct areas of scholarship. As Aparicio has observed, "Latino Studies is an academic imaginary in a very literal sense of the word. It is still in the state of desire, it is still a potential rather than fact, a field very much in its initial makings despite the three decades of scholarly production in Chicano Studies, Puerto Rican Studies, and the emerging Cuban American, Central American and Dominican scholarship" (1999: 4). The field-in-the-making description remains apposite when one considers that the first significant critical texts to take a comparative approach to Latino/a cultures appeared in the late 1980s, with a steady increase in publication density ever since. Over the same period sector-specific studies have continued to shape the evolution of Latino/a Studies.

To speak of Latino/a Studies and to work under that rubric present practitioners with a number of challenges, beyond the community divisions that marked the field's genesis and influenced its development. Perhaps the most significant challenge arises because Latino/a Studies cannot be located unequivocally in any one discipline or university teaching and research structure.

Investigative and critical work in Latino/a Studies, especially the cultural and literary terrains dealt with in this book, span a multidisciplinary spectrum. That multidisciplinarity requires of Latino/a critics, by necessity, broad research and theoretical capacities. One practical result of this situation is that practitioners of Latino/a Studies may continue to encounter a range of institutional obstacles derived from the inherent disciplinary unhomeliness of the field. For example, do Latino/a literary studies, which deal with texts written in English, Spanish, or Spanglish, or any or all of those options in combination, belong in Departments of English or American (US) literature, or their Spanish and Latin American equivalents, or both? As Debra Castillo argues, "beyond the mere modifying [of] existing curricula and introducing texts," studies of Latino/a literature, especially that written in Spanish, which tends to be neglected in English-dominant American literary studies, require "changing ways of thinking in the academic sites where authority is vested in particular disciplinary and departmental divisions of labor" (2005: 194). For Castillo, a "larger pan-American critical context for scholarly inquiry" is required in order to better accommodate the multiple geocultural and linguistic drives of much Latino/a cultural and critical practice (2005: 194).

Yet, underwriting Castillo's criticism of institutional limits is her recognition that the inherent border-disturbing multidisciplinarity of Latino/a Studies also gives the field its fundamental strength. Latino/a Studies designates a rich body of critical work whose geopolitical, transcultural, and linguistic drives often target the structural and discursive borders of the USA. That geopolity, it must be emphasized, provides the national base in and against which Latino/a has arisen as a meaningful, yet disputed, mutable and strategically adopted identificatory and communal option. In that national setting, "America" functions as a key locus of dispute in the field. Latino/a cultural and critical work has a potentially productive, because disruptive, critical, and imaginative relation to the purportedly fixed boundaries of the state—and its predominant culture, language, and discourses of belonging—that has made "America" its formal and informal name. Poblete argues that Latino Studies engages in this political and imaginative struggle from a location "in the borders of ethnic and area studies" (2003: xv). That borderline emplacement offers practitioners an "analytical space where borders themselves can be investigated and with them all kinds of transnational, translingual, and transcultural phenomena. Thus Latino/a studies can, in this view, perform the very healthy job of criticizing the nation-centered limitations of area and ethnic paradigms" (2003: xv). Important Latino/a critical work against dominant national, area, and ethnic paradigms is exemplified, to name only three examples, by the borderlands as a geospatial concept in Chicano/a Studies, by LatCrit Theory, which has critiqued the Black/White Paradigm in legal discourse, and by the Latino Cultural Studies Working Group and its development of the concept of cultural citizenship (Flores and Benmayor 1997). Such critical drives have broad implications for global understandings of the USA and its latinized place in the Americas.

Another challenge arises out of the very name that defines Latino/a Studies, and that provides the field with its ostensible subjects *and* objects of study: Latino/a. Who and what are included under that rubric is neither unproblematic nor self-evident. Do large numbers of recently arrived migrants from Mexico, Central America, the Caribbean, and such states as Peru and Colombia, fall automatically into the Latino/a category, particularly given that many of these migrants may be indigenous and speak their own languages rather than Spanish? Do the Chicano/a and Puerto Rican historical minorities continue to have a shaping role in the changing discourses of Latinidad? How do the factors of class status, gender, desire, generation, length of familial residency, Spanish-language proficiency, processes of racialization, panethnic interactions, and new transnational constructions of family and community affect the terrains of *lo latino* and associated critical practice? Do sector studies (for instance, Chicano, Cuban American, Nuyorican Studies) make much sense, given the increasing demographic dispersal and intermixing of these and other Latino/a communities, the inevitable quotidian relationships that those communities have with non-Latino/a sectors, and the complex modes of identification and structures of feeling that link peoples and places across geopolitical borders?

Disputes about the parameters of Latino/a continue among Latino/a critics and in the broader terrains of sociocultural, economic, and political life. Much of that terminological argument arises because the term jostles against—and is often cast as a critical, political, and imaginative rival to—Hispanic, the word preferred by government, media, and commercial apparatuses alike, and which inevitably evokes and privileges the Spanish sociocultural and linguistic base or inheritance. This is not simply a semantic squabble, however: "Latino/a" is a self-chosen designation whereas "Hispanic" is a state-imposed one. As Noriega points out, the strategic adoption of Latino arose in the 1980s "because—in the popular imagination, governmental classification, and mass media distribution—specific Latino/a groups are not understood in national terms" (1993: 46). For Noriega Latino/a does not signify an ethnic identity that overrides the specific national or ethnic categories of Chicano/a, Mexican, Puerto Rican, Cuban, Dominican, Colombian, and so on. Rather, Latino/a connotes "the hilo/thread for a social movement to remap 'America,' and—in a more immediate sense—for negotiating the representation of specific histories/identities as part of the national culture" (1993: 46). This is a crucial, but highly debated, point. For many commentators the political bedrock of Latino/a Studies is located in the civil rights struggles of the 1960s and 1970s, and the attendant nationalist and antiracist drives of the Chicano and Puerto Rican movements in particular (Aparicio 1999; Oboler 1999). The explicit political basis of Latino/a Studies in that era is recalled whenever practitioners attempt to keep the memory and achievements of former struggles alive and meaningful for younger generations, Latino/a and otherwise, in the century in which Latinos became the USA's largest collective minority. It seems appropriate here to recognize that for the rest of the twenty-first century, the diverse Latino/a sectors will continue to grow in number and influence. While noting the epistemological problems of Census Bureau categories, and the census's routine undercounting of Latino/as, most observers accept census projections that the combined Latino/a population will represent one quarter of the total population by, or before, 2050. Note that this is not intended to replicate what Juan Flores calls the demographic mentality that reduces the multiple axes of Latino/a "unity and diversity" to a statistical subset (2000). Rather, it is to recognize that those developments will modulate, if not transform, a field that arose from an important moment in modern US history. Confronted by the changing contours of Latinidades (panethnic identifications and affiliations) and their importance in US culture, Latino/a Studies will continue to intervene in and potentially reform such areas of scholarship as "American" and Latin American studies (in all their disciplinary guises), ethnic, race and immigration studies, postcolonial studies as well as studies of national and transnational identity and cultural formation, popular culture, and globalization.

The rapid evolution and internationalization of a field that targets the borders of the "American" trans/national also means that Latino/a Studies is no longer a critical enterprise with US or continental parameters only. The field now has practitioners across the globe, and valuable contributions are being made throughout Europe, as well as in the Caribbean, Canada, Mexico, and

Australia. Latino/a critics have, with qualification, welcomed that internation-alization. Oboler has called for a nuanced multidisciplinary and transnational Latino/a Studies praxis that nonetheless grounds itself in "US Latinos' diverse history, cultures and experiences," while respecting and maintaining the field's "originating *raison d'être* (i.e., the struggle against racism) and the need to reinforce a societal and political response to racism as essential to the strengthening of citizenship" (1999: 23). The field, she emphasizes, "must be rooted in both a national and a hemispheric understanding of the ongoing racialization of people of Latin American descent in the United States" (1999: 24). As Oboler points out, Latino/a Studies must acknowledge the his-torical legacies of US–Latin American relations while attending closely to the national setting in which the entities of "Latino" and "Hispanic" arose as identity or taxonomic categories, variously conceived and deployed to desig-nate racial, ethnic, cultural, linguistic, and/or national differences from a pur-portedly dominant US norm (1999: 35). Oboler's compelling reading of the challenges faced by Latino/a Studies is one that other critics have made when advocating a Latino/a "cultural and political space of transamerican and transatlantic scale" (Poblete 2003: xxi). That said, Latino/a spaces are also at work beyond the Americas and the historical axes of European American and European Indigenous African contact that preoccupy such critics. Alongside the critical tasks identified by such commentators, Latino/a Studies is also impelled to acknowledge how the field's practitioners are implicated in the processes by which the heterogeneous Latino/a entity also influences the oper-ations of cultural imaginaries and critical work beyond the American hemi-sphere. *Lo latino* is no longer an "American" concern.

This extra-American interest in Latino/a Studies, and the need for that interest, can be illustrated by numerous examples. A case in point since the 1980s has been the German embrace of Chicano/a theoretical positions when explaining the Turkish *Gastarbeiter* (guest worker) predicament. Translations of the borderlands concept have also been applied to the Palestinian and Israeli conflict, and it is increasingly common to encounter that concept in European cultural and immigration studies. Another example is provided by the migra-tion trajectories at work in such states as Canada, Spain, and Australia, where the categorical trouble inherent in and to "Latino" is being felt and managed by Latin American-origin populations. All three states have growing commun-ities derived from Latin America. Indeed, Spain has seen the arrival of large numbers of Latin American immigrants since the early 1990s, Ecuadorians now jostling with Moroccans for most populous minority group. Many of those migrants have Latino/a relatives in the USA, and it is increasingly common to encounter people in Spain whose worldview spans three states, their lived practices and identificatory shifts challenging nation-based discourses of belonging. Canada has seen a rapid growth in its Latino/a population since the 1970s, and Canadian Latino/a cultural productions are now attracting the attention of scholars interested in the transnationalization of Latinidades (Habell-Pallán 2005). In Australia, the word Latino/a has become common-place in the quotidian life of Sydney, which hosts a "Latino" festival each January, and which has seen the rise of "Latino" magazines and community organizations. Like the country as a whole, Sydney has also witnessed a pop-ular cultural obsession with Latin/o culture, as attested by the proliferation of suburban salsa schools and by the fact that Spanish has become one of the most popular languages of choice at university level.

While such phenomena have not yet attracted the deep critical attention they merit, it is arguable that they signify the emergence of new Latinizing transnational links, communal relations, and cultural flows spanning the Atlantic and Pacific Oceans. Such phenomena may also signpost the ways by which Latin American-origin communities are inserting themselves into the options provided them by local official discourses of multiculturalism, dis-courses whose bureaucratic evolution do not replicate US paradigms or strug-gles. Yet the appearances of "Latino" in a state such as Australia could also be interpreted as evidence of the USA's global pop cultural and capitalist influence. By this I mean the process by which a specific US identificatory term—along with the erotic-exotic aura and cultural capital that gets attached to its bearers—is received and remade on local terms without due awareness or discussion of the term's complex circulations, and fraught historical origins, at home. Indeed, given that Latino/a cultural productions made inside US borders are circulated in a global capitalist system that has long stopped regarding state frontiers as a barrier, those mobilities inevitably generate ques-tions about the local, national, and transnational meanings, values, imaginative uses, memories, and locations that accrue to Latino/a cultural products and to the Latino/a critical modes that have sought to interpret them. This pre-amble is one way of saying that Latino/a Studies is a central enterprise in the broader critical drive to forge new transnational and transcultural under-standings of US and trans-American sociocultural life, and of the USA's global reach as well.

Overview of *Key Terms*

Key Terms in Latino/a Cultural and Literary Studies is intended as a contribution to a rich field that is by turns local, regional, national, hemispherical, and global in scope and message. In meeting the needs of students, teachers, researchers, and interested readers, the book has a number of overarching aims. It concentrates on Latino/a cultural and literary production and critical developments since the 1960s and the concomitant rise of the so-called Hispanic generation in the USA. This volume provides accessible definitions of critical and cultural concepts in Latino/a cultural and literary studies, and acknowledges the critical interplay between Latino/a, American (US), Latin American, and other cultural studies traditions. *Key Terms* draws sustenance from specific Latino/a sector studies while attending in a comparative sense to the historical, geopolitical, and cultural convergences and divergences of Latino/a experiences. It acknowledges both the multidisciplinarity and the internationalization of the field. The book also accepts that the growing audience outside the USA for Latino/a cultural production and criticism requires particular attention to matters of historical context that might otherwise be taken for granted by US readers.

The glossary of Latino/a cultural and literary studies terms consists of some 230 entries, ranging in length from brief descriptions to extended discussions. Arranged alphabetically (from **ABC Generation, Generation Ñ** to **Zoot Suiters, Zoot Suit Riots**), the content is wide ranging and encompasses Latino/a critical and theoretical concepts, cultural and literary practices and forms, Spanish-origin and Spanglish terms that appear in the critical literature and cultural productions, significant historical terms, and discussions of broader sociocultural and transnational processes. Bold terms in a glossary entry indicate cross-references to other terms in the glossary. For example, the entry on the **Pachuco/a** refers to the **Zoot Suit Riots** elsewhere in the glossary. Given that many excellent "Hispanic" and "Latino" biographical dictionaries, encyclopedias, and library reference works already exist, entries on individual historical figures are not provided in this book. Similarly, the availability of critical glossaries in cultural and literary studies has freed this book from having to replicate material readily found elsewhere. This book complements such resources by providing entry points into Latino/a cultural, literary, and theoretical drives that are routinely omitted in generalist works. Throughout this book I have striven to respect the dialogic qualities of diverse Latino/a critical and creative practices. My aim has been to inform as much as it has been to produce a critical transcultural story. This approach reflects the influence on my own critical practice of the Cuban Fernando Ortiz, who in 1940 coined the neologism 'transculturation' and elaborated on it in, and through, evocative historical and critical story-telling (1940a, 1995). The entries in *Key Terms* aspire to that ideal.

ABC Generation, Generation Ñ

The ABC Generation (American-Born Cubans or Cuban-Bred Americans) designates the US-born and -raised children of the Cuban **diaspora**. According to Pérez Firmat (1994), the ABC Generation has no direct experiences or memories of Cuba and is more at home in the host society than in the parents' transplanted Cuban ambit. The ABC Generation thus occupies the assimilated end of a migratory line that begins with Cuban-born and -raised exiles and moves to the **One-and-a-Halfers**, the Cuban-born but US-raised generation who are comfortable in displaced Cuban and Anglo-American host cultures alike. A related term, Generation Ñ (*Generación Ñ*), refers to the US-born children of the One-and-a-Halfers. De La Torre (2003) notes that although this term signals a Latino/a variant of Generation X (the generation following the baby-boomers), it has been adopted by younger **Cuban Americans** to differentiate themselves from older Cubans. Members of Generation Ñ claim to differ from those of Generation X, and other Latino/as, in four ways: they are (a) bicultural and bilingual, (b) middle class and professional, (c) pro-"American" without accepting an inevitable deculturation of their Cubanness, and (d) lighter skinned than the majority of working-class Latino/as. With these class and racial coordinates, Generation Ñ appears to define a conservative and privileged subset of the ABC Generation.

Active–Passive Matrix

The active–passive matrix is a social science term that describes the sociocultural conventions or bodily economy by which gender and sexual appearances, behaviors, relations, and practices in Latin American and Latino/a societies are popularly structured and interpreted. Sometimes referred to as the Mediterranean model of sexuality, the active–passive matrix allocates positive and negative values to the differentiated social conduct of men and woman. Men are presumed to be bearers of the active (penetrative) sexual principle, typified by the hypermasculine conventions of **machismo**, whereas women are considered as bearers of the passive (penetrated) principle (*marianismo*). Proponents argue that all Latin American gender behaviors are interpreted as either passive or active according to the logics of the matrix, and that penetrable bodies of either sex are situated on the same depreciated continuum in opposition to the *machista* paradigm (Lancaster 1992). Manzor-Coats (1994) notes that the lesbian in this system falls outside the social codes governing gender and sexual behavior; yet, her very unthinkability and unnameability in dominant gender-sex terms threatens those very codes. In explaining Chicano gay identifications, Almaguer (1991) proposed a sexual-identity spectrum: the fully assimilated Chicano gay male, three categories of increasing **assimilation**, and two Latin American categories defined by the active–passive matrix. The spectrum structures the interplay between sexualized and ethnicized identities, such that the assimilated Chicano gay male attains that identity by losing his Chicanoness and embracing the "more egalitarian norms of the North American sexual system." Román (1997) argues that Almaguer's typology perpetuates a notion of Latino homosexuality as negativized, repressive, and unimaginable unless the Latino is delatinized and assimilated. Bustos-Aguilar (1995) is even more critical of what he sees as the neocolonial and exoticizing critical trend among US-based anthropologists to treat Latin America as a sexually charged zone in which an undefined, but sexually rampant, machismo reigns supreme and makes all Latin Americans and Latino/as into subjective prisoners of rigidly maintained active/passive and hypermasculine/hyperfeminine logics.

Adelita, Soldadera

La Adelita is the term given to a woman who is said to have fought in the **Mexican Revolution** and who has been celebrated in Mexican folklore, film, and *corridos* (Herrera-Sobek 1990). The term *las Adelitas* also signifies dance and music associated with the revolution, which were performed and kept alive in the *ballet folklórico* tradition. La Adelita has popularly come to symbolize all *soldaderas* (female soldiers) throughout the revolutionary period who followed or accompanied their male partners to the battlefronts, and who, aside from attending to domestic duties in the field, at times bore arms and fought. These women were known by a range of names—*amazonas* (amazons), *soldaderas* and *soldadas* (female soldiers), *guerilleras* (guerillas), *coronelas* (colonels), the more popular *adelitas*, as well as less active terms such as camp followers—which testify to the challenge they posed to traditional gender mores (Salas 1990). However, in many Mexican films about the Mexican Revolution, la Adelita has been portrayed in romantic terms as a passive rather than an active agent. That is, she appears as a dutiful and honorable woman who supported or followed her man's involvement in the twined revolutionary and nation-building projects. In Mexican and Chicano/a popular discourse, la Adelita's name is often invoked to characterize a woman's ideal behavior, her remaining steadfast to her men or country, particularly in the face of familial and national crisis. Cantú (1986) identifies what she calls the "Adelita Complex," by which Chicanas were excluded from or accorded minor roles in **Chicano Movement** activism and cultural production. Nonetheless, in her more active guise, la Adelita has provided a positive model for many writers, an important example being Josephine Niggli's 1936 play *Soldadera* (1938).

Afro-Latino, Indo-Latino

Afro-Latino and its variants Afro-Caribbean and Afro-Latin American are black Latino/a identity terms that announce a reclamation of, and sense of pride in, the African heritage as well as identificatory connections with African Americans based on the legacies of slavery in the Americas and shared historical experiences of racial discrimination (Dzidzienyo and Oboler 2005). Indo-Latino is a recent identity term for indigenous Latino/as, for instance, Mexican Mixtec communities in California (*Oaxacalifornia*). Afro-Latino and Indo-Latino complicate understandings of Latino/a **ethnicity** and **racialization**, and challenge homogenizing uses of Latino/a and definitions of Latino/as as a mixed-race constituency.

AIDS/HIV

AIDS (Acquired ImmunoDeficiency Syndrome) is the name for the complex disease cluster that results from infection with HIV (Human Immunodeficiency Virus). Its Spanish equivalents are *el SIDA* (*Síndrome de Inmunodeficiencia Adquirida*) and *VIH* (*Virus de la Inmunodeficiencia Humana*). The HIV virus (or related viruses) associated with AIDS works by targeting and undermining the body's immune defense system, thus exposing the body to potentially fatal secondary infections. Responsible for killing millions of people and infecting millions more across the globe since the early 1980s, the AIDS pandemic has given rise to the epochal descriptor—the AIDS era. HIV is transmitted by the exchange of body fluids, for example, through unprotected sexual contact, use of unsterilized needles, infected blood transfusions, and from mother to child during childbirth. People living with HIV do not necessarily have AIDS, but HIV infection is the necessary precondition for AIDS. First identified among gay men in 1981 in North America, the term AIDS entered medical discourse in 1982. Although gay men have accounted for the majority of infected people in the USA and other Western countries since the 1980s, this has not been the case elsewhere; the vast majority of HIV/AIDS cases worldwide (most clustered in sub-Saharan Africa) are transmitted through heterosexual contact or from mother to child. HIV/AIDS has been a significant medical and sociopolitical issue in the USA since the early 1980s. Gay men responded to the AIDS crisis by politicizing the system of medical treatments, lobbying for fast-tracked distribution of drug therapies, and forging affiliative activist groups, such as ACT UP to fight for nondiscriminatory responses from the health-care apparatus. Such responses reflect the fact that gay men succumbed to AIDS in large numbers before the introduction of HIV-suppressant medications prolonged life expectancies, especially among middle-class gay men. A particular concern for medical prevention and treatment programs, however, is the overrepresentation of HIV in African American and Latino/a communities. Current infection and death rates for the disease cannot be separated from broader socioeconomic and political issues of poverty, access to adequate health care, and institutionalized racism that may influence state responses to the pandemic in certain communities. Specific sociocultural understandings of desire among Latino/as may also mean that men who have sex with men do not conceive of themselves as gay (in identity terms) and therefore at risk (Alonso and Koreck 1993; R. Díaz 1998). A rich body of

Latino/a cultural work has arisen in response to HIV/AIDS since the early 1980s (Román 1998). Much of that cultural work has taken the form of AIDS testimonials that aim to overcome the taboos and silence about both AIDS and queerness in many Latino/a communities (Sandoval-Sánchez 2005). Notable examples of this trend include *City of God* (1994), from the Chicano Gil Cuadros (who died with AIDS in 1996), and the work of the Los Angeleno Luis Alfaro (1994). A performance from the mid-1990s, "Quinceañera" (Araiza et al. 2002), features a group of Chicanos who celebrate a queer version of the *quinceañera* as a ritual of survival in the fifteenth anniversary of the AIDS era. The Cuban *marielito* Reinaldo Arenas confronted his experiences with AIDS in his autobiography *Antes que anochezca* (1992), which later formed the basis of the film *Before Night Falls* (dir. Julian Schnabel, 2000). The evolution of the **voguing** dance culture among gay men of color in the 1980s represents, in part, a response to the HIV/AIDS pandemic in the US northeast.

Ajiaco, Ajiaco Christianity

Ajiaco is a traditional Cuban stew that has become a culinary symbol of Cuban culture. It is made from a base vegetable stock (using corn on the cob and root vegetables, which give the stew a thick consistency) to which meat and other ingredients are added, depending on the season and availability. In theory the stew's life can be extended with the introduction of new ingredients; in practice *ajiacos* tend to be cooked for special occasions and large gatherings, with little if anything left over. *Ajiaco* entered the critical lexicon in the work of Fernando Ortiz (1940b), for whom *ajiaco* signaled the transformative and constantly augmented process of Cuban racial and transcultural intermixing between **Taíno**, European, and African peoples, without any foreseeable or definitive end point. Pérez Firmat (1989) argues that Ortiz's *ajiaco* metaphor designates the "openness and receptivity" of Cuban transcultural realities. *Ajiaco* announces a rhetorical and political rejection of epistemologies imposed on Cuba from outside by signposting new modes of Cuban self-expression drawn from local vocabulary. For Pérez-Firmat, *ajiaco* provides a concrete form to the discourse of **transculturation** that Ortiz also pioneered. De La Torre (2003) adapts the *ajiaco* metaphor in his notion of Ajiaco Christianity, an alternative to Mulatto Christianity (Caribbean forms) and Mestizo Christianity (Mexican, Central American, and Andean forms). The last terminologies are burdened by the racializing discourses of Spanish colonialism that first gave rise to *mulato* (African European mixture) and *mestizo* (Indian European mixture). Ajiaco Christianity connotes the ways by which Cuba's multiracial peoples have contributed to heterogeneous religiosity on the island. Ajiaco Christianity is further transformed in south Florida, where it generates a conviction that displacement, and diasporic well-being, is the result of a godly versus godless battle, *la lucha*, between exile Cubans and island Cubans (darkness, evil). The trouble with the *ajiaco* metaphor, however, is that it is not immune to the same homogenizing and romanticizing problems that beset any application of culinary analogies to describe transcultural realities. Given that food preparation has been the social function of women under patriarchy, how does the gendered division of labor influence the use-value of *ajiaco* to describe Cuban cultural identity? Moreover, the *ajiaco* metaphor does not account for the deep social divisions and intermittent conflicts along class, racial, and gender lines that have marked Cuban history since the Spanish conquest, and in the island and diaspora alike.

Alamo

Derived from the Spanish word *álamo* for cottonwood tree, the Alamo in San Antonio, Texas, was part of a Spanish mission founded in the eighteenth century that became the site of a famous battle between Texan and Mexican forces in 1836 during the Texan Revolution (1835–1836, the Texan Republic being declared on March 2, 1836). For 13 days from February 23, 1836, the Texan garrison of some 200 Anglo and Mexican Texans was besieged before Mexican troops overwhelmed the building on March 6 and all but one defender were killed. Among the Texan dead were such well known, but not yet mythologized, figures as David Crockett, William Travis, and Jim Bowie. The battle was a minor setback for independence forces, which defeated Santa Ana in April 1836 at the Battle of San Jacinto, the subsequent Treaty of Velasco confirming Texas's brief independence (the Republic was annexed by the USA in 1845). The Alamo remains a deeply politicized symbol of the clash between Anglo and Mexican peoples in North America, a clash alluded to whenever Texans invoke the phrase, "Remember the Alamo!" Richard Flores (2002) argues that the Alamo master narrative as understood today is the outcome of a complex and cumulative history of representations and revisions. Crystallized by the early 1900s, the Alamo narrative had shifted from an account of a military defeat to a national tale of heroism against the odds. Flores plots that shift in relation to the transition of Texas from a rural cattle-based economy to a modern industrial and agricultural system in the late 1800s and early 1900s. In that era, the legacies of Anglo-Mexican relations once encoded in the Alamo were renarrativized in a power hierarchy between dominated Mexican and "masterful Anglo." Mexicans now symbolized the nonmodern (backward, treacherous, undemocratic, alien) in the rise of a Texan and a national discourse of modernity, progress, and belonging. The reading of the Alamo defenders as state and national heroes, and of the Alamo as a sacred national site, is replicated in numerous popular-cultural and critical responses to the battle (Hansen 2003). *The Alamo,* the 1960 film directed by John Wayne, portrays the battle as a Manichean struggle between good and evil, with the Anglo-Texans defending liberty against overwhelming odds. Such representations contrast with the Mexican historical record, which has interpreted the battle as a justified response to an illegal secessionist movement. A remake of *The Alamo* in 2003 (dir. John Lee Hancock) provided a less hagiographic account by attending to Mexican and Anglo involvement in the Texan independence movement. Joseph Tovares's documentary *Remember the Alamo* (2004) also focuses on the **Tejano** contributions to Texan independence that remain unknown to US audiences. In Laura Esparza's "I DisMember the Alamo: A Long Poem for Performance" (2000), she reinserts her family's forebears into the conventional Alamo narrative. The piece ends with a ritual recounting of the identities that converge on the performer's body (*mestiza, india, gringa,* Chicana), which thus becomes a corporeal palimpsest of a Texan history marked by waves of territorial conquest and competition.

Altars, *Ofrendas*

Altars (*altares*) or shrines are an important folk art in Mexican and Chicano/a communities, with roots in indigenous Meso-American traditions in syncretic union with Spanish Catholicism. In Caribbean-origin Latino/a communities, altars are also part of lived daily practices, with their symbolism and imagery mixing Afro-Caribbean and Catholic traditions. Although the *ofrendas* (offerings) made to celebrate the **Día de los muertos** (Day of the Dead) in Mexico are perhaps the best-known form, altars are found in Mexican, Chicano/a, and other Latino/a homes, shops, and public spaces (wall recesses, sites of car accidents, courtyards, and public building entrance ways). Home altar-makers (*altaristas*) are usually women, and the altar-making process itself is most often an ongoing and evolving affair, with photographic records of important family events (births, graduations, weddings, and deaths) added to the altar over time in what amounts to a three-dimensional palimpsest of familial memory. Home altars vary in size and can come to dominate a particular room (R. Castro 2001). Mesa-Bains (2003) argues that since altar construction and main-tenance is one of many folk cultural practices undertaken by Latinas in the home, the neologism *domesticana* designates the art practices based on women's **domestic** cultural labor. Mexican and Chicano/a altars feature images of the **Virgen de Guadalupe**, as well as saints, votive candles, *calaveras* (skeletons), flowers, papier-mâché fruit, *papel picado* (paper cut outs), and objects of personal significance. Although the altar tradition has its origins in popular Catholicism, it is common to encounter secular home altars that com-bine religious and secular images and objects. The *ofrendas* associated with the Mexican *Día de los muertos* celebration are characterized by the display of *calavares* and skulls made from such materials as papier-mâché, plaster, alu-minum, and sugar that remind everyone involved of the meeting between living and dead realms, and of human mortality. Like home altars, *ofrendas* feature representations of the Virgen de Guadalupe and patron saints, but given their role in a cultural tradition that remembers and honors the dead, *ofrendas* are also decorated with photographs of dead relatives and friends, along with per-sonal belongings, *pan de muertos* (bread of the dead), and corn drinks such as *atole* to nourish the souls of the deceased (R. Castro 2001).

Alter-Native

Alter-Native is Gaspar de Alba's (1998) descriptor for the ways by which Chicano/as are at once "alien and indigenous" in and to the USA. Alter-Native evokes a number of binaries to designate the mutable and contradictory Chicano/a historical experience: insider/outsider, visible/invisible, main-stream/marginal, and dominant/subordinate. Those binaries demand a critical gaze, the Native "Eye/I," that insists on the fundamental "Americanness" of Chicano/a communities and the cultural work they produce. Gaspar de Alba regards Alter-Native as an alternative, ethnographic praxis—a way to acknowledge an alternative US-culture rather than a sub-American culture—that is rooted in the making-do sensibilities of **rasquachismo**. As a working-class and vernacular cultural practice, *rasquachismo* announces a community-centric response to dominant-cultural protocols. Alter-Native also connotes flux, difference, and adaptation as well as also evoking a Chicano/a "alter ego" or alterity, a Chicano/a **subaltern** communal reality that emerges from the competing historical geographies of New Spain, Mexico, the US southwest, and the Chicano/a **Aztlán**.

Ambiente

El ambiente is the Spanish-language term for environment, atmosphere, or milieu. In Latino/a, Latin American, and Spanish queer cultures, however, to be *en el ambiente* also signifies the occupation of a space of queer possibility. In cultural criticism, the term announces a queering project that according to Ellis (2000) shifts from US understandings of sexuality in identity terms to a more fluid conception of the shifting Latin/o locations in which queer sexualities may emerge and operate. That is, as opposed to an Anglo-American conception of ontological sexual identity that exists irrespective of the closet, *el ambiente* implies that sexuality becomes meaningful only in a communitarian social setting, as a way of knowing. *El ambiente* is not predicated on a purported sexual core but rather on a "process of generating a social space and infusing it with a sexuality of inclusiveness." The term thus signifies a process by which sexuality per se emerges not as a matter of individual choice but as an identification that can only gain meaningfulness in a social or communal context. As a challenge to the Anglo-American notion of the sexualized closet, *el ambiente* evokes the *zaguán* (L.G. Gutiérrez 2006). Literally a vestibule, entrance, or waiting room in a house or home, a *zaguán* occupies a liminal domestic space that provides a mediating point of entry and departure between inside and outside, private and public. As an alternative for closet, *zaguán* implies that the conventions by which sexualities are regarded as legible and meaningful in Anglo-America may not apply in Latino/a cultural spaces where different orderings of public and private space may pertain, and sexual behaviors and conventions may not be legible as identities in ways popularly understood in the USA.

America/*América*

America (in Spanish, *América*) is the name for the North and South American continents, and derives from the Italian explorer Amerigo Vespucci who, in the employ of the Spanish crown, undertook three voyages to the Americas between 1499 and 1503. He was the first European to realize that the insular territories encountered by Columbus and his successors nestled against a large continental land mass unimagined by Europeans. America is also a shorthand term for the United States of America (USA), a usage as old as the country and one that occludes the long history of Latin American uses of América when referring to their continental location and identity. That usage reflects what has been called American exceptionalism, the idea that the USA is unique among geopolitical states, not only in terms of its political institutions and ideals but also in terms of its purported national character and geographical location. When invoked, American exceptionalism often suggests that the USA's national success and unparalleled civilizational capacity have arisen on home-grown terms by virtue of the country's worldly place, and its particular national origins, history, religious makeup, and institutionalized belief in democratic processes, economic freedoms, and individual self-fashioning. Rowe (2000) notes that the doctrine of an exceptional America is enshrined in two foundational national documents, George Washington's "Farewell Address" from 1792, in which he advised against US involvement in European affairs, and the **Monroe Doctrine** of 1823. Much attention has been paid to "America" in Latino/a and American Studies. As Moraga describes the semantic struggle between "America" and "América" at work in her own sense of national place, the discourse that Chicano/as and other Latino/as do not belong to the US national community impels her to embrace an identity as "an Amerícan con acento" (1993). Moraga's point is that America/América is a false dichotomy that obscures how neither "America" nor "América" has been categorically, geopolitically, spatially, or culturally distinct. The transnational turn in American Studies since the mid-1980s has encouraged a move away from references to the USA as "America," and cut to the heart of the question of the USA's own history and governing mythos. Critical enterprises, such as Chicano/a studies, **Critical Race Theory**, Black Atlantic studies, postcolonial studies, and feminist and queer approaches, have also challenged the "American" identity (white, male, heterosexual, middle- or upper-classed, and English speaking) at the subjective heart of nation-centric American Studies (Ridway 1998). José Saldívar (1991) argues that the attention to the dialectic between America and América permits a critical resemanticization of both entities with important lessons for "American" literary and cultural studies. New modes of comparative criticism arise from a remapping of the continent that would recognize historical and literary similarities, disparities, intersections, and flows, without reducing the Americas to a homogeneous whole or a mere space of diversity. Poblete (2003) similarly argues that the borderline emplacement of Latino/a Studies between race and ethnic studies provides a productive location from which to challenge nation-centered models of ethnicity, citizenship, and cultural interaction. This drive animates much Latino/a cultural production. For example, Californian performance ensemble Culture Clash's deployment of AmeriCCa (as in Culture Clash in AmeriCCa) demonstrates that the semantic struggle over "America" forms part of a cultural-political struggle to insert Chicano/a cultural practices and aspirations into national debates on citizenship and belonging.

Americanization

Another word for **assimilation** within the USA, the term Americanization may also connote **cultural imperialism** and a US-dominated **globalization**. Americanization may thus encapsulate both the generalized global influence of the USA and the forceful imposition of "American" cultural values and political and economic interests beyond US borders, and on the country's historical minorities and immigrant communities. In Puerto Rico, Americanization designated the governmental policies applied after the US takeover in 1898 in order to assimilate island residents into capitalist "American" modernity. Americanization policies targeted the education system from 1898 to the early 1950s, exemplified by the official role granted from 1898 to 1948 to English as an official language of instruction. For the first half of the twentieth century, the island's schools functioned as the key state apparatus by and in which young Puerto Ricans were taught about US values, often in English (Fernández et al. 1998). Americanization continued with the **Estado Libre Asociado** after 1952 and underwrote such modernizing programs as **Operation Bootstrap**. Ambivalent local reactions to Americanization are revealed in Esmeralda Santiago's memoir *When I Was Puerto Rican* (1993), in which she talks about the arrival of *americanos* in the town of Macún in the early 1950s. School children encounter classes in English, a language they do not yet understand, and are required to attend the local community center each morning for a nutritious breakfast of "American" food. The center is also the site in which mothers and children are given lectures by *americanos* about hygiene and nutrition, the recommended foods on display (lettuce, apples, pears, broccoli, sliced bread, cornflakes, and the like) as yet unavailable in the local shops.

At one stage the young Esmeralda notices a new poster that shows a nuclear family surrounded by US commodities and food, and "the Puerto Rican seal, flanked by our flag and the Stars and Stripes . . . like a lamb on a platter." The scene demonstrates how the discourses of civilizing benevolence and dependency that typified the US colonial system were translated to the Puerto Rican population. George Sánchez (1993) points out that similar Americanization programs were applied to Mexican immigrants in Los Angeles between 1900 and 1945, but with the aim of enforcing Mexican assimilation. Such policies reflected widespread social and governmental attitudes on the part of health and education professionals, church leaders, and academics. Americanization in this era regarded immigrants as an unruly sector requiring both directed assistance and benevolent treatment in the process of becoming "American." Mexicans were singled out as a problem "alien" category in terms of distance from perceived US cultural values and normative Protestant work ethics. Americanization programs after World War I aimed at deculturating *Mexicanidad* (Mexicanness) in order to produce a compliant labor force. Specific programs targeted Mexican women and the family home, the Mexican "wife" and "mother" being regarded as the lifelines to the next local-born generation, as attested by a line from a 1923 master's thesis from the University of California: " 'Go after the women' and you may save the second generation for America" (G. Sánchez 1993). Sánchez also traces the defeat of Americanization programs. Large-scale migration from Mexico contributed to the maintenance of cultural traditions and language, and new transgenerational modes of *Mexicanidad* challenged orthodox expectations of immigrant assimilation.

Anglo-American, European American

Anglo-American, or Anglo, designates US residents whose primary language is English. Among Latinos, Anglo or Anglo-American may also signify white. Alternatives are European American and Euroamerican, which accept that the "Anglo" designation obscures the complex European origins of many millions of "Americans." Related to Anglo-American is WASP, the acronym formed from White Anglo-Saxon Protestant. This identity string is most often deployed to indicate (both positively and negatively) the ideal or standard "American," the bearer and embodiment of Americanness. To that identity string is often appended the word "Male." A WASP purview continues to underwrite a great deal of discussion about immigration, especially Mexican immigration, and **bilingualism.** Latino/a culture has generated numerous euphemisms for Anglo-American, many of which can also be applied to assimilated Latino/as. The most widespread is *gringo/a*, which in Mexico and for many Chicano/as designates white North Americans, especially people from the USA. Typically, but not invariably, the use of *gringo* is pejorative. For Armando Rendón (1971), identifying the *gringo* "enemy" was a crucial aspect of Chicano/a resistance—hence his distinction between Anglos (a general ethnic category) and *gringos*, individuals and institutions that enacted and upheld the oppressive policies toward the Mexican American population. A related term, *agringamiento* (becoming *gringo*), signifies **assimilation**, with *agringado* referring to Latino/as who have lost Spanish and who may have Anglicized their names. *Güero/a* (whitey) was also used during the Chicano Movement era to label light-skinned Chicano/as as traitors to the cause and the Chicano "race." Another term, Amerikkka/n, is encountered in Chicano/a and Nuyorican writing, a case in point being the Young Lords' "13-Point Program and Platform" from 1969, which states that Latino/as and Latin Americans "are oppressed by amerikkkan business" (Melendez 2003). The replacement of "c" with "kkk" (invoking the Ku Klux Klan) thus resemanticizes "America" into a racist, white supremacist enterprise. *Tinajuaco* is used in some parts of the Puerto Rican **diaspora,** such as Chicago, for a white American. *Bolillo* (the crusty white Mexican bread used to make *tortas,* sandwiches) is a Chicano/a and Mexican euphemism for an Anglo or white person, or a gringofied Mexican, as is evident in Rolando Hinojosa's novel *Querido Rafa* (1981). *Gabacho/a* (or *gavacho/a*) is Chicano Spanish for a white person. *Gabacho/a* can also be used to describe a Chicano/a who passes or identifies as white, as in *agabachado/a*. Yet another term, *judío/a* (a Jewish person) is used by Dominicans in New York to refer to any white American, a usage that reflects the preponderance of Jewish people in the neighborhoods in which Dominicans first settled in large numbers in the 1960s.

Assimilation, Acculturation

The terms assimilation and acculturation had wide currency for much of the twentieth century in anthropology and ethnography as conceptual means for describing the transformation of one culture as it comes into contact with another. Critical use of the terms implied a unidirectional or asymmetrical process that affected a weaker culture as it became indistinguishable from, or absorbed into, a more powerful culture. The dominant or stronger culture was not regarded as being transformed by such contacts. Acculturation has also been applied to colonial subjects said to have lost their local native or traditional ways of life in the face of stronger hegemonic metropolitan culture. In the USA, the concept of acculturation was applied by anthropologists, ethnographers, and "race" scholars to the processes by which European migrants adapted to the host society, and the term was also routine in ethnographic scholarship up to the 1980s to describe the experiences of historical minorities, notably Native Americans, Chicano/as, and Puerto Ricans. In all of these guises, acculturation functions as a conceptual ally of assimilation, the process by which migrants and minorities become integrated into a host society. As Suárez-Orozco (2000) notes, like acculturation, assimilation was first deployed in social science research to assess the adaptation to the host society made by European immigrants, the aim being to test the success of integration into the US mainstream. The concept implied immigrant adaptation to the host society to the point of being indistinguishable from existing populations. In some critical uses, acculturation provides a precondition for assimilation as migrants adapt to and adopt a host society's social conventions, dominant linguistic modes, and value systems, and also assume a role in economic, political, and educational life. Thus, a person or a particular group may be acculturated (able to survive in the host culture and language) without being assimilated (integrated into the host culture and language). In these senses, assimilation and acculturation are often understood as antonyms for pluralism and multiculturalism. Contemporary anthropology and cultural studies have disputed the Eurocentrism or US-centrism underwriting some uses of acculturation and assimilation—whereby purportedly weaker nonmetropolitan cultures succumb to dominant and more successful or civilized European or European-derived cultures—and developed more nuanced understandings of **transcultural** adaptations, identifications, and communal connections across geopolitical borders. Similarly, Latino/a critics also point out that ongoing immigration has meant that Latino/a communities are not necessarily abandoning or losing Spanish-language facility, cultural traditions, or primary identifications with countries of origin. Nonetheless, assimilation has provided a significant vector of resistance on the part of Chicano/as and Nuyoricans, in particular. During the 1960s and 1970s, Chicano activists targeted Chicanos perceived as having sold out to **Anglo-Americans** and argued that enforced assimilation must be resisted if Chicano/as are to assert their place as a distinct people, with their own languages, traditions, and cultural habitus. Many terms rose to semantic prominence in this era, and continue to be used, reflecting a widespread purview that assimilation equals **Americanization** and/or becoming white: *agringado* (gringofied), *bolillo* (the Mexican crusty white bread used to make *tortas*, sandwiches), coconut (brown on the outside, white on the inside), *tío taco* (a parallel to the Uncle Tom of African American cultural discourse), **malinche**, and *vendido/a* (traitor, sellout). Some conservative Latino/a critics, however, have argued that assimilation is the only viable means for facilitating "Hispanic" integration. Linda Chavez (1992) links such initiatives as affirmative action and **bilingual education** to leftist or liberal strategies intended to maintain Latino/a socioeconomic subordination through a discourse of communal victimhood that prevents individuals from taking advantage of the opportunities offered by "mainstream America." Chavez's emphasis on individual self-reliance ignores the structural and discursive barriers to class mobility and social acceptance confronting millions of Latino/as. She also presupposes that there is such a thing as a "mainstream" culture with fixed values, and that the mainstream is as unaffected by transcultural adjustments as the Latino/a population. Countering such logics, and at the same time also revealing complex modes of resistance to assimilatory pressures, concerns Norma Cantú in *Canícula: Snapshots of a Girlhood en la Frontera* (1995). A more recent variation on the assimilation model is retroassimilation, the process by which younger generations reject assimilationist pressures and adopt an ethnically marked consumerist ethos. Among Mexican Americans, retroassimilation involves new or renewed interest in learning Spanish, consuming Mexican and Mexican American music and media products, and claiming Mexican, Chicano/a, and broader Latino/a identifications. Mayer (2003) argues that retroassimilation arose in the wake of a previous generation of Mexican American media workers who established a Mexican American presence in the media industry, while facilitating the emergence of a "Hispanic market" and consumer acceptance of ethnicity as a selling point. Mexican American retroassimilation is paralleling the moves made by many young Anglo-Americans to learn Spanish and to recognize that their socioeconomic welfare depends on Spanish and English bilingualism.

Aztecs

Aztec (*Azteca*, also *Mexica* and *Tenochca*) is the name given to a people who wielded imperial hegemony over the central valleys and highlands of Mexico at the time of the Spanish conquest in the 1500s. Tenochtitlán (place of the cactus, current-day Mexico City), the Aztec capital, was founded around 1325 as the culmination of the Azteca migration, begun in the twelfth century, from the original homeland of **Aztlán**. Tenochtitlán was located on swampy ground in the middle of a lake; over time the Aztecs built large rafts on which buildings could be erected and crops could be grown, with floating causeways connecting inhabited and agricultural areas. Aztec society was organized along caste lines, had a strong military culture and associated practice of sacrificing captured enemy combatants, and produced a rich mythology and cosmology. The Aztec empire, which reached its peak in the 1400s, was maintained by a combination of military conquest, alliances, and tribute demands on neighboring people. The Aztecs were overthrown by Spanish forces under Hernán Cortés in 1521, with the assistance of local peoples who relished the prospect of ending the tribute system. The account by a conquistador who fought with Cortés, Bernal Díaz del Castillo (1963), provides an important historical record of Spanish insights into Aztec society and culture, and of the teeming and impressive city of Tenochtitlán, thought to have had a population of some 250,000 when the Spaniards arrived. Aztec perceptions of the conquest survive in a number of codices (pictographic texts). The Aztec inheritance was mythologized by successive Mexican governments in the 1930s and 1940s as one of the indigenous bases upon which modern Mexican identity and nationhood could be built. Aztec cultural traditions and mythology, most notably that pertaining to Aztlán, were similarly appropriated by Chicano activists in the 1960s and 1970s to underwrite the redefinition of Chicanos as national claimants to lost territory, and to provide the **Chicano Movement** with a set of unifying symbols. Chicano/a critical work since the 1960s has maintained this appropriation, as is evident in the many critical concepts drawn from Aztec culture and the **Náhuatl** language: **Coatlicue state**, *nepantla*, *el quinto sol*. The term Aztec also appears routinely in Chicano/a literary texts, films, and **murals** and is used as a synonym for Chicano/a in Chicano/a **rap and hip-hop**.

Aztlán

Aztlán (**Náhuatl** for white place, or place of the white herons) is one of the most powerful and resilient symbols of Chicano/a identification and mobilization. The use of the concept by Chicano/as signals a cultural appropriation of the **Aztec** name for their mythic homeland, from which the Aztec tribes migrated south in the twelfth century in their search for the promised land, to be identified by the sign of an eagle, perched on a cactus, devouring a snake. Surviving Aztec codices (pictographic texts) assert that the Aztecs established their promised land and new capital around 1325 at Tenochtitlán, current-day Mexico City. Although debate continues among historians about the likely location of the original Aztlán (Anaya and Lomelí 1989), the term entered Chicano/a consciousness in the 1960s when it was adopted as an alternative name for the US southwest. Aztlán thus designated a specific geocultural space and a new Chicano nation that was separate from both the USA and Mexico, but fortified by cultural links to the latter. Aztlán also metaphorized the Chicano struggle against racism and socioeconomic, political, and cultural subordination by joining an indigenous past, current activism, and a liberated future into a discourse of collective resistance to the US state and its dominant culture. In geographical, nationalist, and utopian senses, Aztlán defined Chicano/as as the colonized residents of occupied territory now prepared for a material and metaphorical reclamation (Acuña 2000). Those precepts were outlined in the *Plan Espiritual de Aztlán* from 1969. Daniel Alarcón (1997) points out that in nationalist definitions from the 1960s and 1970s, Aztlán was constructed as a unitary myth for all Chicano/as, irrespective of intercultural differences, and with a number of exclusionary consequences. The idealization of the indigenous past failed to address or admit the competing historical narratives grouped under the Aztlán rubric. Chicano/a uses of Aztlán may not align with Aztlán's symbolic function in Mexico, where it has signified the pre-Columbian base on which modern national unity is to be constructed. The original adherents of Aztlán also failed to interrogate Aztlán's function as a master narrative of *Chicanismo*; not all Mexican Americans were granted access to Aztlán. For example, Aztlán's location in the southwest disenfranchised Chicano/as who lived elsewhere, the large Mexican-origin community in Chicago a case in point. Finally, the nation signposted by Aztlán, a brown fraternity, ignored the many axes of identification that challenge the imagined male-dominated collectivity. The fraternally encoded Aztlán glossed over gender and sexual differentials, distinct processes of racialization, and disparities in Chicano/a class status and regional affiliation. Since the 1960s, Chicana feminists have critiqued Aztlán and related Movimiento symbols and rhetoric for failing to include and address the positions and struggles of women. More recently, advocates of a Queer Aztlán have emerged, similarly concerned to counter the marginalization of queer Latino/as in the evolving Aztlán (Moraga 1993).

The constant revisions of Aztlán confirm the observation made in Rudolfo Anaya's 1976 novel, *Heart of Aztlán* (1988), that new generations need to unravel the meanings of the Aztlán legend. Arrizón (2000b) argues that the genealogy of Aztlán now not only redefines the spaces in which Chicano/a critical and creative practice emerge but also influences diverse modes of Chicano/a cultural identification, from the ethnonationalist to the radical feminist and the queer. A constantly contested and transmutable place, utopian destination, and metaphor for collective politicization, Aztlán continues to serve diverse aspirations. As the performer El Vez put it in "Aztlán," from his 1994 CD *Graciasland*, "I'm going to Aztlán, where I wanna be."

B

Bachata

Bachata is a working-class music that arose in the Dominican Republic in the early 1960s, a decade of extreme economic hardship on the island. By the 1990s *bachata* had become one of the most popular dance styles in Latin America. According to Pacini Hernández (1995) *bachata*'s origins lie in traditional romantic guitar music played by trios or quartets with one or two guitars, and at times other stringed instruments, plus percussion (*maracas, claves,* bongo drums, scraper or *guiro, marimba/ula*). *Bachata* evolved into an urban dance form by the 1970s, having drawn on and assimilated musical styles from Cuba (*bolero, son, guaracha*), Puerto Rico (*plena*), Colombia, and Mexico (*ranchera, corrido*). The word *bachata* is Dominican idiom for a good time or fun, and the term stuck to the Sunday get-togethers among working-class people at which *bachata* outfits played. For much of its history *bachata* was dismissed by the island's elites and middle classes as an unsophisticated, debauched, and vulgar country or *campesino* music; this attitude also reflected the racialized divisions on the island, *bachata*'s popular base being working-class Afro-Dominicanos, many of whom had migrated to the island's cities and towns in search of work. Pacini Hernández suggests that the lyrics of the male-dominated *bachata* responded to class and racial disparagement, and to unemployment and poverty, by adopting a hypermasculine stance that celebrated sexual prowess, drinking, and **machismo.** Despite the neglect of the music by island TV and radio stations, *bachata* began to gain international audiences in the 1980s and 1990s, a reputation in no small part due to the Dominican diaspora that introduced the music to local Latino/a audiences. *Bachata* achieved a level of social respectability in 1992, when the *bachata* singer Juan Luis Guerra won a Latin Grammy Award for his album *Bachata Rosa*.

Ballet folklórico

Ballet folklórico refers to the traditional regional and local dances, and the dance groups or troupes that perform them, found throughout the Spanish-speaking world. *Ballet folklórico* traditions, which are closely related to local musical and dress traditions, are particularly strong in Mexico and among Mexican American populations, where they function as an important medium of local and regional identity. *Ballet folklórico* groups traditionally perform on national holidays and on important dates in the religious calendar, for instance, as part of *Las Posadas*, the traditional Mexican Christmas pageant. After the Mexican Revolution of 1910, folk dance and music forms in the north of Mexico called *las Adelitas* became the repository of story-telling about the revolution, and did much to keep the memory of female revolutionary figures alive (***Adelita***). The postrevolutionary period also saw a surge in popularity of *ballet folklórico* troupes across the country. In Mexico, the shift from local and regional significance to national importance occurred in the mid-twentieth century, as exemplified by the *Ballet Folklórico de México* in Mexico City. Founded in 1952, this troupe represents one of many cultural initiatives sponsored by the Mexican government in its ongoing construction of a national project anchored in regional and indigenous cultural traditions. At the local level throughout Mexico, *ballet folklórico* companies maintain and pass on Mexican dance traditions, and middle-class Mexicans (and increasingly Mexican Americans) routinely send their children to *ballet folklórico* classes. Rafaela Castro (2001) notes that while folk dances were maintained in Mexican American **barrios** and *colonias* for many decades, a resurgence of interest in folk dance and music occurred in the 1960s as part of the **Chicano Movement**'s recuperation of Mexican traditions.

Balseros

Balseros (rafters, from *balsa*, raft) is the name given to the third significant wave of Cubans to arrive in the USA, the first occurring in the years following the **Cuban Revolution** and the second being the *marielitos* of 1980. Related terms are *lanchero,* which designates anyone who leaves Cuba by paying a speedboat (*lanche*) owner to take them to Florida or another Caribbean destination, and *botero,* which signifies anyone who leaves Cuba by boat. The *balsero* pheno-menon is usually dated to the economic travails associated with the so-called Special Period in Cuba from 1990 to c. 2004, an era in which many hundreds of thousands of Cubans left the island. The year 1994, in particular, was a key or "crisis" year, with some 35,000 Cubans attempting to leave Cuba by boat for Florida in a few weeks from August. The most famous *balsero* to date has been Elián González, the Cuban boy who survived the crossing of the Florida Strait in November 1999 and, as a result, became a cause célèbre in a bitter custody battle fought across national lines. The term *balsero* is also used to designate other people who move from country to country in the Caribbean by boat or raft, for instance, Dominicans making the sea crossing to Puerto Rico. Another term, "reverse *balseros,*" refers to Cubans who make the sea crossing to Florida but subsequently return to the island. For some commentators (Greenhill 2002; Henken 2005), the *balsero* phenomenon, like the earlier Mariel boatlift, is explicable in terms of the complex and often tacit or quasi-formal relations between the USA and Cuba in the context of the official US embargo of the island. Greenhill (2002) describes the *balsero* exodus as an "engineered migration," in that the Castro regime has periodically relaxed the legal obstacles to Cuban emigration in times of social restlessness, with the aim of gaining concessions from the USA and policy changes vis-à-vis Cuban nationals and the embargo itself.

Banda

Banda, Spanish for a band or musical ensemble, is also the name of a Mexican form of music with a number of subcategories and offshoots. Traditionally *banda* designates the brass-band music from the northwestern Mexican state of Sinaloa (*banda sinaloense*), but related *banda* forms also evolved elsewhere in Mexico. Although many critics assert that *banda* was influenced by German and Austrian migrants in the nineteenth century who popularized the use of brass instruments and polka rhythms, Simonett argues that local traditional music forms in cities such as Guadalajara were more likely the original source (2001). She notes that brass bands were introduced to the Americas in the 1800s as a European cultural export; by the early 1900s, virtually every Mexican village and town had its own brass band. Over the decades the *banda* style absorbed musical influences from *cumbia*, *corrido*, and the Mexican *bolero*, a reflection of how *banda* outfits would shift genres during a performance as a result of crowd expectations. *Technobanda*, a contemporary by-product of *banda*, became popular in Mexico and the USA in the 1990s among working-class and immigrant Mexicans. This fast-paced dance music incorporated yet more influences (Brazilian *lambada*, flamenco, tango, *cumbia*, *salsa*, and a range of Mexican regional genres), and is associated with the acrobatic dance called the *quebradita* (little break). *Technobanda* outfits retained the double-headed bass drum (*tambora*) of traditional *banda* but added a synthesizer and electric bass guitar. The *technobanda* phenomenon was notable for the fashion style adopted by musical ensembles and audiences, which derives from the Mexican *vaquero* or cowboy tradition. Simonett (2001) describes the evolution of *technobanda* as one of transnational and transcultural interchange. Arising from Guadalajara, it spread north, where new practitioners and audiences in Los Angeles, Chicago, and the US southwest took to *technobanda* and the *quebradita* dance, after which *technobanda* traveled south again to find new audiences in the nightclubs of most Mexican cities. A key to that popularity was the willingness of Spanish-language music radio stations in southern California to play *technobanda*, to the point that *technobanda* came to occupy a central cultural role in what Simonett calls "Nuevo L.A.," or the Los Angeleno neighborhoods dominated by recent Mexican immigrants.

Barrio, Barriology, Barrioization, Barrio Logos

Barrio is the Spanish term for a neighborhood, district, or suburb. In the USA a barrio is the name given to a neighborhood in which the Latino/a population is predominant. In popular parlance, barrio may be synonymous with ghetto and evoke images of an inner-city zone marked by governmental and commercial neglect, and social problems such as **gangs**, crime, violence, familial breakdown, and drug use. Media and scholarly focus on such issues has tended to overlook the fact that the vast majority of barrio residents conduct peaceful and uneventful lives, and in many parts of the country have sustained the barrios as important sites of community cohesion and cultural production. Indeed, some barrios have played pivotal roles in the development of Latino/a culture and its dissemination to other parts of the country: El Paso's Chicano/a and Mexican barrios, East LA, Miami's Little Havana, New York's *Loisaida* (Lower East Side, Manhattan), and Dominican-dominant Washington Heights.

In New York City, the capitalized *El Barrio* sometimes denotes two important Latino/a neighborhoods: Harlem (Spanish Harlem) and the Bronx (El Bronx). An alternative to barrio is *colonia*, which also signifies a neighborhood, local community, or housing estate. US federal and state governments, however, use *colonia* to define any unincorporated migrant-dominant community, within 150 miles (240 kilometers) of the US–Mexico border but outside metropolitan areas of more than 1 million people, that lacks basic amenities, such as electricity and water supplies, adequate sewage infrastructure, and robust housing. In Chicago by the 1920s, established Mexican barrios, such as Hull House, Irondale, East Chicago (Indiana Harbor), and Gary, were referred to as "colonies" (from *colonia*) by town planners and academics of the time (Arias Jirasek and Tortolero 2001). As a site of socioeconomic and political **marginalization**, and resistance, the term barrio has provided a spatial basis for a number of important theoretical approaches in Chicano/a studies: barriology, barrioization, barrio logos, and Chicano/a reworkings of the **internal colonization** model. Barriology derives from the satirical magazine *Con Sapo*, which was established in 1969 in East LA by a collective of artists and students. The term referred to a fictive new social science by which Chicano/as could learn about, and assess the strength of, their *Chicanismo* and knowledge of Chicano/a barrio culture and daily life. With that focus, barriology targeted and parodied the epistemological drives by which Mexican Americans had been known and represented in various branches of scholarship. Barrioization was developed by Albert Camarillo (1979) to refer to the processes by which, since the middle of the nineteenth century in southern California, Mexican populations were barrioized by processes of urban and political segregation and ethnic separation from the wider Anglo-American community. Barrioization thus evokes the Chicano/a critical notion of the barrio as an internal colony proposed by Barrera, Muñoz, and Ornelas (1972). Building on barriology and barrioization, Villa's (2000) concept of "barrio logos" regards barrios as dynamic cultural sites of spatialization governed by a barrioizing dialectic of imposed pressures and internally generated responses on the part of barrio residents to those pressures. Barrios register the broader social marginalization and discrimination of Chicano/as through counteractive processes of communal formation and the construction of distinct barrio uses of space, and new imaginaries of barrio communal identity. For Villa, barrio logos provides a useful deromanticizing corrective to many celebrations of the barrio as neatly contained sites of Chicano/a resistance. Barrio logos denotes the tension between barrioizing pressures (deformative) and barriological (affirmative) practices, out of which emerges the barrio's physical form and meaning.

Baseball

Baseball, a quintessential "American" sport, is now a popular sport in the Spanish-speaking Caribbean, much of Latin America, and in such countries as Japan and South Korea. Baseball games involve two teams, each consisting of nine players, on a diamond-shaped field the corners of which represent the bases (three plus the home plate), and a position for a pitcher in the infield of the diamond, and another for a catcher behind the home plate, where team batters stand. A team wins by scoring more runs than its rival (after a successful hit a batter must try to complete a circuit of the bases to the home plate). Games last for nine innings, each inning ending when three members of the batting team are declared out, which can happen for a range of reasons: the hit ball is caught; the batter earns three strikes (fails to hit pitched balls within the strike zone); the fielded ball arrives at first base before the batter or at the base to which one of the runners from another base is attempting to reach (Montague 2004). Baseball developed from the English game of rounders, which English settlers brought to the North American colonies. The rules of baseball as understood and recognized today were formalized by 1845. The National Association of Professional Baseball Players (later the National League) was formed in 1871. The American League was established in 1901, and since 1903 teams from the American and National Leagues have participated in the World Series (Montague 2004). Policies of racial segregation ensured that the sport was theoretically "white" until African American Jackie Robinson joined the Brooklyn Dodgers in 1947, thus opening up the game for black Americans who had been relegated to their own "Negro League." The Latino contribution to baseball has been immense, with many Latino players becoming stars in the major leagues, and league team officials often scouting for talent in the Hispanophone Caribbean. One of the greatest baseball players, the Puerto Rican Roberto Clemente, became the first Latino admitted to the National Baseball Hall of Fame in 1973. Burgos (2002) notes that despite the official baseball color bar, Mexican Americans and Cubans played for US League teams as early as the 1870s, although there was disquiet in the media about their involvement, which Burgos attributes to the disruption such players posed to the black/white logics determining participation in the game. Baseball was introduced to Cuba in the 1860s, with the Cuban professional league being formed in 1878 (Ruck 1999). González Echevarría (1999) argues that the popularity of baseball in Cuba was in part linked to the independence struggle, whereby Cuban nationalists rejected Spanish-origin pastimes such as the bullfight in favor of "American" cultural and social practices. Cuban émigrés fleeing the civil conflict on the island in the latter decades of the nineteenth century also played a role in introducing the sport to the Dominican Republic and Puerto Rico. Louis Pérez (1999) demonstrates that Cuban baseball was always connected to the game in the USA, with interchanges and relationships at club level, and much US interest in island teams and players. Those connections characterize the relationship between US and Dominican, Puerto Rican, and more recently, Venezuelan baseball systems. Pérez also points out that, by the 1870s, the more acceptable presence of Cuban players in the US League inspired some African American teams to pass as Cuban in order to enable their travel and competition against white teams. As with many team sports, part of baseball's historical allure derives from its potential to provide players from racial, ethnic, and/or working-class communities a means of mobility, security, and acceptance (Regalado 1988). Given that baseball is regarded popularly as the national sport, the game has served as a key venue in which audiences could witness the performative interplay between national, masculine, and racial ideals (Burgos 2002). Baseball is a salient site for cultural analysis of how Latino baseballers interrupt the black/white discourses of national belonging that play out in baseball matches and in the imagination of the game's spectators.

Basketball

Basketball was developed in 1891 at the behest of the Young Men's Christian Association. A physical educator called James Naismith from Springfield, Massachusetts, devised the rules of the game. By the end of the 1890s, the sport had become popular in schools across the country. The National Basketball League was founded in 1937, and in 1946 the Basketball Association of America was established, both organizations merging in 1949 as the National Basketball Association (Montague 2004). Played at amateur and professional levels in the USA, the sport has different rules and conventions depending on those levels, while the rules of international competitions again differ. Generally, however, basketball is played on a court between two teams of five, each team attempting to throw the ball through its designated basket and thus scoring more points than its rival. Basketball is played at a fast pace and is characterized by the constant shifts in direction of the ball as players intercept it. Matches tend to be close due to the balance of defending and attacking skills of team members. Basketball is increasingly having a Latino/a presence, with a number of players in the major US leagues coming from Latino/a communities or from Latin American countries. Basketball has also become a quasinational game in Puerto Rico, and many Puerto Rican star players are recruited by US League teams.

Bato/a, Vato/a, Batos locos

Possibly derived from the potentially insulting *chivato*, goat, in Chicano Spanish a *bato/a* (or *vato/a*) signifies a young man or woman. In contemporary use, *bato* is rap and hip-hop slang for a homeboy. Related terms include *bato loco* (a crazy guy, connoting coolness and unpredictable independence), *bato tirilí* (**pachuco**), and *bato tirilongo* (hood or **gang** member). The expression *bato loco* (plural *los batos locos*) has a long history as a signifier of streetwise and untrammeled *pachuco* or Chicano masculinity, and regularly appears in cultural texts since the 1940s. The narrator of Oscar "Zeta" Acosta's 1973 novel, *The Revolt of the Cockroach People*, provides a sense of the masculinity that *los batos locos* purportedly embody: "They are *vatos locos*! Nobody tells crazy guys what to do" (see Acosta 1989). A synonym for *bato* is *chulo*, which can signify a pimp, homeboy, cool guy, dude, or bad guy. Rapper Kid Frost's 1991 hit, "La Raza," typifies this usage: "*Vatos, chulos, call us what you will.*"

Bilingualism, Bilingual Education

Bilingualism, sometimes called bidialectism, refers to the ability of a speaker to inhabit and function in two distinct languages. Multilingualism refers to the same process but involves two or more languages. For most of the world's population, the ability to speak more than one language is a norm, although in many parts of the Anglophone world, monolingualism has historically been the reality. Yet, even in Anglophone countries, middle- and upper-class English speakers have valued the acquisition of other languages. In the USA, a monolingual ethos has shadowed definitions of the nation, as in, "America" is a monolingual English-speaking country. Current debates over the national language are linked to and influenced by anxieties over the changing demographic landscape of the USA since World War II, and a concomitant fear that national values are somehow under threat from bearers of languages other than English, most notably Spanish. Debates over bilingualism at government and education levels are of great concern and relevance to many millions of Latino/as who operate in both Spanish and English. The anxieties unleashed by bilingual education (schooling where a proportion of lessons are conducted in Spanish) and bilingual government practice are exemplified by the rise of the **English-Only Movement** in the 1980s, whose proponents regarded bilingualism as contrary to the English-language bedrock of the nation (Crawford 1992; M. Davis 2000). The corollary of those debates is that Latino/a cultural practice and production have historically embraced a bilingual ethic that also permits **code switching** and the practice of **Spanglish**, as the title of the Nuyorican poet Victor Hernández Cruz's *By Lingual Wholes* (1982) suggests. That relationship nonetheless points to the imaginative challenges that Spanish–English bilingualism poses to accounts of "American" history and culture. For Arteaga (1994b) the presence of millions of Spanish speakers inside US borders confronts Anglo-America with an alternative linguistic and cultural tradition and mode of national discourse. Debra Castillo (2005) argues that the rich US literature in Spanish, as well as numerous literary texts that switch codes or utilize Spanglish, require a profound readjustment of the disciplinary and epistemological approaches that dominate "American" literary studies.

Black Legend, *Leyenda negra*

The Black Legend (*La leyenda negra*) is the name of an anti-Spanish discourse said to have arisen in Europe in the sixteenth and seventeenth centuries, an era of constant warfare and competition between western European powers, and of conflict between **Catholicism** and Protestantism. Some historians have also identified variants of the Black Legend in Catholic-dominant France, Italy, and Poland. Institutions such as the Inquisition and the Catholic Church, the intermixing of Spanish, indigenous, and African peoples in the Spanish empire, and a history of racial, religious, and cultural **syncretism** in Spain, were regarded elsewhere in Europe as signs of an inherent and intractable cultural and racial deficiency. The heterogeneous peoples and cultures of both Spain and its empire were found wanting when compared with

the purportedly purer, more benign, and humanistic northern European imperial enterprises. Anti-Spanish Europeans demonized the Spanish imperial project in the Americas as inhumane, cruel, violent, irrational, and concerned only
with exploitation and rapacious profit making. The term Black Legend was
introduced in 1914 by the Spanish historian Julián Juderías y Loyot (1974),
who wanted to disarm what he regarded as the antipathy toward Spain, and
Spanish **Catholicism**, among European historians. He noted that the imperial
projects of all European powers had catastrophic consequences for native peoples, and that to single out the Spanish for criticism provided northern
Europeans with an alibi for downplaying their own excesses and brutalities.
Juderías y Loyot thus inaugurated a Spanish counterdiscourse called *La
leyenda rosa* (the Pink Legend, commonly known as the White Legend), which
cast the Spanish conquest as a benign and civilizing mission. Hillgarth (2000)
proposes that the Black Legend arose as a propaganda exercise intended to
garner international support for the Dutch in their sixteenth-century revolt
against the Spanish. Fernández Retamar (1979) argues that the Black Legend
drew attention away from the interest groups that would benefit from the displacement of Spain's imperial hegemony: the northern European agents of
early capitalism. Juderías y Loyot and later historians trace the Black Legend
back to the Dominican Friar Bartolomé de las Casas's 1522 *Brevísima
relación de la destrucción de las Indias* (Brief Account of the Destruction of
the Indies), one of the first accounts of the devastating impact on native
Caribbean peoples (1999). Subsequent translations into various European languages were cited as evidence of Spain's violent and uncivilized record in the
Americas. Fernández Retamar (1979) proposes that the Black Legend per-
sists in the racializing discourses circulating in the USA that continue to de-
nigrate Latin American and Latino/a peoples, and that have helped to justify
US interventions in Latin American states since the early 1800s. He regards
the use of **Hispanic** and **Latino** in the USA as evidence of the homogenizing
"disdain" by which certain communities, Chicano/as and Puerto Ricans in particular, have been rhetorically located in the parts of the Americas that were
marked by the uncivilized, barbaric Spanish. For Maltby (1971), the Black
Legend, or anti-Hispanism, overdetermined British relations with Spain from
the early 1500s, and ensured the persistence in Britain—and later the USA—
of stereotypes about Spanish capriciousness, fanaticism, cruelty, hot-blooded-
ness, and untrustworthiness. Powell (1971) argues that US relations with
Latin American states, Mexico in particular, have also been modulated by

a deep-seated belief in the Black Legend. Extending from previous studies, DeGuzmán (2005) proposes that anti-Spanish discourse was pivotal in the evolution of the USA's national myths, Spain providing the racialized "black" counterego to national ideals of (white) selfhood and **citizenship**.

Black/White Paradigm

The Black/White paradigm is regarded in many branches of Latino/a Studies as one of the discursive hallmarks of US national history, culture, and politics, by which the USA is discussed and imagined in black and white **race** terms only. Although the paradigm reflects the unresolved historical legacies of slavery and the role played by African Americans in the evolution of the US state and its culture and economy, it nonetheless erases from the national debate communities that either sit outside or trouble the categories of black and white. Aside from many Latino/as, these excluded communities include Native Americans, Asian Americans, Hawaiians, and Pacific Island Americans. As Arrizón (2000a) succinctly put it, official US Census definitions confirm that Latino/as "are not 'Black enough' for the civil rights model, and we are not 'white enough' for the immigration model." Juan Perea (1997b) argues that the Black/White paradigm prevents Latino/as from contributing to race debates, thus perpetuating both the paradigm's survival and the production of negative representations of Latino/as as an "alien" threat to the nation. Perera calls for a sustained critical shift away from the Black/White paradigm of race that nonetheless remains focused on challenging white racial privilege. However, Valdes (1997) warns that the deconstructive project with regard to race needs to critique the Black/White paradigm's "truncation" of race without discounting African American struggles and aspirations. See **Critical Race Theory**.

Blowouts, Walkouts

Blowouts or walkouts were a tactic—a form of *huelga* (strike) or *protesta*—used by Chicano/a high school students in Los Angeles, California, in the late 1960s. The walkouts were motivated by widespread student anger at the failure of the Californian educational system to acknowledge and cater to the needs of Chicano/as. The first and most famous blowouts began in East LA on March 8, 1968, and over the next ten days involved hundreds of students from a number of inner-city high schools. In some cases, police called by school administrators responded with violence to the demonstrating students, and there were numerous arrests. Typical demands of the students included the establishment of Chicano/a studies programs, increased funding to repair poorly maintained school infrastructures and to improve educational resources, more Chicano/a teachers in schools with significant Chicano/a student populations, an end to racist practices in the classroom and school system, and, most fundamentally, access to a better education. After the initial blowout, the student protests continued throughout Los Angeles and California over the following year. The blowouts, which involved thousands of Chicano/as, are considered by Chicano/a historians to have been an integral aspect of the **Movimiento Chicano** (Haney López 2003). A literary representation occurs in Luis Rodriguez's *Always Running. La Vida Loca: Gang Days in LA* (1993), where the blowout is described as "a walkout for our self-respect." The 1969 skit (*acto*) *No saco nada de la escuela* (I Get Nothing from School) by el **Teatro Campesino**, transmits a sense of the growing politicization of Chicano/a students in the 1960s (Valdez 1990). The blowouts inspired the 2006 film *Walkout* (dir. Edward Olmos), which is based on the experiences of student activist Paula Crisostomo, a leading organizer of the East LA blowouts in 1968. The film's ending features short interviews with Crisostomo and other activists, including Crisostomo's teacher at Lincoln High School, Sal Castro, who, at some risk, encouraged the student protests. The walkout tradition was revived by high school students in California and the southwest in 2006 in support of the mass demonstrations by **undocumented workers** that took place from March onward. Those demonstrations and walkouts opposed the Republican-sponsored Sensenbrenner Bill (November 2005), which aimed to felonize "illegals," and anyone who employs or assists them, and to further extend the border wall between Mexico and the USA.

Bolero

The term *bolero* is used throughout the Spanish-speaking world to designate a range of local music forms, although the Spanish *bolero* is unrelated to Latin American *boleros*. The Cuban form has been particularly important in the history of musical cross-fertilization in the Americas. Orivio (2004) claims it was the first Cuban style to achieve international recognition. The Cuban *bolero* is a slow- to mid-paced dance music in 2/4 time with European and Afro-Cuban musical forebears that emerged in the late nineteenth century in the eastern Cuban city of Santiago. The genre evolved in the first half of the twentieth century, a key innovation being the adaptation of lyrics drawn from the works of noted poets, with the consequence that the rhythms began to follow and support the lyrics rather than predetermine their writing and delivery. By the 1950s the Cuban *bolero* had become a popular dance and singing style in Mexico (where Agustín Lara composed many now famous *boleros*), the Caribbean, and much of Latin America. The genre survives as a classic (some critics would say sentimental) part of the musical repertoire throughout the Hispanophone world, its traces evident in such mutations as the *bolero-mambo.*

Borderlands, *Borderlands/La Frontera*

A borderland or borderlands designate the territories abutting a geopolitical divide or frontier between two states. In North America, the term borderlands normally designates the territories that extend on either side of the border between the USA and Mexico: the states of California, Arizona, New Mexico, and Texas on the US side and the states of Baja California, Sonora, Chihuahua, Coahuila, Nuevo León, and Tamaulipas in northern Mexico. The borderlands are a historical legacy of the treaty provisions of the **Mexican–American War** (1846–1848), which compelled Mexico to cede its northern half to the USA. The borderlands region is characterized by the presence of sizeable twin cities, the largest being San Diego/Tijuana on the Pacific coast and El Paso/Ciudad Juárez on the Texas–Chihuahua border. Since the early 1980s the borderlands has been a site of enormous demographic and economic transformation, with the Mexican side in particular experiencing massive population increases, largely as a result of the expansion of the *maquiladora* or assembly plant sector. Much of the border that runs through the borderlands is heavily militarized, especially at twin-city sites, and the landscape ranges from coastal temperate in the west, through mountains and deserts until the border fence joins the Rio Grande and extends through the lower Rio Grande valley to the Gulf of Mexico. The term borderlands is arguably one of the most widely used critical concepts in Latino/a cultural studies, particularly in Chicano/a studies, and in **border theory** more generally. Many Chicano/a critics argue that as a geopolitical place and contact zone, the US–Mexico borderlands have exerted a definitive hold on Chicano/a and Mexican cultural typologies and perceptions of self and place since 1848. Such critics have also regarded the borderlands as an imaginative trope, a metaphor of liminality, multiplicity, fluidity, flux, and possibility, whose applications may not require the US–Mexico border as referent (Pérez-Torrez 1995b). José Saldívar goes further, arguing that the "American" (US) imaginary itself is founded on the profound "discontinuity" between Anglophone and Hispanophone Americas, or the frontier versus *la frontera* (1997). Such critical positions confirm Claire Fox's (1999) thesis that the borderlands, and not **Aztlán**, now provide the spatialized metaphor of choice for many Chicano/a critics and cultural workers. Although the critical prominence of the borderlands concept is attributable to Gloria Anzaldúa's *Borderlands/La Frontera: The New Mestiza* (1987), the origins of the concept lie in earlier decades. The historian Herbert Bolton (1921) is credited with developing the idea of the Spanish borderlands as a coherent geographical region. For Bolton, the Spanish borderlands designated the northern reaches of the Spanish empire, now the northern states of Mexico and the region from California to Texas. Later US historians and ethnographers began to utilize the notion of the borderlands when referring to the territories and peoples around the geopolitical frontier established in 1848 (Truett and Young 2004). A borderlands-like approach is evident in the work of Américo Paredes (1976, 1987), who contrasted the term **Greater Mexico** with the border, thus implying that a cultural notion of Mexicanness has transnational attributes. Chicano/a understandings of the borderlands draw on this critical tradition. Anzaldúa's (1987) approach is deeply marked by an upbringing in south Texas along a border that she describes as an open wound "where the Third World grates against the first and bleeds." Anzaldúa approaches the US–Mexico borderlands as a historical-material location and as a trope for cultural flux, and for identity destruction and reconstruction. Anzaldúa's borderlands are fear inducing, oppressive, and prone to violence and state-sponsored discipline. The borderlands are populated by **subalterns** whose cultural practices, language, skin color, gender, sexuality, and ethnicity are devalued. Faced with that predicament, Anzaldúa enacts a complicated recuperation of the disparaged aspects of her own identity (Chicana, female, queer, dark skinned) in order to represent a new borderlands subject, *la nueva mestiza.* Throughout *Borderlands/La Frontera,* the geopolitical border and its divided "lands" appear metonymically as a slash (/) between Spanish and English expressions, thus providing Anzaldúa with a dominant trope, a sign of the linguistic and cultural limits constantly breached by borderland residents.

Typography reflects topography, and it also characterizes Anzaldúa's border-lands epistemology as "a shock culture, a border culture, a third country, a closed country." A tactical response to this zone is the deployment of border crossing as a governing metaphor for her desired identity reinvention. Another tactic is the metaphorization of the borderlands itself to signify any split iden-tity condition (physical, psychic) that nonetheless encodes within itself the pos-sibility of accommodating those fractured selves in a less damaged whole. Anzaldúa's figurations of the borderlands as a venue for multivalent identity fashioning are decidedly ambivalent and contradictory, at once utopian in their aspirations, and yet withholding from claiming a utopic fix. Her desired *nueva mestiza* is deferred as an ongoing, incomplete project. Acknowledging Anzaldúa's influence, José Saldívar (1997) argues that the frontier/*frontera* discontinuity has permitted US hegemony in the hemisphere by upholding a radical disjunction between Anglophone and Hispanophone Americas. This position typifies the cultural political uses to which both the border and the borderlands have been put in much Chicano/a studies. The borderlands concept thus functions in the critical field as both fact and trope, a double usage that recognizes that the border and life along it have profoundly marked Chicano/a national, collective, and personal identifications. The cultural appeal to the borderlands as fact and trope nonetheless carries a number of risks. Once the US–Mexico borderlands are regarded as a paradigm of national imaginary formation and transcultural signification, the trope may potentially overdeter-mine the communal and personal relations to the USA of other Latino/as (notably those from the Caribbean) with no historical-material relation to, or imaginative investment in, the land frontier or its adjacent terrains. Caribbean-origin Latino/as may have a different geospatial and cultural sense of their place in relation to the state in which they reside (Allatson 2002). Another risk in the culturalist use of the borderlands as fact/trope has been raised by ethnographers who are highly skeptical of the claims made about the peo-ples and cultures of the border region, not only in Anzaldúa's conceptualiza-tion, but also in the work of cultural critics (Rosaldo 1989; J.D. Saldívar 1997). Vila (1995, 2000) and Ortíz-González (2004), for example, regard the culturalist approach to the borderlands as reductive, homogenizing, and out of step with on-the-ground realities. That approach, they argue, reifies the borderlands as a coherent space (a third country) of identity production and cultural resistance in defiance of the complex modes of identity fashion-ing that takes place in distinct border locales. Moreover, proponents of the borderlands "third space" may not recognize that the conceptual and national protocols governing that space are anchored on the northern side of the geopolitical line, and in US identity and cultural discourses, that rarely translate neatly to terrains to the south. That said, male critics of Anzaldúa's borderlands/*frontera* concept often overlook the complexity of her feminist framework, and potentially misread her ambitions as merely advocating borderlands reconciliation and hybridity.

Borderotics/*Fronterótica*

Borderotics/*fronterótica* is a bilingual neologism coined by Susana Chávez-Silverman (2000) to designate a libidinal reformulation and problematization of the **borderlands** when treated as a utopian liminal space enabling Chicano/a identity construction and healing. Running counter to that treatment, borderotics/*fronterótica* signifies a space of discursive ambivalence and irresolvable differentiation. This reformulation is enabled when the border, as textualized by traditional Chicano writers, converges with another border constructed along gender and sexual lines in the work of Chicana lesbian writers. In turn, those writers negotiate the borders erected by Anglo-lesbian feminism and Chicana heterosexuality. *Borderotics/fronterótica* thus announces the impossibility of theorizing Chicana lesbian desire in terms of its essentialist separatism from other logics of desire and epistemological production in multiple borderlands. Indeed, the ambivalences, breaches, and inherent incoherencies of the borderlands, at once a geocultural zone and trope of desire, are foregrounded when the purportedly utopian promise and policing function of both zone and trope are ungrounded by the dialogic operations of Chicana lesbian sexuality and textuality. Borderotics/*fronterótica* is thus evocative of *sitios y lenguas*.

Border Patrol, *Migra*

Since its official formation in May 1924, the US Border Patrol, called *la migra* in Chicano/a and northern Mexican Spanish, has been the mobile policing body responsible for monitoring, overseeing, and controlling the cross-border movement of peoples and goods. For most of its history the Border Patrol formed a branch of the Immigration and Naturalization Service (INS). The INS was, from its earliest incarnation in 1891 until its absorption into the

Department of Homeland Security after 2001, the government bureau responsible for processing immigrants, tourists, and other visitors, assessing naturalization and residency status, and apprehending "aliens" without documentation (M. Smith 1998). After September 11, 2001, the INS and the Border Patrol were subsumed under US Customs and Border Protection, in the new Department of Homeland Security. Since the 1920s, the Border Patrol has had two headquarters: El Paso on the Mexican border and Detroit on the Canadian border, the latter border receiving most of the Border Patrol's attentions during the Prohibition era. The Border Patrol was officially incorporated into the new INS, in the Department of Labor, in 1933, and the first Border Patrol Academy was established in the following year in El Paso. Since World War II, the Border Patrol has concentrated on combating unregulated immigration and apprehending drug traffickers and smugglers of contraband. The Border Patrol provided the central force in one of the biggest anti-immigrant crackdowns in US history, **Operation Wetback** in 1954 and 1955. This clampdown on Mexican "aliens"—between 1 and 1.3 million people were repatriated to Mexico—did much to cement the negative reputation of the Border Patrol among many Mexicans and Chicano/as. In the 1990s federal and state administrations began approving a range of operations intended to stop undocumented workers from crossing the border in twin-city zones. The first of these was Operation Hold the Line in El Paso, Texas, in 1993, which established a template for later operations in the mid-1990s: Operation Gatekeeper in San Diego; Operation Safeguard in Nogales, Arizona; and Operation Rio Grande in south Texas. These operations, which coincided with the implementation of **NAFTA** (North American Free Trade Agreement) in 1994, amounted to a full-scale militarization of the border, as evident in the technologization of surveillance operations and the construction of walls and razor-wire fences with materials recycled from the Gulf War, and intended to prevent border crossing in specific urban areas. The reality has been that undocumented workers and other immigrants without papers now cross the US–Mexico border in underpopulated desert or mountainous terrains. Such immigrants not only include Mexican and other Latin American nationals, but also increasing numbers of people from Asia and other parts of the world, the latter referred to by the Border Patrol as "Other Than Mexican." The Border Patrol's official history is posted on the US Government's Customs and Border Protection webpages (www.cbp.gov); that history is also celebrated in the US Border Patrol Museum and Memorial Library, near El Paso.

La migra has been a constant presence in northern Mexican and Chicano/a cultural texts since the 1920s. Mexican **corridos** have long chronicled the activities of *la migra*, and Border Patrol abuses were common motifs in Chicano/a murals. A subgenre of Hollywood films has also focused on the Border Patrol, with varying degrees of empathy for the plight of apprehended **undocumented workers** (Maciel and Herrera-Sobek 1998). Rafaela Castro (2001) notes that the phrase "Te vaya a llegar la migra" (*La migra* are coming to take you away) has been used for decades by Chicano/a parents to scare their children into behaving, and that a common **barrio** game is "La migra chasing the Mexican," a variant of cowboys and Indians. Characters based on *la migra* have appeared as stock baddies in Mexican *lucha libre* and are often referred to in *telenovelas* that are either set in the USA or that feature Mexicans who have worked in the USA and returned. However, not all Chicanos/as regard the Border Patrol with suspicion, fear, or antipathy. Many border patrollers have come from the ranks of Chicano/as and share the idea that the US–Mexico border is a threatened line of national defense. This fact challenges assumptions that there is a clear-cut division between European American and Mexican American imaginaries of national place, and that there is a natural affinity between Chicano/as ("citizens") and Mexicans ("aliens").

Border Theory

Border theory is the name for a critical field that focuses on, and draws lessons from, the US–Mexico border and its surrounding geocultural terrains, and increasingly other geopolitical and geocultural lines as well. The origins of border theory lie in **frontier** historiography, the pioneering work on the Spanish **borderlands** by Eugene Bolton (1921) and his successors (Truett and Young 2004), and in the post-World War II period, the ethnographic work done by Américo Paredes. The latter's 1958 *With His Pistol in His Hand* (1986) is widely regarded as a foundational work in Chicano/a ethnographic studies into the folklore and vernacular oral traditions of border communities in the Rio Grande valley of south Texas. In that text, Paredes also alluded to a new transnational geocultural formation, **Greater Mexico**, which he subsequently elaborated on (1976), thus establishing a Chicano/a mode of theorizing the border region as a continuous and interactive cultural zone. This understanding of the region is implicit in the work of Gloria Anzaldúa (1987), perhaps the most influential culturalist border theorist. Anzaldúa's influence is evident in numerous border-centric studies that similarly regard the US–Mexico borderlands as a coherent geocultural space, while also drawing metaphorical and theoretical lessons from the border. Such critical moves are evident in readings of the **coyote** as "cross-border" smuggler of resistance, José Saldívar's frontier/*frontera* discontinuity (1997), Mignolo's border gnosis (2000), Rosaldo's **border zones**, and Vélez-Ibáñez's (1996) concept of cultural bumping. They are paralleled by García Canclini's designation of Tijuana/San Diego as a border "laboratory" of postmodernism (1990, 1995), and the performance work of Guillermo Gómez-Peña (1993, 1996, 2000), who celebrates the San Diego/Tijuana section of the borderlands as a paradigm of postmodern and postnational cultural hybridity. Indeed, Gómez-Peña's (1996) "border paradigm" designates a dialectic between borderlessness, the drive to dismantle or dispense with geopolitical borders, and borderization, the disciplinarian practices along extant state frontiers and the construction of new geopolitical, racial, and cultural divisions. This paradigm has led some observers to warn that the universalizing figuration of the border has become detached from historical-material terrains, and can thus be applied neoimperialistically anywhere and everywhere (C. Fox 1999). Countering this critical tradition is the work of ethnographers who take issue with the culturalist notion that the US–Mexico borderlands is a coherent geocultural region and a productive metaphor for intercultural processes. Pablo Vila (2000, 2005), who has conducted empirical research in El Paso/Juárez, concludes that the identity categories favored by border theorists on the US side (an antagonistic stand-off between Mexican/Chicano and Anglo), are not to be discovered on the ground, or in the ways borderlands residents speak about themselves and their social relationships. Vila points out that the *fronterizo* Mexican (*fronterizo* signifying a northern Mexican identity option that is not replicated in the USA) and the Chicano/a on the other side of the border are more likely than not inhabitants of separate borderlands worlds, as are the residents of El Paso's Chicano/a and Mexican immigrant **barrios**. On both sides of the border, complex and surprising modes of relational and oppositional identification are at work, and those modes conform to distinct historical contexts and local conditions throughout the border region. Vila also argues that the culturalist wing of border studies is hampered by its failure to actually cross the border into Mexico. That is, much of the theoretical power invested by cultural critics in the borderlands, and the border itself, enacts a "confusion" of the US side with the borderlands as a whole. Ortiz-González (2004) argues that the culturalist wing of border theory not only remakes the region for the benefit of an exploitative "somewhere" else under the current global order, but also glosses over the existence and realities of local residents, while ensuring that the border region remains understood as "an open space of constant takeovers." The militarization of the US side of the US–Mexico border since the early 1980s also militates against transborder borderlands conceptualizations by ensuring the radical incommensurability of north and south (Andreas 2000; Magaña 2003; D. Peña 1997). Criticisms of the culturalist wing of border theory also emanate from cultural studies, such as that of Michaelsen and Johnson (1997), who reject the notion of the borderlands as a universal paradigm for transcultural production or identity subversion.

Border Zones

The concept of border zones was developed by Renato Rosaldo (1989) to signify regions that cannot sustain the idea that "cultures" are distinct, different, pure, coherent, and readily observable and meaningful. Border zones are marked by the tension between cultural invisibility and visibility. That is, border zones, and the people who reside there, are marked as "cultured" by outsiders, whose ranks may include the ethnographer, who operate under the assumption that they themselves lack culture, and that the true bearers of culture are to be found elsewhere and therefore studied. Rosaldo links this perception to the ways by which national discourses of citizenship (rationality, belonging, not having culture) arise in dialectical relation to discourses of cultural visibility (irrationality, not belonging, being seen as having culture). Chicano/as, and Indian populations in Mexico, exemplify peoples read by dominant cultural protocols as having "culture." The cultural visibility of such peoples arises out of their fraught historical relation to, and colonial production by, the state that contains them. Rosaldo argues that the cultural visibilities and invisibilities that characterize border zones make them a particularly useful general model for social analysis that explicitly regards the notion of cultural purity, homogeneity, and difference as tenuous and unhelpful. Rather, border zone movements and incoherencies are emblematic of all human interaction. Attention to culture itself as the product of border zone times and spaces thus exposes to scrutiny the cultural invisibilities that tacitly inform much critical practice. See **Cultural Citizenship**.

Boricua, Borinquén

Boricua is a synonym for Puerto Rican and derives from the **Taíno** name for the Puerto Rico, *Borinquén* (*Borinkén, Borikén, Boriquén*). Use of these terms suggests a nationalistic and proindependence position on the question of the island's political status, and implies a sense of national cultural pride. *Boricua* and *Borinquén* are common terms in much Puerto Rican and Nuyorican literary and musical production, including **rap and hip-hop** lyrics, and sometimes appear in combination with Carib, as in *Boricua y Carib*. The term also provides the name of the island's national anthem, "La Borinqueña," which was composed by D. Felix Astol in 1867.

Boxing

Boxing-like traditions have been practiced for millennia in many parts of the world, but the modern sport derives from Great Britain, where the use of a boxing ring was popularized, and boxing academies and schools established, in the eighteenth century. At that time, boxing was essentially a working-class male free-for-all fight, in which wrestling holds, eye-gouging, kicking, and biting were permitted, and a winner only declared by the knockout or resignation of an opponent. Similar free-for-all forms of boxing were also popular in Britain's colonies. The rules governing boxing matches were steadily reformed in Britain in line with the increasing interest of middle- and upper-class spectators, the most important innovation being the Marquis of Queensberry's codifications of 1867, which established the basis of the modern sport (Montague 2004). Boxing now consists of amateur and professional categories, with both divided up into title competitions based on weight categories. Professional boxing matches or bouts comprise up to 12 three-minute rounds in a roped and raised boxing ring (actually an oblong 16 by 20 feet; 4.9 by 6.1 meters), and participants are required to wear padded gloves. Winners are declared after an opponent is either knocked out or one fighter earns more points than his rival for clean hits (Montague 2004). Boxing's codified violence and working-class base have, at times, offended middle-class taste; the sport has been burdened by historical associations with organized crime, and has also attracted criticisms from health professionals for the injuries, brain damage, and, at times, death, incurred by participants. Boxing remains one of the world's most popular spectator sports, and US contributions have been vital in achieving that global popularity. As with many other sports, boxing has provided a means by which working-class and/or minority participants may find social acceptance and an escape route from poverty and quotidian discrimination. The history of boxing in the USA is of note for its disturbances to practices of segregation, with many African Americans reaching champion status in the boxing ring. Latinos have also been involved with the sport for many decades and are well represented among the sport's champions in various weight categories: the Puerto Ricans Carlos Ortiz, Wilfredo Gómez ("Bazooka"), Héctor Camacho ("Macho Man"), and Felix Trinidad; and the Chicano Oscar de la Hoya. Boxing has played a role in what Gregory Rodríguez calls the shift from a limited ethnic imaginary to a recognition that Mexican Americanness and **Latinidad** also have a place in the postindustrial, mass-mediated, and corporatized world that generates such boxing celebrities as de la Hoya (2002). The Chicano Floyd Salas was an amateur boxer, and insights from boxing inform his novel *Tattoo the Wicked Cross* (1967) and memoir *Buffalo Nickel* (1992). The documentary *Split Decision* (2000, dir. Marcy Garriott) traces the experience of Mexican-born but Chicago-raised Jesús "El Matador" Chávez, whose boxing career was curtailed when he was deported to Mexico in 1997. The film *Undefeated* (2003, dir. John Leguizamo, who also plays the lead role) fictionalizes the story of a Nuyorican boxer for whom boxing provides an escape route into the American Dream. The film *Girlfight* (2000, dir. Karyn Kusama), features Michelle Rodríguez, a young Nuyorican from the projects of Brooklyn, who finds in boxing an avenue to manage her anger with the world and circumvent the limited socioeconomic options available to her as a Latina. Yxta Maya Murray's novel *What it Takes to Get to Vegas* (1999) focuses on Rita Zapata who similarly sees in boxing an escape route from East LA.

Bracero, Bracero Program

A *bracero* (from *brazo*, arm) is a Mexican day laborer who is most commonly employed in the agricultural and construction industries. The Bracero Program (1942–1964) was an official migrant regulatory program by which the US and Mexican governments agreed to a formalization of the cross-border migrant economy so that Mexicans could be recruited to work in the industrial and agricultural sectors. The impetus for this initiative (Public Law 78) was the shortage of labor due to the mass mobilization of troops following the US entry into World War II in December 1941. The Bracero Program was organized as a contract system, in Spanish. In theory, the contracts were supposed to establish fair pay rates, define hours and periods of work, provide health care and housing, cover transportation costs, and guarantee basic living conditions. After contracts expired, the *braceros* were required to return to Mexico. In practice, many farm workers found themselves working in conditions of servitude with little or no legal redress, or what activists in the 1960s called legalized slavery. The corollary of that exploitation was that many thousands of Mexicans opted to stay after their contracts terminated. It has been estimated that some 5 million Mexicans worked in the USA under the program. After the official termination of the program, *braceros* continued to cross the US–Mexico border in response to demand for labor on the US side, and their own desires for socioeconomic betterment. The exploitation of *braceros* in the agricultural sector animated the **United Farm Workers** in the 1960s, and inspired el **Teatro Campesino**'s work on behalf of the union. Herrera-Sobek (1979) regards the *bracero* novel, an autobiographically modulated genre about migratory labor, as a significant narrative trend in Mexican literature. Chicano/a literature has also generated a rich body of *bracero* novels, testimonies, and memoirs, as attested by four random selections: Raymond Barrio's *The Plum Plum Pickers* (1969), Victor Villaseñor's *Macho!* (1973), Ramón "Tianguis" Pérez's *Diary of an Undocumented Immigrant* (1991), and Rose Castillo Guilbault's memoir *Farmworker's Daughter* (2005). Alex Rivera's *Why Cybraceros?* (1988) is a film (part documentary, part science fiction) that parodies the US ambivalence about Mexican workers, and the increasing visibility of Mexicans in public space, by imagining a postcorporeal future in which Mexican labor is employed and put to virtual work over the internet, with the effect that Mexican workers are no longer obliged physically to cross the US–Mexico border. In a similarly satirical vein, *A Day Without a Mexican* (2004, dir. Sergio Arau), is a fictional documentary about the fate of California when dawn breaks and every person of Mexican origin or Mexican American identification has disappeared, with devastatingly comic consequences. See **Mojado/a, Operation Wetback**.

Brown, Brownness, Brown Pride, Brown Out

The term brown was adopted by Chicano/as in the 1960s and 1970s in line with the Chicano Movement redefinition of Chicano/as as a *mestizo/a* people.

This racialization also signaled an attempt to insert a third racial category into US racial discourses and debates alongside black and white. The civil rights' celebratory slogan Brown Pride typified this redefinition. Joining and complementing **Chicano Movement** uses of *raza* (race, people), brownness became a routine descriptor of the Chicano/a people in literature associated with, or influenced by, the Movement, Oscar "Zeta" Acosta's *The Auto-biography of a Brown Buffalo* (1972) being a typical example. Since the 1970s, brownness has also been metaphorized to connote communal safety and belonging, as is clear in Sandra Cisneros's novel *The House on Mango Street* (1984). The obverse of the deployment of brownness as a name for a people, or a metaphor for communal familiarity and security, is that pale-skinned Chicano/as (*güero/as*) had difficulties in being accepted as members of *la raza* in the Movement era. Moraga (1983), for example, confesses that a combination of light features, lesbianism, and an inability to speak Spanish, precluded her participation in Chicano/a activism, and disabled her self-iden-tification as a (brown) Chicana. Richard Rodriguez, an advocate of "Hispanic" assimilation in the 1980s and 1990s, appears to have modulated his ideas on the status of "brown" people in his third volume of autobiography, *Brown* (2002). Rodriguez regards the trope of brownness as a sign of the USA's mixed-race present and future, and a means of moving beyond the **Black/White paradigm** that dominates national debates. Rodriguez makes of brownness a broad racial category that encompasses many Latino/as, Asian Americans, and people from other immigrant communities. Brown Out is the name for a campaign to draw public attention to the dearth of Latino/as in English-language television programming, and to encourage more representa-tions of Latino/as in primetime. The first Brown Out was organized by a coali-tion of groups, including the National Council of the Raza and the National Hispanic Media Coalition, in September and October 1999, and took the form of a boycott of the television networks by thousands of Latino/a viewers.

Brown Berets

The Brown Berets (1967–1972) was a militant nationalist Chicano organiza-tion inspired in part by the African American Black Panther Party (1966–1971). The Brown Berets formed in East LA in 1967 under the leader-ship of college student David Sánchez, with many members drawn from earlier youth activist groups. By the end of the 1960s, Brown Beret chapters had been established from California to Texas. While men dominated the organization, chapters for women were also formed. Characterized by their paramilitary uniform and ubiquitous brown beret, both of which evoked the Latin American revolutionary icon, Che Guevara, the Brown Berets adopted an ethos of local community mobilization as they tackled such issues as Chicano/a marginalization in the Californian school system, state neglect of **barrio** infrastructures and health care, and police violence and intimidation. The Brown Berets' agenda aimed at practical outcomes: improving the socioeconomic status and base wage of Chicano/as; introducing Chicano/a studies to school curricula; and improving barrio dealings with state authorities, the last demand evident in calls for police to deal with Chicano/as in Spanish (E. Chávez 2002). Brown Beret members took part in the Californian student **blowouts** and the anti-Vietnam War Chicano Moratorium. At large-scale demonstrations, Brown Berets often took the role of self-appointed community police, ensuring maintenance of order (I. García 1997). Perhaps the group's most famous and widely publicized feat was the 1972 occupation of Catalina Island off the California coast, and the renaming of the island as "**Aztlán** Libre" (Free Aztlán). Police harassment and infiltration of the group, as well as internal disagreements and tensions, contributed to the disbanding of the Brown Berets at the end of 1972. In April 1994, a new Brown Beret organization, explicitly modeled on its predecessor, was established by school students in Watsonville, California, its aims being to encourage a sense of community among Chicano/a youth in an area beset by **gang** violence, police intimidation, and state neglect. As both a political example and an epochal icon, Brown Berets have been a constant presence in Chicano/a cultural production since the 1960s. Alfredo Ramos's play *The Last Angry Brown Hat* (1993) recreates the funeral of an ex-Brown Beret 25 years after the organization disbanded, at which a group of ex-members meditate on the organization's achievements and failures, and its messages for new generations. Similar concerns animate the autobiography by the Brown Berets' founder, David Sánchez (1978).

C

Caló

Caló is a Spanish word that originally denoted the Gitano or gypsy dialect in Spain. However, among Chicano/as *caló* refers to the working-class urban Chicano-Spanish dialect (also known as *pachuco* in Texas), and is often used synonymously with **Spanglish** as well. Aside from retaining many archaic words not used elsewhere in the Spanish-speaking world, *caló* is characterized by an inventive and playful approach to verbal communication, from **code switching** between English and Spanish to punning, the generation of neologisms, and the borrowing and adaptation of words, phrases, and pronunciative conventions from English. In the *colonias* in the border cities of northern Mexico, *caló* may be used to signify local Spanish dialects influenced by proximity to English.

Cannibal, *Canibál*, Caliban

Cannibal derives from the Spanish word *caribál* (*canibál*), which debuted in Columbus's journal from his first voyage of 1492–1493, as the name for an indigenous people, the caribs, purported to eat human flesh. Rouse (1992) notes that during the first century of European exploration and conquest in the Caribbean, carib was applied indiscriminately to any people who attacked or resisted Europeans. The figure of the cannibal—which quickly replaced the English word for eater of human flesh, anthropophagite—survived in the European imagination from the sixteenth century as the embodiment of New

World monstrosity, barbarism, primitiveness, and cultural lack (Hulme 1992). The cannibal, a discursive and textual invention, became the "Other" of Europe, a function that has inspired a range of counterdiscursive responses (Barker et al. 1998). An important manifestation of this trend was the Brazilian modernist movement of *Antropofagia* (cultural cannibalism), which originated with Oswald de Andrade's 1928 "Manifesto Antropófago" (Bary 1991). De Andrade called on Brazilian writers and artists to engage in an indiscriminate consumption and transubstantiation of European cultural forms and ideas. Underwriting *antropofagia* was a debate about the possibility of establishing an independent local or native national Brazilian culture. An overt borrowing of cultural cannibalism by Latino/as is Coco Fusco and Nao Bustamante's performance *Stuff* (2000), which parodies the sexual commodification of Latin American and Latina women within the transnational sex tourism industry. The performance utilizes *antropofagia* rhetoric in order to permit the objectified Latina to "consume" the masculine upholders, beneficiaries of, and participants in the sex trade in places like Cuba and Mexico. A widespread response to the European invention of the cannibal is the tradition of writing back to Shakespeare's *The Tempest* and its representations of Caliban (an anagram of the Spanish *canibál*). The Uruguayan Rodó (1900 [1988]) counterposed *The Tempest*'s Ariel (the cultured, civilized Latin American intellectual) with the barbaric and materialist North American Caliban. For the Cuban Fernández Retamar (1979), Caliban embodies a Latin American identity generated by European colonialism and subject to US neocolonial hegemony. Rejecting that trend, Eliana Ortega (1989) proposes Anacaonian liberation as a feminist praxis based in Puerto Rican oral traditions and historical memory. Ortega's aim is to find an alternative to patriarchal and androcentric Latin American intellectual traditions, notably Uruguayan critic Rama's "lettered city" (1996), and the practice of drawing on European literary and cultural models. Ortega proposes the **Taíno** figure of Anacaona (from Hispaniola, in what is now the Dominican Republic) as a more viable symbol. Anacaona survives in oral traditions and folklore as a rebel ruler who, despite being killed by Spanish forces, commanded great respect, defied the Spanish and her male kin alike, and embraced her sexuality. As a forebear of the Puerto Rican woman writer in the USA, and a model for all Latin American women, Anacaona and the liberation she configures signifies a critical praxis for writers wishing to target dominant cultural protocols.

Canon

The term canon derives from the Greek *kanon* (rule or edict), and originally signified those religious books (e.g., the key texts in the Jewish and Christian traditions) whose authority and authenticity were debated, assessed, and confirmed by religious leaders and scholars. In literary studies, the canon refers to the body of writing (or art or music) that is accorded authoritative or classic status, with the additional connotation of purportedly encoding the desired and desirable values or ideals of a particular community, people, nation, or linguistic tradition. Thus, such notions as the Western canon and the English canon designate sets of literary (and at times historical and philosophical) works and writers on which the civilized base of the West or the Anglophone world rests. The project of canon formation is exemplified by the production of literary anthologies and series of "classic" writing, the inclusion of certain texts and authors in school and university curricula, and the selection of texts and authors studied by scholars. Guillory (1993) defines canonicity in terms of the exclusionary processes by which literary cultural capital is made, circulated, and consumed. For Guillory, the hegemonic use made of the literary text—the commodity used, for example, in the school system to regulate and valorize literacy and social status—transforms that text into linguistic capital (socially valued speech) and symbolic capital (knowledge that brings rewards to well-educated people). Since the 1960s, the idea of a universally applicable or meaningful canon has been disputed. Critics have argued that the question of what and who is included in, and excluded from, the canon is intrinsically tied to struggles for socioeconomic and political power, privilege, and cultural value. Feminist, Marxist, ethnic, and postcolonial critics have challenged the traditional or classic Western canon's domination by European and/or white men (Edgar and Sedgwick 2000). These critical drives aimed either to expand the traditional canon in order for it to accommodate previously neglected writers and texts, or to construct alternative canons, for instance of women's, African American, and postcolonial writing. Latino/a critics have also struggled to gain spaces for Latino/a texts and authors in the American canon, while also constructing a new Latino/a canon, and Chicano/a, Nuyorican, and Cuban American canons. Entities such as the Recovering the US Hispanic Literary Heritage Project, based at the University of Texas, Houston, have also contributed to the development of a Spanish-language canon of US literature. Latino/a canonical debates are complicated by the long tradition of Latino/a literary production in Spanish, English, and switching between or mixing the two idioms. How the US literary and educational apparatuses deal with Spanish-language and mixed-language texts remains an important critical issue (D. Castillo 2005; Pérez Firmat 2003). Moreover, Latino/a texts may also be allocated places in the Latin American canon, the broad Hispanophone canon, as well as the national canons of countries such as Mexico, Cuba, and the Dominican Republic. The status of Puerto Rican literary production is particularly contentious. While the island has a rich Spanish-language literary tradition, the Nuyorican literary tradition has evolved in Spanish, English, and Spanglish. However, in both the USA and Latin America, island literature has often been relegated to the "other" America. In Chicano/a literary studies, the canonical place of *literatura chicanesca* was a notable concern in the 1970s and 1980s. Some Chicano/a authors were excluded from the Chicano/a canon, the argument being that their texts failed to address Chicano/a quotidian realities by focusing on other identity modes. This logic has resulted in the ambivalent canonical status of John Rechy and Sheila Ortiz Taylor, responsible for the first literary explorations of gay male and lesbian themes in Chicano/a writing (Bruce-Novoa 1986).

Carnalismo

Carnalismo, an ethic of fraternal solidarity or brotherhood (from *carnal*, of the flesh, blood brother), was a key force of constructed homosocial kinship during the **Chicano Movement**, and was often used by male Chicano activists to define the binding qualities of *Chicanismo*. This explicitly androcentric approach alienated women and gay Chicanos, and inspired feminist critiques of the Chicano civil rights project. More generally, the term *carnalismo* signifies the close local and friendship ties that may bind men in Latino/a communities. See **Comadrismo**, **Compadrazgo**.

Casita Movement

The *casita* movement is the name for an urban folkloric tradition on the part of New York-resident Puerto Ricans who began to construct little houses (*casitas*) and gardens in abandoned lots and derelict spaces in the 1970s and following decades. The *casita* movement arose as a Nuyorican popular cultural response to the downsizing of the industrial sector in the 1970s and 1980s, and the resultant increase in unemployment, and the reduction in **barrio** space due to demolition programs and urban renewal initiatives. As Aponte-Parés (1998) notes, the *casita* movement represents a collective response to the devastation of Nuyorican neighborhoods. An attempt to claim, reshape, and repair damaged barrio ground, the movement announces a cultural reclamation and resemanticization of public space, and a resistance to further destruction and deculturation of that space. Based on traditional island models from the countryside that are brightly colored and constructed by collective teams out of whatever materials are at hand, *casitas* are often given names such as "Villa Puerto Rico" that self-consciously announce a sense of cultural pride and identity anchored in island origins. Often accompanied by gardens where vegetables are grown and chickens raised, *casitas* provide a site for communal interaction (parties, barbeques) and construction that would otherwise be unavailable to participants. Juan Flores (2000) regards the *casita* phenomenon as a performative tradition by which "Puerto Rico" is staged and transformed in the barrio setting. The *casita* phenomenon has been an important drive in the community garden movement in New York City; it has also attracted periodic attacks by New York City authorities who have claimed that *casitas* are eyesores, or sites of illegal squatting and land appropriation. As a consequence many famous *casitas* have been bulldozed or demolished at city orders.

Catholicism, Protestantism

Due to the colonial division of the Americas between Catholic powers (Spain, Portugal, and France) and Protestant states (Britain and Holland), the Americas are often thought of as replicating rigid historical religious divisions, with Protestant North America arranged against the Catholic South. However, though the vast majority of Latin Americans is Catholic, a significant number is Protestant, and since the 1960s, Latin America has seen a dramatic rise in charismatic and evangelical denominations, particularly in Central America. Similarly, the Catholic Church has been a significant religious force in US history, a position secured by mass migration from European Catholic states such as Ireland, Italy, and Poland, and from Latin America. The USA currently has the world's third largest Catholic population, after Brazil and Mexico. Antipathy between Protestants and Catholics has nonetheless marked historical relations between the USA and its Latin American neighbors, leading some commentators to detect an anti-Spanish and anti-Catholic discourse, the **Black Legend**, in Anglo-American attitudes to the south. That legend, and the historical rivalry between Catholicism (headquartered in Rome with a Pope as Supreme Pontiff) and Protestantism it exemplifies, derives from the Reformation that began in Europe in the sixteenth century, which coincided with the first century of European colonization in the Americas. This was the era after the Renaissance when the power and teachings of Catholicism were disputed (protested) by religious figures and thinkers, the most important being Martin Luther and John Calvin. These critics agitated for Church reform along simpler, more fundamental lines. They argued that the practice of faith should proceed without interference from the traditions, rituals, dogma, and hierarchical, bureaucratic, and often corrupt institutions that had come to dominate Catholicism. As a result of the Reformation, many Protestant denominations were established in the 1500s and subsequent centuries, and adherents of Protestantism (such as the Puritans) spearheaded British and Dutch colonial settlement of the east coast of North America. Today, while there is disagreement about which of the many thousands of Christian denominations reside under the Protestant rubric, historically the term has been applied to any western European denomination that either broke away from Catholicism during the Reformation, or evolved from those denominations in subsequent centuries. Protestantism thus spans a religious spectrum from the highly institutionalized and Catholic-like Church of England (Anglicans), through Lutherans, Pentecostals, Calvinists, Presbyterians, Episcopalians, and Methodists, to the small and socially progressive Quaker faith. Due to Spanish and Portuguese colonization, many parts of Latin America are deeply marked by the Catholic inheritance. That inheritance is perhaps most visible in the cults associated with Virgin Mary and her many American variants (**Virgen de Guadalupe**, *Alta Gracia, Providencia, Caridad del Cobre*), and those cults' influence on the operations of *marianismo*. However, it is difficult to speak of Catholicism as a monolithic apparatus or homogeneous belief system. At times, Catholic clergy have defied the authority of the central Church in Rome in order to work with poor and marginalized communities in the American continent, a trend exemplified by 1960s liberation theology. Moreover, as a consequence of centuries of adjustments between European, indigenous, and African peoples, complex forms of popular Catholicism evolved. This is a broad designation for a range of everyday cultural traditions and productions marked by the **syncretism** of belief systems, traditions, and imagery. Often produced or displayed in the domestic space, these practices include altars, *retablos, santos*, and *Día de los muertos* celebrations in Mexican and Chicano/a communities. Catholic influences are also evident in non-Christian religious systems, as exemplified by the adoption of Catholic saints in Afro-Cuban *santería*. Although Catholicism is the dominant faith in all Latino/a sectors, recent studies have confirmed that approximately one-quarter of Latinos/as define themselves as Protestant or some other non-Catholic faith (Mormon, Jehovah's Witness). Indeed, Mexico is the source of the largest number of Catholic and Protestant immigrants to the USA. Today, pentecostal or evangelical Latino/as account for 85 percent of the total Latino/a Protestant population, and, nearly 40 percent of Latino/as (Catholic and Protestant) define themselves as evangelical or "born-again" (Espinosa et al. 2005). Although there is some concern in the Catholic Church that Latinos/as are shedding Catholicism in favor of Protestant denominations, immigration rates have nonetheless ensured that Catholicism remains the main Latino/a religion, and Catholicism remains a significant mode of identification for many Latino/as (Vila 2005).

Census

The US Census is routinely conducted every 10 years (the last occurring in 2000) to gather statistical information about the US population. The first census was conducted in 1790, when the population registered 3.9 million. Its parameters have expanded in response to the changing demographics of the US population, and to changing government expectations of the data it regards as relevant and useful for policy work and planning. Among the significant data currently collected by the Bureau of Census are age, place of residency, occupation, income, household composition, religious affiliation, country of origin if not US-born, and race and ethnicity. According to the 2000 census, Latinos or Hispanics numbered 35,305,818, or 12.5 percent of the total US population. While challenged by demographers for consistently undercounting the Latino/a population, the Census Bureau's forward estimates provide a sense of the future significance of Latino/a communities: by 2050, Latino/as will represent at least 25 percent of the population. Latino/a observers have criticized what they regard as the homogenizing aims of the census, which in 2000 provided three terms of purported equivalence—Spanish, Hispanic, Latino—by which respondents could self-identify. The Census Bureau's conflation of Latino, Hispanic, and Spanish suggests that this particular US state apparatus regards identifications based on linguistic (Spanish,

Hispanic), national (Spanish), and ethnocultural (Hispanic, Latino) factors as synonymous (Grieco and Cassidy 2001). Respondents could also nominate more than one racial category, the census in theory thus permitting identifications along mixed-race lines. Latino/a critics also point out that wider political and cultural debates about race and ethnic identity have been played out in the categories deployed by the census over many decades with regard to the country's minorities. Clara Rodríguez (2000) argues that census categories demonstrate how dominant ideals and belief systems about identity, and public assumptions and consensus about how to measure identity, inform government classifications. Census categories on race and ethnicity have changed over time, and moved people into and out of "white" and "black" and other options, thus betraying the inherent mutability and sociocultural constructedness of the categories popularly deemed to be essential, natural, and fixed. At the same time, confusion between what the census categories of race and ethnicity are supposed to designate also arises from, and reflects, broader social conflations of those categories (Dávila 2000). That confusion is evident in the changing terminologies and values presented by the census since its inception, the only category immune to amendment and adjustment being white. For Oboler (1995), the proliferation of census categories, and their ever-morphing contours, iterates the disjunction between imposed identities and the ways by which Latin American origin people define or talk about themselves.

Cha-Cha-Chá

Along with **mambo**, cha-cha-chá was one of the Cuban music styles to gain international popularity in the mid-twentieth century, particularly in European and US dancehalls. With its origins in the *danzón* and the *son*, the cha-cha-chá differed from the faster-paced mambo in its slower and less syncopated rhythmic drive (with emphasis on the first beat) that enabled the repetition of the characteristic three-step dance movement (the *cha-cha-chá*). The style is attributed to Enrique Jorrín who between 1948 and 1951 experimented with the *danzón* form in order to provide a more danceable alternative to the *danzón-mambo* (Orovio 2004).

Charco, Brincando el charco

El charco translates as "the puddle" or "the lake" and is used by Puerto Ricans on and off the island to describe the distance between the USA and

Puerto Rico, and the traversal of that distance. Typical expressions derived from this term are *cruzando el charco*, crossing the puddle, and *brincando el charco*, jumping/hopping over the puddle. An important filmic representation of the ambivalent Nuyorican identity is Francés Negrón-Muntaner's *Brincando el charco: Portrait of a Puerto Rican* (1994), a fusion of documentary, autobiography, and fiction that follows a US-based Puerto Rican lesbian photographer as she crosses *el charco* in order to attend her father's funeral on the island. In much Nuyorican cultural criticism, the constant movement of many Puerto Ricans back and forth across *el charco* functions as a trope for the mutable and divided Puerto Rican condition, and a metaphor for the ways by which connections between island and mainland Puerto Rican identities and cultures are maintained and rejuvenated. Mexicans also use the phrase *brincar el charco* when referring to the crossing of the Río Grande/Río Bravo del Norte into the USA. The phrase also signifies migration north from Mexico and Central America in a more general sense. See **Guagua aérea**, **Vaivén**.

Chicanismo

During the **Chicano Movement** and concomitant **Chicano Renaissance**, *Chicanismo* was the ideological force that propelled activism and political art. Roughly translated as the state of being Chicano, the term encoded within it a notion of Chicano identity forged out of oppositional politics. A typical usage from the Movement era comes from the 1969 **Plan de Santa Barbara**, which distinguished Mexican Americans/Hispanics from Chicanos. The former lacked the political consciousness of the latter whereas the radical politicization, self-respect, and ethnic pride of the latter underscored their *Chicanismo*. *Chicanismo* thus provided an organizing rubric for the main precepts of a new communal identity formed by *mestizaje*, the sense of belonging to the US southwest as a homeland (***Aztlán***), and a consciousness of Chicano history as marked by two conquests (Spanish and USA) and decades of labor exploitation. For Bruce-Novoa (1982), the term *Chicanismo* provided the conceptual base for understanding Chicano/a literary texts, primarily poetry, as an expression of Chicano/a socioeconomic, cultural, linguistic, and national liminality. That is, Chicano/a literary texts occupy an "interlingual space" exemplified by English–Spanish **code switching**, and characterized by an ambivalent relation to the Mexican cultural inheritance, and an acceptance of the inevitable neoculturation of *Mexicanidad* (Mexicanness) in the US setting. Many femi-nist critics, however, regarded *chicanismo* as an exclusionary and sexist dis-course on account of the androcentric and heteronormative protocols by which Chicano/a identity was imagined and proclaimed. A feminist alternative to *Chicanismo* is Xicanisma. Coined by Ana Castillo (1994), the term Xicanisma announces a woman-centered critical and creative-cum-spiritual project to attain voice and effect social change. By placing Chicanas at the center of the project, Castillo also distances Xicanisma from Chicana feminism, a form of feminism that she regards as hampered by its origins in the nationalist politics of the Movement era. Xicanisma therefore parallels, but is distinguishable from, other forms of political consciousness organized along *mestizo/a* (mixed race), *mejicano/a* (Mexican), and Chicano/a nationalist lines. Xicanisma rep-resents a specific political and creative feminist praxis that values coalitionist and affiliative initiatives across gender lines.

Chicano/a, Chicana/o, Chican@

Chicano/a is a neocultural sign, and a neosubjective outcome, of a history of conquest, transcultural contact, and **migration**, spanning more than 150 years. Originally a term of disparagement for working-class Mexican Americans, Chicano was adopted as a collective identity marker in the 1960s by the **Chicano Movement**. The term announced a break along generational and aspi-rational lines between Mexican American student and worker activists, and older Mexican Americans. It also signified a desire to differentiate Mexican Americans from other Latino/a sectors and to affirm Chicanos as a distinct US minority formed by invasion, colonization, and capitalist exploitation. Under this name, activists attempted to politicize a community, now recast as a people. Rafaela Castro (2001) describes three possible origins of the term dating from the early twentieth century. First, Chicano may derive from a fusion of the Mexican City of Chihuahua with Mexicano (Chi- and -cano). Second, the word may derive from the *Mexica* (indigenous people) and the **Náhuatl** convention of pronouncing "x" as "sh" or "ch." A third theory posits that Chicano derives from *chico* (Spanish for boy), a disparaging term used by Anglo-Americans in the US southwest in the nineteenth century when referring to a Mexican American. The third explanation may also account for the resist-ance on the part of older Mexican Americans to adopt a term they regarded as demeaning and insulting. Although Chicano is now commonplace, having given its name to the field of Chicano/a Studies, the term has had a contested history since the 1960s. Acuña (2000) suggests that the **Chicano Movement** may have erred in dispensing with Mexican as a marker of a distinct ethnic identity. Nonetheless, Acuña continues to use Chicano/a in honor of the term's reclamation by Movement activists. Although it is routine to encounter the single masculine noun Chicano in critical and cultural work, variations that acknowledge gender differences are also commonplace: Chicano/a, Chicana/o, and Chican@. Xicano/a is an alternative spelling, the use of the "X" (which follows Náhuatl orthographic conventions) reminding of the Mexican base and acknowledging the importance of indigenous ancestry and traditions for many Chicano/a identifications.

Chicano Movement, *Movimiento chicano*

El Movimiento Chicano or Chicano Movement refers to a range of Chicano activist drives in the 1960s and 1970s. Many critics regard the movement as historically embedded in the "Mexican Americanization" of people of Mexican descent, and anchor the movement in earlier civil rights activism. Some historians trace this communal consciousness back to the post-1848 era, with a range of bandit resistances, oral and musical accounts of resistance to *gringos,* and the founding of local Spanish-language newspapers, that helped forge a sense of Mexican American community. Other historians argue that the consolidation of Mexican Americanness occurred in the 1920s, a result of mass migration across the border in the wake of the 1910 **Mexican Revolution.** As these migrants joined established Mexican American communities, and their children were born and raised in the USA, a sense of communal difference from Mexico also developed, as exemplified by the establishment of Mutual Aid Associations in the 1920s and 1930s. An important example was The League of United Latin American Citizens (LULAC), formed in 1929 in Texas by middle-class Mexican Americans with the aim of fostering community economic development through education and a vigorous work ethic. LULAC worked to end segregation in southern Californian schools as early as 1946, a continuation of its campaign against segregation in Texas in the 1930s and 1940s. World War II also played a role in the politicization of Mexican Americans and the consolidation of a Mexican American consciousness based on collective opposition and resistance to perceived Anglo-American hegemony (Rivas-Rodríguez 2005). In California, the **Sleepy Lagoon** Murder Case (1942) and the **Zoot Suit Riots** (1943) highlighted systematic abuses of Mexican Americans and did much to encourage in younger Mexican Americans a sense of opposition to the US state and Anglo-American culture. Given the high level of Mexican American male involvement in the armed services, Mexican American women, like many women from other communities, were impelled to take on social roles traditionally foreclosed to them—factory work and other wage-earning activities, community organization leadership, responsibility as family heads—all of which contributed to a growing sense of communal transformation. After the war, the Félix Longoria controversy was a notable example of a mobilization around a specific issue that attracted national attention and high-level political intervention (Carroll 2003). Longoria was a Mexican American serviceman killed in the Philippines during World War II. In 1949, when his body was finally returned to his family, the local funeral parlor in Three Rivers, Texas, refused to accept the body and host the wake his relatives wanted. This refusal was regarded by many Mexican Americans as an act of racism, and caused widespread protest and the eventual intervention from the then senator Lyndon B. Johnson, who organized Longoria's burial at the Arlington National Cemetery. This incident was a watershed in the politicization of Héctor García's American GI Forum beyond the interests of returned servicemen. Many other organizations emerged across the US southwest in the 1940s and 1950s, exemplifying the growing Mexican American mobilization against structural discriminations. These organizations were paralleled by the establishment of Spanish-language newspapers, radio, and TV stations, and increasing Mexican American involvement in the political system at local, state, and federal levels (Meier and Gutiérrez 2000). Indebted to earlier Mexican American activism, the Chicano Movement comprised a set of political drives with no centralized organization. These enterprises included the **United Farm Workers** (UFW), which was formed in 1965 in California to fight for better pay and working conditions for agricultural laborers. The term *La causa* (the Cause) was often applied to the UFW, although it could also refer to any movement enterprise. Significant, too, were the student boycotts or **blowouts** of 1968. Related to the broader civil rights enterprise was the Chicano Moratorium of 1970, an anti-Vietnam War demonstration organized by a coalition of student groups, unions, and other organizations, who regarded the war as an imperial enterprise that Chicano/as, being a colonized sector by virtue of an imperial act in the nineteenth century, did not support. Across the US southwest and Texas, specific organizations with civil rights agendas were also formed in this era, notable examples being the Colorado-based Crusade for Justice, the National Council of La Raza (formed in 1968 in the southwest, but becoming national in 1973), and the New Mexican Alianza Federal de Mercedes (Federal Alliance of Land Grants). The Chicano Movement spawned a number of political parties, such as La Raza Unida Party in Texas, which sought to advance Chicano rights through direct involvement in political processes at local and state levels, and the **Brown Berets**, which took a community mobilization approach to Chicano civil rights. Such enterprises reflected a widespread sense of Chicano/a solidarity with **decolonization** movements in the Third World, as well as with armed struggles against totalitarian regimes throughout Latin America, with activists linking those liberation struggles to Chicano experiences under US suzerainty since 1848. The Chicano Movement also designates the cultural political productions of the **Chicano Renaissance**, which did much to popularize such unifying discourses as *mestizo* identity or **brownness**, a national homeland, **Aztlán**, and transnational solidarity with Third World liberation movements (Mariscal 2005). Already in circulation by the mid-1960s, these ideals were formalized in El **Plan Espiritual de Aztlán**, from 1969. The various drives of the Chicano Movement combined to insert Chicano/as into the national consciousness as an oppressed and exploited minority, and a colonized people and nation defined by indigenous ancestry and connection to the land. Despite the factional demise of many organizations associated with the Chicano Movement in the late 1970s, the ongoing critiques leveled at *chicanismo* since that time confirm that *Movimiento* legacies continue to inform activism and cultural discourse in many ways. The androcentric and patriarchal credentials of Chicano nationalism, as well as the male-dominated structures of most organizations, inspired feminist disputes with *Movimiento* rhetoric and structures from the late 1970s. Alongside Chicana feminist interventions into Chicano/a identity debates, cultural work, and political activism, queer critics have also challenged the *machista* and homophobic contours of *Movimiento* activism, as exemplified by the queering of Aztlán (Moraga 1993). Critics have recognized the tendency of Movimiento practitioners to gloss over the role of Mexican *mestizos* in the conquest of native peoples. More complex assessments of Chicano/a and indigenous relations, made without appeals to native status or appropriations of indigeneity, are now routine, as are readings of Chicano experiences of racialization that recognize multiracial identifications. The Movimiento reduction of the Chicano predicament to a Chicano–Anglo dichotomy of antagonism is recognized to have undervalued productive **panethnic** relations and potential conflicts, between Chicanos and other ethnic and racialized communities: African Americans, Asian Americans, Native Americans, other Latino/as, and immigrants from Mexico and Central America. Many critics have challenged the *Movimiento* celebration of a unitary Chicano/a collective, as opposed to a set of communities with divergent historical experiences of US residency and subordination, and subject to internal divisions along class, gender, sexual, racial, generational, and regional lines. As these critical trajectories suggest, post-Movimiento Chicano political and cultural work against state and dominant cultural imperatives continues on multiple fronts in the new millennium.

Chicano Renaissance

One of the key manifestos produced by the student wing of the Chicano Movement, el **Plan de Santa Barbara** from 1969, opened with the lines: "For all peoples, as with individuals, the time comes when they must reckon with their history. For the Chicano the present is a time of renaissance, of renacimiento." The use of the word renaissance (rebirth) here typified Chicano/a activist sentiment in the 1960s and 1970s that those decades were witnessing not only the coming to political voice of Chicanos/as, but also a cultural and critical flowering on numerous fronts: literature (especially poetry, but also the novel and short story); the establishment of Chicano/a publishing houses, literary magazines, and academic journals; music; **murals**; theater (such as el **Teatro Campesino**); films and documentaries; visual art; and Chicano/a studies itself typified by the founding of Chicano/a, Mexican American, and Hispanic research centers in universities across the US southwest and Texas. The term Chicano Renaissance now routinely designates the cultural output that coincided with, and that was politically tied to, the various drives of the Chicano Movement and the militant notions of *chicanismo* that the movement spawned. Maciel et al. (2000) note that Chicano/a cultural workers regarded their practices and outputs as an intrinsic feature of the movement, and themselves as agents by which to assist in the project of community politicization and building ethnic pride. Differing from commentators who assert that the Chicano Renaissance ended in the late 1970s, Maciel et al. argue that the cultural renaissance has continued unabated, thus generating an artistic and political continuum linking generations of art workers since the 1970s.

This view of an ongoing cultural renaissance expands on the four evolutionary stages in Chicano/a cultural and critical practice since the 1960s identified by Ignacio García (1997): a critical and revisionist phase in which Chicano/as disputed the historical record and scholarly representations of Chicano/as, most notably notions of **assimilation** and **acculturation**; the quest for critical models (such as **internal colonization**) for understanding the historical oppression of Chicanos/as; a phase of affirmation and celebration in Chicano/a culture, typified by the reclamation of Mexican cultural traditions and legacies; and finally, a phase of oppositional and liberatory politics, organized under the **Aztlán** rubric, by which activists and cultural workers targeted structures of domination and discourses of racism.

Cholo/a

Cholo is a word used in much of Latin America to designate a *mestizo*, and at times, an Indian who has adopted European language and culture or been in some way assimilated. However, regional and dialectical factors throughout the Americas dramatically transform the term's usage. In Mexico and Central America, *cholo* normally signifies a half-breed, a *mestizo*; as an insult this use emphasizes indigenous ancestry over European and draws attention to purported racial and cultural contamination. The term has also connoted a Mexican who has adopted US youth styles and tastes. Indeed, in the border regions of northern Mexico, *cholismo* has had currency since the 1970s to indicate local youth cultural forms and identities that incorporate dress styles, cultural symbols, idiom, and musical forms derived from, or influenced by, the Chicano/a and Mexican **barrios** of the USA. In the Andean region (Peru, Ecuador, Bolivia, parts of Chile, and Colombia), *cholo* traditionally signified an indigenous person and/or a poor peasant. However, with increasing migration to the cities in Peru and Bolivia, *cholo/a* may be a positive identity label, which is reinforced by distinct and widely recognizable dress codes. In the Andean states the word is often directed at people perceived to have aspirations beyond, or who may have strayed from, their "proper" social place. That straying may include moving from the country to the city, or the adoption of "foreign" practices, notably from contact with US consumer products and values. The insult is thus based on racial and class logics of purported superiority. In Chicano Spanish, since the mid-nineteenth century, *cholo/a* has had numerous significations in addition to, but always modulated by, *mestizo*, and it appears as a racially and class-framed insult in Anglo-American texts from the 1840s right through to the 1960s as a generic term for any working-class or poor Mexican American. Some critics claim that *cholo* became particularly prevalent during the **pachuco** era (Vigil 2002). Depending on context and period, when used by Chicano/as the term may designate variously: a Mexican American or Chicano/a, a term of pride, and a synonym for **pachuco** and **pocho** (terms that predate and overlap with Chicano); a **gang** member (an insult if used by Anglos, a positive term of personal and collective identification if used by *cholos*); someone who is particularly cool or good-looking; and most recently a **homeboy**/girl, again emphasizing a certain look in terms of hairstyles, dress codes, and street sensibilities. The Chicano gang use of *cholo* has also begun to permeate the Mexican side of the border. A synonym for *cholo/a* is *chulo/a* (a cool, slick, pretty, flashy, streetwise person, a **bato**).

Choteo

Choteo is a Cuban expression, claimed by the Cuban ethnographer Fernando Ortiz (1924) to derive from African Cuban idiomatic speech, that variously connotes the act of "tearing, talking, throwing, maligning, spying, and playing" (Muñoz 1999). Jorge Mañach (1940) defined *choteo* as a collective street-level antiauthoritarian sensibility that mocks and satirizes its targets, the agents of social order, decorum, and power. Although for Mañach the expression *choteo* designated an ambivalent, unserious, and potentially pathological aspect of the Cuban national character, the Cuban American José Muñoz (1999) argues that it is a transcultural signifier, encoding within it the long historical interplay between African and Spanish peoples in Cuba. Muñoz further regards *choteo* as a Cuban variant of camp, in that like camp, *choteo* can at once mock or satirize agents and forms of dominant culture and take the form of a menacing countercolonial mimicry of those agents and forms. *Choteo* for Muñoz thus becomes a key strategy for self-assertion, identity construction, and critique of dominant cultural protocols, and an important mechanism in the resistant drives of **disidentification** evident in much Cuban American queer cultural production.

Chusmería

Chusmería is a Caribbean Spanish term that, according to José Muñoz (1999), designates unconventional, impolite, and unrefined behavior and that, when used critically (as in "*¡no seas tan chusma!*"), reflects middle- and upper-class disparagements of such behavior. As Muñoz describes it, *chusmería* is a cover-all for a range of stigmatized social sectors (the working classes, black people) and their public appearances. The term may also be applied by Cuban exiles to newly arrived Cubans who have yet to access the codes of "Americanness," and also to Cubans who are hypernationalist. Onlookers may apply similar notions of excess to people whose sexual and gender behavior they regard as flagrantly departing from conventional mores. Many of those connotations are evident in *Chicas 2000*, by noted performance artist Carmelita Tropicana. Muñoz argues that this performance announces a self-conscious recuperation of *chusmería*, one that enables the artist's **disidentification** with a dominant cultural imperative in the US host society to appear "larger than life" because she is a Latina. Carmelita Tropicana toys with the Cuban logics of *chusmería* in order to mock and damage the "burden of liveness" that regards her as mere exotic spectacle. The play includes a succinct definition of *chusmería*, delivered to the audience in a staged news broadcast that warns "Americans" of one of the "deviant" *chusma* gene responsible for the *chusmería* disease: "shameless, loud, gross, tacky behavior, in short, tasteless with attitude" (2000).

Citizenship, Cultural Citizenship

Citizenship is a product of the rise of geopolitical states and national communities in the eighteenth and nineteenth centuries (B. Anderson 1991), hence the orthodox understanding of the concept as a universal norm by which, in theory, all residents of a particular state are equal members of a geopolitical order. Citizenship generally implies political and legal status and recognition, participation in national institutions, and access to government services such as welfare, health, education, and civil and military protection (Bennett et al. 2005). However, the ideal of universal political (legal) citizenship is paralleled, and disrupted by, other modes of citizenship (economic or class, ethnic and racial, cultural, linguistic, and human rights models) by which particular sectors may be either excluded from or granted partial access to citizenship. Immigrants, refugees, and asylum seekers, for example, might be admitted into a particular state without political citizenship (Bennett et al. 2005). Working-class or poor sectors might regard their capacities as citizens to be hampered by poverty and class exploitation. Ethnic and racialized communities, and colonized subjects, might regard racializing discourses and structures of domination

as precluding their unequivocal citizenship. In the USA, citizenship has provided a vector of contention, and long-standing struggle, on the part of
Latino/a historical minorities (Chicano/as and Puerto Ricans) and immigrant
communities. Discourses of belonging that define US citizenship in terms of
legal and **illegal alien** status are of particular concern for the millions of
undocumented workers in the USA, as exemplified by the mass demonstrations by hundreds of thousands of such workers across the country from March
2006 onward, and their demands to have access to the "American Dream."
Similar struggles over citizenship erupt in the debates over the national language and **bilingualism**. The Latino Cultural Studies Working Group regards
cultural citizenship as a particularly important response to the historical
denial, or partial granting, of political citizenship to Latino/as. Cultural citizenship refers to the ways by which Latino/a sociocultural practices establish
distinct venues of belonging that, in turn, challenge dominant political discourses about citizenship that have historically excluded Latino/as from the
national realm. Cultural citizenship thus designates the political and social
function of cultural practices (traditions, daily life, artistic work, language
use) in the formation of Latino/a identifications and consciousness. Flores and
Benmayor (1997) argue that cultural citizenship aims to counter the
Black/White paradigm in debates over citizenship, which operates by silencing
or occluding Latino/a cultural, ethnic, and linguistic aspirations and contributions. Cultural citizenship also aims to counter **nativist** attempts to restrict
immigrant rights. The conjunction of "culture" and "citizenship" thus seeks to
challenge unitary and universal understandings of "American" community and
citizenship. The conjunction foregrounds the dialectic between, on the one
hand, the discourses by which Latino/as are constructed as an "alien"/"illegal" constituency, and, on the other hand, quotidian responses to such discourses, for instance through countercultural practices aimed at refiguring
Latino/as "as legitimate political subjects" deserving of rights as "Americans"
(Flores and Benmayor 1997). This approach builds from Rosaldo's (1989,
1997) argument that cultural citizenship mediates the power dialectic
between "citizenship" and "culture." Sectors with full citizenship are regarded
as lacking culture, whereas ethnicized or marginalized groups that have
culture are lacking citizenship. Rosaldo (1997) points out that this dialectic
derives from the historical construction of the ideal citizen as white, male, and
middle classed, thus excluding the claims to citizenship of others along gender,
race, and class lines. Reacting against that exclusion, subordinate groups

aspire to their own enfranchised and socially valued spaces of productive belonging as part of a broader national community. Cultural citizenship emerges in sociocultural practices and notions of belonging as managed, articulated, and understood in local communities. Critical cultural citizenship involves heeding the claims made by Latino/as, and understanding the limits to, and potential for, Latino/a agency on individual, familial, and communal levels, as Latino/as insert themselves into, reconfigure, or work around citizenship debates (Flores and Benmayor 1997).

Class

In its general sense, a class designates a social division or order, as is colloquially encoded in the tripartite social division of upper, middle, and lower classes. In Marxist theory, however, classes exist, and become meaningful, only in direct relation to other classes, which in turn depend on their relation to the modes of production that themselves conform to an overarching order of socioeconomic and political organization. Under capitalism, a capitalist class controls capital, or the wealth enabling and financing economic production, a ruling class or bourgeoisie controls the institutions of state, and enjoys social and cultural prestige, whereas the most populous class, the working class or proletariat, survives by selling its labor (Bennett et al. 2005). There may also be a middle class between the bourgeoisie and the working class. Historical relations between the classes are marked by antagonism and conflict, hence the theory that the working classes must develop a class consciousness of their exploitation that will enable their collective mobilization and the overthrow of the capitalist order, thus establishing the preconditions for a classless socialist order. The sociological tradition derived from Max Weber regards classes as orders of rank and privilege arranged from an aristocracy through a middle class or bourgeoisie to the lower or laboring classes (Bennett et al. 2005). The Weberian notion of classes regards them not as relational economic categories but as social ranks whose members have more or less access to what the market can provide, and, accordingly, more or less decision-making capacity about all aspects of their daily lives (Bennett et al. 2005). Under the influence of the culturalist turn in many disciplines in the 1970s and 1980s, class was routinely regarded as one axis of identification among many (**race, ethnicity, gender**). Critical emphasis on one of these categories at the expense of others often attracted admonition. For example, a standard criticism of Marxist or sociological class-based approaches to Latino/a communities was that oppressions along race, ethnic, gender, and sexual lines were overridden by the attention to class struggles. Darder and Torres (2003) claim that such disciplinary pressures, and the rise of cultural and identity politics, has meant that Latino/a studies have tended to regard class as irrelevant and outdated. Darder and Torres, however, argue that it is not a reductive enterprise to treat class as inherent to social relations. Class remains a viable mode of analysis of how such relations are "configured, dialectically, within the context of contemporary capitalist social formations."

Coatlicue State

One of many influential concepts developed by Gloria Anzaldúa (1987), the Coatlicue state represents a feminist Chicana reworking of the goddess Coatlicue's status in **Aztec** mythology. Roughly translated as Serpent Skirt, Coatlicue was the Aztec mother goddess who gave birth to celestial bodies as well as such gods as Huitzilopochtli (God of the sun and war), Quetzalcoatl (the feathered serpent), and Xolotl (Lord of the underworld and the god of lightning). Like all Aztec gods, Coatlicue was the personification of duality. As the Goddess of Life, Death, and Rebirth, she was life giver and destroyer, and that double role was evoked in her visual manifestations in Aztec art as a bare-breasted woman with clawed hands (to dig graves), wearing a skirt made of writhing snakes and a necklace of human skulls, hearts, and severed hands. Coatlicue metaphorized the cycle of life and death and served as a reminder that all life comes to an end. Anzaldúa attends to Coatlicue as an archetypal synthesis of duality in order to undo what she regards as the historical mistreatment of Coatlicue before and after the Spanish conquest. In her earliest incarnations, Coatlicue was the synthesized embodiment of creation and destruction. Over time, patriarchal Azteca-Mexica society downgraded her status in a pantheon that had once balanced male and female. Coatlicue's positive life-giving aspects were eventually transferred to one of her offshoots, Tonantsi, the good mother, while Coatlicue was cast as the dark and malevolent monster destroyer. After the Spanish conquest, the cult of Tonantsi (life giver) fused with the Catholic cult of *la* **Virgen de Guadalupe** (chastity, purity, dutiful maternity). Thus, the contradictory qualities once embodied by Coatlicue were separated into acceptable form (Guadalupe) and unacceptably dangerous, treacherous forms such as Coatlicue, la **Malinche**, and la **Llorona**.

Anzaldúa regards the Coatlicue state as a metaphor for a ***nueva mestiza*** consciousness of plural and contradictory selfhood. The Coatlicue state signifies the eruption of repressed and painful memories, and it also denotes a liminal space of self-awareness, *la facultad*, outside the imposed discourse of Western rationalism, in which the Chicana subject's identity guises can be acknowledged. Anzaldúa emphasizes that the Coatlicue state signals a way to deal with **borderlands'** structures of oppression that have made of the Chicano/a subject a divided, fearful self. The Coatlicue state also functions as a model for a new Chicana writerly praxis, based on an acceptance that the historical, cultural, and personal blocks to Chicana self-expression are themselves Coatlicue states.

Cockfighting

Cockfighting (*peleas de gallos*) is a popular entertainment in much of Asia, Africa, parts of Europe, Latin America, and the USA (Dundes 1994). Although cockfights are a traditional entertainment in many Latino/a and Asian American communities, and were introduced into the Americas by the Spanish, fighting birds were also among the most highly prized animals brought from England to its American colonies. In the nineteenth century, President Andrew Jackson was known to stage cockfights at the White House (Gilb 2003). A typical cockfight involves placing two roosters specially bred for fighting in a ring or fighting pit, each rooster being armed with sharpened silver spurs called gaffs (or in Mexican cockfights, specially designed knives) attached to their feet. Cockfighting birds are highly prized and lovingly handled, and often sell for huge sums of money, with large wins and losses also possible for spectators who bet on likely winners. Before a bout, handlers remove the wattles from beneath the roosters' beaks, pluck much of the plumage, and toughen up exposed areas of skin with special chemical solutions. The birds then attack each other until one is killed or seriously weakened, usually from loss of blood, internal injuries, and exhaustion. Cockfighting is illegal in all US states barring New Mexico and Louisiana, but is legal in Puerto Rico, Mexico, and most Latin American states. Jerry García (2004) notes that the ban on cockfighting has not been accompanied by a ban on the breeding of gamecocks, and a transport network has arisen to move the fighting birds to states where the practice is illegal and where clandestine cockfights are held. The prevalence and symbolic importance of the cockfight among working-class Mexican

American men reflects how the sport and traditional codes of Mexican masculinity reinforce each other. For García, the "resistance masculinity" on show at a Mexican American *pelea de gallos* signals a defensive gesture by which male participants may assert cultural resilience in the face of daily socioeconomic marginalization and cultural disparagement.

Code Switching

Code switching (or switching) refers to the interlingual capacity to shift in and between two or more language communities. Understood as both a linguistic and a social "contact phenomenon" that conforms to tacitly understood conventions and rules (Duranti 2001), code switching is a common occurrence among the children of first-generation immigrants, residents of multilingual societies, and inhabitants of frontier zones where language communities interact or overlap. The practice of code switching is complex and fluid and depends on many factors: physical location; **class**, gender, and age status; the depth of the relationship between speakers; the formal or informal parameters of a conversation; the modifying presence of monolingual speakers; the perceived insider/outsider status of speakers and addressees; and the levels of competence and confidence in the languages involved. Code switching is a **bilingual** reality for many Latino/as who move back and forth, creatively and easily, between English and Spanish in their daily lives. Some commentators claim that code switching provides **Spanglish** with its distinctive communicative feature. Code switching is commonly encountered in much Latino/a literature and performance work. Chicana writer Susana Chávez-Silverman (2004) exemplifies the creative possibilities of code switching: "So here I am, gente, dizque back home, just north of Route 66 — la Foothill Blvd. — right on the easternmost edge del condado de Los Angeles, right smack on the edge, también, del Evil — que digamos, del *Inland* Empire." For many Latino/a writers, code switching, and the refusal to translate for monolingual readers of either Spanish or English, is a highly political practice. Anzaldúa (1987) argues that the right to use and shift between multiple codes cuts to the heart of personal and communal legitimacy for many Chicano/as. The question of legitimacy indicates that the struggle for linguistic rights cannot be disentangled from broader struggles against discrimination in the US setting. Code switching between languages at once upholds and challenges sociocultural boundaries, and thus may have sociopolitical costs depending on how such linguistic boundary transgression is perceived in a particular time and place.

Colonialism, Neocolonialism, Postcolonialism

The orthodox understanding of colonialism, or colonization, is of a form or subset of **imperialism**, a mode of domination by which an imperial power assumes and gains control over a conquered territory by establishing its own colonies there, and thus transferring settlers, institutions, goods, and value systems from the metropolis to the new peripheral site. Settler societies such as Canada, New Zealand, and Australia conform to that definition. However, colonialism may also signify a condition of subordination that can be enacted and maintained by an imperial entity without establishing colonies. In this case, colonization may proceed by the imposition of political, legal, and economic institutions, cultural practices, language, and values on a subject populace, as has occurred with Puerto Rico under US colonial rule since 1898. A related term, coloniality designates the colonial-like experiences and quotidian conditions of certain populations that have not been formally colonized. For example, in the USA, legal and juridical apparatuses, racial and ethnic discourses, and media representations may treat Latin American-origin immigrant communities as new additions to already colonized sectors, hence the Chicanoization of Central Americans in California and the Nuyoricization of Dominicanos in New York (Grosfoguel et al. 2005). A different conceptualization, **internal colonization**, arose in the 1960s to designate the subordination of certain populations in their traditional lands, or of groups such as slaves, displaced inside the colonizing power itself. Although colonialism is closely associated with a European mode of domination across the world from the fifteenth to the mid-twentieth centuries, neocolonialism refers to the contemporary condition of colonial-like economic and political dependency experienced by many Third World, and ostensibly independent or decolonized, countries after World War II. Postcolonialism is a critical discourse that emerged in the late 1970s in the Anglophone world with the publication of Edward Said's *Orientalism* (1978), as a means of theorizing the effects of European colonization on subject peoples, including their resistance and accommodation. The "post" in the equation is semantically ambiguous, implying a critical gaze that either traces the modes of colonial power from the outset of colonization, or that tracks the legacies of those modes after colonialism has formally ended.

Postcolonial discourse is particularly influential in Anglophone criticism, with much of its analysis attending to British colonialism and the postcolonial experiences of ex-colonies after **decolonization**. However, the application of postcolonial discourse and analytical approaches to the Americas, and to Latino/a populations, inevitably confronts the fact that all but two of Spain's American colonies (Cuba and Puerto Rico) achieved their independence by the 1820s. While western European powers such as Britain and France were embarking on the greatest acquisitions of overseas territory and empire building in Europe's history, most Latin Americans were grappling with a postcolonial epoch and nation-building projects, well before other parts of the colonized world. That divergent hemispherical experience raises questions about the application of postcolonial discourse to American terrains. What do the terms "colonial" and "postcolonial" signify in relation to the Americas, and for the peoples subsumed into the USA by such moments of territorial acquisition as the **Treaty of Guadalupe Hidalgo** and the annexation of Puerto Rico in 1898? These questions inevitably intersect with longstanding historical debates over the USA's own imperial identity, and, within Latino/a Studies, over how imperial legacies play out in the contemporary receptions and status accorded to Puerto Ricans, Chicano/as, and other Latino/as, and those communities' attempts to decolonize themselves (Grosfoguel et al. 2005).

Comadrismo, Compadrazgo

The Spanish term *compadrazgo* refers to the Latino/a kinship system of co-parenting or godparenting, and which amounts to a ritualized communal relationship that preserves and bolsters normative gender and familial structures. The practice of *compadrazgo* was historically more prevalent among working-class Latino/as than the middle and upper classes, given its social function as a formalized system of mutual aid and extended community support (R. Castro 2001). Conventionally, all children baptized in the Catholic Church are allocated a *comadre* or *padrina* (godmother) and a *compadre* or *padrino* (godfather), the understanding being that all sides in the relationship bear certain mutual obligations and responsibilities. Godparents are expected to assist the biological parents in the raising of the godchild, contributing funds to pay for such events as the baptism, a *quinceañera*, graduation, and wedding, and, in the event of death of the biological parents, bringing up the children. Godchildren are required to treat their *compadres* with the same respect as they would their biological parents, and are expected to help out in times of illness or emergency. *Compadrazgo* arrangements traditionally bind the bride's parents to their daughter's husband, while at weddings, the best man and the maid of honor may also become *compadres* to the married couple (R. Castro 2001). Outside the *compadre* relationships framed by Catholic ritual and familial ties, *compadrazgo* has the additional meaning of signifying any deep fraternal relationship between men, with one of the men serving as a *compadre* figure to the other men. *Compadrazgo* thus has affinities with **carnalismo**. Bourgois (1996), for example, describes the *compadrazgo* relationship as a Puerto Rican tradition of reciprocity between men along traditional familial and blood-kin ties, yet flexible enough to include "fictive kinship" arrangements. Many **gangs** are organized according to fraternal, *machista*, and homosocial rather than blood-kin arrangements. The female equivalent *comadrismo* may also refer to the complex set of relationships, reciprocal duties and dependencies, and mutual support networks and friendships between women that are not necessarily determined by the obligations of traditional godmother status or familial ties, but which nonetheless confirm a place in a constructed community of women. See **Machismo**.

Comics

A highly popular cultural form across the world, the comic designates a sequence of pictographic images, often but not invariably boxed, that forms a narrative. Such comics may also contain text. Comics may be serialized, as in newspaper comic or cartoon strips (*Peanuts*, etc.), televised as cartoons (*The Simpsons, South Park, Dora the Explorer, Mucha Lucha*), and printed in magazine or book formats. Generally, a printed comic is distinguishable from a printed cartoon (a single image/text), as exemplified by the editorializing cartoons in newspapers that respond to current events or debates. That distinction is illustrated by the work of the LA-based Chicano artist Lalo Alcaraz. His collection of stand-alone political cartoons about immigration issues, *Migra Mouse* (2004b), contrasts with the evolving narrative of the comic strip *La Cucaracha* (2004a). In Latin America, *historietas* (small comic booklets) and *novela semanales* (serialized comic-strip novels) that target specific class and gender markets are sold weekly in many millions of copies. The Mexican comic artist Rius (Eduardo del Río) made of the comic a didactic genre by which to inform readers about political events, ideas, and thinkers, as exemplified by his *Cuba para principiantes* (1965, Cuba for Beginners) and *Marx para principiantes* (1976, Marx for Beginners). The production of political comics in Latin America in the 1960s and 1970s contrasts strongly with the US experience, where the market was dominated by such corporations as Warner Brothers and Disney. Leftist Latin American critics often regarded the cartoons produced and exported by these corporations as emblematic of US **cultural imperialism** (Dorfman and Mattelart 1971). Cultural critics today would argue that cultural texts that emanate from the imperium are taken into unforeseen terrains, and accorded local meanings, by transcultural processes of adaptation and transformation. For example, the US cartoon *The Phantom*, which debuted in 1936, was exported almost immediately to Mexico where it had an aesthetic influence on *lucha libre*. Rius was also responsible for the first comic-book account of Chicano/as, *The Chicanos* (1973). An updated translation into English of the original Spanish-language comic in Rius's "Los Agachados" series, *The Chicanos* is informed by a leftist political agenda that targets the US "government and its imperialist policies." The comic advocates a transborder alliance between Mexican workers and intellectuals and the Chicano workers and activists in the north. *The Chicanos* is self-consciously didactic and utilizes recurring characters and icons to construct its historical narrative of *gringo* exploitation and victimization of Chicano/as. The format provides a tacit blueprint for the later *Latino USA: A Cartoon History* (Stavans 2000). In the 1980s and early 1990s, both the comic magazine and the comic book or graphic novel enjoyed a renaissance of sorts, with thousands of underground practitioners emerging across the country. A number of Latino/a cartoonists appeared at this time, perhaps the most successful being the brother team of Jaime and Gilbert Hernández, responsible for *Love and Rockets* (Fantagraphic Books, Seattle), a multiplotted comic series from 1982 to 1996, and which was revived in the early 2000s. *Love and Rockets* comprises a range of parallel and occasionally intersecting plots, with the brothers issuing magazines and book collections either singly or in collaboration. Particularly renowned is Gilbert Hernández's transgenerational saga of Palomar, a fictitious village located somewhere in Central America, where daily life evokes the stylistic devices favored by **magical realism**. Jaime Hernández's work focuses on a group of Chicano/as in post-punk, panethnic, and sexually liberated southern California. The tightening of the comic market and declining readership in the late 1990s resulted in a return to independent comic production, and the establishment of Latino/a comic support organizations such as PACAS (Professional Amigos of Comic Art Society), which uses the internet to circulate the work of Latino/a cartoonists.

Conjunto

Conjunto is a Texan folk music style and forerunner of *tejano*, and a variant of *norteño*, that has been compared to zydeco and blues. A working-class music, the conjunto emerged in the late 1920s as an improvisational form characterized by its use of the accordion, with accompanying guitar, *bajo sexto* (traditional Mexican 12-stringed guitar), and *tambora* (drum). In the 1930s, proponents such as Narciso Martínez, the "father" of conjunto, were recording and popularizing the genre. By the 1950s conjunto had evolved into a modern dance ensemble form, by which time it was regarded by many working-class Mexican Texans as the music that best represented and reflected their social concerns and realities after decades of rural to urban migration, and of increasing social stratification between Anglo and Mexican Texans (M. Peña 1985). The conjunto is a hybrid style, with elements drawn from European-origin styles such as the waltz, mazurka, and polka, *mariachi*, and *ranchera*, as well as influences and instrumentation (e.g., the drum kit) drawn from US pop music. Manuel Peña's studies of the form reveal the complex evolution and geospatial convergence of the conjunto with other music styles (1985, 1992–1996, 1999a, 1999b). Conjunto was carried by *Tejanos* from the Rio Grande valley to other parts of Texas, the southwest, California, and the Midwest, where it provided a means of maintaining a sense of community at the social occasions (weddings, baptisms, *quinceañeras*) where conjunto ensembles traditionally played. Peña also notes that in the wake of the 1960s **Chicano Movement**, younger Chicano/a audiences throughout the southwest began to support conjunto, as part of a trend to reclaim folk traditions. Dorsey (2005) argues that, like many Mexican-origin music forms, the gendered logics at work in the male-dominated conjunto replay the tension between Anglo and Mexican notions of nation and community. Conjunto's heyday was the 1950s and 1960s, after which the rise of other musical forms, including the Mexican *cumbia* introduced by Mexican migrants to Texas, as well as the migration of Tejanos to other parts of the USA in search of work, reduced the popular appeal of conjunto ensembles. Conjunto nonetheless continued to evolve as a folk form well into the 1980s and 1990s, with local adherents across the south of Texas, while its influence can be detected in many of the musical trajectories included under *norteño*.

Corrido, Narcocorrido

The *corrido* is a traditional border folk music that has narrated and memorialized working-class life since the mid-nineteenth century and played a role in the maintenance, and development, of Mexican and Mexican American communal identities. *Corridos* also have a formative role in the evolution of Chicano/a Studies, as exemplified by the foundational reputation accorded to Américo Paredes's *With His Pistol in His Hand: A Border Ballad and Its Hero* (1958 [1986]). That text was later used as the basis for the film *The Ballad of Gregorio Cortez* (1982, dir. Robert Young). Paredes (1979) regarded the *corrido* as the most important cultural influence in the evolution of Chicano/a literature. Ramón Saldívar (1990) argues that since *corridos* narrated **subaltern** Mexican American opposition to Anglo-American state apparatuses and assimilationist pressures, and that given *corridos* were passed down to new generations of singers and interpreters, they provided the nineteenth-century "subtexts" for the Chicano/a novel in the twentieth century. Derived from the Spanish *romance* tradition, *corridos* have a waltz or polka rhythm over which the lyric narrative is sung according to an ABCB rhyming structure. *Corridos* relate significant events (social conflicts, natural disasters, political issues, individual crises, brushes with the law, the death of a local personality), and often focus on a protagonist who faces and surmounts great obstacles. After the **Mexican–American War** (1846–1848), the popularity of *corridos* among Mexican Americans rose in tandem with the consolidation of Anglo-American control over the annexed territory, particularly in south Texas. In the late 1800s, popular *corridos* celebrated the extralegal exploits of such folk heroes as Juan Nepomuceno Cortina, Joaquín Murrieta, and Gregorio Cortéz. After the **Mexican Revolution** of 1910, many *corridos* were composed in honor of revolutionary figures (Francisco Villa, Emiliano Zapata, Felipe Angeles) and La **Adelita.** *Corridos* have functioned historically as an oral and memorializing tradition, a musical equivalent to the newspaper. They have chronicled the undocumented migrant economy, contraband smuggling across the border, and the travails of working-class and rural labor, as exemplified by such early twentieth-century classics as "El lavaplatos" (The Dishwasher) and "El deportado" (The Deportee). *Corridos* have exposed the abuses of the **Texas Rangers** and the **Border Patrol**, and exploitative bosses and corrupt government officials. The attacks of September 11, 2001, inspired a number of *corridos*, including "La tragedia de Nueva York," by the Sinaloan group El As de la Sierra. In 2003, Pedro Rivera from Fresno, California, penned the first *corrido* about the Iraq War, "War for Peace," which he dedicated to the Latino/as in US forces killed or wounded in the conflict. Highly topical in 2004 was the *corrido* from the famous US-based Los Tigres del Norte, "Las mujeres de Juárez" (The Women of Juárez), at once an account of the brutal murders of hundreds of young women in Ciudad Juárez since the early 1990s, and a critique of binational legal and police agencies that have yet to bring the perpetrators to justice. An important trend in the evolution of *corridos* was the rise of *narcocorridos*, or *corridos* about drug trafficking, which are also called *corridos pesados* (heavy *corridos*) or *corridos bravíos* (fierce/savage *corridos*) (Edberg 2004; Wald 2001). The *narcocorrido* tradition was inaugurated in the 1970s when the most famous *corrido* band, Los Tigres del Norte, released "Contrabando y traición" (Smuggling and Betrayal). Unusually for *corridos*— a hypermasculinist, heteronormative genre (Herera-Sobek 1990)—the song featured a protagonist, Camelia La Tejana, who has been interpreted as a feminist icon on account of her refusal to be a passive victim of the male-dominated drug world (Wald 2001). The *narcocorrido* phenomenon has been criticized for its celebration of drug cartel violence, and at times banned by radio stations on both sides of the border. Such moves have not dented the genre's popularity. *Narcocorridos* are often produced and disseminated in the underground economy, and sold in pirated form in Mexican street markets; and many Mexican films are based on popular *narcocorridos*. The Spanish writer Arturo Pérez-Reverte's 2002 novel, the corrido-influenced *La reina del sur* (The Queen of the South), deals with narcotrafficking in the Americas and the Mediterranean. Brady (2002) describes the *narcocorrido* phenomenon as a cultural symptom of the "narcoglocalization" of the US–Mexico border region caused by the symbiotic war on drugs and drug-trafficking economy.

Coyote

Coyote is a term for someone who, for a fee, smuggles undocumented migrants (*pollos*, chickens) into the USA. Related expressions include *pollero* (chicken man) and *pasa pollos* (chicken smuggler). A recent term, *chiquipollo* (little chicken), designates teenage males between the ages of 13 and 17 enlisted by trafficking syndicates to take migrant workers across the US border. *Chiquipollos* operate out of the *colonias* of such border cities as Mexicali and Tijuana, their function in the transborder economy assisted by the fact that their youth protects them from prosecution if apprehended on the US side. Coyote has entered the transnational Spanish lexicon. The term is used, for example, by Ecuadorian migrants in Spain when referring to the people they paid to organize their migration outside official channels. The coyote also has a reputation in the critical and fictional literature as a trickster figure in the **Borderlands**, thus paralleling the place of tricksters in African American and Native American cultures, whereby the trickster represents an icon of, and a metaphor for, resistance to Anglo-American cultural paradigms (Reesman 2001). At times the coyote is regarded as a symbol of Chicano/a and Mexican identity reconfiguration, resistance, and subversion. These figurations in part reflect the perceived qualities of the animal itself. The wily and wide-ranging species of North American wild dog or prairie wolf (*Canis latrans*) has adapted to urbanization throughout the US southwest while remaining at home in less populated natural habitats, from deserts to prairies and wooded mountain ranges in the USA and Mexico. Pérez-Torres (1995a) argues that the coyote metaphorizes a range of border-crossing practices in a Borderlands that requires subjects to adopt disguises, shift between cultural systems, and dodge alien significations. A typical example is the undocumented Mexican who adopts the semiotic dress codes of Chicano/as in order to blend into the streets of US towns and cities and thus avoid detection from the **Border Patrol**. For Pérez-Torres, a coyote cultural praxis signifies the smuggling of minority discourses across multiple borders in order to disrupt and dispute the material manifestations of those boundaries and the logics that maintain them. Nonetheless, missing from this optimistic description is any sense of the coyote's disciplinary function as a figure who may regard migrant border-crossers as an exploitable, and at times violently secured, financial, and sexual resource. In Chicano/a literature and literary criticism, the coyote is a stock figure. Luis Pérez's *El Coyote: The Rebel*, from 1947, describes the life of a Mexican nicknamed "El Coyote" because of his cunning and survival tactics during the **Mexican Revolution**, who crosses the border to forge a new life in the USA. For Alire Sáenz (1994), the coyote as trickster best describes his own relation to the literary **canons** on both sides of the US–Mexico border, as well as indigenous oral and narrative traditions. Those canons and traditions fail either to regard Chicano/a writers and texts as worthy of inclusion or to provide spaces adequate enough for describing Chicano/a communal realities and cultural and racial complexities. The Chicano/a writer, by implication, has an intimate knowledge of the trans-American literary traditions that would exclude him/her, and an ability to negotiate in, around, and outside them in order to construct Chicano/a writerly spaces.

Creole, *Criollo*, Creolization

Creole and its Spanish equivalent *criollo* were terms for defining local-born European inhabitants of the Americas during the European colonial era. The term distinguished local-born Europeans from those born in the imperial center, as well as from indigenous, African, and mixed-race colonial subjects. Similar colonial-era uses of Creole to designate an American-born European exist in French (*créole*) and Portuguese (*crioulhu*). In all of these languages, however, the term Creole was at times extended to non-European colonial subjects, or any person born in the American colonies irrespective of race. In linguistics, Creole denotes a hybrid or pidgin idiom with roots in two or more other languages; it also provides the name for the language and culture of the French-speaking community in Louisiana, and of Haiti. As with many terms that arose to define subjects of European empires in the Americas, the term Creole has had a metaphorical life to signal the cultural intermixing and transformations that occurred under colonialism: *creolization* (English), *criollaje* or *criollazación* (Spanish), and *créolité* (French). *Creolization* and *créolité* were important concepts in the Anglophone and Francophone Caribbean in the post-World War II period, and are now regarded as key terms in Caribbean postcolonial studies, with roots in the earlier discourse of *négritude*. Both terms have affinities with the cultural discourse of **mestizaje** in Mexico and other parts of Latin America, and its French equivalent of *métissage*.

Critical Race Theory, LatCrit Theory

Critical Race Theory (CRT) is the name for a broad denomination of interlinked critical enterprises that focus on the discursive relations between race, racism, and power, and that seek to dismantle those relations (Delgado 1995; Delgado and Stefancic 2001). Emerging from legal studies in the 1970s, CRT questions the production and function of race in legal discourse, and its basis in such principles as equality, neutrality, rationality, and liberalism as they have influenced US history, and given rise to the tensions between individual and group self-interest. According to Delgado and Stefancic (2001), CRT has three tenets. First, racism is an ordinary feature of daily life for people of color. Second, racism brings material benefits to white elites (self-interest) and psychic rewards to working classes (a sense of security, the promise of integration or higher living standards) in what amounts to a system of ''interest convergence'' that permits white people to rule over people of color. Third, race is a mutable and adaptable social construction. Added to these tenets, CRT also explores the processes of "differential racialization," whereby different groups are racialized in distinct ways and along multiple axes of identity ascription, conflict, loyalty, and affiliation (Delgado and Stefancic 2001). A theoretical approach and an activist drive, CRT aims to expose the national operations of white supremacy, and to shatter the deep relation between law and white power (Crenshaw et al. 1995). CRT's theoretical and activist origins lie in the African American civil rights movement, and evolved out of the liberal, but white-male dominated, Critical Legal Studies organization in the late 1970s. However, CRT departs from "traditional civil rights discourse," exemplified by the "liberal" struggles over affirmative action, and the use of stock terms as "integration" and "color-blindness" by civil rights activists and liberal legal scholars alike. CRT advocates argue that a radical re-engagement with structures of racism and racialization is required in order to achieve fundamental social change, hence the CRT's critique of the liberal legal tradition, and its exposure of the mechanisms by which the law has upheld white power through a neutral or "aracial" legal lens (Crenshaw et al. 1995). This position recognizes that the US legal system has been a key state apparatus in perpetuating and reinforcing the discourses of racial difference, the structures of racialized power, and the production of "race" itself in US history. Since CRT emerged in the 1980s, other critical groups have formed under the CRT rubric. Critical Whiteness Studies, for example, is concerned with unmasking the operations of whiteness as a pervasive trope of social power (Delgado and Stefancic 1997, 1998, 2001). Other significant CRT projects include TribalCrit (Native American approaches), QueerCrit (Queer positions), Asian American jurisprudence, and LatCrit Theory, all of which are concerned with "outsider jurisprudence." LatCrit Theory designates legal scholarship that focuses on the status of Latino/as in legal discourse in order to assist Latino/as surmount the legal and social obstacles they face in the USA (Valdes 1997). LatCrit Theory engages with CRT in order to ensure that the differential legal and policy treatments of Latino/as are not occluded by a **Black/White paradigm.** LatCrit Theory, which maintains a critical web site (www.latcrit.org), has a number of concerns not shared by other CRT enterprises: reframing discourses of immigration away from illegality, the politics of bilingual education and language, seeking redress for Mexican Americans whose ancestors were disenfranchised in violation of such legal documents as the **Treaty of**

Guadalupe Hidalgo, intervening in the debates over US **Census** categories and their influence in shaping perceptions of Latino/as, and countering **nativism** and vigilante groups.

Cuban American

Cuban American is a term used by, and often imposed on, anyone of Cuban descent in the USA. Within the Cuban community there is a widespread preference to use Cuban before Cuban American, especially among members of the older generation. Many synonyms for Cuban American have arisen since the early 1960s. Cubanglo is a fusion of Cuban and Anglo. YUCA is an acronym for Young Urban Cuban American, and circulates as a variant of Yuppie (Young Urban Professional). Current in Florida since the early 1990s, YUCA forms part of the **One-and-a-Halfer** generation, in contrast to the **ABC Generation**. This use of the term should not be confused with the *yuca* plant (yucca or manioc), a staple source of starch in Caribbean cuisine. Miami Mafia is the derogatory epithet favored by the Castro regime when speaking of Cuban American political organizations that support the US government's diplomatic and economic isolation of the island, and that aspire to overthrow the Socialist government. The term is also used in the USA by critics of the Cuban American community's influence in local, state, and national politics, particularly in the Republican Party. Hardline Cuban Americans are also known as *duros*, whereas *gusano/as* (worms) designate Cubans perceived to have betrayed, opposed, or fled the **Cuban Revolution**. A related term, *gusañero/a*, a fusion of *gusano* and *compañero/a* (comrade) arose in the 1990s to define exiles who sent **remittances** back to Cuba in exchange for the right of unrestricted travel to the island. Since the early 1990s, *mariposas* (butterflies) have also gained currency in Cuba to designate exiles. The use signifies a softening attitude of sorts, although since *mariposa* is also a euphemism for queer, the term may be perceived as an insult in a largely homophobic community. *Dialoguero* is applied to Cuban Americans who favor dialogue between exile and island Cubans, and may advocate an end to the economic and political embargo of the island. Within the exile community the term is often used as a synonym for traitor directed at people perceived to be soft on the Castro regime. In January 2006, *dialoguero* reached national headlines with the arrest of two Miami academics and well-known *dialogueros*, Carlos Álvarez and Elsa Prieto, a married couple accused of spying for the Castro government.

Jubano/a is used by Jewish Cuban Americans and reflects a Jewish Cuban identification (*Jubanidad*) constructed in exile (Bettinger-López 2001).

Cuban Revolution

The Cuban Revolution (January 1, 1959) was the outcome of a political struggle in the 1950s on the part of a leftist rebel movement to overthrow the US-backed dictatorship of Fulgencio Batista, who had seized power in a coup in 1952. The rebels aimed to establish a regime independent of US government influence that would recognize and legislate worker and peasant rights, and end the historical exploitation of the island's economy and people by US corporate interests and the Cuban elite alike. The revolution was preceded by unsuccessful attempts on the part of insurgents, whose members included Fidel Castro and his brother Raúl, to overthrow the dictatorship. In July 1953 the attack on the Moncada Barracks in Cuba's Oriente Province, which the Castro-headed rebel group of some 150 had hoped would inaugurate a popular uprising, ended in failure for the rebels, and imprisonment for the survivors who became known as the heroes of the "Movimiento 26 de Julio." A popular campaign to free the Moncada rebels, including Castro, led to an amnesty, the prisoners leaving Cuba for exile in Mexico. The revolution resumed in December 1956 when Castro's force (82 people, including Ernesto "Che" Guevara) returned to Cuba, and began a guerilla campaign from their bases in the Sierra Maestra mountains. The rebel cause was assisted by popular antipathy toward the Batista regime's often brutal attempts to quash dissidence and punish rural populations thought to have assisted the rebels, while groups not linked to the guerilla struggle, such as student associations, unions, intellectuals, and some elements from the middle class, also began to demonstrate and agitate for regime change in the late 1950s. After many months of struggle and growing popular opposition to the dictatorship, Batista eventually recapitulated, seeking asylum in the Dominican Republic on January 1, 1959. That date ended the revolution and inaugurated the period of revolutionary consolidation. This period was characterized by the passing of legislation intended to reform Cuba for the benefit of its peasant and working classes. Urban housing and agrarian reform laws were enacted, and, in the face of US opposition to such laws in 1960, further legislative moves were made to ensure Cuban control of the national economy (the formal nationalization of the banking and trade sectors, the nationalization of the sugar industry and US-owned oil companies having already occurred). The revolutionary government outlawed prostitution, and embarked on programs to ensure universal literacy, and establish free health care and education for all Cubans. Such moves accompanied, and in some instances were triggered, by US opposition to the revolutionary government, also saw Cuba aligning itself with the Soviet Union. That alignment became permanent after the abortive Bay of Pigs Invasion in April 1961, and played a key role in the Cuban Missile Crisis of 1962. The Cuban Revolution encapsulated the hopes of a generation not only in Cuba, but also throughout the Americas and elsewhere. Many Latin Americans saw in the revolution a sociopolitical, economic, and ideological alternative both to the US capitalist model of governance and to corrupt and totalitarian regimes in the continent. Yet, while the revolution was hailed in the Americas as a cold war victory against US interference in Latin American states, it also led to the mass exodus from Cuba of the island's white upper and middle classes, who sought haven for the most part in the USA, and also in Mexico, Puerto Rico, Spain, Italy, France, and other countries. Other waves of exodus from postrevolutionary Cuba have augmented the original exile community with Afro- and working-class Cubans. Today the Cuban exile community accounts for some 10 percent of the total Cuban population.

Cultural Imperialism

Cultural imperialism is a critical concept that emerged in the 1960s, with numerous approaches and understandings in circulation since that decade, and an implicit influence on such Latino/a critical approaches as **Latinismo** and **tropicalizations**. Recent critics of cultural imperialism argue that it is burdened by the definitional elusiveness of its component parts: culture and imperialism. Faced with that difficulty, Tomlinson (1991) suggests that cultural imperialism is best understood as a discourse about domination with different applications. He identifies four discourses of cultural imperialism, which say more about proponents than the purported sources of imperial power. Media imperialism designates the ways by which the media apparatus (film, television, radio, the press) may function on a global level as an apparatus of domination, achieved either through political-economic means (the saturation of local markets with metropolitan programming) or cultural means (through the messages encoded in that programming). This approach is exemplified by Dorfman and Mattelart's (1971) leftist critique of the Disney comic as a mass cultural form disseminated throughout the Third World with the aim of transmitting "American" political and cultural values. Dorfman and Mattelart's stance may also be read as a critique of **Americanization**, understood as the export of US-"friendly" cultural products and the USA's capacity to exercise its political will in other states. The discourse of nationality approach proposes that the "nation" or the local is under threat from an external and more powerful imperial culture. Again, Dorfman and Mattelart's position could be understood in relation to this discourse. A third approach regards cultural imperialism as a symptom and sign of global capitalism. By identifying capitalism as the source of the cultural imperial drive, this approach accepts a priori that global capitalism is an inescapable political and economic system, superseding both the media apparatus and the national realm. The fourth discourse links cultural imperialism to modernity, that is, as a global phenomenon characterized by increasing homogeneity in the ways by which people live anywhere. In this discourse, cultural imperialism can manifest itself through the global networks of capitalism, urban development and renewal programs are replicated across the world, the mass communication industry, organizations of social space and notions of the worldly place of the individual and/or local community (Tomlinson 1991). This schematic overview, Tomlinson warns, does not solve the definitional problems inherent to "cultural imperialism." Each discursive position focuses on specific or generic sources of domination, and thus may ignore other sources. Each approach is haunted, too, by the empirical and epistemological difficulty of measuring the effects of domination on the target populations and communities. Another challenge for proponents of cultural imperialism is how to account for resistance to domination, and for alternative readings of "imposed" cultural texts or discourses uncountenanced in the purported centers of domination.

Cultural Politics

Cultural politics refers to any political enterprise that either regards cultural work as an intrinsic part of activism, or defines cultural work itself as inherently political (as opposed to conforming to, or arising out of, an aesthetic tradition or discourse only). However, this broad understanding of cultural politics does not necessarily explain what culture or cultural work, or politics, denote, either singly or in combination, or in theoretical and practical terms. These semantic and practical difficulties are irresolvable features of the uses that

cultural workers and critics make of a "cultural politics" in particular historical material times and places. Proponents of a cultural political position may
argue that under **globalization**, the collapse of temporal and spatial barriers to
the circulation of mass-produced goods, ideas, and peoples has globalized culture and homogenized the everyday practices of life. In response, advocates of
cultural politics might argue that (autonomous) local cultural practices and
traditions need to be preserved and fostered in order to counter (nonauton-
omous) globalizing imperatives. Whether or not the autonomy of cultural
work can be maintained under globalization remains a debatable concern.
Similar arguments about the need for autonomous cultural political action and
production characterize a number of movements that targeted the cultural traditions and values inherited from imperial and colonial regimes, or those imposed
and championed by national elites. For example, Brazilian *antropofagia* or
cultural **cannibal**ism, and certain applications of **transculturation**, sought to
construct aesthetic and critical models for new cultural practices on local
terms either unbeholden to the valued "foreign," or remaking the "foreign" for
local consumption. Cultural workers associated with specific political movements might regard artistic endeavor as a key venue for disseminating movement ideals and aspirations. This approach typifies the artistic production
associated with the **Chicano Movement** and **Chicano Renaissance**, which also
revalorized and reclaimed cultural traditions and folkloric practices as integral
features of a politicized communal and cultural imaginary. Nuyorican poets in
the 1970s developed **Nuyorican aesthetics** as a cultural political response
to quotidian marginalization. States, too, may yoke culture and politics, as
occurred in postrevolutionary Mexico in the mid-twentieth century, when successive administrations reconstructed *Mexicanidad* (Mexicanness) by funding
and celebrating regional and indigenous folk traditions (*mariachi, ranchera,
ballet folklórico*), constructing museums as national monuments to the indigenous base, and redefining the national in terms of a discourse of resolved *mestizaje*. The political uses to which cultural forms and traditions are put in the
service of the "nation" have been criticized for celebrating indigenous culture,
while not attending to the poverty and sociopolitical discrimination of indigenous peoples. The post-1952 reclamation of the **Taíno** as an emblem of Puerto
Rican cultural identity similarly raises questions about the appropriative uses
to which the "native" can be put. In their advocacy of a cultural politics of transculturation, Sandoval-Sánchez and Saporta Sternbach (2001) identify and
build on four modes of minority cultural political praxis in the USA since

the 1960s: the politics of representation, identity, location, and affinity. The politics of representation denotes a dual mode of working with dominant cultural stereotypes of Latino/as and revising and rearticulating them in new ways (**disidentification, tropicalizations**). The politics of identity permits a particular subject to adopt a tactical speaking position and "identity" in relation to extant power relations and dominant discourses. The politics of location situates a subject in a specific location in order to draw attention to the localized play of power relations and their effect on subject formation. Many cultural political praxes anchored in the **borderlands** conform to this mode. Finally, the politics of affinity recognizes both the possibilities and limits encoded in the concept, and politics, of identity difference. For example, Román's "politics of affinity" refers to the political and activist coalitions or affiliations forged by members of disparate minority groups (1998). Indebted to Chéla Sandoval's **oppositional consciousness**, Román proposes that tactical affiliations—for instance, queer coalitionism, **AIDS** activism, panethnic antiracist organizations—are predicated on shared experiences of oppression and resistance against specific targets. For Sandoval-Sánchez and Saporta Sternbach, the politics of affinity is evident in Latino/a performances whenever a coalitionist and dialogic sensibility enables social players to recognize identificatory differences without glossing over or ignoring the operations of racism, sexism, homophobia, AIDS stigmatization, and classism (2001). The politics of difference asserts that minority subjects have the right to be unlike other subjects, particularly representatives of a dominant culture. However, when those proponents of identity difference enter into coalitions across political lines of identity engagement, they must accept that affinity raises the risk of encountering other modes of discrimination and discourses of disparagement (Sandoval-Sánchez and Saporta Sternbach 2001). All of these approaches are nonetheless haunted by the tension between cultural political transformation and historical material constraints. Cultural politics may succeed in enabling the coming into voice, discourse, and representation, but the cultural act may not in itself have the substantive capacity to challenge historical material structures of domination, discrimination, and exploitation. This limitation raises the vexed question of how cultural work might enact, and exact, fundamental sociopolitical change. The difficulties posed by that question are nonetheless of a different order to the pressing issue of why cultural political work matters. As the Cuban American performance artist Coco Fusco argues, culture remains perhaps the most important vector for political struggle over identity in the USA (1995).

Culture of Poverty Thesis

The Culture of Poverty Thesis (CPT) was, and in some circles remains, a popular twentieth-century sociological concept for explaining the cross-generational prevalence of poverty in certain communities in the United States (Puerto Ricans, African Americans, Native Americans, Mexican Americans, poor whites in the US south) and in other countries (for instance, slum dwellers in Mexico City). The CPT was first proposed by the influential anthropologist and pioneer of the participant observer method, Oscar Lewis, in his 1959 study *Five Families: Mexican Case Studies in the Culture of Poverty*. He elaborated on the CPT in "The Culture of Poverty" (1964), and in the introduction to *La Vida: A Puerto Rican Family in the Culture of Poverty— San Juan and New York* (1965). In the latter study, Lewis argues that poverty is best understood "as a subculture with its own structure and rationale" that is passed on in families down generational lines. For Lewis, poverty is not a "matter of economic deprivation," despair, and lack (1965); the culture of poverty also has positive and enabling features that permit the poor with limited or no prospects to survive in capitalist societies characterized by rigid class hierarchies and an individualist rather than communal ethos. The culture of poverty has four main features. First, it arises when the poor are unable to participate in, or are excluded from, enabling social institutions (education system, the market, banks, the medical apparatus), as opposed to disabling ones (the police and judicial systems). Second, the culture of poverty obliges families to live in overcrowded and unserviced housing that limits their capacity to organize or participate in associations beyond the family unit. Third, the culture of poverty eliminates the protective "life stage" of childhood, so that children enter into the sexual economy at an early age, traditional families break down, and female-headed families predominate. Fourth, individuals in the culture of poverty feel marginalized, silenced, helpless, apathetic, inferior, fatalistic, and unable to see or plan for the future (1965). All of these attributes, Lewis says, exemplify the pragmatic "making-do" aspirations of the poor. For Lewis the CPT explains why some communities never develop an international, historicized or **class**-based sense of their predicament, and fail to benefit from the solidarities offered by participation in such organizations as church groups, unions, and political or neighborhood associations. Thus, the CPT does not explain poverty per se, but rather why certain sectors are condemned to poverty across generations. Lewis felt that his thesis could assist government and social policy in tackling entrenched poverty in the most socioeconomically deprived communities. From the early 1960s, the CPT attracted a great deal of critical, media, and government support for its suggestion that the cycle of poverty can be attributed to the cultural qualities, traditions, beliefs, and behavior patterns affecting specific communities, and that the cycle could be broken by attending to that "culture." However, the CPT was criticized in later anthropological discourse for not attending to the structural causes of socio-economic subordination. Nuyorican critics have also disputed the CPT, and the discourse of blame that later observers extrapolated from it. Juan Flores (1993) describes Lewis's *La Vida* as a "social pathology" that in tandem with popular filmic representations of Nuyoricans, such as *West Side Story*, entrenched in the wider society a view of Nuyorican culpability for their own predicament. Two more limits of the CPT may be noted. Lewis's CPT is under-written by a tacit faith in the discourse of US-led development and forced modernization, which he regarded as having improved life in Puerto Rico in the post-World War II era (1965). At the same time, Lewis did not scrutinize his own narratorial function and presence vis-à-vis his own participant observer methods. He assumed that he could unproblematically excavate and mediate the purported truths of the poverty experienced by the family members whose stories were relayed in studies such as *La Vida*. See **Americanization**.

Cumbia

Cumbia is an Afro-Colombian dance music that, since the 1940s, has become one of the most popular dance forms in the Hispanophone world. Originally the local music of Colombia's coastal and African-dominated communities, *cumbia*'s popular evolution began with rural to urban migration in the twenti-eth century. *Cumbia* outfits are small with drums, percussion, guitar, and bass guitar underwriting the moderate to fast dance tempos, an accordion that produces the *cumbia*'s distinctive melodies, and a vocalist. *Cumbia* now has regional and national variants, with lyrics reflecting local concerns and topical issues: *cumbia mexicana*, which comprises *cumbia norteña* from Mexico's north, and the *sonadero*, from the center of the country, which adds keyboards to the traditional *cumbia* instruments; and *cumbia villera*, a form popular in the shanty towns of Buenos Aires.

D

Danza, Danzón

The *danza* is a music style with variants in Cuba and Puerto Rico, and whose influence can still be detected in such contemporary styles as salsa. A popular ballroom music in nineteenth-century Cuba, the *danza* was danced to a fast tempo with couples facing each other, without touching, in line or square formations. The origins of the *danza* are said to lie in courtly or country dances brought from Spain. Today the Cuban *danza* survives as part of the island's "classical" music repertoire. Orovio (2004) notes that the *danza* retained its popularity until the 1870s, when the *danzón*, another form of ballroom dance, superseded it. The *danzón*, which also influenced the *mambo*, developed from the *habanera*, which in turn derived from the *contradanza*, a ballroom line or square dance introduced to Cuba from Spain, with new impetus from the French in the late 1700s. Given that most ensemble players were African Cubans, African Cuban instrumentation and rhythmic structures infiltrated into the *contradanza* and *danzón*. The Cuban *danzón* was introduced to Mexico in the late 1900s; it remains the name of the local dance form in Vera Cruz, as is clear from the 1991 film *Danzón* (dir. María Novaro). The Puerto Rican *danza* was a highly stylized form of ballroom line or square dancing that may have derived from Spanish country dance forms modulated over time by movements introduced by émigrés from Colombia and Venezuela. Aparicio (1998) argues that the *danza* became the signature music of the island's plantocratic elite, and was thus constructed as Puerto Rico's national form in the late 1800s and early 1900s. That elite function survives today with the *danza's* reputation as a classical, not a popular, music. The *danza* has been treated as a feminine and "white" form (the "other" of *plena* and *bomba*) by numerous Puerto Rican cultural critics. Aparicio nonetheless points out that a revival of interest in the *danza* in the late twentieth century has been responsible for new *danza* forms that are political and anti-imperial in intent. This revival, and recent historical revisions (Quintero Rivera 1987, 1998), have foregrounded the *danza*'s African influences and the genre's capacity to function as a socio-cultural record of Puerto Rican race relations since the mid-nineteenth century.

Decolonization, Decolonial Imaginary

Decolonization refers to the process by which colonized peoples achieve self-determination or independence, as occurred with the political and juridical struggles of Europe's colonies throughout the so-called Third World to achieve their independence in the post-World War II era. Decolonization also describes the ongoing project of dismantling **colonialism**; independence does not in itself end colonial structures of political, economic, and cultural domination, or preclude the circulation of colonized senses of worldly place. Nor does it preclude neocolonial dependency under global capitalism. Decolonization may also underwrite the political and cultural struggles of peoples for whom national self-determination is not an option, given those peoples' subsumption into, or **internal colonization** by, geopolitical states. In the case of the USA, those peoples would include Native Americans, African Americans, Chicano/as, and Puerto Ricans. Many Latino/a critics argue that in the current era of globalization and transnational migration, new immigrant groups are obliged to manage preexisting conditions of "coloniality" in the host society (Grosfoguel et al. 2005). Those conditions are overdetermined by the historical treatments of four communities: African Americans (displaced by slavery), Chicano/as and Native Americans (the "minority" byproduct of conquest), and Puerto Ricans (the denizens of an island colony). Programs of decolonization are thus required to counter the colonial logics that have racialized and ghettoized, **barrio**ized, or reservationized African Americans, Chicano/as, Puerto Ricans, and Native Americans, and, by extension and discursive application, later immigrant groups (Grosfoguel et al. 2005). Decolonization for many critics thus marks a critical and political response to the "US power of coloniality," the multiple modes of dependency, exploitation, racialization, categorization (as **Hispanics**), and national incorporation, that overdetermine, and imbricate, the national experiences of distinct immigrant and minority communities. Decolonization designates an unfinished project of intervention against the "US empire" and the many structural and discursive venues (male dominance, white supremacy, class privilege, epistemologies of difference) in which that power is upheld. A decolonizing praxis would also expose the ways by which Latino/as may uphold the "power of coloniality," for instance, when Euro-Latino/as discriminate against Afro-Latino/as and Indo-Latino/as (Grosfroguel et al. 2005). Historian Emma Pérez (1999) uses the term decolonial imaginary to define a historiographical practice by which history itself is reconceived in order to assist the Chicano/a project of social transformation. Pérez's concept is predicated on the existence of a traditional US history—a Chicano/a-unfriendly colonial imaginary—founded upon concepts such as the **frontier** and the **West**. This colonial imaginary has contained and constructed Chicano/as as a subordinate or **subaltern** sector without the power to access modes of historical representation or to construct counterdiscourses against colonial historiography. Pérez argues that Chicano/a historical work must occupy the temporally and epistemologically disruptive time lag between the colonial and the postcolonial in order to open a representational space for the voices that the traditional historical imaginary has ignored or silenced, most notably, the voices of Chicanas. Influenced, among others, by Foucault's notion of an archaeological and nonlinear approach to understanding and representing the past, as well as by Bhabha's third space of **hybridity**, Chela Sandoval's **oppositional consciousness**, and Chicana feminism, the decolonial imaginary signifies an alternative historiographical practice to traditional history. It represents a method by which "to write a history that decolonizes otherness" (1999). This method is at once elusive and intangible, for it deals with fragmented and mutable identities, lived experiences, and understandings of the purported "real," out of which may emerge a nontraditional practice by which to elude and resist colonized and colonizing logics. This project also entails a gendering of the decolonial imaginary, so that the Chicana subject can move into alternative representational and historical-material spaces of resistance, identity transformation, and agency.

Día de los muertos, Day of the Dead

El día de los muertos (The Day of the Dead) is celebrated in Mexico and among the Mexican **diaspora** on November 2 each year. The Day of the Dead corresponds with the Catholic All Souls' Day, and is close to All Saints' Day (November 1) and Halloween (October 31), hence the term *Todos santos* for designating the entire period. Many observers regard the Day of the Dead celebrations as a syncretic amalgam of pre-Columbian and Catholic religious beliefs and rituals. Rafaela Castro (2001) argues that the indigenous influence is evident in the belief that the souls of dead people visit their relatives once a year to receive "an *ofrenda*, an offering to the soul." However, Lomnitz (2005) cautions against approaching the Day of the Dead as proof of an Aztec ritual base and belief system over which Spanish Catholicism was simply laid. Rather, the evolving Day of the Dead celebrations are symptomatic of death's function in Mexico as the national totem; death itself provides the key to the modern Mexican national imagination in mutually affective popular and statist terms. The Day of the Dead celebrations involve families picnicking in cemeteries where they offer food and drink to nourish the souls of dead relatives and the construction of **altars** or *ofrendas* on graves and in the family home (Castro 2001). The folk tradition of *El día de los muertos* has been a constant presence in Chicano/a cultural production, and it has also been the target of political resemanticization. Among gay Chicano/as, for example, the practice of building *ofrendas* became an important mode for ritualized mourning during the **AIDS** epidemic in the 1980s and 1990s. That reclamation of folk traditions provides the subject for Lourdes Portillo's 1989 film *La Ofrenda*, which follows a group of Latinos in San Francisco as they construct a queer version of the Day of the Dead rituals.

Diaspora

Diaspora, which derives from the Greek words *speirein* (to sow) and *dia* (over), implying a migratory or colonizing dispersal, has been applied to the Jews, the paradigmatic diasporic people. Diaspora in the Jewish case defines Jewish history, lore, and communal identity as having been forged historically by enforced exile, expulsion, and population displacement, with the additional connotation that a return to the homeland will one day be achieved. Other groups, such as the Armenians, African peoples subject to slavery, and the Palestinians, have been designated victim diasporas (Cohen 1997). Since the 1980s, diaspora has passed into the critical vocabulary to designate any condition of communal displacement that evokes, but is not necessarily like, **exile**. Diaspora is also deployed to signify any large population that has left its homeland and settled elsewhere, or been displaced and scattered over a number of territories in substantial numbers. Despite its generalized usage, the term diaspora tends to connote the residual or persisting sense of communal attachment to the homeland, and thus is often applied to **transnational** immigrant communities (Puerto Rican, Dominican, Mexican) that maintain cultural, familial, and other connections with their country of origin. An example of the popular uses to which the term diaspora has been put is the neocultural term Diasporican (a Puerto Rican resident of the USA).

Dichos

Dichos (sayings or proverbs, refranes) pepper the Spanish of Latino/as from all communities. The Mexican-origin communities of Texas and the US southwest are a rich source of dichos that reflect quotidian communal concerns, and that often derive from forms of Spanish no longer heard elsewhere in the Spanish-speaking world. Many dichos are of note for their punning and rhyming qualities. Due to their generic significance as a repository of local folk and oral culture, and of generational differences in language use, ethnographers and linguists have collected dichos for decades, and many Spanish-language dictionaries contain appendices of popular dichos. Rafaela Castro (2001) notes that among Chicano/a and Mexican American populations the rhetorical function of dichos and refranes enables speakers to evoke a sense of shared community in their daily speech; only those in the community will understand the underlying import of the local dichos. At times, dichos provide an oratorical means by which political activists and politicians make readily understood points to local audiences. Similar claims can be made of Cuban, Dominican, and Puerto Rican communities, whose dichos also confirm the profound influence of Afro-Caribbean oral culture.

Disidentification

Disidentification is a critical concept that has two influential applications in Latino/a Studies. The earliest use was by the Chicana feminist theorist, Norma Alarcón (1991), who regarded the **Third World Feminist** or Women of Color Movement as a critical drive of disidentification in which "multiple-voiced subjectivity is lived in resistance to competing notions for one's allegiance or self-identification. It is a process of disidentification." For Alarcón, disidentification denotes a cultural-political praxis on the part of women of color as they acknowledge the "multiple registers of existence" by which their subject positions and identity claims emerge and become meaningful, against the grain of the identity drives emanating from mainstream European-America, white feminism, or men in their own communities. In a different vein, José Muñoz (1999) regards disidentification as a minority praxis of resistance to dominant cultural protocols that make of Latino/a identity a "toxic" identity, and deny Latino/as a say in the representations that construct them for popular cultural consumption. Disidentification, therefore, becomes a Latino/a performative tactic for reworking and resemanticizing dominant cultural codes, **stereotypes**, and tropes of Latinidad, in order to gain control over the representation of Latino/a subjectivities. Disidentification aims to open up new spaces in which minority identities may be empowered through the act of breaking open, and then appropriating, dominant cultural codes that assume a universal and exclusionary identity space. See **Cultural Politics, Identity, Oppositional Consciousness.**

Domestic, *Doméstica*, Domesticana

The adjective domestic designates the private or family sphere, the home. It also has national applications, as in domestic or internal affairs, or the domestic economy—domestic signifying the opposite of foreign. As a noun, domestic refers to a woman employed by a family to work in the family home as a maid, nanny, cleaner, cook, child-minder, or some or all of those in combination. Domestics (*domésticas*) may be hired on a live-in basis, their food and lodging costs thus forming part of their salary, or they may be employed on hourly or daily rates with no expectation that they will live with their employers. Poverty is the underlying factor in the rise of the industry across the globe, as women with limited prospects are impelled to leave their own families and communities to seek employment with middle- and upper-class families in their own countries, or abroad. In Latin America and the USA, many domestics are indigenous women, who move from rural to urban sites, and across national borders, in order to find work. The global domestic service industry has a reputation for exploitation and insecurity, in that domestics may lack unionized protection or the security of legal status, and employers may not include in pay structures such benefits as holiday or sick leave, health-care coverage, or contributions to social security, pension, or superannuation plans. Since the 1960s, the domestic service sector in the USA has been dominated by Latinas and by immigrants from Latin American (Mexico, Central America) and the Caribbean states, such as Jamaica, Haiti, and the Dominican Republic (Grasmuck and Pessar 1991). This demographic profile may reflect a historical process of domestic "succession," whereby new immigrants fill the employment gaps left by previously dominant groups, for instance African Americans, as they move into other more desirable areas of employment (Wilson and Wilson 2000). Romero (2002) argues that the demographic profile of the industry is tied to the issue of **citizenship**, and the lack of it, undocumented domestics in partic- ular being constrained in terms of their capacity to negotiate better work con- ditions or enjoy job security. Romero also demonstrates that the intersections of race, ethnicity, class, and gender further underwrite the experience of domestic workers on a spectrum from vulnerable to privileged. For Romero, the domestic sector plays a pivotal role in what she calls the "social repro- duction of family, community, and nation," hence the importance of studying the experiences of domestics and gaining insights about their socioeconomic role from domestics themselves. Hondagneu-Sotelo (2001) endorses that position, arguing that Latina domestics are rendered invisible or overlooked in a country whose social and economic survival depends on their labor. The documentary *Maid in the USA* (2004, dir. Anayansi Prado) tracks the experi- ences of three domestics in California and foregrounds the operations of the Domestic Workers Project (DWP), one of many support organizations for domestics to have emerged since the 1970s with the aim of fighting for improved work conditions, pay, and worker rights. Eulalia Camargo's play, *Call Me María* (featured in *Maid in the USA*), centers on Superdoméstica, a domestic super hero. Notable novelistic treatments of the domestics' condition include Chicano John Rechy's *The Miraculous Day of Amalia Gómez* (1991), the Nuyorican Esmeralda Santiago's *América's Dream* (1996), and the Cuban American Oscar Hijuelos's *Empress of the Splendid Season* (1999). Extrapolating from the uses of domestic to signify the private home and fam- ily realm, Mesa-Bains (2003) proposes the neologism "domesticana" as a feminist version of the Chicano/a "making-do" aesthetic of *rasquachismo* that can account for a range of women's home-art practices and sensibilities. Domesticana toys with the notion of mexicana, the name for the **kitsch** art objects and souvenirs manufactured for, and sold in, the tourist economy as embodying an authentic "Mexican" reality. Mesa-Bains plots a range of art prac- tices and traditions under the domesticana rubric: **altars**, home decorations (niches, *ofrendas*, **retablos**), *curanderismo* (healing traditions), yard shrines, and even "feminine pose and style." "Domesticana chicana" functions as a home-based response by women to the pressures of assimilation, and a defiance against Chicano/a gender mores. Many Chicana artists draw upon the site-specific making-do traditions of Chicana domestic labor, thus extending the domesticana aesthetic into the fine-art realm.

Dominicano

Dominicano, or Dominican, is the name for someone from the Dominican Republic. *Dome* is a colloquial **Spanglish** term, current in the Washington Heights district of New York City, for a Dominican American. Dominicanyork is the term for Dominican New York City and can also refer to Dominican residents of the city. *Nueba Yol* is another Dominican American term for New York City that approximates a Caribbean Spanish pronunciation of the city's name. *Nueba Yol* is also the title of a film directed by Ángel Muñiz (1995), which deals with the travails of a Dominican immigrant in search of the "American Dream." See **Quisqueya.**

Duranguense

Duranguense is a fast-paced and percussion-led dance music that arose in the 1990s in the Mexican state of Durango; it has become popular on both sides of the US–Mexico border, with an increasing number of US-based practitioners, including El Grupo Montez de Durango from Chicago. A neocultural music form that incorporates elements of *banda*, *cumbia*, *ranchera*, and polka, *duranguense* employs brass and woodwind instruments, electric keyboards, and multiple sets of snare drums. Among the popular Mexican proponents of *duranguense* are Alacranes Musical, Patrulla 81, and K-Paz de la Sierra.

E

English-Only Movement

English-Only is the name for a movement that aims to enshrine English as the sole official language at city, county, state, and/or federal levels. These campaigns, which began in 1980, aim to repeal or prevent official **bilingual education**, remove local community signs in languages other than English, and prevent government dealings with citizens in languages other than English, primarily Spanish. Many commentators regard English-Only as a symptom of a **nativist** backlash against immigration from Mexico and other Spanish-speaking countries, the ostensible focus on "language" by proponents often masking deeper fears about the "nation" under threat from Spanish-speaking peoples (Crawford 1992). At a federal level, English is not the official language of the USA, and any attempt to give English that function would require a Constitutional amendment. However, this is not the case at city, county, and state level across the country, and much of the recent legislative success to enshrine English as the official state, county, or city language is attributable to English-Only. As Max Castro points out (1997), the movement was inaugurated in Dade County, Miami, in 1980, in a successful grassroots reaction by non-Cuban sectors against the bilingual policies of local government, the education system, and the media. The Florida example was emulated elsewhere in the country, as exemplified by the formation of influential political organizations opposed to bilingualism: "US English" (1983), "English First" (1986), the "American Ethnic Coalition" (1986), and "Pro-English" (1994). By 2005, 24 states had passed the English First or English Alone legislation, with two

(Arizona and Alaska, 1998) having the result overturned by state Supreme Court decisions in 1998 and 2002, respectively. Hawaii and New Mexico, however, are officially bilingual. The state constitutions of Nebraska (1920), Illinois (1969), and Massachusetts (1975) also regard English as official languages. A countermovement called "English Plus" began in Florida in 1987 as a coalition under the auspices of the Spanish-American League Against Discrimination. English Plus emphasized the pedagogical and social benefits of bilingualism and attempted to demystify the misconception that Latino/as do not want to learn English or speak Spanish only. English Plus has achieved state-level support in New Mexico (1989), Oregon (1989), Washington (1989), and Rhode Island (1992). A number of critics point out that the English-Only Movement was preceded, and paralleled, by the imposition of English on Puerto Rico as an official language and medium of instruction in schools in the decades after the US takeover in 1898. The struggle between English and Spanish at official levels and in the education system has continued in Puerto Rico since 1949, with the official status of Spanish and English changing at regular intervals (Crawford 1992; Negrón-Muntaner 1997; Urciuoli 1996). In May 2006, the release of a Spanish-language version of the "Star-Spangled Banner" reignited calls to make English the national language. Critics of the song described Spanish as a "foreign" idiom, their arguments again confirming that the language issue cannot be disentangled from broader discourses of political and cultural **citizenship**.

Estado Libre Asociado

El Estado Libre Asociado de Puerto Rico (ELA, Free Associated State), or the Commonwealth of Puerto Rico, defines Puerto Rico's formal relationship with the USA. The declaration of the ELA in 1952 represented a political attempt to redefine Puerto Rico's colonial status, inaugurated by the US annexation of the island in the **Spanish–American War** of 1898. However, many Puerto Rican nationalists claim that the ELA designation sidestepped the issue of **colonialism**. For these critics, the ELA was an imposed political name and governing structure impelled by the USA's own self-serving concerns in the Cold War era to avoid appearing as an imperial power unwilling to grant the island either independence or greater autonomy. The change to Commonwealth status was nonetheless approved in a referendum of the island's voters before being ratified by the US Congress, and was enshrined in the island's new constitution that described Puerto Rico as a "self-governing unincorporated organized territory" that "belongs" to the USA. That formal declaration of territorial ownership gives Puerto Rico the same status as the US possession of the Northern Mariana Islands in the Pacific Ocean. The use of the term "unincorporated" means that the island is neither on track for incorporation into the USA as a state, nor free. Given that the original ELA statute and associated island constitution defined Puerto Rico as a US territory, and that Article IV, Section 3, of the US Constitution states that only the US Congress can dispose of national assets and territories, attempts on the part of Puerto Rican political leaders since the 1950s to achieve greater autonomy or alter the island's political status (the string of plebiscites that give Puerto Rican voters the choice of ELA status, statehood, or independence) are potentially unconstitutional and unlikely to succeed. The result is that Puerto Rico remains locked into colonial status.

Ethnicity, Panethnicity

Often contrasted with **race**, ethnicity designates the set of characteristics (cultural practices and traditions, language, shared ancestry, religion, national or regional origin and location) that combine to define or identify a particular group. As opposed to racial categorizations that define peoples according to supposed natural or essential biological, genetic, and physical criteria, ethnicity is normally regarded as an identity that is claimed and constructed by particular groups, or imposed on them, in order to distinguish ethnic self from ethnic other. However, for some peoples, ethnicity is related to nationality itself, an application that reflects the origins of the word in the Greek *ethnos*, nation; for others, ethnicity may be anchored in a particular region, language, religious affiliation, or racialized identification (Bennett et al. 2005). Ethnicity may reflect how dominant populations define themselves as nonethnic bearers of "national" qualities, and dismiss other groups as "ethnicities," the implication being that the latter challenge, contradict, or fail to embody the "national." In popular understandings, ethnicity may provide an identity vector for emotive investment, political defense, and, at times, violence against other ethnic groups (pogroms, ethnic cleansing, **nativism**). In current critical applications of the term, ethnicity is often treated as a fluid mode of identification that responds to changing historical material and socioeconomic circumstances, such as immigration (Nelson and Tienda 1997). However, the purported difference between racial and ethnic categorizations may not be clear cut. For example, the US **Census** regards **Hispanic** and **Latino** as ethnic markers, to be distinguished from race. However, in the popular imagination and media, both Hispanic and Latino are treated as racial categories, hence the widespread use of "Hispanic" as of the same order as black and white. Panethnicity refers to identifications and/or relations that span ethnic- or national-origin groups. Panethnicity may designate new identity formations—**Latinidad**, **situational alliances**—by which individuals perceive themselves to be part of a larger "Latino/a" community. Noriega and López (1996) argue that complex and contradictory interethnic relations determine the identifications available to Latino/as. That is, Latino/a ethnicity and panethnicity are explicable in "the matrix of differential histories" by which the names adopted by Latino/as also multiply and shift. This matrix has four levels: ethnic or subnational (Chicano, Puerto Rican, Cuban); interethnic (relations along gender, class, sexuality, racial lines), panethnic (Latino, Hispanic) within a national US frame; national mainstream (American); and transnational or hemispherical (Latin American). None of these axials of identification overrides or overdetermines the other possibilities. Klor de Alva (1997) identifies a range of ethnic "corporate identifications" at work in particular places for particular people. A *Tejano/a* in south Texas, for example, may have a micro-ethnicity anchored in the local community, a regional or nationalist identity as a Chicano/a, a macroethnicity as a Latino/a or Hispanic/a, and a range of "meta-ethnicities" as someone of Mexican descent (Mexican), a US citizen (American), and a resident of the Americas. Those ethnic strata may also give rise to identity options defined in opposition to other local groups on either side of the border. Vila (2000, 2005) emphasizes that ethnic and other identities in El Paso/Juárez arise from a matrix of differentiated, and often antagonistic, local relations. Panethnicity, or interethnicity, can also refer to Latino/a relations with other US sectors. Long histories of interethnic cooperation, transcultural interchange, and political affiliation have characterized local relations between African Americans and Latino/as in many of the USA's largest cities. Historians of the Chicano and Puerto Rican Movements of the 1960s and 1970s have demonstrated the fundamental influence on those movements of African American civil rights struggles (Mariscal 2005; Torres and Velázquez 1998), while panethnic collaboration and affiliation characterized **Third World Feminism.** Nuyorican and African American cultural interchanges enabled by demographic proximity provided the transcultural conditions for the rise of **rap and hip-hop**. Vaca (2004), however, contends that the belief that African Americans and Latino/as were "brothers under the skin" united in opposition to white hegemony was widespread in the 1960s. Nonetheless, that fraternal ideal may have belied fundamental minority differences (for instance, between African Americans and Cubans in south Florida) and overlooked the potential for divergent nodes of activism, for example, immigrant status and bilingual education. Many **Chicano Movement** era critics proposed that Native Americans and Chicano/as were territorial minorities with panethnic affinities (De la Garza et al. 1973), a reading that also reflected a movement belief that Chicano/as were, in part, a native constituency. Noting that Latino/as and Asians will provide over half of the USA's population growth in the first half of the twenty-first century, a process well underway in California, some critics have called for new theoretical understandings of the influence of "new immigration" on panethnic relations (Hamamoto and Torres 1997).

Ethnopoetics, Mythopoetics

Ethnopoetics (or mythopoetics, ethnonationalism) is a term often used by Chicano/a critics to describe the ritual, mythical, and cultural characteristics, many derived from indigenous and popular cultural traditions, of Chicano/a poetic production since the 1960s. Candelaria (1986) identified three interrelated stylistic qualities in "Chicano poetics" or "ethnopoetics" that distinguish Chicano/a poetry from other literary approaches. First, Chicano poetics is multilingual and anchored in quotidian realities. Second, its symbolism underwrites *Chicanismo*, hence the drawing of images and figures from Meso-American myth and culture, discourses of *mestizaje*, and **Chicano Movement** political activism, in order to generate an anticolonial sense of communal identity. The widespread references in Chicano/a cultural work to **Aztec** culture and myth typify this drive. Finally, Chicano poetics is ritual and tradition based, a means of maintaining links between people across historical eras. Pérez-Torres (1995b) argues that the ritualistic and performative drive of much Chicano/a poetry must dispute modernist understandings of the poetic text as somehow detached from material history, and enable an overt political critique of Anglo-American constructions of knowledge. Pérez-Torres takes issue with Candelaria's celebration of ethnopoetics as a means to evoke or intervene in an uninterrupted cultural tradition that conjoins pre-Columbian and contemporary Chicano/a poetic practices. That view, he argues, glosses over an intervening history of discontinuities and ruptures (conquest and colonization by both Spain and the USA), and ignores how the ethnopoetic gaze in Chicano/a cultural work has always grappled with those cultural breaks and violence. Chicano/a ethnopoetics thus provides one possible poetic mode among many possible options within the multivalent and dialogic terrains of Chicano/a cultural production.

Exile

Exile is conventionally defined as banishment, a geographical dislocation and a physical separation from home enacted by, or elected in response to, a state regime's political, legal, and policing apparatuses. When imposed, exile is intended to prevent certain social actors, groups, and sometimes entire communities from effecting national or regime change. When chosen, exile may provide an escape from unbearable or life-threatening circumstances, and permit opportunities for political activism and resistance impossible at home. Kaminsky (1999) argues that physical displacement is a necessary prerequisite for exile, and that exile's effects are felt on and by the displaced body. Given the political framework in which exile takes place, and with great personal cost, critics distinguish exile from other categories of displacement: refugee status, migration, guestwork, tourism, short and extended travel, professional postings abroad, and expatriate status. A number of other terms either parallel, or overlap with, and even supersede exile (**diaspora**), while others differentiate between structures of displacement (**transnationality,** nomadism, cosmopolitanism). Moreover, exile may be regarded metaphorically as a sign and symptom of modernity, thus connoting a sense of identity unease, pain, and alienation at, and from, home. Exile has also been figured as a condition of the productive and creative possibilities and pleasures, afforded by physical or psychic alienation. Political exile has been a significant force in the historical evolution of numerous Latino/a communities. Cuban independence and nationalist advocates, such as José Martí, found save havens in the USA in the nineteenth century. Large numbers of Mexicans crossed the border into exile to avoid the social upheavals and violence stemming from the **Mexican Revolution** (1910). In the 1970s and 1980s, many Latin Americans arrived in the USA as political exiles from military dictatorship (Argentina, Uruguay, Chile) and civil war (El Salvador, Guatemala, Nicaragua). However, the Latino/a community most closely associated with exile is the Cuban sector.

After the 1959 **Cuban Revolution**, hundreds of thousands of upper- and middle-class Cubans fled to the USA, most settling in Florida. This community has defined itself as a "political exile" formation and has often drawn parallels between the Cuban predicament and Judaic notions of a communal identity profoundly marked by exilic displacement and a hoped-for return to the homeland. The exile designation has nonetheless proved difficult to maintain as the Cuban exile community has evolved into one immigrant sector among many (Rivero 1989), with younger generations growing up with limited or no direct memories of Cuba, and emigration from Cuba since the 1980s motivated by economic, rather than political, imperatives. In Latino/a queer studies, the term sexile or s/exile designates the chosen exile of Latino/as whose migration is motivated by a desire to escape the homophobic environments of their home cultures and to establish new queer identities and communities in the host society (Guzmán 1997; Sandoval-Sánchez 2005).

F

Folklore, Folk Culture

Folklore (folklife, folk culture) refers to cultural practices by and in which communities share past knowledge, make sense of the world, and pass on community values, identities, and traditions across generations. The concept of folk culture presupposes a distinction between industrial culture and that of the folk or people who may be thought of as preserving preindustrial or premodern cultural practices. Folk culture is said to reside, and be perpetuated through, the oral preservation, transmission, and teaching of stories, tales, and legends (e.g., tales about folk heroes, fables, *dichos*, ghost or supernatural stories told to children), community and familial history, material cultural practices (cookery, artisan work and crafts, housing design and construction, dances, music, and so on), social customs and rituals (*quinceañera*), and women's domestic labor and cultural practices (Abarca 2006; Mesa-Bains 2003). Some critics regard the folk traditions of rural and ethnic communities as an integral part of popular culture, although the latter term tends to signify mass-mediated cultural productions and their reception and consumption. In the evolution of the folklore concept since the late 1700s, the term has often encoded within it a sense of unease about, and critique of, modernity. The concept has also provided some proponents with a potent tool for ideological and political manipulation, for example, in nation-building projects that find in folk traditions an ''authentic'' base on which the nation can be imagined and the state cohered. The Mexican government's sponsoring of *ballet folklórico* troupes in the mid-1900s, and the naming of *mariachi* as the national music, for example, are emblematic of this appropriation of folklore. Paredes (1986) regarded the study of folklore as a means of confirming the historical vitality of Mexican American communities and cultural practices. Such research was a necessary political enterprise, given the historical disparagement of Mexican Texans since 1848, and the resilient legend of Anglo-Texan superiority (exemplified by the cry, "Remember the **Alamo!**" and the heroization of the **Texas Rangers**) that had silenced or ignored Mexican American contestations of the historical record, such as those recorded in *corridos*. Chicano/a and Latino/a scholars have produced a rich body of work that explores the importance of folkloric practices and traditions for communities faced by imposed **assimilation**, socioeconomic marginalization, informal segregation, state-sanctioned violence, and European American cultural hegemony.

Football, *Fútbol*, Soccer

Football (soccer), or *el fútbol*, is the most popular, and one of the most lucrative and corporatized, spectator sports in the world. The modern sport derives from a British game that developed over centuries as a communal village affair characterized by its free-for-all violence (Montague 2004). By the early 1800s the game was being played in public schools. Game rules were codified at the Cambridge University in 1843, and revised in 1863, the latter date also marking the foundation of the British Football Association. A standard football match consists of two teams of eleven players on a field divided into two sides; each team attempts to win by kicking more goals than its rival into a goal area that is backed and sided by a net. Matches last for 90 minutes and are divided into two halves. A referee on the pitch and linesmen or assistant referees on the sidelines arbitrate the conduct of the match and attempt to ensure that rules are followed. Football is not a high-scoring game, given the balance between teams and the players' skills at defense. Often, matches end in draws. Players are not permitted to use their hands, with the exception of goalkeepers, and balls are passed by kicking or by bouncing off the upper torso and forehead. Football was exported to Britain's colonies in the heyday of the British Empire in the nineteenth century. Given Britain's domination of the world economy in that era, the sport was introduced to local communities when British ships stopped at ports and trading centers. The Fédération Internationale de Football Association (FIFA) was formed in 1904, and it remains the international governing body for the game today (Montague 2004). Football engenders extreme passions and loyalties, and national and international competitions in many continents reflect broader political tensions. The Spanish league, for example, is dominated by the historical rivalries between the Catalan team, El Fútbol Club Barcelona (Barça), and the Spanish team, Real Madrid. Those rivalries reflect the center–periphery struggles of Spanish history while also evoking memories of General Franco's support for Real Madrid and suppression of Catalan aspirations. At times, football has caused armed conflict, as occurred with the so-called Fútbol War of July 1969 between El Salvador and Honduras. Today football is a big transnational business, with players in the major national leagues paid in millions and enjoying global superstar status. Football is making extraordinary inroads into USA's sporting life and public consciousness, in no small part due to the Latino/a spectatorship. Shinn (2002) posits that the transnational media is enabling recent immigrants to follow their home national teams. At the same time, *el fútbol* in the Latino/a context not only facilitates the maintenance of national identifications in a transnational framework, but it also assists the formation of new panethnic, albeit masculinized, imaginaries that regard the USA as the "other" *fútbol* homeland.

Frontier

The frontier, like the **West**, is an important geospatial concept in US historical and national debates. The US frontier traditionally designated the edges of civilized or settled lands, on the other side of which resided indigenous peoples. The era of the frontier lasted from the eighteenth to the nineteenth century, the closing of the frontier dated to 1890, when the US **Census** announced that the frontier had disappeared. The origin of the frontier thesis lies in the 1893 essay by Frederick Jackson Turner, "The Significance of the Frontier in American History" (1994), which argued that "American" civilization was founded on the natural and inexorable spread of the nation westwards, domesticating land and making "Americans" of the people involved in the process. In the westward movement of the frontier, Turner argued, lay the foundational qualities of the "American" national character: rugged individualism, exceptionalism, adaptability, and inherent democratic tendencies, all of which differentiated "Americans" from Europeans. Frontier historiography designates that branch of US history that explores the idea of the frontier, either in dialogue with Turner or diverging from him. As with the discourse of the West, this has had to grapple not only with the "frontier's" conceptual and geospatial resistance to definition, but also with a historical recognition of other contact zone axials, such as the north–south encounter between Mexican and Anglo peoples (disavowed in the work of Walter Prescott Webb [1931, 1935]), Native American occupations of continental space, and migrant trajectories east across the Pacific. Revisionist history for many decades has been confronted by the challenges posed by such alternative frontier narratives and by the creation of the US–Mexico **borderlands** as a new species of frontier after the **Mexican–American War** of 1846–1848 (Garza-Falcón 1998). The Turnerian frontier thesis has even been "Latinized" by Latino/a critics. For example, Flores and Yúdice propose the "living border" as a supplement to the "moving frontier" effect celebrated by Turner. This "living border" signifies the historical movement of the frontier from an oceanic limit or margin of exploration for Europeans, to the westward occupation of the North American continent by European Americans, and finally to a new frontier margin as defined and resemanticized by the **Latinization** processes at work inside US borders (Flores 1993). See **Border Theory.**

G

Gachupín

Gachupín (and *gachupina*) is a pejorative term for a Spaniard that dates from the colonial era in Mexico and other parts of Latin America (Stephens 1989). One popular theory (common on the internet) posits that the term derives from the **Náhuatl** word *catzopini*, a contraction of *cactli* (shoe) and *tzopini* (a sharp object), an allusion to the Spanish habit of wearing spurs. An alternative explanation is that *gachupín* is a medieval word for a Spaniard of "pure" blood from Cantabria. By the early 1800s, *gachupín* had come to designate a dishonest or uneducated Spaniard, and was also a stock figure of mockery in Mexican burlesque poetry. *Gachupín* survives in Mexican and Chicano/a Spanish as a synonym for Spaniard or someone who speaks with a Spanish accent. The term was common during the **Chicano Renaissance**, as exemplified by Rodolfo "Corky" Gonzales's 1967 poem, "I am Joaquín / Yo soy Joaquín" (2001).

Gangs, *Maras*

The Latino/a gang is a controversial topic in Latino/a Studies given that dominant cultural discourses have long placed Latino/as on the "bad" edges of the law and nation. In the popular imagination, media, and legal discourse, "Hispanic" often functions as a euphemism for criminality, organized or not. Those portrayals predate the popular success of *West Side Story* (1961), after which Nuyoricans were popularly regarded as a gang-ridden populace.

Hollywood films in the early 1900s had already established templates for equating Mexicans with *banditos* and illegal border crossers, and thus as an inassimilable criminal constituency. Gang scholarship has contextualized gang culture in relation to communal experiences of **marginalization** and structures of poverty, racism, and discrimination. Faced with those conditions, gang culture generates its own semiotic codes, informal and formal regulations, cultural capital, territorializations, and idiom. Bourgois (1996) describes a Nuyorican gang "street culture of resistance" that does not represent a coherent oppositional habitus. Rather, rebellion and nonconformity provide identificatory vectors of group cohesion that at times preclude viable resistances to structures of oppression. Vigil (1988) proposes that gangs must be understood as an adaptive response to "multiple marginality." The LA Chicano/a gang tradition, for example, represents a sociocultural reaction against the limited physical mobilities permitted by a history of ethnocultural, linguistic and economic marginalization. Continuing migration from Mexico has also contributed to an intergenerational "gang" continuum by which newcomers are acculturated into Chicano/a gang structures. Vigil (2002) calls that process *choloization*, from *cholo*, Chicano/a idiom for a gang member. The formal and informal customs and traditions in Chicano/a gangs derive from cultural mixing between Mexicans, Chicano/as, and other groups, adaptations of Anglo-American cultural forms, and the evolution of street-level codes, structural conventions, and names in specific **barrios**, "urban, rural, suburban, classic, modern" (Vigil 2002). Gang membership is not fixed and immutable. Participants move in and out of gangs depending on circumstances, group sizes vary, territories shift or disappear, and organizational structures range from the loosely run to highly corporatized hierarchies involving 80–100 participants. Moreover, different codes and conventions apply to male and female participants, as is evident in the adolescent initiation customs in many Chicano/a gangs ("courting in" or "jumping in," the beating of new recruits), which also confirm the importance for participants to conform to hypergendered norms (Vigil 2002). Among Chicano/as, *la clica (la klika*, clique) designates the subgroups that comprise a gang; with origins in the **Zoot Suit** era, the term is commonly used by prison inmates in California and the US southwest. *Clica* can also refer to any close group of friends. **Graffiti** artists in or associated with gangs have developed complex graphic codes for writing or "hitting up" their clique names (*placas*) in clique territory. Similarly, many gang members bear tattoos identifying their clique affiliation. The term *la eMe* is a shorthand for the Mexican Mafia, the dominant Mexican American gang in US prisons in California, Texas, and other states. Another consequence of the gang continuum has been the rise of transnational gangs called *maras*, or Central American urban-youth street gangs. *Maras* arose among Central American immigrant and refugee communities in the USA in the 1980s and early 1990s in an era of civil war and military dictatorship. Due to US deportation policies of "criminal" migrants, and the increase in flows of travel and circular migration between the USA and Central American states, *maras* spread back to Central America, with El Salvador having the greatest density (Bruneau 2005). *Maras* represent a legacy of US interventions in Central America, and, for some commentators, a sign of new transnational criminal links across Central America, the USA, Canada, and Mexico. The highest concentration of *maras* in the USA is found in California, one of the largest gangs in the Los Angeles area being the El Salvadorian Mara Salvatrucha (Vigil 2002). Latino/a gangs are a routine presence in Latino/a cultural production, from film and literary explorations and autobiographical accounts, to art, music, and **graffiti**. Gang culture provides a significant thematic strand in the Nuyorican **mean streets** genre, which has its Chicano/a counterpart in urban narratives about gang life (Brown 2002). The Chicano gang continuum provides the focus of the epic saga *American Me* (1992, dir. Edward Olmos). Set in East LA, the film, which uses young actors drawn from local gangs, attempts to historicize the criminalization of Chicano youth that began with the **Zoot Suiters** in the 1940s.

Globalization

Globalization is a ubiquitous term in public discourse, the media, government circles, and numerous disciplines; it is also a term that has generated a huge amount of critical debate about what globalization is, and how individuals and communities might recognize or make sense of its effects and driving properties (Robertson 1992). There is general agreement, however, that certain features of contemporary life changed in the twentieth century in unprecedented ways, and that globalizing pressures now touch everyone in the world. For some critics, globalization designates an economic phenomenon, a synonym for global or international capitalism, which is represented by multinational companies that can, and do, disregard state boundaries in the construction of a worldwide market, while exploiting disparate peoples and natural resources.

Some observers define globalization as an era in which time and space have collapsed, the mass-mediation and the technologization of communication channels enabling contact between people across the world at the push of a button, and generating a widespread sense of interconnectedness, and even a sense of the global homogenization of everyday life. Other commentators describe globalization as the relentless incorporation of local cultures into a global cultural order or market comprising distinct cultural practices, traditions, and values; that fate is evident, for example, in the history of **salsa**, which cannot be homed in a single nation or musical tradition. Yet other critics take the line that globalization is synonymous with a productive **hybridization** or bricolaging of daily life. Against such views, some notions of globalization regard it as in dialectical tension with the local, or between the regional and the local; the global requires the local to be located in order to deal with it, while the local wants access to the global without losing its historical material identity. Globalization may designate the increasing transnational movements of goods, peoples, and ideas—mobility being a sign of the inexorable weakening of geopolitical state power to stem the flows. Indeed, globalization is often used synonymously with **transnationality**, or to designate a postnational realm. For some critics, globalization defines a US-dominated global order, characterized by the pressures of **Americanization** and the application of US military hegemony wherever US interests are threatened. Such understandings of globalization as a threat to people and cultures have inspired a range of (and, ironically, globally connected) antiglobalization movements, typified by the indigenous Zapatista Rebellion in southern Mexico since 1994, demands to cancel Third World debt, and organizations opposed to the World Bank and such trading entities as **NAFTA**.

Graffiti

Graffiti refers to the process of marking, writing, or producing text and images on walls and other surfaces. Often regarded as a youth cultural phenomenon now found in urban settings across the world, graffiti nonetheless designates a range of distinct writerly enterprises: political graffiti (for instance, the "*Viva la raza!*" slogans of the **Chicano Movement**), **gang** graffiti, and graffiti art. Graffiti is often regarded as a social problem, a symptom and symbol of antisocial behavior on the part of vandals and criminals who are said to deface and disfigure public space, and who show lack of respect for property.

Graffiti writing has thus become a criminalized practice, with graffiti writers aware of their outsider or socially illegitimate status. Graffiti production is a complex social, aesthetic, and communicative practice characterized by the innate ephemerality, and rapid production, of graffiti (which can be written over, destroyed by weather and construction work, or interrupted by the police). It is indicative of the evolving relationships and dialogues that occur between wall writers and the communities in which they reside. In US gang parlance, writing on walls with spray paint is called wall banging (wallbangin'), a term that Phillips (1999) argues involves two related activities: writing initials (tags, or *placas*), numbers, and codes on walls in order to announce and identify a gang's or a gang member's presence and to establish spatial and social boundaries (hitting up, *plaquear*); and the crossing out of the writing done by other gangs. These activities reinforce intergang power relations. Local graffiti may not be legible to outsiders, thus constituting a communicative code that conforms to the organizational institutions, rules, and purviews of gang cultures in African American, Latino/a, and other communities. Graffiti produced by hip-hop artists represents a different aesthetic practice, its prac-titioners calling it aerosol or spray-can art, and organizing and identifying themselves as crews. Hip-hop graffiti's origins lie in the **rap and hip-hop** cultures of inner-city New York in the 1970s, but the practice has spread with the **globalization** of rap and hip-hop and is now a familiar feature of the urban landscape across the world. As Phillips notes, hip-hop graffiti generates its own terminology, but involves three distinct types of writing: (a) intricate and detailed "pieces" (masterpieces) combining text and image, and produced by writers; (b) "tags" (from nametags, *placas*), which can also be highly detailed; and (c) "throw-ups" (graffiti quickly "thrown up" on a wall). Other terms include "bombing" (putting a lot of work into producing graffiti in limited space and time) and "killing" (crossing out or spraying over another graffiti artist's name and work).

Gran familia

Literally the great or large family, *la gran familia* is a Spanish-language euphemism for the nation or, to use Benedict Anderson's wording, the national imagined community (1991). Evocative of such terms as **Greater Mexico** and **Greater Cuba**, which designate national populations that exceed state bound-aries, *la gran familia* most often signifies the familial base, anchor, or unifying structure in nation-based identifications (*Mexicanidad, Cubanidad*, and so on). Those ideals of nationality are often the focus of self-conscious construction on the part of postrevolutionary regimes, as occurred after the **Mexican and Cuban Revolutions**. In both countries, notions of nationality were anchored to the indigenous (*Mexicanidad*) and African (*Cubanidad*) base whereas local cultural traditions and folkloric practices were reified as symbols of national character, sovereignty, and unity, especially in Mexico. The purported unity signaled by *la gran familia* is predicated on faith in the patriarchal structures, and heteronormative reproductive logics, that undergird the ideals of both family and nation. In this respect, the fact that national communities are increasingly split and splintered across geopolitical lines and that families themselves take myriad forms that may challenge and dispute the patriarchal structure of home and family, further indicate how the concept fails to accredit transnational and transcultural complexities.

Greaser

Since the mid-1800s greaser has been a term of disparagement for Mexicans and Mexican Americans, and at times for other Latino/as. The word—and its relative grease-monkey—also has a broader usage for indicating a working-class male who works with machines. In its application to Mexicans, the term may indicate working-class or laboring status, or it may be linked to the unfounded stereotype that Mexicans have oily or greasy appearances. Bender (2003) points out that in the nineteenth century, the term had legal ramifications, as exemplified by the 1855 California Vagrancy Act, or Greaser Act, which defined greasers as people of mixed Indian and Spanish "blood" who are armed and "not peaceable and quiet persons." The act was perhaps the first instance of a US law that treated Mexican Americans as a criminalized sector that merits constant police surveillance and attention. The act is of note, too, for linking the term greaser (a synonym for half-breed) to *mestizos*, this usage thus betraying Anglo-American anxieties about miscegenation and racial contamination. In US popular culture, particularly film, the Mexican greaser has featured as a stock stereotype since the late 1800s.

Greater Cuba

The term Greater Cuba signifies a notion of *Cubanidad* (the purported quality of being Cuban) that, since the 1959 **Cuban Revolution**, cannot be contained to or on the island state, given that exile communities (some 10 percent of the Cuban population) form part of a larger Cuban whole. Ana López (1996) argues that Greater Cuba designates the extra-insular exile community at the edges or margins of the *cubanidad* propounded by the Cuban state. That community mirrors national codes, traditions, discourses, and symbols, and supplements them with its own. Greater Cuba thus indicates that Cuba now "exceeds national boundaries," and that the exile communities in South Florida and elsewhere are symptomatic of, and a significant force in, the transnational transformation of Cuban identities since 1959.

Greater Mexico

Greater Mexico designates a Mexican national cultural entity that exceeds geopolitical borders. Greater Mexico thus includes Mexico and the Mexican and Chicano/a communities in the USA, the latter swelled by the migration of some 20 percent of the Mexican population in the twentieth century. The origins of the term are attributed to Américo Paredes's 1958 study *With His Pistol in His Hand* (1986), in which Paredes counterposed Greater Mexico with the border, thus implying that Greater Mexico signifies the Texas–Mexico **borderlands**. Paredes later defined Greater Mexico as a transborder community of Mexican people united by shared cultural traditions and practices (1976). For Calderón (2004), Greater Mexico designates the Mexican diaspora wherever it may be found, a broadening of the concept from the region that anchored Paredes's usage, the lower Río Grande valley in Texas. Limón (1998) argues that Greater Mexico is even more complex than Paredes accredited, for its operations and appropriations in Anglo-American cultural texts confirm the long presence of Mexico as an internalized "Other" presence in US imaginaries of national and worldly place.

Great Migration

The Great Migration designates the mass migration of Puerto Ricans to the USA between 1946 and 1964, the era following the *pionero* phase and preceding what some commentators call the "revolving-door phase" of migration. During the Great Migration most Puerto Rican immigrants settled in New York and elsewhere in the US northeast, with the result that by 1964, New York's Puerto Rican population was close to ten percent of the city total (Sánchez Korrol 1994). By 1980, 2 million Puerto Ricans were living in the USA, some 860,000 in New York alone. The causes of the Great Migration can be traced back to 1917, when the **Jones Act** granted Puerto Ricans nominal US citizenship, thus eliminating legal obstacles to movement to and from the USA. By the 1940s, many Puerto Ricans regarded emigration as an escape route from poverty on the island. That escape was also impelled by **Operation Bootstrap**, and by the introduction of affordable and regular flights between San Juan and New York. The term Great Migration also designates the mass movement of some 2 million African American farm and rural workers from the southern states to northern industrial cities, and to such states as California, between World War I and the advent of the Great Depression in 1929. That migration was fueled by the desire for better socioeconomic conditions and employment, and an equally powerful wish to escape from a part of the USA where racial segregation (Jim Crow) policies were rigidly and violently maintained.

Green Card

The green card is the document by which immigrants attain "Lawful Permanent Residency" status, thus ensuring they can work legally and gain access to government and social services. The Bureau of Citizenship and Immigration Services (www.uscis.gov) provides detailed information on the various paths of immigration that lead to green card status. These avenues include the family reunion program, employer sponsorship, investment, the Legal Immigration Family Equity Act, an Immigration Court Order, asylum or refugee status, the Diversity Lottery, international adoption, the Violence Against Women Act, and "Special Immigrant" status. Green cards are also available to immigrants applying under a Country-Specific Adjustment, such as the Cuban Adjustment Act, which has enabled Cubans to fast-track residency if they reach dry land, as opposed to being intercepted at sea (the Wet-Foot/Dry-Foot law). Among Mexicans, a green card is referred to as *la Mica* whereas a *miquero* is someone who sells *Green cardas* on the street.

Guagua aérea

La guagua aérea (flying bus) is the Puerto Rican name for the aircraft that connect San Juan and the cities of the US northeast, most notably New York. The term also encapsulates both literally and figuratively a sense of the circuitous connections and migratory movements that bind island and diasporic Puerto Ricans, and that also divide them. Sandoval-Sánchez (1997) argues that the "revolving door" of the airport and the "up-in-the-air" airplane function as liminal sites in which mobile and transitive Puerto Rican identities are affirmed, translated, disrupted, and even destroyed. Unlike the US–Mexico border, or the maritime border in the Florida Strait between Cuba and Florida, the Puerto Rican border is "up in the air." For Sandoval-Sánchez, the Puerto Rican diasporic imagination has constructed a myth of "eternal return" that being "up in the air" will take Puerto Ricans back to the island home and that Puerto Rican identity is not also anchored ambivalently in a US "home." These ambivalences underwrite the metaphorical function of the *guagua aérea* as the moving border space that Puerto Ricans are obliged to negotiate. The most famous literary depiction of the *guagua aérea* is Rafael Sánchez's short story, *La guagua aérea* (1987, 1994), in which the airbus becomes the venue for fragmented Puerto Rican identity, as relayed by the narrator in snatches of overhead conversations and opinion, and observations of the airbus's Anglo-American and Puerto Rican passengers and their interactions. As Duany (2002) notes, the fluid and mutable construction of Puerto Ricanness evident in Rafael Sánchez's story presents a clear challenge to unitary nation-based models of identity formation and meaning. A film version of the story with the same title (dir. Luis Molina Casanova) was released in 1995.

Guajiro/a

In Cuba, a *guajiro/a* refers to a peasant or *campesino* and may connote timidity or bucolic backwardness. *Guajira* is also a Cuban musical style, played at a slow pace, featuring a standard and a tres guitar (a small 12-stringed instrument), soft percussion, and a piano. *Guajira* lyrics include verses of ten lines (*décimas*) and deal with topical issues, making the genre a vehicle of folk knowledge and news transmission. This working-class musical form developed in the twentieth century in line with rural migration to Havana. The most famous *guajira* is "Guantanamera," which was written in the 1930s by the Cuban radio announcer, Joseíto Fernández Diáz, with lyrics based on the first poem in José Martí's *Versos sencillos* (1997). For eighteen years Fernández Díaz used "Guantanemera" to sing the daily news bulletins on his radio program (Calvo Ospina 1995). Although Fernández Díaz's usage consolidated the place of "Guantanamera" in the consciousness of an entire Cuban generation, later versions of the song ensured that "Guantanamera" now circulates as a world-renowned icon of Cuban culture. Perhaps the most famous version was made by Celia Cruz in 1967, but the transnational popularity of the song is also owed to covers by such 1960s folk-singers as Pete Singer, Joan Baez, and the Weavers. In keeping with the song's original fluid and mutable usage, many recordings of "Guantanamera" have added new lyrics. A rap version by Ratclyff Jean (1997) transformed the song into an ode to Latino/a life, with references to Miami, and New York's Bronx and Spanish Harlem.

Hispanic

The term Hispanic derives from the Latin Hispania, the designation for a Roman province on the Iberian Peninsula that coincides with modern day Spain, whose name itself derives from Hispania. A Hispanic may thus signify a Spaniard, a speaker of Spanish (hence Hispanophone, Spanish-speaking), and, in the US context, anyone of Latin American or Spanish heritage. Since its introduction into government and media discourse in the 1970s, and its use in the 1980 **census**, the term Hispanic has become a routine designation. The Hispanic Decade, for example, refers to the 1980s and was routinely heard in the US media and among business interests to indicate the rise to public and media visibility of Latino/as, and their growing economic and political power. The so-called Hispanic Generation was a media and policy term from the 1980s to designate Latino/as who reached adulthood in that decade and who were poised to influence the US political, economic, and sociocultural landscape. Yet another use of Hispanic is encoded in Hispanic Heritage Month, an annual celebration of "Hispanic" culture from September 15 to October 15. Such uses of Hispanic presuppose a homogeneous, meaningful, and identifiable Hispanic sector, untroubled by such complicating factors as gender, age, racial, and ethnic identification, regional location, and familial migration and residency histories. Hispanic has centered a great deal of debate over ethnic labeling and terminology (Giménez et al. 1992; Nelson and Tienda 1997; Noriega 1993; Noriega and López 1996; Oboler 1995; C. Rodríguez 2000). As Dávila (2000) notes, the construction of the "Hispanic" market renders Latino/as into an abstract totality, a domesticated set of consumers that, on the way to becoming **Americanized**, nonetheless always retains its "culture" on the margins of the European American mainstream. Noriega (1993) argues that the terminological debate between Hispanic and Latino signals a struggle between dominant and counterdiscourses: Hispanic names a state policy of social control by homogenization whereas Latino announces a new collectivism seeking fundamental social change. Oboler (1995) notes that Latin American immigrants instantly acquire "Hispanic" status, and are thus caught up in the history of stigmatization that has characterized Mexican American and Puerto Rican experiences. Latino and not Hispanic is preferred by many Latino/as because it avoids the Spanish European shadow that makes Hispanic the attractive option for Latino/a conservatives (L. Chavez 1992; Stavans 1994), government apparatuses, and business interests alike. Unlike **Latino/a**, Hispanic is widely regarded by Latino/as as an imposed identity marker, one that homogenizes diverse Latino/a communities and privileges the Spanish and European imperial, cultural, and racial heritage. Those connotations were endorsed in 1980 by the Spanish American Heritage Association, which asserted that since Chicano/as and Puerto Ricans are "not Caucasians of Spanish ancestry" they are not Hispanics (Hayes-Bautista and Chapa 1987). A contrary stand appears in "Never Been to Spain," a song from the Chicano performer El Vez: "Well I've never been to Spain / So don't call me Hispanic." Yet, as many critics also recognize, the Latino/a versus Hispanic conflict is always in danger of splitting down an either–or axis that ignores other axes of dispute and the divergent historical experiences of Latino/a groups.

Hispanidad, Hispanism, *Hispanismo*

Hispanidad, or Hispanism (*Hispanismo*), designates the shared values and traditions that are claimed to bind people in the Hispanophone world. Most commonly, the discourse of *Hispanidad* operates and circulates in Latin America as a unifying and ethical force or imaginary enabled by Spanish-derived traditions, and a common language and religion. This sensibility was at times regarded as the foundation for a shared **Creole** opposition to Spanish imperialism, and later American imperialism, whether military, political, economic, or cultural, or any of these in combination. Leftists in Latin America from the 1940s to the 1970s often appealed to an anti-imperialist *Hispanidad*. Today the discourse may also describe resistance to the pressures and demands of globalization, widely regarded in Latin America as being related to US state and economic power. That power encompasses the inroads of the English language, the reification of neoliberal democratic and economic policies, and the imposition on the passive (non-US) world population of US cultural forms and habits, from Hollywood film and digital technologies to consumer goods and fast-food outlets. Underwriting some uses of *Hispanidad* may be a Catholic ethos that runs counter to the perceived protestant, and even atheistic, ethos of US capitalism. In the 1800s, *Hispanidad* understood as an ideal of political unification was evident in the **pan-American** nationalism of Simón Bolívar and José Martí. Whatever form it takes, the discourse of *Hispanidad* is often predicated on an idealistic, and at times utopian, fantasy of unification despite irreducible diversity. Glossed over in the discourse is a range of factors that undermine the unified Hispanicist dream: class, racial, gender, sexual, generational, interregional, and regional. Since the 1970s a variant of *Hispanidad* has circulated in the USA as the name of a discourse by which the government, commercial conglomerates, the media, and many middle- and upper-class Latino/as use **Hispanic** to define a homogeneous minority constituency. Rejecting that broad and simplifying inclusivity, many Latino/a critics and cultural workers oppose Hispanic, and by implication, *Hispanidad*, favoring instead the term **Latino/a**. A more optimistic approach is taken by Debra Castillo (2005), who argues that the long history of Spanish language, bilingual and **Spanglish** literature produced inside US borders challenges orthodox understandings of *Hispanidad* as a unifying imaginary that stops at the US–Mexico border. Arguing that traditional *Hispanismo* needs to accommodate the multi-lingual and transcultural project of **Latinidad**, Castillo proposes that Latino/a-centered epistemologies and reading practices may, in fact, provide the conceptual and critical means for overcoming the nation-centric and disciplinary barriers that have obstructed pan-Hispanic and pan-American intellectual interchange.

Hispano

Hispano is the name adopted by many Mexican-origin inhabitants of New Mexico and southern Colorado, and is most often claimed by people who trace their ancestry back to the Spanish colonizers of New Spain, and not to the region's Indian and *mestizo* peoples. *Hispano* has similar connotations to Spanish American and Hispanic American, which also emphasize European at the expense of indigenous, African, or mixed-race ancestry. Historians trace the origins of *Hispano* to a romanticizing but pragmatic myth of Spanish Americanness by which elite and middle-class Mexican Americans managed their interactions with working-class Mexicans, Indians, and Anglo-Americans (J. Chavez 1984). By insulating themselves from the accusation of being like Indians, the bearers of *Hispano* were at once perpetuating racial stereotypes and attempting to preclude racist attacks on their own class identities, particularly in the decades following the **Mexican–American War** when Anglo-American authority in the conquered territories was consolidated. An alternative term for a New Mexican is *Manito/a*.

Homeboys, Homegirls, Homies

Most generally, homeboy and homegirl (and the related homey or homie) are idiomatic African American street-slang terms that arose in the early 1980s. The terms now signify someone from the same local neighborhood or community, or someone with whom the rapper or speaker has a personal affinity or friendship. Originally the term was applied as an insult for people who did not go out much, but it was resemanticized into a positive moniker for a friend or close acquaintance by the mid-1980s. Homeboy and homegirl may also designate members of, or people known to, a particular street gang. Evidence of the transcultural transferal of the term from African American cultural terrains to other groups is provided by homies and Mijos, the names for the small collectable plastic figures, some two inches or five centimeters tall, that became popular in the late 1990s. Designed by Chicano artist David Gonzales, the first series of six Homies (attached to keychains or stand-alone figures) was released in 1998 via gum-ball machines. The series attracted national media attention in response to public statements in May 1999 from the Los Angeles Police Department, which claimed that the homies perpetuated stereotypes of Chicano/as as violent gang members and should be removed from stores. Gonzales's trade description of Mr Raza, from Series 1, would belie such claims. Boasting degrees in Chicano/a, Latin American, and pre-Columbian history, Mr Raza works tirelessly to politicize young Chicano/a homies and ensure that they gain a decent education (www.homies.tv). Since 1998 more homies series have been released, with characters ranging from traditional Mexican and Chicano/a "types" to workers and professionals. Gonzales has also produced sets of Mijos (from *mis hijos*, my children), Palermos

(Italian mobster figures from the 1940s), Hoodrats (Latino/a characters with the bodies of rats), and the Dogpound series (**barrio** dogs doing time in the dogpound).

Hometown Associations

Hometown Associations (HTAs) are the organizations set up by Mexican and Central American workers in the USA to facilitate and fund community development projects in the home town or pueblo and to offer assistance for migrant workers from that town or pueblo in the US host society. Sometimes referred to as *Clubes de oriundos* (Native Clubs), and similar to the Mexican American mutual aid societies in the first half of the twentieth century, HTAs have been an integral feature of the Mexican American experience since the 1950s. By 2004 some 600 HTAs were registered with city administrations across the USA, with large clusters in Los Angeles and Chicago (Bada 2003). Often inspired by a deep community and collective ethos, HTAs have become a philanthropic hallmark of the new transnational communities and identities generated and enabled by the circuitous migration and work itineraries of many millions of Mexicans and Central Americans. For such workers, HTAs provide a means to maintain links with their home communities and to construct viable extensions of that community in the USA. Alex Rivera's documentary *The Sixth Section* (2003) focuses on the Mexican HTA Grupo Unión in Newburgh, New York State, and its funding of a football stadium, an ambulance, and other infrastructural improvements in the group's hometown of Boquerón, Puebla. The "sixth section" is the Grupo Unión's term for the Newburgh community as the sixth district of Boquerón, which consists of five sections.

Hybrid, Hybridity, Hybridization

Ubiquitous terms in contemporary cultural theory, hybridity and hybridization designate any process of intercultural transformation that produces new cultural forms, and subjectivities, out of distinct cultural parents, and that thus challenges the very notion of cultural essentialism or purity. The discourse of hybridity emerged within the interwoven histories of European **imperialism**, **colonialism**, **slavery**, and discourses of economic and civilizing progress and racial classification. That history shadows, and potentially burdens, cultural uses of hybridity (Young 1995). The primacy of hybridity in cultural and post-colonial criticism since the early 1990s has been attributed to Homi Bhabha (1994), who argued that hybridity is the hallmark of the contemporary post-colonial world, the colonial effect that estranges and subverts the rules of colonial engagement and power by marking spaces as sites of hybrid production. Those spaces—the in-between, the liminal stairwell, the Third Space—elude authoritarian systems of classification and representation. They emerge in the enunciative moment to transgress the spatial and temporal frameworks of communication between dominant and dominated, colonizer and colonized, thus confirming the impossibility of an original or "pure culture." In turn, the hybrid cultural form or subject represents an estranging presence, for it renders impossible the quest to identify distinct cultures and define them as "different." Among many dissenters, Coco Fusco (1995) critiques two official uses of hybridity in the Americas: the first, the US government's embrace of cultural pluralism rather than its targeting of racialized poverty; the second, the ideological manipulation of *mestizaje* as a means of containing the threats embodied by black or brown people. For Fusco this official *blanqueamiento* (whitening) rhetoric underwrites the idea that blackness (and Indianness) are qualities that Latino/as must remove cosmetically before attaining rights as "Americans." Noting the racialized origins of *mestizaje*, García Canclini (1995) prefers the term hybridization for indicating "diverse intercultural mixtures" rather than racialized ones. But he also cautions that people cannot live with permanent transgression and indeterminacy, or the collapse of cultural traditions and identities announced by "excessive hybridization" (1990). The critical appeal to cultural hybridity is often used simplistically to signify a successful challenge to the historical material structures of power beyond the hybrid subject, culture, or cultural text. Moreover, proponents of cultural hybridity often sidestep the possibility of hybrid hegemony; hybridizing discourses (cultural pluralism) may recognize and discipline unacceptable hybrids, and some "hybrids" may assert their cultural essence in the face of hybridizing sociocultural forces (Fusco 1995; Werbner and Modood 1997).

Hyphen, Hyphenation

The concept of the hyphen, or the hyphenation of "American" identities, has engendered a great deal of debate among cultural critics. Pérez Firmat (1994) argues that the Cuban exile condition is metaphorized by the hyphen between "Cuban" and "American." That is, a displaced *Cubanidad* emerges in the interstices between two cultural and national entities as neither one nor the other, but somehow contaminated by, and conjoined to, both. For Pérez Firmat, the hyphen in Cuban-American signifies an appositional rather than oppositional state where it is impossible to determine which side of the bicultural equation has more power or influence. Other critics, however, argue that any term yoked to "American" implies the inevitable **assimilation** of the lesser entity into the more powerful "America." An orthographic response has been to avoid the hyphen, or, as with Chicano/a and Latino/a, to dispense with "American" altogether. Some identity terms have never had the luxury of rejecting the hyphen. Options like "Puerto Rican American" are rarely if ever used. As Juan Flores (2001) puts it, US Puerto Ricans "live off the hyphen," that is, outside the debates that confer "American" status. Critics of the hyphen also argue that the practice provides no options for people of mixed race or ethnicity; how, for example, does someone with an African American and a Chicano/a parent determine the appropriate hyphenated-American designation? Conservative critics, however, regard the proliferation of hyphenated "Americans" (Anglo-American, Italian-American, Irish-American, Polish-American) as a fracturing of a purportedly cohesive "American" national identity and culture.

I

Identity, Identification

Identity is the name for the imagined, yet often deeply and necessarily felt, sense of personal sameness, over time and place, that enables a person to differentiate himself or herself from, or liken himself or herself to, another person. A similar process of imaginative investment operates at the level of family, village, community, and even **nation** (B. Anderson 1991). The identity of a person, community, or nation appears in contrapuntal relation to an other (or others) that is not I (us), or, that is not I (us) but like me (us). However, popular understandings of identity might not recognize identity described this way. Identity is so taken for granted that it appears as an essence, authentic and unchanging, a set of core attributes, a truth that defines a person, group, community or nation, especially against other like entities. Identification denotes the sociocultural processes by which identity itself is imagined, felt, invested in, changed, rejected, and collapses. The identities that emerge from processes of identification can, and do, have political consequences. States ascribe identities to subjects and sometimes to entire communities and require subjects to have proof of their identities, particularly at crucial places such as border-crossing checkpoints or when boarding international flights. Vectors along which processes of identification conventionally run in the West include gender, sexuality, **race**, and **ethnicity.** In other places and times, those vectors might include religion, language, cultural practices, age, physical incapacity, and occupation. The politics of identity ascription and adoption is a particular concern for so-called minority subjects who, recognizing that identities are processed in particular historical material and cultural settings, may tactically claim an identity in order to speak or intervene in structures of domination (Sandoval-Sánchez and Saporta Sternbach 2001). Latino/as who are the recipients of imposed **stereotypes** may play with the protocols of identity ascription through a praxis of **disidentification** or **cultural politics.**

Illegal Alien, Legal Alien

"Alien" is a routine US government and legal designation for any person who is not a citizen by birth or by the naturalization process. There are two official categories of "alien": (a) the "illegal alien" or **undocumented worker**, resident, or denizen and (b) the "legal alien" who is entitled to live and work in the USA due to possession of a **green card**. The use of "alien" to define the legal status of noncitizen residents burdens a largely immigrant population with the negative connotations accruing to the word. Standard dictionary definitions of "alien" range from foreign (foreigner, stranger) and extra-terrestrial (not of this world, not human) to anything or anyone that is excluded, inconsistent, repugnant, estranged, opposed, hostile, and simply strange (in appearance or character). The government use of "alien" dates back to the 1798 "Alien and Sedition Acts," which defined aliens as potential enemies of the state. For many Latino/as the widespread use of "alien" is intimately related to broader discourses of denigration and othering that regard all Latino/as as an "alien" constituency, and thus as somehow non- or un- and even anti-American. The operations of these discourses erupted in full force with media and political reactions to the mass demonstrations by **undocumented workers** in US cities that began in March 2006.

Imperialism, Empire

Imperialism designates a system of control by a people or country (the center of empire) over other people and territories. Imperialism may take the form of a colonial system of domination, which involves the establishment of colonial settlements in the empire, but colonization is not a precondition for imperialism (see **Colonialism**). Imperial power is conventionally maintained and dispensed from the imperial or metropolitan center through political, legal, and juridical institutions, the deployment of armed forces, control over the means of production and colonial economy, religious institutions (conversion), and the use of such apparatuses as the education system to instill the values and language of the center. The peoples in the composite territories of the empire, the periphery, are kept in a subordinate condition through a systemic application of these forces. Contemporary uses of imperialism often refer specifically to the acquisition of overseas territories and colonies by various European powers since the late fifteenth century, with the most intense period of territorial acquisition occurring in the late 1700s and 1800s. This era coincided with the Industrial Revolution and the international expansion of the capitalist system, thus ensuring that the exploitation of resources and peoples characterized most western European empires. The nineteenth century also saw the rise of a new imperial player, the USA, its national territorial expansion on the North American continent coinciding with European imperial consolidation elsewhere in the world. The **Mexican–American War** (1846–1848) and the **Spanish–American War** (1898), in particular, played decisive roles in the evolution of US hegemony in the hemisphere. Kaplan (1993) proposes that American Studies scholars have tended to overlook the history of US diplomacy and international relations—typified by the **Monroe Doctrine** and **Manifest Destiny**—and perpetuated a notion of "America" as exceptional and self-contained, and, thus not an imperial player since the early 1800s. The challenge that this purview poses, however, lies in eschewing a simplistic understanding of US imperialism in terms of an all-powerful state arraigned against passive targets, as opposed to focusing on the complex processes by which the USA's shifting political, economic, and cultural hegemony is managed and felt in the hemisphere (Joseph et al. 1998). Providing critical explanations of US imperial hegemony in relation to Latino/a community experiences underwrites various Latino/a approaches to **decolonization**. In the 1960s, the critical discourse of **cultural imperialism**, which is often deployed as a synonym for **Americanization**, arose to designate modes of domination that work through culture, the media for example, and without the need for an empire per se.

Insularismo

Insularismo refers to a Puerto Rican cultural discourse from the 1930s that implies the quality of belonging to or being produced by an island culture, and of being shut off or isolated from the wider world. The concept's architect was Antonio Pedreira, whose 1934 *Insularismo* (1992) attempted to explain

Puerto Rican national and cultural identity by way of the insular metaphor. *Insularismo* was marked by a pessimistic vision that saw the island as cast adrift from global history. Dependent on great powers (Spain, the USA), debilitated by centuries of racial admixture, and emasculated and feminized by colonial domination, the island's character had become enfeebled, unmanly, indecisive, and moribund. Pedreira singled out popular cultural forms like the *danza* as symptomatic of the national crisis, arguing that the genre was feminine, bland, and sentimental, and thus unsuited to the development of a vigorous national culture. He coined the neologism *aplantanamiento* (bananization) to characterize the island condition, and thus established a critical tradition among Puerto Rican intellectuals to elaborate on the weaknesses of Puerto Rican identity, as exemplified by René Márquez's essay, "El puertorriqueño dócil" (The Docile Puerto Rican) from 1962 (1966). Pedreira argued that the island's sterile identity and culture could only be redeemed by a superman capable of mediating the island's realities with vigor and virility. His rhetoric is marked by an elite and patriarchal purview that disparaged popular cultural traditions and regarded the nation as a male domain. Nonetheless, Pedreira's *insularismo* has influenced all later discussion on the national question. As Duany (2002) says, *Insularismo* functions as a foundational text of Puerto Rican identity, as is evident in its continued use in the school curriculum, and the persistence of Pedreira's pet metaphors in national and cultural debates on and off the island.

Internal Colonialism or Colonization

The theory of internal colonialism or colonization arose in Latin America in the late 1950s and 1960s to explain Latin America's uneven experiences of development and modernization. Proponents of the concept, such as the Mexican González Casanova, argued that the Spanish imperial epoch had produced societies stratified not by class divisions, but by rural/urban, cultural and ethnic (European and indigenous) divides (Kay 1989). The internal colonies in such societies are located in rural areas and consist of subsistence farmers or farmhands who are indigenous or *mestizo/a*, and whose languages and cultural traditions further differentiate them from the broader society. The predominant social groups and the owners of capital regard these internal colonies as an exploitable and expendable labor market and source of cheap materials. Members of internal colonies experience ethnic discrimination on

the basis of their racial and cultural appearances and identities, further precluding their mobility and ability to attain a viable working-class status (Kay
1989). Highly influential in the 1960s and 1970s, Latin American applications of internal colonialism nonetheless attracted a number of criticisms. The
internal colony model downplayed class factors in its bid to account for ethnic
discriminations. The theory was not historicized to account for differential
regional and local experiences of Spanish colonization. Proponents tended to
homogenize all residents of internal colonies as similarly marginal, with no
capacities for complicity, redress, or resistance (Kay 1989). The theory of
internal colonialism was taken up, and modified, in the 1960s and 1970s as
a means of explaining the historical subordination of immigrant and ethnic
communities in the UK and the USA, in the latter case, African American,
Chicano/a, Native American, and some Asian American populations. For US
critics, internal colonization designated the subordination of three groups:
populations in their traditional lands, such as Native Americans; sectors inside
US borders due to territorial annexation, such as Chicano/as and Hawaiians;
and African Americans, whose colonial predicament arose because slavery displaced them inside the colonial power and later locked them in urban ghettoes
(Carmichael and Hamilton 1967). Barrera et al. (1972) argued that the urban
barrio was an internal colony characterized by residents' political incapacity
to influence either barrio institutions or the external institutions that affect
barrio life. The authors disputed **assimilation** and accommodation explanations for Chicano/a socioeconomic and political subordination, and proposed
that Chicano/a communities are subject to the entrenched structures of colonial
rule, with no possibility for liberation from the colonizing state. The barrio as
internal colony thesis went out of favor in the 1980s and 1990s (Hernández-
Gutiérrez 1994), with some critics arguing that Chicano/as were dealing not
with extant colonialism, but rather with the subtle and multivalent nodes of
subordination emanating from a pluralistic state in a postcolonial context
(Cervantes 2002). The internal colony model has been revived and modified to
account for barrio-led resistances to structural domination (Villa 2000).

J

Jíbaro/a, Gíbaro/a

Jíbaro/a or *gíbaro/a* is a Puerto Rican term for a *campesino* or someone from the rural and mountainous center of the island; in recent decades, the term has also become a generic name for any Puerto Rican, whether on the island or in the diaspora. Traditionally, the term *jíbaro* conveyed a sense of a rural-based island character as poor, humble, fatalistic, unknowledgeable about the wider world, and yet stoic and endearing (Fernández et al. 1998). This character is celebrated in Puerto Rican literary texts and music from the early 1800s, a tradition exemplified by Manuel Alonso's *El Gíbaro* from 1849 [1974]. *Jíbaro* is also a rural folk music derived from the Spanish *decimal*, a ten-line verse genre, which often required singers to improvise; it is played in small groups with guitar, percussion, and at times woodwind instruments. *Jíbaro* groups have been a feature of the Nuyorican musical community since the 1970s.

Jones Act

The Jones Act (formal name: the Jones-Shafroth Act) was a key legal document that defined Puerto Rico's colonial status between 1917 and the declaration of the **Estado Libre Asociado** in 1952. The Jones Act modified the Foraker Act (1900), by which US colonial control over Puerto Rico was formalized after the **Spanish–American War** of 1898. Signed by President Woodrow Wilson on March 2, 1917, the Jones Act granted Puerto Ricans nominal US citizenship, although without the power to elect the island's governor or to vote in US presidential elections. Coming into force after the US entry into World War I, the act enabled the drafting of Puerto Rican men into the US military. It also provided for the establishment of an island bicameral legislature (House of Representatives and Senate), although the US Congress retained the right of veto over legislation, and controlled the island's budget, immigration, defense, and economic matters.

Joto/a

Joto/a is American Spanish idiom for a male homosexual, the feminine form traditionally signifying a man who appears to be feminine in appearance (similar to the English word queen) or, like *loca*, someone who passes as a woman. *Joto/a* (the Jack or knave in a deck of cards) also popularly connotes someone who is sexually passive, although the **active–passive** distinction does not fully account for the range of sexual roles played by *jotos* and *jotas*. *Joto* is often deployed as a homophobic insult, equivalent to the English-language terms faggot or queer when used deprecatingly. One theory of origin is that *joto/a* derives historically from Mexico City's Federal Penitentiary, where cell block "J" (*jota* also denotes the Spanish letter "j") was reserved for homosexuals (Prieur 1998). Like the English word queer, *joto* has been reclaimed as a positive identity moniker, as exemplified by the "Lesbian and joto caucuses" of the National Association for Chicana and Chicano Studies.

K

Kitsch

Kitsch arose in the nineteenth century as a pejorative term for works of art and other material objects that were in some way tasteless or tacky, sentimental, shoddily or cheaply made, unattractive, or flamboyantly decorative. In much modernist art criticism, kitsch was regarded as an evil or dangerous totalitarian aesthetic, the mass-produced or working-class "other" of avant-garde art production, or, a deception, a means of escape from the real. Some critics have regarded kitsch as the (sad) essence of modernity itself (Dorfles 1968). The critical literature has tended to regard kitsch in terms of an art/kitsch binarism that evokes other binaries, each casting kitsch into the realm of the negative: elite/popular; good/evil; rich/poor; enduring/transient; high/low; serious/laughable; beautiful/ugly; valuable/worthless; unique/mass produced; art/not art. Such readings of kitsch are made in defiance of the difficulty, if not impossibility, of defining either term in the art/kitsch dyad (Calinescu 1987). Similar problems pertain to kitsch's synonyms in other languages, including the Spanish *cursilería*, or *cursi*, which has many significations: the rococo; bad taste; camp (effete, something queer); anything that is derivative; and even someone, or a class, that is dependent on foreign things and styles (Valis 2002). The aesthetic conundrum of how objects and practices become socioculturally valued underwrites critical attention to Latino/a kitsch cultural practices. Olalquiaga (1992) regards kitsch as the hallmark of a Latino/a aesthetic, which can be graded by degrees of "difference between reality and representation," from the "mere substitute" of the real object such as the home **altar**, through the "neo-kitsch" object, like tourist kitsch, in which the representation becomes the referent, to the third-degree kitsch object, transformed by the hybrid significations determined by its artist maker. While this formulation has influenced reassessments of *rasquachismo* as similarly marked by degrees of signification (Gaspar de Alba 1998), some critics propose that *rasquachismo* is kitsch, or a Chicano/a version of camp (R. García 1998). José Muñoz (1999) identifies two dominant cultural aesthetic modes, the "kitsch = ethnic protocol" and the "camp = queer protocol," which are rarely conjoined by critics of either kitsch or camp. As Muñoz argues, Sontag's notion of camp (1994) defines an aesthetic sensibility of "artifice and exaggeration" while remaining politically "disengaged" and de-ethnicized; Olalquiaga's degrees of Latino/a kitsch are hampered by a heteronormative gaze that ignores camp in the cultural scenes she surveys. Muñoz identifies a mode of Latino/a camp that defies "dominant culture's identity-denying protocols." Latino/a camp purportedly redresses the apolitical, aesthetic, and de-ethnicized notion of camp, and a desexualized aesthetic notion of kitsch, by ensuring that camp permits a minority culture to appropriate, recycle, and rework dominant cultural forms.

L

Latin America, Latin/o America

An apparently coherent regional designation, "Latin America" changes shape and location depending on the perspective taken, and the context in which it is used. Latin America is commonly counterposed with Anglo-America or North America (USA and Canada). When Latin America is opposed to North America, Mexico and the other states of Central America have a tenuous relation to the north, whereas the island states and dependencies in the Caribbean may not be included in either north or south. Latin America may refer to those countries in the Americas where Spanish and Portuguese are spoken. This approach would exclude countries such as Belize and Guyana (English), French Guiana and Haiti (French and French Creole), and Surinam (Dutch, Papiamento), and deny indigenous languages and peoples a place in broad "American" geospatial denominations. From the US perspective, Latin America may simply define all the states and peoples south of the US–Mexico border. Each of these approaches demonstrates that "Latin America" is neither self-evident nor fixed, and exemplifies what Mignolo (2005) argues is the production of the Latin American "idea." For Mignolo, Latin America is a set of geocultural, spatial, and conceptual imaginaries, an invention. This idea is a product of imperial and colonial histories and logics, by which the continent was named "America" and assimilated into a Eurocentric discourse of civilized capacity, modernity, and, subsequently, peripheral position in a world system or order. A response to this "idea" is "Latin/o America," coined by Chicana critic Diana Taylor (1994). Latin/o America represents an attempt to find an orthographic solution to the binary formed by America/Latin America, and **America/América**, whose use implies separate geopolitical and cultural terrains, rather than a continental space subject to transcultural flux and interchange. Taylor's Latin/o America also acknowledges the central place of Latino/as in the mutually transformative history of North and South American continents. An alternative—Latin(o) America—has also appeared.

Latinidad, Latinismo

Latinidad, and the less common Latinismo, are designations for panethnic Latino/a identifications, imaginaries, or community affiliations that encompass, but do not supersede, diminish, or destroy, national origin or historical minority identifications. The critical debate over Latinidades followed Felix Padilla's (1985) coining of the term Latinismo, or "Latino ethnic consciousness", to designate the types of panethnic identifications that arise from the interactions between two or more Latino/a groups in a particular neighborhood or city, and that may involve periodic or extended **situational alliances** over a particular issue (provision of social services, **bilingual education**, transport improvements, and so on) that affects the groups concerned. In their study of Latinas in Corona, Queens, New York, Ricourt and Danta (2003) show that a broad Latinidad has arisen among women in this immigrant neighborhood because no single group predominates, and Spanish provides a medium of communication and community cohesion across group lines. Noriega and López (1996) define Latinidad as "an available cultural identity, political affiliation, or expressive genre" encompassing but not superseding particular groups. For Flores and Yúdice (Flores 1993), Latinidad names a cultural political project aimed at resemanticizing "America," extending the nation's imaginary frontiers, and demanding recognition of cultural pluralism. Noriega (1993) links Latinidad to the ideal of pan-American political unity propounded by Simón Bolívar and José Martí, which inspire attempts to conceptualize Latino/a populations in both national and continental terms. Noriega nonetheless cautions that whenever Latinidad is evoked it encodes within itself a dialectic between an imagined Latino/a community and the different historical material realities and experiences of diverse Latino/a communities. Román and Sandoval (1995) argue that the invocation of Latinidad rarely questions its own ideological and exclusionary premises, particularly with regard to gender and sexuality. Building on that critique, Aparicio and Chávez-Silverman (1997) insist on the pluralization of Latinidad into Latinidades as a means of indicating the multiple tropes of "Latino-ness" produced by dominant cultural forces and Latino/as alike. That position gestures toward recognizing the limits of Latinidad(es) as geocultural and panethnic imaginaries, and of the ways by which local Latinidades may be subject to transcultural disjunctions and mis-readings, for instance, when Latino/as travel between the east and west coasts.

Latinization

Latinization designates the socioeconomic, political, cultural, and linguistic transformations of the USA spearheaded by the country's Latino/a popula-tions. The term may also shift semantic register to identify the transformations supposedly effected by specific Latino/a groups: Mexicanization in California, the southwest, Texas, and Chicago; Cubanization in south Florida; Puerto Ricanization in New York; and the Chicanoization of Central Americans in California, the Cubanization of Nicaraguans in Florida, and the Nuyoricanization of Dominicanos in New York (Grosfoguel et al. 2005). Latinization may refer to the formation of panethnic affiliations and identifications (**Latinidades**). Other observers define Latinization as the process by which a new "Hispanic" or "Latino" constituency is constructed as a voting bloc, a community of con-sumers, or a coherent population to be studied. For some critics, Latinization denotes new transnational and trans-American patterns of integration and connection (cross-border communities or *comunidades satélites*, circular migratory routes, and pan-national identifications). Conservative and nativist commentators, however, utilize Latinization as a euphemism for an alien inva-sion from the Latin American or Mexican south, and thus as a process that will lead to a nation disunited along cultural, linguistic, and communal lines. According to Noriega (1993), mainstream uses of the Latino/a sleeping giant metaphor are symptomatic of the treatment of Latino/a sectors as either "potential citizens" or a sector about to overrun the USA from within. Amexica, Mexamerica, and Mexifornia are also used as scare words by conservative and anti-immigrant spokespeople who claim that Mexican immi-gration is destroying the so-called White Anglo-Saxon Protestant (WASP) bedrock of US society. Flores (2000) identifies three modes by which Latini-zation is popularly and critically discussed. First, the demographic approach tends to unify Latino/as as an amorphous mass and gloss over factors that interrupt or discredit the idea of unity, thus reducing Latino/as to countable units. Second, the analytical approach pretends to eschew this universalizing and reductive construction of Latino/as by focusing instead on constituent parts (subgroups, class status, income, countries of origin, settlement patterns); this approach is nonetheless also predicated on faith in the objective reality and coherence of the parts being discussed. Third, the imaginary approach diverges from the first two imposed approaches by regarding Latinization as an evolving history of community formation and potential as perceived, articulated, and molded by Latino/as themselves. For Flores, the imaginary approach—the recognition of Latino/a imagined community/ies— avoids the statistically overdetermined truth-claims of the previous two approaches. Latinization designates the possibility of a constructed sense of unity based on shared memories, aspirations, community struggles, and experiences of socioeconomic and cultural marginalization. Understanding Latinization thus requires "attention to cultural expression and identity claims" so that Latino/a relations to the state that hosts them, and to broader panethnic and transnational identifications, can be recognized and mapped.

Latin Jazz

A fusion of Latin American rhythms and percussion conventions and jazz be-bop improvisational styles and harmonies, Latin Jazz emerged as a neocultural musical drive in the late 1940s and became popular in dancehalls and concert halls across the USA, Europe, and Latin America in the following decades. Latin Jazz drew on Brazilian samba and bossa nova, and such Afro-Caribbean genres as the **mambo**, **rumba**, **cha cha chá**, **bolero**, and *son*. Key names in the evolution of Latino Jazz were Stan Keaton ("The Peanut Vendor"), Dizzy Gillespie, and the New York-based ensemble Machito and His Afro-Cubans (Roberts 1999; Waxer 2002).

Latino, Latino/a, Latina/o, Latin@

Latino/a is the broad panethnic identity term that includes the Chicano/a and Puerto Rican historical minorities and any citizen or resident with Latin American heritage. Latino is the preferred term of many Latino/as when adopting a panethnic identification or speaking of self and community in national terms; it thus circulates as a self-adopted alternative to the government-imposed and media-preferred **Hispanic**. The political uses to which

Hispanic and Latino/a can be put, and the significations accruing to them, have attracted a great deal of critical debate among scholars and cultural workers. Since Latino/a provides the nominal base for the panethnic sensibility, imaginary and potential vector of community affiliation, a key debate in Latino/a Studies has concerned the viability, potential formation, and meaning of **Latinidades.** The orthographical convention of replacing Latino with Latina/o or Latino/a, and Latin@, reflects a widespread political gesture against the gender power of the noun's masculine form to signify all Latinos, irrespective of gender, and to acknowledge Latinas as an essential component of the panethnic designation.

Literatura chicanesca, Chicanesque Literature

La literatura chicanesca or Chicanesque literature refers to texts by Anglo-Americans that deal with thematic and geocultural territory similar to that found in Chicano/a writing. At times, those writers may even present or pass themselves as Chicano/as. Lomelí and Urioste (1976), who coined the term, defined *literatura chicanesca* as writing by Anglo outsiders who attempted to capture Chicano/a communal realities, but only managed to attain a superficial resemblance to those realities because they did not live as Chicano/as. Zimmerman (1992) provides a list of chicanesque writers whose texts focus on Chicano/a characters and predicaments (Paul Horgan, Gordon Kahn, Oliver LaFarge, Eugene Nelson, John Nichols, Jim Sagel, and Frank Waters), and two authors who adopted a Chicano persona (Amado Muro AKA Chester Seltzer and Danny Santiago AKA Daniel L. James). Danny Santiago, the author of *Famous All Over Town* (1983), was a controversial figure due to the 1984 revelation that he was an Anglo-American Yale graduate. The subsequent public controversy over the revelation generated a great deal of debate about the ethnic boundaries and authentic credentials of Chicano/a writing, and of the Chicano/a **canon.** Márquez (1989) broadly defines Chicanesque writing as texts by Anglo-Americans that perpetuate stereotypes of Mexicans and Chicano/as, a tradition inaugurated by travel narratives in the early 1800s.

Llorona

La Llorona, the weeping woman who searches in vain for the children she has killed, is a ubiquitous presence in Mexican and Chicano/a culture. The legend

that deals with her plight possibly has both **Aztec** and European origins.
A weeping woman like la Llorona was the sixth omen of impending disaster
before the Spanish arrival in Aztec territory in the sixteenth century, as
recorded in the *Codex Florentino* and the *Historia de Tlaxcala* (León-Portilla
1962). Other theories suggest that la Llorona is a synonym for la **Malinche**,
the consort of and translator for Cortés, or a neocultural version of the Aztec
deity Cihuacoatl, responsible for overseeing childbirth (R. Castro 2001). The
legend of la Llorona, which was told to children as a warning about the risks
of transgression, takes numerous versions, with la Llorona appearing as a
beautiful woman dressed in white who becomes ugly or morphs into a skele-
ton, an old Indian woman, or a terrifying witch-like creature, if approached by
the living. Rafaela Castro (2001) notes that the legend centers on the fate of
a woman abandoned by her husband or lover. Enraged by the betrayal, the
woman drowns or kills her children, only to go mad and henceforth wander
the streets and countryside at night in search of her dead children, her presence announced by plaintive, spine-chilling cries of remorse. Chicana feminists
have reworked the myth against the grain of the traditional story's figuration
of a hapless and tragic victim of patriarchy. The title story in Sandra Cisneros's
Women Hollering Creek (1991) exemplifies this drive. During the **Chicano
Movement**, la Llorona was also adopted as a symbol of the Chicano/a
predicament, a means to express a communal sense of orphanhood or loss
(Chicano/as as la Llorona's children) due to assimilationist pressure and historical discrimination (Rebolledo 1995). This approach animates Rudolfo
Anaya's *The Legend of la Llorona* (1984). Moraga's (2000) revision of la
Llorona as a Mexican Medea is set in a post-US future, where Medea, her
lover Luna, and Medea's son reside in Tamoanchan, the place to which all gays
and lesbians of color were banished after the secession of Chicano **Aztlán**, in
the old southwest. Moraga's Mexican Medea reconceives the Chicano/a
Movement reading of la Llorona as a communal symbol by drawing an analogy between Chicano/a queer subjects and la Llorona's predicament.

Loco/a

The Spanish word *loco/a* literally means mad or crazy, as encoded in the well-
known phrase *la vida loca* (the crazy life), which is historically associated with
the Chicano/a **bato**. *Loca* is also a euphemism for queer, functioning much like
the English term *queen*, adopted by gay men who may prefer to be sexually
passive or are feminine in appearance. More specifically, *loca* is the preferred

name of transvestites in many Latin American and Latino/a communities, although some *travestís* (men dressing and/or living as women) do distinguish themselves from *locas* (queens). Puerto Rican author Mayra Santos-Febres's *Sirena Selena vestida de pena* (2000) is a notable literary exploration of the *loca* identity. The novel problematizes the popular conception that all *locas* comply to the binarized distinctions between sexual activity/passivity, and male/female, that their social appearances may imply.

Low Rider, Low Riding, *Onda bajita*

A resilient cultural tradition among Chicanos, low riding refers to the customization of cars so that the car chassis is hydraulically lowered as close to the road surface as possible, hence the term *la onda bajita* (the low wave) to describe the practice. A low rider can signify either the customized car (*carrito, carrucha, ranflas*) or the car's male driver or owner (Stone 1990). Cars are lovingly tended and highly decorated with neon lights, painted murals, and designs on the chassis, and etched images on the windows. Historians have traced low riding back to the 1930s and the **barrios** of Los Angeles, a hub of Mexican American migration to other parts of the state and the southwest. The style is popular from California to Texas and has distinct regional characteristics. Many critics regard low riding as a significant manifestation of a Chicano working-class masculine cultural habitus, one that appropriates and Mexicanizes mainstream US car culture and the status that car ownership can provide (Parsons et al. 1999; Plascencia 1983; Stone 1990). The low rider has attracted critical attention as a folk phenomenon that exemplifies the making-do aesthetic of *rasquachismo*, a means by which working-class men assert their cultural worth and ingenuity despite poverty. Low riding has been celebrated in numerous cultural texts, from Cheech and Chong's *Up in Smoke* (1978, dir. Lou Adler) and *Mi vida loca* (1994, dir. Allison Anders), to "Low Rider," the 1970s ode to low riding from the East LA group War. The main media organ for practitioners has been the *Lowrider Magazine*, which maintains its own website (www.lowridermagazine.com); amidst the sexist images and advertisements, the site contains a useful history of the low-riding phenomenon.

Lucha libre

Lucha libre (free struggle; free-form fighting) is a Mexican form of wrestling whose popularity is surpassed only by **football** in the national sporting imagination.

The sport has generated a huge support industry that produces magazines, comic books, films, dolls, and masks. *Lucha libre* matches are screened regularly on Spanish language television in the USA, and the popularity of this televisual entertainment is increasing in the USA, helped in no small part by the children's television cartoon, *Mucha lucha* (Warner Brothers), which debuted in February 2003 and which at once celebrates and parodies the phenomenon. Some Mexican *luchadores* (wrestlers) achieve national fame, and cross over from the wrestling scene into film and television acting, as happened with perhaps the most famous *luchador* of all time, El Santo. Other *luchadores* have used their fame as a springboard for political activism. These activities are assisted by the *lucha libre* conventions of wearing masks and adopting a stage name and persona, which ensure that individual identities are normally unknown to audience or state authorities. However, not all *luchadores* are anonymous. In the 1990s, for example, the Catholic priest Sergio Gutiérrez Benitez adopted the name Fray Tormenta, his participation in *lucha libre* matches intended to raise money for the orphanage he runs near Mexico City. Levi (2001) proposes that the sport was inaugurated in September 1933, at the initiative of a promoter, Salvador Lutteroth, who brought US wrestlers (and the mask convention) to Mexico after seeing matches in Texas, and who subsequently helped found the sport's main organization, the *Empresa Mexicana de Lucha Libre*. The evolution of *lucha libre* was also influenced by popular cultural phenomena. After its debut in 1936, the US comic *The Phantom* was exported to Mexico where it created a demand for masked avengers that the new wrestling scene could fulfill. Another famous *luchador*, El Enmascarado de plata (The Man in the Silver Mask), is said to have been inspired by Alexander Dumas's novel *The Man in the Iron Mask*, a popular text in translation in 1930s Mexico. By the 1950s the phenomenon had generated an entire genre of Mexican wrestling films and *luchador* comic books, which followed the melodramatic exploits of the most famous *luchadores* as they combated crime, righted social wrongs, or fought vampires, headhunters, zombies, werewolves, Martians, and other characters derived from Hollywood horror and science fiction films. El Santo, for example, starred as himself in over forty wrestling action-cum-crime busting films until his death in 1984. In Mexico, in 1991, the resumption of television broadcasting (matches had been televised in the 1950s before being banned as unconducive to national culture) helped to broaden the sport's audience beyond its traditional working-class base (Levi 2001). *Lucha libre* is by turns acrobatic, melodramatic, comical, excessive, noisy, and chaotic, with *luchadores* cast in the character roles of either *los técnicos* (good guys/heroes; technicians or "faces") or *los rudos* (bad/rough guys). Audiences are vocal and physical, and throw *tortillas* onto the wrestling arena as a sign of anger or displeasure. *Lucha libre* is characterized by the breakdown of barriers between wrestlers and audiences, which thus implicates everyone in the "morality play" of matches (Levi 2001). Aside from one-on-one matches, bouts may also consist of tag-team matches, which are known inexplicably in Mexico as *relevos australianos* (Australian tag-team matches) and outside Mexico as *trios* matches. Such matches have three rounds and involve two teams of three wrestlers, each with a nominated captain. A win is accorded when one team has either pinned down two opposing team members, or one team's captain has pinned down the rival team's captain. Some matches feature teams of four players. At times, matches can be organized as mask against mask contests, with the loser having to remove his mask in what amounts to a public revelation of his "real" identity and collapse in *lucha libre* status. US-derived characters are being introduced into the *luchador* repertoire, as attested by *rudos* modeled on the **Texas Rangers**, **Border Patrol**, and LA police. Also of note is the rise of female *luchadores*, some of whom have achieved transnational fame. The *lucha libre* phenomenon has spread throughout Latin America where it has been adopted in the poorest neighborhoods of the largest cities, and even to Japan where the local form attracts large audiences.

Machismo

Machismo is the conventional term for the codes, ideals, behaviors, and appearances by which masculinity is structured and assumes meaning in Latin American and Latino/a societies. For Evelyn Stevens (1973b), machismo designates a Latin American "cult of virility" with origins in Mediterranean gender mores. This cult is characterized by aggressive and "intransigent" relations between men that also overdetermine men's sexually aggressive and arrogant treatment of women (1973b). Underwriting machismo is a discourse of shame, which erupts when men fail to uphold or defend familial or communal reputation and honor. For Stevens machismo operates in ideological consort with *marianismo*, the value system by which women abide in Latin American societies. Lancaster (1992) differs from Stevens by suggesting that machismo does not structure male–female power relations, but rather those between men according to an **active–passive matrix**. The failure of men to perform in such acts as drinking, fighting, being assertive, and seducing women leads to a loss of social power in the eyes of other men. The conceptual viability of the term machismo and of the machismo/*marianismo* dyad have been disputed. Some critics point out that the machismo model is rigid, simplistic, and universalizing, and thus inadequate to the task of explaining either the complex sociocultural and political meanings that accrue to masculinity, or the equally complex relations between men and women. Machismo is further burdened by the term's entry into English to signify any hypermasculine male, an added implication being that all Latino and Latin American men are bearers of the virile macho principle, irrespective of factors to do with class, race, age, education, regional location, social setting, and sexual preference. Bustos-Aguilar (1995) argues that critical deployments of machismo are untheorized and implicitly racist as they target the cultural lacks of "tropical others." Other critics suggest that while machismo has some conceptual value as a synonym for sexism, there is also a need to recognize the complex interplay between hegemonic and alternative Latin American masculinities, and their relations to multiple modes of femininity (Baca Zinn 1982; Gutmann 1996, 2003; Mirandé 1997; R. Ramírez 1999). Américo Paredes (1993a) intervened into debates on machismo in the 1970s by arguing that a notion of Mexican hypermasculinity only emerged in the 1930s and 1940s as a nationalist response to the hypermasculine model emanating from the USA. After the violent territorial conflicts of the 1800s (**Mexican–American War**, American Civil War, Indian wars, **Spanish–American War**) had been settled in the USA's favor, a mythologized model of gun-toting masculinity became entrenched in the US national imagination and cultural texts, such as film, which were exported widely. The national celebration of the *macho* in Mexican film, music, and literature in part signified a counterreaction to the images arriving from the north. The ambivalence of Mexican masculine conduct is evident in many Chicano cultural texts. Victor Villaseñor's 1973 novel *Macho!* (1991) recounts the journey north of Roberto García as an undocumented worker, and his unsuccessful attempt to walk away from the oppressive codes of honor by which he is judged by family and community. Ana Castillo (1994) claims that machismo among Chicanos derives from the legacies of two systems of colonization, Spanish and US, which replay in the Chicano/a family as a gendered division of labor. However, Moraga (1983) argues that the presence of a Chicano patriarch is not a precondition for the rigid regulation of gender and sexuality. She points out that in her family, whose father was Anglo not Chicano, the task of educating the children in line with gendered behavioral codes was invested in her mother. Such approaches confirm the importance of challenging what Stevens called the "semantic deformation" evident in popular and critical understandings of machismo (1973b).

Magical Realism

Magical realism is a literary genre that attempts to account for realities characterized by the pluralization of worlds and signifying traditions, the intersections between rational and prerational epistemes, and the hybridization of modern and traditional cultural practices. While the concept of the "magical real" had earlier proponents in Europe in the 1920s, the genre came to international attention with the so-called literary boom in Latin American writing of the 1960s and 1970s, and has since been identified by critics in many national literatures (Bowers 2004; Zamora and Faris 1995). In Latin America some critics reject the term's usage, while others dispute the term's use by critics outside the continent to homogenize Latin American literary productions, or, indeed, all "Third World" literatures and cultural work, as national allegories (Jameson 1986). Latin American magical realism is marked by a range of recurring narrative and plot devices: the collapse of time; the normative integration of supernatural events and figures into daily existence; transformative shape changing; miraculous coincidences; false appearances and their unmasking; the conflation of high and low, elite, folk, and popular cultural forms and worldviews; and the hybrid incorporation of indigenous, African, and European perspectives and cultural practices. The genre has a theorist and exemplary writer in the Cuban Alejo Carpentier, who in the 1940s asked, what is Latin American history if not a "crónica de lo maravilloso en lo real?" (a chronicle of the marvelous in the real), and a paradigmatic novel in Colombian Gabriel García Márquez's *Cien años de soledad* (One Hundred Years of Solitude) from 1967. Zamora and Faris (1995) argue that the trope of "magic" serves as a narrative clue for readers to question "realistic conventions of causality, materiality, motivation." For these critics, the genre's magical elements are the matter of everyday occurrences and appearances that erupt in, and challenge, the rationalism of realist literary mode. Magical realism has also been an important aesthetic drive in Latino/a literature, film, and art (F. Aldama 2003; Lomas Garza 1987).

Malinche, Malinchismo

Malinchismo refers to the Mexican discourse of national and gender treachery centered on the historical figure of la Malinche (c. 1500 – c. 1527). As Hernán Cortés's native translator and consort, la Malinche has been blamed in the Mexican popular imagination for the Spanish conquest of the **Aztecs**. The conquistador Bernal Díaz del Castillo's (1963) contemporaneous account describes how la Malinche was given, his euphemism for sold, by her aristocratic Aztec parents to the rulers of Xicalango, who then dispatched her to

Tabasco in the Mayan region, where, in turn, she was sold to the Spanish in March 1519, when she was 18 or 19. Since she spoke **Náhuatl**, the Aztec language, as well as Mayan, she was able to translate for the Spanish through the mediation of a Spaniard who had been shipwrecked on the Mayan coast and learned Mayan. La Malinche quickly learned Spanish, and thus became an indispensable figure for the Spanish by the time they arrived in the Aztec capital of Tenochtitlán. An indication of the power la Malinche wielded due to her linguistic abilities and mediating function is provided by surviving Aztec codices, which confirm the Aztec preference for referring to and addressing Cortés as and through Malinche. Cortés fathered la Malinche's son, Martín. Born in 1522, Martín is often regarded as the symbolic first *mestizo*. After the defeat of the Aztecs, Cortés passed la Malinche on to a Spanish officer, Juan Xaramillo, who married her in 1524 and may have fathered a daughter in 1526. La Malinche disappeared from Spanish records in that year, and it is thought that she died in 1526 or shortly after. As a result of this complex history, la Malinche's many names attest to her multiple transcultural locations and identities: Malintzin Tenépal or Malinali Tenépat, her Aztec names; la Malinche (possibly the Spanish pronunciation of Malintzin); Doña Marina or Mariana, her Catholic conversion names; and last, la Chingada (the fucked one), her disparaged name in Mexican and Chicano/a cultures today. La Malinche's reputation as an icon of negativity and national shame was outlined by Octavio Paz in his 1950 *El laberinto de la soledad* (1999). For Paz, the processes of *mestizaje* ensured that, at least symbolically, Mexicans were the illegitimate children of the raped indigenous mother and the conquering European father. *Mestizo* illegitimacy underwrites *malinchismo*, by which Mexican women are always open to the accusation of treachery whereas Mexican men are defined as the sons of la Chingada, the psychologically damaged products of conquest, rape, and deception. Thus, la Malinche potentially gives her name to all traitors, to all Mexicans who have been contaminated or seduced by foreign people, cultures, and values (also called *entreguismo*), especially those emanating from the USA. This narrative of blame ensures that la Malinche survives as a disputed historical subject and object of mythification in Mexico (Glantz 2001). Norma Alarcón (1983) claims that la Malinche also occupies the symbolic center of Chicano/a gender and familial disputes in the wake of both the Spanish conquest and the US conquest of Mexico's northern half by 1848. Those disputes erupted in the 1960s and 1970s when male activists demonized feminists as *malinchistas* and enemies of the Chicano race (Rendón 1971).

Such claims inspired a feminist tradition of contesting androcentric uses of the historical record. Chicana writers have sought to reclaim la Malinche as a powerful icon of female agency, and to iterate the ways by which patriarchal structures have demonized or marginalized women, especially indigenous women, in the nationalist projects of both Mexico and **Aztlán** (Anzaldúa 1987; Cypress 1991; Del Castillo 1977; Herrera-Sobek 1985; Moraga 1983; M. Sánchez 2005). In Mexican and Chicano/a Spanish, dozens of derogatory terms are based on the verb *chingar*, thus confirming the shadow that la Malinche discourse casts over the idiom; but many uses can also be positive, admiring, or playful, depending on context (*¡Qué chingón/a!*), as exemplified by Latino rap artist Chingo Bling from Houston, Texas, the *chingo* signifying "a lot."

Mambo

The term mambo originally designated a priest in Afro-Cuban *santería*. In musical terms, a mambo signified the entry of a group of instruments into the final parts of a particular song. In the twentieth century, mambo came to describe a set of innovative dance rhythms introduced by musicians and composers such as Orestes López (credited with inventing the genre with his 1938 *danzón* "Mambo"), and refined by Dámaso Pérez Prado, who was responsible for remodeling the mambo outfit in line with big band jazz conventions, and for introducing the new dance rhythm to US audiences (Orovio 2004). By the 1950s, a popular mambo craze had developed, characterized by a fast pace and complicated dance steps. Since then, the mambo has traveled to and from multiple sites and influenced other musical styles across Latin America (Salazar 2002). Pérez-Firmat (1994) regards the mambo as emblematic of Cuban American culture, a musical form that is "a **one-and-a-halfer**, born in Cuba but made in the USA." A revival of interest in the mambo occurred in the 1980s and 1990s, and the genre is a constant presence in literary texts, a notable example being *The Mambo Kings Play Songs of Love* (1989) by Oscar Hijuelos, the first Latino/a to win a Pulitzer Prize for literature. Sandra María Esteves's poetry collection *Bluestown Mockingbird Mambo* (1990), makes of the mambo a rhythmic frame for her explorations of Nuyorican identity from female perspectives. Actor-comedian John Leguizamo had a successful off-broadway show in the 1990s called *Mambo Mouth*.

Manifest Destiny

Manifest destiny is a nineteenth-century term that denoted the USA's purported moral and cultural right to expand across and civilize the North American continent. Manifest destiny encodes within it a sense of divine providence, and also a sense that the expansionist drive is related to a national civilizing and developmental mission that the USA's continental competitors—Britain, France, Spain, Russia, and later Mexico—could not provide. The term is attributed to the journalist John O'Sullivan, whose 1839 article, "The Great Nation of Futurity," proposed that the USA needed to expand in both territorial and moral senses if its fundamental democratic and free enterprise ethos was to move into and improve new lands. Such inevitable progress and improvement was required if the USA was to become *"the great nation* of futurity" that its early history had promised. In his 1845 article, "Annexation," O'Sullivan elaborated on manifest destiny in the context of the heightened tensions between the USA and Mexico caused by the independent Texan Republic (1835–1845). O'Sullivan supported the annexation of Texas, arguing it would better prepare the union for a peaceful usurpation of the Mexican territory from Texas to California. Anglo-Saxon initiative and the civilizing spirit of millions of enterprising new settlers in Mexico's neglected and underpopulated north would guarantee the USA's future national and international power. O'Sullivan's main targets in this essay were the European states (France, England) with the capacity to prevent "the fulfillment of our manifest destiny to overspread the continent allotted by Providence." O'Sullivan made similar claims in the 1840s about the need to absorb the Oregon territory, at the time a British possession. Manifest destiny was subsequently taken up by politicians of all persuasions to justify expansionist ventures, beginning with President Polk in 1845 who urged Congress to follow the spirit of the **Monroe Doctrine** and support US designs on Mexican territory, which were achieved with the **Mexican–American War** (1846–1848). The loss of half of Mexico's national territory became proof to many Mexicans that manifest destiny was a euphemism for US imperial aggression.

Marginality, Marginalization

The terms marginality and marginalization have widespread critical currency to indicate the subordination of one social group by a more powerful, dominant, or central group. Marginality implies lack of access to social and political power and privilege, and invisibility in modes of representation. It also implies that the dialectics of political and socioeconomic power play out between the center and the margins or peripheries. Some theories of modernization, for instance, dependency theory in the 1960s and 1970s, viewed the Third World as exploited by, and therefore peripheral or marginal to, the center occupied by the capitalist First World. In feminist, ethnic, minority, and queer studies, marginalization may designate a peripheral and disparaged status or identity as opposed to a dominant sociocultural sector. In the USA, Latino/as and other communities of color are often regarded as locked out of dominant cultural institutions, prevented from accessing the seats of national power, and demeaned or stereotyped in the media. A geospatial understanding of margin-alization informs the idea that the US–Mexico **borderlands** have been treated as a marginal national site when compared with the centers of US power and significance. Marginality may also denote an effect of colonial domination, by which the imperial or colonial center renders its colonies into peripheral zones of control and exploitation onto which metropolitan cultural values and lan-guages can be imposed. The notion of **internal colonization** reflects, in part, that understanding. However, the idea that power resides in a center and that groups lying outside the center are denied power implies that the center is untouched by the mutually affective transcultural relationships between all entities involved, and that marginal sectors are lacking agency, voice, or the capacity to intervene in the structures of domination in ways not determined by the center. Critical emphasis on Latino/a marginality may also overlook the growing economic and political influence of the Latino/a middle class, a his-tory of successful community activism, and traditions of cultural production that do not assimilate into Anglo-American cultural norms. The critique of marginalization vis-à-vis multiple axes of domination desimplifies understand-ings of the historical alienation of Latino/as from the US national project.

Mariachi

An iconic and yet, at times, clichéd signifier of authentic Mexicanness both in and outside Mexico thanks to its use in Mexican and US film, *mariachi* is a group-musical style with origins in the *jaliscienses*, a nineteenth-century folk music from Guadalajara. *Mariachi* bands or groups consist of anywhere between three and 20 or more performers—guitar, violin, harp, cornet, and trumpet players—many of whom also contribute to the distinctive singing harmonies of the *mariachi* style. *Mariachi* music became popular in the first half of the twentieth century and was designated the official national music of Mexico after the **Mexican Revolution.** *Mariachi* repertoires nonetheless comprise a range of folk and regional genres, from the Mexican **bolero** and *ranchera* to *corridos* and polkas (Burr 1999). The popularity of *mariachi* in the USA is often attributed to such trends as the evolution of Los Angeles into a de facto Mexican city by the 1940s, and the Hollywood **Western**'s use of *mariachi* music when invoking ideas of Mexicanness. *Mariachi* bands today throughout the USA play at such social events as weddings, christenings, and birthday parties, and are a popular entertainment in Mexican restaurants. *Mariachis* wear distinctive *charro* suits and sombreros derived from the *vaquero* tradition. *Mariachi* has been a male-dominated tradition, although all-female groups have existed in Mexico for many decades, perhaps the first being Mariachi Las Coronelas in Mexico City from the 1940s. Throughout the USA *mariachi* festivals and new ensembles have proliferated since the 1970s. Notable outfits include the LA-based Mariachis Sol de México, the Campanas de América, from San Antonio, Texas, and the all-female Mariachi Las Generales, also from LA. Laura Sobrino, a *mariachi* violinist, and founder of The Mariachi Publishing Company (www.sobrino.net), has done much to unearth and preserve women's contributions to *mariachi* history. Sobrino was named Los Angeles' "Mariachi Queen" in 1995 by the *Los Angeles Times*.

Marianismo

Marianismo (or Mariology) is the name for the social conventions, divisions of labor, and gendered spatializations said to govern the role and status of Latin American and Latina women. The gender regime of *marianismo* both stems from and underwrites the associated cult of the Virgin Mary, and her many guises throughout Latin America (Poole 1995; J. Rodríguez 1994; Tweed 1997). *Marianismo* designates a Roman Catholic derived valorization of feminine chastity, purity, obedience, sacrifice, and nurturing maternity. These values conform to two dichotomies. First, women's social functions and values are encoded and located in private or domestic spaces, which are the spaces of familial and communal reproduction, as opposed to the masculine domination of the public realm, the site of economic production and political power. Second, women are passive social actors whereas men are regarded as active social agents, including, as some commentators suggest, in the sexual sphere. Most critical understandings of *marianismo* derive and depart from Evelyn Stevens (1973a, 1973b), who regarded the dialectic between *marianismo* and **machismo** as a powerful social mechanism regulating Latin American societies. *Marianismo* functions by determining the social behaviors, appearances, and conduct by which women are judged and controlled under Latin American patriarchy. *Marianismo* emphasizes such qualities as maternal and familial duty and sacrifice, self-deprecation, fatalism, purity, chastity, obedience, goodness, humility, and, when occasions merit it, quiet suffering, and accepting of male behavior (aggression, violence, selfishness, wickedness), all of which paradoxically enshrine women's innate superiority to men (Stevens 1973a). For Stevens and many later commentators, the exalted rhetoric and social status of motherhood means that Latin American women enjoy a measure of social power in the domestic sphere, despite the limits to women's public movements and agency. However, *marianismo* also ensures that women are complicit in maintaining oppressive gender structures. This collusion arises out of "a reciprocal arrangement" between *marianismo* and machismo, which ensure that neither women nor men are willing to surrender their social status and the differential modes of power they occupy (Stevens 1973b). A number of critics have challenged aspects of the *marianismo* thesis. Ehlers (1991) argues that Stevens downplayed the role of class status and socioeconomic position in the complex, and mutable, play of gender values and structures in Latin America. Middle-class families are more likely than working-class families to require women to remain in the domestic sphere, hence Stevens' descriptions appear to pertain more to relatively privileged social sectors. Ehlers also posits that Stevens assumes that the domestic sphere is invariably a site of power that women want to occupy, and that the relations between men and women in Latin America are not responsive to changing historical material contexts. Despite Stevens' argument that maternity is regarded as a sacred enterprise, her thesis does not account for how severe social and personal penalties may come to women who fail to live up to the saintly ideal. That failure can lead to accusations of being a whore, a bad mother, wife, or daughter, and justify domestic violence against women. Other critics argue that *marianismo* might be better understood as a set of social strategies that women pragmatically adopt, depending on economic, familial, and age circumstances, in order to overcome the limited options provided them by men when negotiating the local economies in which they must survive (Andrews 1997). These coping strategies also include the methods by which Chicana feminist writers and artists negotiate the Mexican variant of marianismo based on the cult of the **Virgen de Guadalupe** (Guadalupismo), and appropriate and rework her image in progressive ways (Rebolledo 1995).

Mariel Boatlift, *Marielitos*

Marielitos is the term for the Cubans who arrived in the USA during the Mariel Boatlift in 1980, and thus distinguishes this generation of immigrants from previous and later waves. The boatlift began in Mariel harbor on Cuba's north coast, in April 1980 in the context of a deteriorating island economy and growing dissent. After a bus crashed through the gates of the Peruvian Embassy carrying six Cuban asylum seekers on March 28, Cuban President Castro (April 4) ordered the removal of the Cuban guards from the Embassy perimeter, a sign that was interpreted by many Cubans that they could now leave the island through Embassy channels. Over the next two days, 11,000 Cubans moved into the Embassy compound and requested asylum; most were airlifted to other countries. On April 20, Castro "invited" Cuban exiles in Florida to sail to Cuba and collect anyone who wanted to depart. By October 31, 1980, when Mariel harbor was closed, 125,000 Cubans had made the crossing in this way. Many commentators regard the Mariel Boatlift as a larger-scale reprise of the Camarioca Boatlift of 1965, when some 3,000 Cubans left the island by boat. Unlike previous exiles from Cuba, most *marielitos* were poor and Afro-Cuban. They were also burdened by media claims that Castro had simply emptied the island's mental hospitals and prisons and exported the inmates. Those claims derived, in part, from sensationalist coverage of the fact that some 23,000 *marielitos* had prior criminal convictions in Cuba, most for petty and/or political offenses. Newspapers such as the *Washington Post* reported that 20,000 *marielitos* were "homosexuals," thus adding to the widespread perception that the *marielitos* were "social deviants" (M.C. García 1997). The *marielitos* also received an ambivalent response from the established exile community, which regarded the largely working class and Afro-Cuban *marielitos* through the lens of class and racial privilege. The *marielito* exodus included a number of important writers, musicians, artists, and filmmakers. Bertot (1995) identifies a group of writers as the Mariel Generation: Reinaldo Arenas, Carlos Victoria, Miguel Correa, Reinaldo García Ramos, Juan Abreu, and Roberto Valero. The filmmaker Juan Carlos Zaldívar subsequently made a film, *90 Miles*, about the boatlift. Other renowned *marielitos* were the singer and percussionist Felipe García Villamil, and the visual artist Carlos Alfonzo. The Mariel Boatlift inspired one of the most controversial films of the 1980s, *Scarface* (dir. Brian de Palma, screenplay Oliver Stone). This violent rags-to-riches narrative set in the world of organized crime and drug-trafficking follows the life of Tony Montana (Al Pacino), a hired killer permitted to leave the island as a *marielito*. *Scarface* did much to cement US and international perceptions of Miami as a crime-ridden city controlled by the Cuban mafia.

Matrícula

La Matrícula Consular de Alta Seguridad (MCAS, *la Matrícula*, or High Security Consular Registration Card) is the official identity document that the Mexican government issues to Mexican citizens working or resident in the USA. While ID cards or documents have been produced for Mexicans abroad since 1871, the MCAS was introduced by the Fox administration in March 2002 in the wake of the September 11, 2001 attacks on New York City and Washington, DC, and the George W. Bush administration's redefinition of the US–Mexico border as a potential line of terrorist entry. The MCAS may be regarded as a tactical response by the Mexican government to a post-9/11 climate resistant to formal recognition of the undocumented migrant economy. The Mexican Instituto de los Mexicanos en el exterior (Institute of Mexicans Abroad) estimates that by July 2004, *Matrículas* had been issued to 4 million Mexicans, and that hundreds of US cities and counties, 33 states, nearly 1,200 police departments, and 178 financial institutions had accepted the MCAS as a valid form of identification (portal.sre.gob.mx/ime/pdf/mcas.pdf). The MCAS has enabled Mexican nationals to gain access to a range of social services, obtain drivers' and business licenses, open bank accounts, register children in schools, and send **remittances** more securely. US supporters of the MCAS argue that the cards assist banks and law enforcement agencies in monitoring and combating criminal activities such as money laundering, while also enabling productive workers gain access to social services otherwise denied them. They further argue that the MCAS announce a quasiformal bilateral recognition of the reality of the immigrant economy and the rights of the workers involved, as well as of the benefits those workers bring to home and host countries alike. However, anti-immigration groups have suggested that the

MCAS signals the Mexican government's desire to export its poorest citizens and economic problems, thus threatening the very fabric of US society. Such critics also see in the MCAS trend a quasilegal means by which terrorists and criminals might infiltrate the USA, although such claims have been made without substantive evidence. See **Nativism**.

Mean Streets

"The mean streets" is a term for a strand of **Nuyorican** prose that arose in the 1960s and that focuses on the criminalized and socioeconomically deprived experiences of Puerto Ricans in New York City. Nuyorican "mean streets" texts draw attention to the racist and structural impediments facing Puerto Ricans. Most commonly autobiographical in scope, or structured as coming-of-age stories, mean streets narratives focus on a male protagonist who struggles to survive the transition from boyhood to adulthood, a transition that may involve participation in the homosocial world of **gangs** and the informal economy of drug dealing. Frequently, mean streets narratives chart family breakdown and dysfunctionality, as well as brushes with the law, and, at times, incarceration. These male-centered narratives also foreground such social issues as racism, poverty, and unemployment. The landmark text in the genre is *Down These Mean Streets*, by Piri Thomas (1967), an autobiographical narrative that charts the fraught and often violent experiences of young Puerto Rican men in the era of the **Great Migration**. Many Nuyorican mean streets narratives followed Thomas's text, notable exponents being the novelists Edwin Torres (1975) and Abraham Rodriguez (1993), the playwright Miguel Piñero (1974), and the Nuyorican-influenced Ecuadorian American Ernesto Quiñonez. It is arguable that the genre has its Chicano/a counterparts (Brown 2002). See **Nuyorican Aesthetic**.

Melting Pot

The term "melting pot" had widespread popular and critical applications in the twentieth century to designate the transformation of the USA as it incorporated larger numbers of immigrant peoples. The melting pot analogy derives from metallurgy, where it means the pot in which metals are subject to intense heat, melted, and then compounded into new alloys and forms. The popularity of the metaphor has been traced to the popular play *The Melting Pot*

(Zangwill 1933), first performed in 1908. In practice, the melting pot functioned as a euphemism for **assimilation**, its underlying assumption being that immigrants would lose their original cultural and ethnic traits in the process of becoming "American." As early as 1963, however, Glazer and Moynihan argued that the melting pot idea was neither useful nor credible. Immigrant communities undergo constant, and unpredictable, adjustments, with concomitant adaptations on the part of the "America" in which they live.

Merengue

Merengue is a dance music, a fast two-step form with horn choruses, that originated in the Dominican Republic, and that now has practitioners and audiences in the USA and throughout the Spanish-speaking world. A related dance-music arose in Haiti, and Venezuela, Colombia, and Puerto Rico also have local styles. Originally a music of the rural poor, Dominican merengue is regarded on the island as the national music form. According to Austerlitz (1997), the genre originated in the nineteenth century out of Afro-Dominican and possibly Haitian forms, with influences from European ballroom dances such as the *danza*. In the first decades of the twentieth century, the rise of *merengue* songs with explicitly anti-American lyrics demonstrated that the genre had become inextricably linked to Dominican perceptions of the island's uneasy relationship with the USA, particularly during times of military occupation. With the first mass emigration from the island to the USA in the 1960s, merengue was transported to cities such as New York, the center of the Dominican **diaspora**. It also became popular in neighboring Puerto Rico and other parts of Latin America. Such transnational movements were responsible for the multiplication of merengue into subgeneric forms, for instance, *pop merengue* and *merengue típico moderno*, and for expanding the range of instruments that groups could play. The genre has influenced new Dominican dance-music styles such as the *bachata*.

Mestizo/a, Mestizaje

A *mestizo/a* is a person of mixed race, and most commonly refers to someone of mixed European and indigenous ancestry. *Mestizaje* refers to the process of racial intermixing, and it also has the added connotations of cultural admixture, a Latin American synonym for **hybridity** or **syncretism**. In many parts of

Latin America with large *mestizo/a* populations, *mestizaje* has been adopted by architects of the nation as an official discourse, a purported means of demonstrating that the state is based on a foundation of racial tolerance, diversity, and pluralism. In practice, the discourses of racial miscegenation were based on elaborations of *mestizaje*, such as the Mexican Jose Vasconcelos's *la raza cósmica*, which claimed that the degenerate Indian side of the admixture would be bred out by the higher civilized capacities of the European element in the racial concord. This discourse ignored the subjugation of indigenous and African peoples by reifying the *mestizo* as the nation's only active historical agent. By contrast, Chicano/a uses of *mestizaje* (**brown,** *la **nueva mestiza***) aimed instead for new communal affiliations and plural-identity formations in uneasy defiance of "constraining social relations" (Pérez-Torres 2006). Anzaldúa's attempt to construct a *nueva mestiza* consciousness and identification typifies that drive.

Mexican American

The term Mexican American refers to any member of the heterogeneous Mexican-origin population in the USA. While **Chicano/a** also designates this population, especially in California, much of the US southwest, Chicago, and southern Texas, the overt political connotations of Chicano/a since the 1960s have led some Mexican Americans to self-identify as Mexican rather than Chicano/a. In New Mexico, Mexican-origin people may prefer **Hispano** to either Chicano/a or Mexican American. Middle- or upper-class Mexican Americans may also prefer Hispanic when describing their sense of national place. Numerous variant terms have arisen since the 1960s. Blaxican refers to someone of mixed African American and Mexican heritage, and commonly appears in Californian Latino/a rap lyrics. *Mechicano/a* combines Mexican (*Mejicano/a*) with Chicano/a to connote a politicized identity that affirms cultural and historical connections between all Mexicans, irrespective of their location. Fregoso (2003) proposes the orthographic and gendered alternative *MeXicana* (pronounced Mechicana) to indicate that the Mexican/Chicano dichotomy obscures the complex historical and cultural imbrication of Mexicans and Chicano/as. *MeXicana* signifies the production of subjects through complex processes of **transculturation**, socioeconomic interdependency, and structures of **borderlands** domination. Fregoso's application of this subjectivity-in-formation to the *MeXican* woman (Fregoso does not deploy *MeXicano*) points to a feminist dispute with the patriarchal ideals of nationhood emanating from the USA, Mexico, and the Chicano "nation."

Mexican–American War

The Mexican–American War (1846–1848), or the Mexican War, resulted in the incorporation of independent Mexico's northern half into the union. That incorporation was achieved under the **Treaty of Guadalupe Hidalgo** and the subsequent Gadsden Purchase (1853). In part, the war was a legacy of the Texan independence movement, which had declared the Texan Republic in 1836 and defeated Mexican forces to guarantee its independence. Debate over whether to admit the new republic into the Union as a state mounted in the 1830s and early 1840s, with opposition to Texan statehood emanating from anti-slavery advocates. On March 1, 1845, under the Polk administration, the US Congress approved the annexation of Texas as a new state (ratified December 29, 1845), despite opposition from the Mexican government. With the addition of Texas to the union, the USA now abutted its southern neighbor, Mexico, although both countries disputed the location of the geopolitical divide: Mexico claimed the border lay along the Nueces River, while the USA argued that the Rio Grande formed the boundary. US forces entered Mexican territory in early 1846, and after a minor battle between US and Mexican troops, the USA declared war on May 12. Between May 1846 and September 1847, when US forces occupied Mexico City and effectively ended the war, Mexican forces suffered a series of setbacks. US-sponsored conflict erupted between US-origin settlers and pro-Mexican sectors in California in June 1846, in the Bear Flag Revolt. This led to the declaration of an independent Californian Republic on June 14, 1846, but Mexican armed resistance to that declaration and to the annexation of California by the USA on July 7 prolonged the war in the area. Los Angeles was captured in January 1847. The Treaty of Guadalupe Hidalgo, which was signed in February 1848, transferred to US control the area now covered by California, Arizona, New Mexico, Utah, Nevada, Colorado, Wyoming, and a significant portion of Texas. The Mexican–American War resulted in perhaps the most significant territorial expansion in the USA's history, one that transformed the country into the territorial form recognizable today. In Mexico, however, the war established a legacy of bitterness and a widespread suspicion of US motives in the continent. The war's other significant legacies were the creation of a Mexican minority in the annexed territories, and the transfer of numerous indigenous peoples and homelands to US control. The Gadsden Purchase (Treaty of La Mesilla) was the 1853 treaty (ratified by Congress in early 1854) between the USA and Mexico by which the former acquired some 30,000 square miles (48,000 square kilometers) of Mexican national territory. This area, which lies south of the Gila River, and extends from El Paso, Texas, to the Arizona–California border, now forms the southern sections of Arizona (including Tucson) and New Mexico.

Mexican Revolution

The Mexican Revolution inaugurated in 1910 is widely regarded as one of two continentally influential revolutions in the twentieth century, the other being the **Cuban Revolution**. The term revolution in the Mexican case encapsulates the bitter civil conflict between rival ideological forces that began in 1910 and continued for the following two decades until stability was established when the Partido Nacional Revolucionario (PNR, National Revolutionary Party, the antecedent of the Partido Revolucionario Institucional) took power in 1929. At stake in the Mexican Revolution was not simply which political force would govern the state, but what ideological shape the state, and with it, a paternally guided notion of *Mexicanidad* or Mexicanness, would take. The revolution of 1910 ended the *Porfiriato*, the long dictatorship of Porfirio Díaz (1876– 1880, 1884–1910), which had been characterized by a highly centralist administration, a guided economy and commitment to economic and infra- structural development, and an intolerance of dissent. Under such policies the gap between the rich and poor widened, and popular disgruntlement mounted over the regime's unwillingness to deliver on the land-reform measures en- shrined in the 1857 Constitution, or to pursue the secularization policies of Díaz's predecessor, Benito Juárez. Civil conflict erupted in 1910 after Díaz won office for the sixth time. Known as the Epic Revolution (1910–1920), this period of civil war was fought along guerilla lines, with forces under Francisco "Pancho" Villa in the north, and others under Emiliano Zapato in the south arraigned against Díaz's armies. Both figures met violent ends, but would be memorialized in numerous *corridos* and films. Díaz was forced out of office in 1911 and succeeded by the democrat Francisco Madero, who was murdered in 1913. Thousands of Mexicans moved to the USA as **exiles** in this decade, in- augurating a pattern of large-scale emigration that would continue throughout the century. A progressive constitution, which formalized land redistribution and enshrined an anticlerical secularism, was promulgated under President Carranza in 1917. The period from 1920 to 1934 (revolutionary reconstruction or institutionalization) was also marked by outbreaks of violence, as exemplified by the Cristero uprising (1926–1929) of priests opposed to government policies aimed at curtailing the power and wealth of the Catholic Church. National stability was restored when the PNR took control of the country's central administration in 1929. The years from 1934 to 1940 are dubbed the years of radicalization or reform, when the presidency of Lázaro Cárdenas nationalized the oil industry, embarked on an aggressive program of secularization, redistributed land to *campesinos* (peasants), and established trade and peasant unions. Many historians regard the revolution as culminating in a state-directed project of nation building founded on a discourse of *mestizaje* as racial reconciliation, with new symbols drawn from autochthonous folkloric traditions.

México de afuera, México del norte, México lindo, Otro México

The expressions *El México de afuera* (Mexico Abroad) and *México lindo* (Pretty Mexico) emerged in the wake of the large migrations from Mexico that followed the social upheavals inaugurated by the **Mexican Revolution** of 1910. On joining the existing Mexican American population and contributing to the retention of Mexican cultural traditions in the *colonias* and **barrios** of the US southwest and Texas, these migrants came to refer to themselves, and their neighborhoods, as transplanted parts of Mexico. *El México de afuera* implies that Mexican Americans were highly conscious of their Mexican identities and traditions, not only maintaining them in the USA, but also reconceiving *Mexicanidad* as a form of transnational identification. According to Arturo Rosales (1996, 1999), middle-class refugees from revolutionary Mexico developed the term *México lindo* in an attempt to preserve an idealized sense of *Mexicanidad* in the host society. The nationalist ideology underwriting the use of these terms was bolstered by symbols (icons of national heroes, religious symbols including la **Virgen de Guadalupe**) and maintenance of Spanish. The successful translation of the *México lindo* ideal to Mexican American communities laid the symbolic and discursive "blueprint" for the more radical nationalism of the **Chicano Movement**, as is evident in Rodolfo "Corky" Gonzales's 1967 epic poem "Yo soy Joaquín/I am Joaquín" (2001). *México del norte* (Mexico of the north) and *El otro México* (the other Mexico) also designate the territories of the US southwest and Texas, and encode a historical memory of Mexican territories lost after the secession of Texas (1836) and the **Mexican–American War** (1846–1848). "El otro México" is the name of a famous *corrido* from 1986 by the *norteño* group, Los Tigres del Norte, in which the song's narrator proclaims that Mexican immigrants have constructed a new version of Mexico in the USA, and hence a new model of the USA itself—"el otro México que aquí hemos construido" (the other Mexico that we have built here). Anzaldúa (1987) uses the term as a synonym for **Aztlán**. See **Greater Mexico, Norte**.

Migration

Migration refers to the movement of people from one place to another, emigration designating the outward migratory process and immigration the incoming process. Migration may take internal forms (within a geopolitical state) or external forms (across state borders). Numerous states are founded on conquest and migration, and are often designated immigrant receiving countries (the USA, Canada, Australia, New Zealand, and since the 1960s many states in western Europe). Some critics regard **transnationality** and/or **globalization** as characterized by the mass migrations of peoples across geopolitical borders, and by the imaginaries and sense of connectedness that develop between home and migrant communities. Those connections may involve the formation of **Hometown Associations**, and are typified by the global **remittance** economy. Migrants move from their homes and homelands for disparate reasons, and in response to numerous factors and historical pressures: war and invasion (refugees), political crisis and military dictatorship (political migration, **exile**), bourgeois cosmopolitanism, globalized economic imperatives, neocolonial dependency, demand for cheap labor (*braceros*, **domestics**, the *maquiladora* or assembly plant industry along the US–Mexico border), poverty (economic migration), or any of these in combination. Some critics identify "gendered migration" (domestics, *maquiladora* workers, workers in sex tourism, and other women workers) as a highly significant trajectory (Hondagneu-Sotelo 2001). At times, some migrant sectors or immigrant generations are defined by the specific historical conditions and timing of their migration (Cuban *marielitos*), or by the transport modes they take (Cuban *balseros*, or rafters). Another term, circular migration describes a migratory process by which migrants move constantly between home and host societies, spending short to extended periods in both settings. Such migration, which has characterized Puerto Rican immigration to the USA since the **Great Migration**, differs from one-way migration, in which migrants do not return to their countries of origin, and from return migration, by which after an extended period spent in a host society, migrants return home permanently (Acevedo 2004). Circular migration may also designate the migratory experiences of workers from Mexico, Central America, and the Caribbean, who move to the USA when demand for seasonal labor is high, and return home for the rest of the year. Migration, and the reception and national place of immigrant sectors, is perhaps one of the most important, and potentially divisive, sociopolitical, and economic issues facing many countries in the world today, as attested by the rise of **nativism** in the USA, Australia, and western Europe. Since the early 1980s, the USA has hosted a growing backlash against immigrants from Mexico (the single largest national source of immigrants in US history) and other parts of Latin America. Aside from the rise of nativism and vigilantism in the southwest, that backlash has involved the **English-Only Movement**, the militarization of the US–Mexico border and involvement of the **Border Patrol** in various operations to stem the flow of **undocumented workers** or "illegal aliens," and legislative drives to similarly seal off the southern terrestrial border (the 2005–2006 Sensenbrenner Bill). Many Latino/a critics argue that processes of **Latinization**, and panethnic imaginaries (**Latinidad**), are at once enabled and characterized by mass immigration from Latin American countries. The immigration trajectories that are underwriting the future demographic strength of the communities grouped under the Latino/a rubric have enormous implications for Latino/a studies, most notably in understanding what has been called the neocolonizing "differential modes of incorporation" by which immigrants and existing historical minorities are received, and themselves manage, national debates over race, ethnicity, language, and political and cultural **citizenship** (Grosfoguel et al. 2005).

Minority

The orthodox understanding of minority is a population living within a geopolitical state that is outnumbered by the majority, or that has less sociopolitical power or status than the majority national population. The minority/majority binary implies a position of inferiority, weakness, devalued status, and **marginalization** on the part of the former in comparison to the latter. The adjectives minoritarian and majoritarian designate the processes by which some communities may experience sociopolitical or cultural influence, or its lack, irrespective of their demographic strength. Thus, women may be regarded as minoritized by patriarchal discourses and political and economic exclusion, while some ethnic or racialized minorities (white South Africans in the apartheid era) may wield sociopolitical and economic hegemony and enjoy quasi-majoritarian status (Johnson 2000). The "invisible" or "silent" minority refers to a particular minority's exclusion and absence from modes of representation and power structures, and majoritarian culture's blindness to, and lack of awareness or interest in, minority concerns and aspirations. For example, the **Black/White paradigm** operates by "disappearing" Latino/as from national debates. In Chicano/a studies in the 1970s and 1980s, Native Americans and Chicanos were defined as territorial minorities due to the state production of these "minorities" through conquest and territorial expansion (De la Garza et al. 1973). The use of the term minority when referring to Latino/as nonetheless raises questions about the conceptual, demographic, and geospatial fluidity and valency of purported minority and majority status. Although Latino/as are commonly referred to as a national minority, in cities and towns across the southwest, and in many of the USA's largest cities, Latino/a communities form local majorities.

Mojado/a, Wetback

Mojado/a (wet, soaked, drenched) is the Spanish euphemism for an undocumented Mexican crosser of the Rio Grande length of the US–Mexico border. The shortened form, *mojo/a*, denotes a recently arrived Mexican. Wetback is a colloquial English language insult for a Mexican or Mexican American. Unlike wetback, *mojado* is often a term of endearment used by Mexicans for people who have made the crossing into the USA. One of the first Mexican films to depict Mexican immigration was *Espaldas mojadas* (1954, dir. Alejandro Galindo), which tells the story of Rafael and his attempts to cross into the USA without documentation. The travails of *mojados* have provided a constant theme in Mexican **corridos** since the mid-1800s. An alternative to *mojado* is *alambrista*, which derives from the Spanish word *alambre* (wire), as in someone who climbs over or crosses the wire fence along the border (Cull and Carrasco 2004). The word supplied the title of one of the most important films to deal with Mexican experiences of migration in the 1970s, *¡Alambrista!*

(also known as *The Illegal*, 1977, dir. Robert Young). Yet another term for an undocumented border crosser is *pato/a* (duck). *Patero* is sometimes used to designate the person who assists such border-crossers or who is paid to do so, and thus represents an alternative for **coyote**. In different contexts, *pato/a* is a euphemism for queer. See **Operation Wetback**.

Monroe Doctrine

Named after President Monroe's 1823 address to Congress, the Monroe Doctrine is the name for a foreign-policy agenda by which the USA announced that the era of European colonization had ended, and that further intervention by European powers in the Americas would be resisted by the USA. Monroe's address singled out the Spanish, Portuguese, British, and Russian powers as the old imperial players in the Americas. Monroe was attempting to preclude the Russians and the British from establishing new colonies in the north and northwest of the continent. Monroe was also concerned that Spain, and to a lesser extent Portugal and France, would attempt to reassert their control over their old American colonies, most of which had achieved independence by the early 1820s. Among many notable subsequent appeals to, and amendments of, the Monroe Doctrine were calls to annex Cuba in the 1850s and end Spanish influence in the Caribbean, the 1895 Olney Interpretation that elaborated on the USA's right to settle border disputes between Latin American states, the Roosevelt Corollary of 1904, which claimed the USA had a right to intervene in Latin American states if its interests were threatened, and the 1930 Clark Memorandum, which reversed the Roosevelt Corollary in line with a foreign policy of nonintervention and peaceful coexistence in the Americas. Traces of the Monroe Doctrine may be detected in US foreign policy initiatives in the hemisphere in our era, as illustrated by the USA's maintenance of its embargo on Cuba since 1962, and various acts of legislation intended to discourage and/or penalize states and companies from dealing with the Castro regime.

Mulato/a, Mulatez

Mulatez is a Spanish language term that refers to the intermixing of African and European peoples. A *mulato/a* (mulatto) is a person of mixed African and European descent. In the regions where slavery was most widespread—the Caribbean, the coastal areas of Venezuela and Colombia, parts of Central

America, and Brazil—*mulato/a* remains a commonplace term that most often refers to a person's dark physical appearance. Dozens of related terms deriving from colonial-era discourses of racialized categorization exist to designate degrees of *mulatez*. Like **mestizaje**, *mulatez* also has a metaphoric role in Latin American cultural discourses, in that it designates the heterogeneous and syncretic cultural formations and practices arising from the mixing of African and European peoples. That said, given that the root noun of mulatto is *mulo* (mule, the sterile offspring of a horse and donkey), current cultural and metaphorical uses of both mulatto and *mulatez* may not sidestep or disarm the racist and eugenicist logics that gave rise to such terms.

Multiculturalism

Multiculturalism, which is sometimes regarded as a recognition or defense of cultural or ethnic pluralism, was the name adopted by two distinct activist movements in the 1980s that sought to counteract the US myth of monoculturalism. That is, multicultural advocates attacked monoculturalism as a non-pluralistic system or discourse that treats ethnicity and culture as monolithic, unitary, and exclusive, and as if the dominant culture (white, English-speaking) is the norm and never comes into transformative contact with other cultures. One of the multiculturalist movement's targets in the early 1980s was the school and university curriculum, and its teaching of history and culture as a White Anglo-Saxon Protestant enterprise only. Those struggles also involved minority interventions into the "American" literary **canon**, disputes over what "America" signifies in a continental framework, and a recognition of the USA's historical identity as an imperial power. The second multicultural drive took place in the arts community, the target for artists of color who wanted the US art scene to regard multiculturalism as a sociocultural reality, not an aesthetic trend (Gómez-Peña 1993). Anzaldúa (2000) explains the presence of **code switching** in her texts, and her refusal to translate, as a tactic intended to impel her readers to question the myth of US monoculturalism. In other parts of the world, by contrast, multiculturalism is the name for an official state-sponsored and sanctioned public policy by which ethnic groups are managed and accommodated. This form of multiculturalism purports to move beyond the myth of monoculturalism and accept, tolerate, and support multiple ethnicities within the borders of the geopolitical state. Multiculturalism has taken different forms across the world since its policy introduction in

Canada and Australia in the 1970s. In such countries, multicultural policies assisted ethnic groups to set up community organizations, and funded ethnic radio and television. This mode of multiculturalism has nonetheless been critiqued for assuming that ethnic groups have culture, and that the dominant or receiving societies have neither culture nor ethnicity. Another criticism of these policies is that they assume ethnicity to be fixed and immutable (Bennett et al. 2005). Although it has not been accorded an official or ideological status at the national level in the USA, multiculturalism understood as a broad social recognition and valuing of ethnic and cultural pluralism has been targeted by conservative critics as a symptom of the ethnic and linguistic fracturing of "America," and a means by which the nation will be swamped by immigrants, especially from the Mexican south. See **Nativism**.

Murals

The production of murals (*muralismo*), or large paintings (with or without text) on walls and buildings in public spaces, has been an important aspect of Chicano/a and **Nuyorican** cultural work since the 1960s, most notably in the 1970s and 1980s. Mural artists (*muralistas*) usually produced their public art in working-class and **barrio** communities, and were often linked to the Chicano and Puerto Rican movements and their calls to enlist art practice in the service of community aspirations and struggles. Muralism associated with the **Chicano Movement** drew sustenance from the postrevolutionary Mexican mural tradition and the work of José Clemente Orozco, Diego Rivera, and David Alfaro Siqueiros (R. Castro 2001). However, *muralistas* were also part of a broad art-worker or public art movement in the post-World War II era to produce art of sociopolitical relevance to working-class and minority communities (Cockcroft and Barnet-Sánchez 1990). That political turn meant making art outside the elite gallery and museum system, and collaborating and working with local communities in the design and production of public art works that would survive as intrinsic features of the local urban landscape. Mural artists tended to work in collectives, as attested by the names of important mural-art groups such as Cityarts Workshop (the Lower East Side in New York City), Artes Guadalupanos de Aztlán (Santa Fe), Mujeres Muralistas (San Francisco), and People's Painters (New Jersey). Chicano/a murals were constructed across California, the US southwest, Texas, and in cities such as Chicago, at the height of the public arts movement in the 1970s. These murals often incorporated folk art symbols and imagery, narratives drawn from Chicano/a oral traditions and Mexican history, and references to the **Aztec** inheritance. At times, the highly political messages contained in mural art— for instance, opposition to the Vietnam War, calls to end police violence, asser- tions of Chicano/a pride—attracted the attentions of state officials and the police, and many public murals from the 1970s were painted over or destroyed. Historically significant and new murals nonetheless remain integral features of Latino/a **barrio**scapes across the country. A particularly important example from the 1970s was The Chicano Park Monumental Public Mural Program, in Barrio Logan, San Diego. Much of the **barrio** had been destroyed by freeway and bridge construction in the 1960s, which also left massive con- crete pylons throughout barrio space. After a long struggle with city officials to accede to community wishes for a park, members of such arts groups as Los Artistas de los Barnos, Los Toltecas en Aztlán, and El Congreso de Artistas Chicanos en Aztlán, as well as independent art workers, produced murals in Chicano Park that celebrated Chicano/a movement struggles and history. Chicano Park and its murals are now regarded as important sites of San Diego's cultural history (Rosen and Fisher 2001). Among other mural projects, "The Great Wall of Los Angeles," was conceived and directed with massive community involvement by one of the most renowned Chicana mural- ists, Judith Baca. Begun in 1974 and completed by 1980, "The Great Wall" is located in the Tujunga Wash Flood Control Channel and depicts California's history of ethnic and transcultural relations.

N

Naco

Naco is a Mexican and Chicano/a Spanish term for something or someone considered by the speaker to be vulgar, crass, grotesque, common, stupid, unsophisticated, uneducated, or plebeian. It may connote any or all of those adjectives, but be directed at poor, *mestizo*, or indigenous people, and their cultural practices. In Mexico *naco* is often a racist synonym for *indio* (Indian), or a class-based insult for a poor working-class Mexican, a *naco* signifying the social opposite of a "decent," "well-mannered," and "well brought up" white Mexican (Stephens 1989). The term may have arisen in the region around Mexico City in the mid-1800s as an insult directed at the indigenous Totonaco people. Idiomatic usage today suggests that people become *naco* by drawing public attention to themselves through speaking or dressing in scandalous or nonconventional ways. However, *naco* can also accommodate, in a quasiaffectionate way, a nerdish person, and even **kitsch** practices and artifacts. In cultural criticism, *naco* designates a self-conscious appropriation or transculturation of non-Mexican cultural forms and symbolism, its end-point being the Mexicanization of those forms. A related phenomenon is the *naco es chido* cultural movement that emerged in the late 1970s and early 1980s with such music groups as La botellita de jérez and La maldita vecindad, and artists and filmmakers like Sergio Arau. For these cultural producers, *naco* signified a making-do aesthetic similar to Chicano/a **rasquachismo**.

NAFTA

NAFTA (North American Free Trade Agreement) is the name of the free-trade zone involving Canada, the USA, and Mexico, which came into effect on January 1, 1994. Specifically aimed at reducing and eventually eliminating fiscal barriers to trade (tariffs and other taxes), and encouraging the movement of capital, goods, and labor across geopolitical borders on the North American continent, NAFTA was an initiative of the George Bush administration that was later supported by president Clinton and endorsed by the US Congress in late 1993. Despite its brief to integrate the economies of the three member states, the implementation of NAFTA was also accompanied by a tightening up or militarization of the US–Mexico border, in part a US government response to the reality of large-scale immigration by **undocumented workers** and an attempt to appease US sectors made anxious by migration from Mexico. For many commentators, NAFTA represents a potential rival to other free-trade zones, such as the European Union (Orme 1996). Devon Peña (1997), however, regards NAFTA as a product of a discourse of modernization under **globalization**, by which Third World states are brought into the age of "progress, civility, and modernity" through the industrialization of the economy, and massive foreign investment. In Mexico's case, Peña argues, the modernizing imperative has seen the expansion of the *maquiladora* or assembly plant system along the Mexican side of the border. Such developments have led to an explosion in border-city populations, a rising toll of environmental damage, the entrenchment of poverty among the local labor force due to its exploitation by foreign companies unchecked by labor protection legislation and unions, and widespread corruption on the part of local authorities. Peña also notes that despite the negative operations of the "terror of the [border economy] machine" since the early 1980s, and most notably since the signing of NAFTA, women *maquiladora* workers in particular are developing tactics (cooperative ventures, unions) to counter their exploitation, and are taking advantage of the *maquiladora* system in order to challenge traditional gender and class mores.

Náhuatl

Náhuatl, the language of the **Aztecs** and many other indigenous groups in what is now Mexico, belongs to the Uto-Aztecan group of languages. Náhuatl remains the second most widely spoken language in Mexico after Spanish, with some 1.5 million speakers. A number of Náhuatl terms have entered Spanish, English, and many other European languages, including words such as chocolate, coyote, avocado, and tomato. The survival of Náhuatl after the Spanish conquest, and its close relation to a number of other Native American languages, has been registered in Chicano/a cultural production since the early 1960s. Many Chicano/a writers, for example, have utilized Náhuatl words in their writing, a linguistic tactic that became commonplace in tandem with the reclamation of an Aztec cultural genealogy for the Chicano/a people and '"nation" by the **Chicano Movement** in the 1960s and 1970s. The adoption of **Aztlán**, the mythical Aztec homeland reclaimed by activists as the name for the US southwest, exemplifies this reclamation. Another example is the use of the Náhuatl word *nepantla*, or the space in between, in Chicana feminist writing. See **Quinto sol.**

Nation, State, Nationalism

Nations and states are important units of critical analysis, and sites of critical confusion, as typified by the routine but erroneous conjunction of the two terms, nation-state, which implies a relationship of structural and conceptual equivalence. A state is the name for a historical material entity, a set of apparatuses, institutions, laws, and symbols, by and through which a country is governed and recognized by other states as sovereign. States normally construct their own identity symbols—flag, anthem, coat of arms, military uniforms—in order to distinguish themselves and their official representatives from other states. States are not permanent and can disappear or appear overnight. A nation, by contrast, does not require a state to exist. For some critics, a nation is the name for an imagined community of people who share and invest in the same bounded national space and ideal, in contradistinction to other imagined communities (B. Anderson 1991). A nation is not coeval with a state, as demonstrated by three examples: Puerto Rico (a colony, a Commonwealth associated with the USA) is regarded by many island residents as a nation; the Yaqui Pascua, a nation of indigenous people in southern Arizona; and the **Chicano Movement** that redefined the Chicano/as as a people, with a national homeland and myth of national origin (**Aztlán**). The distinction between a state and a nation is important in another sense. States have historically been the patriarchal preserve of men, and women have historically been denied access to the institutions and apparatuses by which the state is governed and sociopolitical power conferred. Nations, on the other hand, have been traditionally marked by patriarchal logics as feminine, as motherlands or extended families in which the maternal figure symbolizes the nation's reproduction and survival, as is implied in such concepts as *la gran familia*. In its broadest sense, nationalism designates any nation-building project that seeks to establish a state (self-determination), or modify an existing state and its institutions, in line with a particular national imaginary (Bennett et al. 2005). The idea that the nation is an "imagined community," however, should not imply that every member of a "nation" imagines and experiences the nation in the same way, or that national symbols are interpreted homogeneously, and without dispute (Bennett et al. 2005). The Chicano Movement's appropriation of Aztlán to designate a fraternally encoded and united national constituency generated enormous critique on the part of Chicano/as excluded by the movement's rhetoric.

Nativism

Nativism is a xenophobic discourse (fear of foreigners) that most commonly targets immigrants. Nativist drives have occurred throughout US history since the Declaration of Independence in 1796, although the recipients of those tendencies have shifted in line with patterns of immigration, regional realities, and the integration and mixing of older and newer communities. Historically, nativist rhetoric appealed to the working classes in the largest industrial cities who regarded the arrival of migrants in their neighborhoods or cities as a potential threat to their job security. At times, advocates of nativist policies (limits to immigration, enforced **Americanization**) in the nineteenth and twentieth centuries came from the ranks of the political elite on all sides of US politics. In the nineteenth century, Protestants regarded with suspicion the millions of Catholic European arrivals (Irish, Italian, Polish), which at times led to interethnic violence. Later in the century, and in the first decades of the twentieth century, similar suspicion was directed at immigrants from Eastern Europe, whose number included a substantial Jewish population. In California, in the gold rush era of the 1840s and 1850s, Chinese and Mexican prospectors were the targets of nativist attack. Nativist anxiety over immigration from Asia and Eastern Europe influenced a number of laws that prohibited or restricted specific national groups, including the Chinese Exclusion Act (1882), the Emergency Quota Act (1921), and the National

Origins Act (1924). Latino/a sectors, too, have historically attracted the attention of nativist proponents, who have argued that "American" jobs are under threat from Mexicans, and that Latino/as have failed to assimilate and become "American." Mexican Americans were traditional targets of nativism in the US southwest and Texas after the US takeover of Mexico's northern half in the 1830s and 1840s, particularly in times of economic recession. During the Great Depression of the 1930s, some 600,000 Mexicans were repatriated to Mexico, irrespective of their citizenship status; an even bigger repatriation occurred in the 1950s with **Operation Wetback**. Puerto Ricans in New York represent another large group to experience a nativist backlash in a city founded on immigration. A sense of these realities is filtered, albeit through a Hollywood lens, in the popular musical *West Side Story* (1961), and conveyed in such narratives as Piri Thomas's *Down these **Mean Streets*** (1967). At various times in South Florida since the early 1960s, Cubans have been the recipients of nativist attacks, including the successful campaign to repeal government **bilingualism** in 1980. Anti-immigrant nativism has had a revival since the early 1980s, as attested by the **English-Only Movement**, the legislative success of anti-immigrant propositions at state level, and the reemergence of vigilante groups from California to Texas. The "new nativism" (J. Perea 1997) focuses predominantly on undocumented immigration from Mexico and Central America. In all these guises, nativism (or indigenism) understood as xenophobia must be distinguished from a widespread practice in many postcolonial societies that rejects imposed imperial modes of life and revalorizes the pre-European or precolonial past. Postcolonial nativism assumes that the transcultural processes set in motion by colonization can be wound back, and that a native or indigenous past can be resurrected (Ashcroft et al. 1998). Concepts such as cultural **hybridity, creolization**, *mestizaje*, and **transculturation** gesture toward the difficulty of the return to authentic origins. At least strategically, however the nativist impulse has enabled many colonized peoples to challenge the discourses associated with the metropolitan/periphery relationship, and to revalorize ways of life that were repressed or disparaged in that relationship. The **Chicano Movement**'s recuperation of symbolism drawn from pre-Columbian **Aztec** culture exemplifies this strategy. A similar drive is evident in Puerto Rican cultural nationalism since World War II, which has revived the **Taíno** cultural base. Some critics, however, have argued that the Chicano/a reclamation of an indigenous cultural identity overlooks the history of violence between Native and *mestizo* peoples, and potentially fetishizes an indigenous pedigree of purity in an untenable claim of connection to an unrecoverable, because transculturated, past (Alire Sáenz 1997a).

Nepantla

Nepantla is a **Náhuatl** word meaning the space in between or the space in the middle. Anzaldúa (1987) describes *nepantla* as the marginalized effect of a **borderlands** conjunction of three cultural systems (indigenous, Spanish, USA), two forms of colonization (Spanish and USA), two races (Indian and European), two states (Mexico and the USA), and two or more languages. Since this in-between location is manifested psychically, it is also experienced internally as multiple cultural shocks related to multiple structures of domination. Yet for the *mestiza* who seeks to reverse or counter those structures, *nepantla* also designates a pragmatic and adaptable model for the many possible avenues of identity self-fashioning available to her, and for the development of a new *mestiza* consciousness (***nueva mestiza***). This term is not to be understood in a Marxist sense as the coming to political awareness of class position, conflict, and exploitation. Rather, it resonates in an avowedly spiritual sense as the way into a symbolic realm that promises to heal the identity divisions caused by the competing claims made by rival cultural, linguistic, racial, and national systems. Informed by concepts and values derived from a Meso-American indigenous episteme, or worldview, this rendering of *nepantla* in much contemporary Chicana writing has links to contemporary New Age beliefs. Pat Mora (1993) also uses the "in-between" trope to describe her experiences as a product of the US–Mexico border region. Although Mora avoids the overt spiritual character of Anzaldúa's *nepantla*, in her hands the term similarly signifies the ambivalent possibilities for the self enabled by life in the borderlands. It is arguable that Anzaldúa's and Mora's conception of *nepantla* reprise notions of self-autonomy and nonconformity reminiscent of Emerson for their driving logic that liberation is possible outside institutional and discursive constraints. While there are obvious historical, gendered, and ethnicized differences between *nepantla* and Emersonian autonomy, both can nonetheless be read as emerging from a long-standing US discourse of individual self-fashioning.

Norte

An alternative term for the USA in Mexico and Central America, *El norte* not only literally translates as the north, but it also functions as a metaphor for the "promised land" or hoped-for paradise to be found north of the US–Mexico border. The term has been in circulation since the early 1900s and has appeared in much Chicano/a cultural production. The film *El norte* (dir. Michael Nava, 1983) follows the fraught journey of two young indigenous Guatemalan siblings, Rosa and Enrique, through Mexico to their ultimate destination, Los Angeles. Mario Bencastro's novel *Odisea del norte* (1999) provides an account of El Salvadorean migration to a "North" that proves to be a site of broken dreams, disappointment, and illusoriness.

Nortec

A Spanglish neologism formed from the contraction of *norte* (north) and techno, *nortec* (also referred to as Tech-Mex or the Tijuana Sound) is an electronic dance and ambient music that first emerged in the late 1990s among DJs in the clubs and recording studios of the busy tourist, night-club, and red-light areas of Tijuana, Mexico. Highly popular on both sides of the border, and internationally, *nortec* is of note for sampling, and being influenced by, Mexican musical genres such as the **corrido**, **banda**, **norteño**, and **ranchera**, as well as for drawing sustenance from European electronic and pop music traditions. Tijuana resident Pepe Mogt is credited with the first *nortec* productions, and the genre gained international attention with the transnational success of Bostich's "Polaris" in 1999, itself the opening track of the first CD release from the Nortec Collective (Colectivo Nortec), *The Tijuana Sessions: Volume 1*, in 2001. Other volumes have followed, as has a book by the Colectivo Nortec, *This is Tijuana!: El Paso de Nortec* (2003), and a host of other internationally successful music projects. For its practitioners, *nortec* designates a musical and local aesthetic anchored in, and reflective of, quotidian life in the border city of Tijuana.

Norteño

Norteño (northern) is the term for a style of Texan Mexican music closely allied to **conjunto**, with which it is often regarded as synonymous (Peña 1999b). Like *conjunto*, *norteño* was originally a rural and folk dance music form, with ensembles typically including a piano accordion and the 12-stringed Mexican bass guitar (*bajo sexto*). *Norteño* outfits, which are now found from California to Texas, play a range of Mexican musical genres, including the **corrido**, as well as polkas and **cumbias**. For that reason, many Mexicans refer to US-based musical groups that play multiple Mexican musical genres as *norteño*. Some critics claim to detect the differences between *norteño* and *conjunto* in terms of the nasal Mexican accents of the latter, and the former's subtle instrumentation (Burr 1999). *Norteño* has influenced the *tambora* dance style from the Mexican state of Sinaloa, and the *waila* (from the Spanish *bailar*, to dance) music produced by the Tohono O'odham people of Arizona.

Nueva mestiza, Mestiza Consciousness

La nueva mestiza, and the consciousness required to construct her, is an important critical concept derived from Anzaldúa's *Borderlands/La Frontera* (1987), a text that reworks the *mestizaje* championed by the Mexican José Vasconcelos in the 1920s. For Vasconcelos (1997), *mestizos* embodied the world's first racial synthesis, *la raza cósmica* (cosmic race), one to which all people were heading. Sidestepping Vasconcelos's belief that the Indian was a degenerative "race," while acknowledging his influence on Chicano/a discourse, Anzaldúa regenders Vasconcelos's *mestizo* and locates her in the US–Mexico borderlands. In that geocultural zone, cultural and racial intermixture is generating a "hybrid progeny" out of which will emerge an "alien" or new *mestiza* consciousness that will be neither controlled by patriarchal logics nor burdened by logics of racial inferiority and superiority. But drawing from her own experiences as a *prieta* (dark-skinned woman), Anzaldúa notes that in Mexican and Chicano/a cultures lightness of skin is still privileged over dark. The *nueva mestiza* thus represents a new mode of identification that embraces Indian ancestry, and any other socially disparaged or marginalized identity. *Mestiza* consciousness resonates in an **ethnopoetic** sense as a response to rival cultural, racial, national, and linguistic claimants. Anzaldúa returns to the figure of la **Malinche**/Chingada in order to disable her symbolic function as a traitor, and to place her in a native triumvirate alongside la **Virgin de Guadalupe** and la **Llorona**, all of whom have been used to regulate and punish women. Anzaldúa reveals the Aztec deistic origins of the three mothers and redefines them as aspects of **Coatlicue**, a metaphor for the transcultural border-crossing and shape-changing the borderlands demands of its residents. The "dark" side of Coatlicue, or Tlazolteotl, has fed into definitions of la Chingada as the whore and "the Beast." Anzaldúa re-Indianizes la Chingada by making of her a productive link in a chain of female figures within a value system resistant to the Western rational entrapment of the native woman. In order to override the historical betrayal of the Indian woman, Anzaldúa must figuratively excavate her from within herself. The Indian woman is conceived as an origin to be brought into presence and consciousness in a linguistic performance of constant self-fashioning and naming that takes place in liminal states and spaces (**Nepantla**). The contradiction between identity mutability and utopic wholeness permits a tactical move into representation through a polemical and creative use of language as *mestizaje*. **Code switching** and genre shifting—between prose, poetry, oral storytelling, the *corrido*, essay, manifesto, autobiography, myth, anthropology, history—defy the reader to categorize either Anzaldúa's text or her new *mestiza*. She becomes a signifier of uncategorability, or to reword Anzaldúa's conception, of a "total" inauthenticity, an as yet unrealized "total self" that awaits a future day on which all of the "disowned" and "vulnerable" parts of the self will cohere into an "essential dignity." See **Border Theory**.

Nuyorican, Nuyorico

Nuyorican (or Nuyorrican, Neorican, Newricain, Newyorican, Niuyorkan) designates Puerto Ricans in and from New York City (Nuyorico), and differentiates such Puerto Ricans from island residents. Nuyorican has also been deployed to designate mainland Puerto Ricans more generally. However, the latter usage tends to gloss over the distinct geospatial experiences of Puerto Ricans who have established sizeable communities in other parts of the USA (Florida, Chicago, Philadelphia, etc.). The alternative terms Amerícan, Diasporican, Neorican, Otherican, and Rican have arisen to encapsulate these demographic and regional complexities. AmeRícan, or Amerrícan, was coined by the poet Tato Laviera (1985), whereas Neorican appeared even earlier, as exemplified by Jaime Carrero's poetry collection *Jet Neorriqueño: NeoRican Jet Liner* (1964). Diasporican is the invention of the poet Mariposa (María Fernández), who elaborates on the term in her poem "Ode to the Diasporican: Pa' mi gente" (Virtualboricua.org), and in the performance "DiaspoRican Dementia," from 2001. Diasporican is increasingly being used as a more inclusive term for the neocultural identity formations engendered by immigration. Niggerican is a colloquial term from New York City and is evident in the works of hip-hop and rap artists, to describe someone of mixed African American and Puerto Rican heritage, or an Afro-Puerto Rican. A Florican is a Puerto Rican from Florida, while Orlandorican is used by Puerto Ricans from the city of Orlando. The influence of Nuyorican is also evident in the pan-Latino/a term Nuyorlatin, or Niuyorlatin. Originally, Nuyorican was an insult used by island residents to refer to Americanized Puerto Ricans in New York City.

The term was reclaimed and resemanticized into a positive identity marker in the 1970s by writers associated with the Nuyorican poetry and literary movement in Manhattan's *Loisaida* (Lower East Side). This influential movement included Miguel Algarín, Miguel Piñero, Pedro Pietri, Jaime Carrero, and Tato Laviera, all of whom were also involved with the Nuyorican Poets Café, founded in 1973 (now located in 226 East 3rd Street). The movement at once defined and celebrated the Puerto Rican-origin population and heritage of the *Loisaida* and that community's transcultural difference from the originary island home. It is popularly claimed that the name *Loisaida* was first immortalized in Bimbo Rivas's 1974 **barrio** "love-poem," "Loisaida" (Algarín and Homan 1994).

Nuyorican Aesthetics, Cultural Consciousness, Dialectic

Nuyorican aesthetics is a term coined by Miguel Algarín, a key player in the dynamic Nuyorican literary movement of the 1970s. The movement's poets and playwrights attempted to chronicle and comment on their displacement in New York City, not only in relation to dominant Anglo-American culture, but also in diasporic relation to Puerto Rican island culture. Algarín's introduction to the anthology *Nuyorican Poetry* (Algarín and Piñero 1975) defines Nuyorican aesthetics as a mode of expression that reflects Nuyorican experiences of the **barrios** of New York City. The organization of poems in the anthology provides further insights into Nuyorican aesthetics: outlaw poetry (antiauthority or antiestablishment), evolutionary poetry that targets the "system," and dusmic poetry, which refers to the resemanticization of inner-city rage into a strength. Algarín (1987) later argued that Nuyorican aesthetics represented an approach to poetry production beholden to neither the USA nor Puerto Rico, but indelibly marked by both. Nuyorican aesthetics is marked by a commitment to orality in English, Spanish, or both, and to dialogic shifts between English and Spanish and the mutual contaminations enacted on each language by the other. The aesthetic is also affiliative. As Algarín argues, Nuyorican artists collaborate in forming self-supporting and protective belief systems and collective cultural support networks in the face of social sector breakdown and the neglect of the diasporic Puerto Rican population by successive federal, state, and city administrations. Nuyorican cultural consciousness is Juan Flores's (1993) term for the identity outcome that has resulted from Puerto Rican immigrant adjustment to New York City since the 1940s.

Flores identifies three "transitional phases" in the constructions of Nuyorican cultural consciousness inaugurated by Puerto Rican first impressions of a hostile New York environment. Over time, quotidian despair in this setting is countered by personal perceptions of island origin that provide a sociocultural anchor, and allow the recognition and reclamation of African and **Taíno** cultural roots. Alienation is also overcome by fortifying journeys between mainland and island. As a consequence, the "reentry" process itself affirms the indisputability of a Nuyorican bilingual, multiracial, African-inflected, and popular cultural habitus that permits affiliations with other marginalized groups. Nuyorican cultural consciousness also provides a critical counter to the **Culture of Poverty Thesis** and the Nuyorican **mean streets** narrative tradition, both of which may manufacture a superficial image of Nuyorican marginality that is perpetuated in US media representations and popular perceptions alike. Also countering that tendency, Acosta-Belén's Nuyorican dialectic (1992) refers to a range of relational Nuyorican writerly sensibilities that derive from evolving physical and imaginative distances between US mainland and island. Nuyorican identity is fragmented and rendered contradictory by interlingual and spatial shifts, marginalization in both island and mainland contexts, and racialized and class antagonisms. Writers engage with the Nuyorican dialectic in two ways. First, they work with the contradictions and ambivalences of Nuyorican relations with other New York sectors, and second, they utilize return trips to Puerto Rico to search for "biological" and "mythical" connections that may, in turn, provide antidotes for alienation in America.

O

One-and-a-Halfers, 1.5 Generation

The term "One-and-a-Halfers" was developed by Rubén Rumbaut (1991) to describe the children in Indochinese refugee families born in the USA who faced a double hurdle of adjustment: coping with the transition from childhood to adulthood in the host society, and coming to terms with the rival cultural norms of parental and host societies alike. As a result of a displacement that induces identity crisis, the 1.5 Generation is marginal in parent and host societies, and thus not part of either. Adapting the concept of the "One-and-a-Halfers" to Cuban American terrains, Pérez Firmat (1994) diverges from Rumbaut by arguing that whereas the 1.5 Generation is a marginal constituency, it is also arguably the only constituency that is marginal to neither original nor host culture. Cuban American "One-and-a-Halfers" not only circulate in and understand the cultures of displaced parents and US host society, but also shift between them, a resourceful adaptation that is linked to language facility in English and Spanish. The 1.5 Generation thus centers an assimilatory trajectory that begins with Cuban-born and raised exiles, and ends with the **ABC Generation** (American-Born Cubans), which has no direct experiences and memories of the island, and is more at home in the USA than in the displaced-Cuban parental ambit. Pérez Firmat's "One-and-a-Halfers" schema now circulates in Cuban American studies as a convenient explanation for distinct generational experiences of **exile**. However, José Muñoz (1995) has criticized the schema for its assumption that a unitary Cuban American population moves inexorably toward **assimilation**.

Operation Bootstrap

Operation Bootstrap (*Operación Manos de Obra*) is the name for the program of modernization and industrialization that was applied to Puerto Rico between 1948 and 1964 in an age of independence struggles and Cold War rivalries. Maldonado (1997) notes that the program was motivated and orchestrated by two mutually enabling and supporting forces. On the one hand, restructuring of the island economy was a policy platform of Luis Muñoz Marín, the island's governor (1948–1964) and a champion of **Estado Libre Asociado** status, and of his adviser, Teodoro Moscoso (the "architect" of Operation Bootstrap). On the other hand, the program of economic reform was endorsed by successive US administrations, which desired to transform Puerto Rico into the capitalist "Showcase of the Caribbean," an example to states throughout the Americas that might be contemplating a socialist or non-US-friendly form of governance. Operation Bootstrap was managed through the Departamento de Fomento (Industrial), and aimed to transform an economy that after half a century of US control had become a sugar plantation monoculture owned by US companies. The operation offered tax concessions, low labor wages, no import duties, and other incentives to US companies and investors. Some 2,000 US firms established manufacturing plants and factories in Puerto Rico in this period. Puerto Rican workers trans-formed imported raw materials into products for export to the USA. The oper-ation also encouraged the development of the island's tourism sector. However, many of the US firms that invested in Puerto Rico pulled out of the island when the tax advantages came to an end, taking their profits with them, and causing widespread unemployment. Most observers acknowledge that Operation Bootstrap remade the agrarian peasantry into a mobile or floating industrial working class. The operation impelled rural to urban migration on the island, a process that took a mass transnational turn (the **Great Migration**) in response to US policy that saw in the Puerto Rican working class a convenient labor force for the manufacturing industries in the US northeast (Grosfoguel 2003). The structural dependency of the island on the US econ-omy, and Puerto Rico's colonial status, thus ensured that modernization worked against the island population's advantage. The very wording of Operation Bootstrap is telling in this regard; its connotations of pulling a peo-ple up out of poverty and backwardness by their "bootstraps" smacking of a paternalistic discourse of development.

Operation Pedro Pan

Operation Pedro Pan (Operation Peter Pan, *Operación Pedro Pan*) was a covert scheme that brought 14,048 unaccompanied middle-class children from Cuba to the USA between December 26, 1960, and the onset of the Cuban Missile Crisis in October 1962. The scheme's name is attributed to Miami journalist Gene Miller, who introduced the term (derived from the novel by British writer J.M. Barrie) in his article " 'Peter Pan' Means Real Life to Some Kids," in the *Miami Herald* on March 9, 1962. Although the scheme had no official name, it was called *El Rescate de la Niñez* (Rescue of the Children) in CIA documents (Angeles Torres 2003). The operation was facilitated by such figures as George Guarch and Father Bryan Walsh (Catholic Welfare Bureau), and James Baker (who had run a school in Havana for many years). They liaised secretly with Cuban families and government officials in Cuba, the USA, and a number of Caribbean states in order to obtain exit permits and flight reservations, and then met the unaccompanied children on their arrival in Miami or other Caribbean destinations. Many of these children were later reunited with their parents, although a large number were not. Angeles Torres (2003), Conde (1999), and Triay (1983) confirm that many Pedro Pan children experienced great psychological, and at times physical, hardship. For some Pedro Pans, the difficulties of adjusting to the host society without familial support, and initially without English, were exacerbated by placement with non-Cuban foster families, and the loss of Spanish and imaginative connections to Cuba. Among many notable Pedro Pans are the playwright Eduardo Machado and the writer Carlos Eire. Angeles Torres (2003) notes that Operation Pedro Pan now has a foundational function in Cuban exile imaginaries as both "an official narrative" of imposed exile and a metaphor for parental self-sacrifice in the face of an oppressive regime. She argues that the key to understanding Operation Pedro Pan lies in a discursive and ideological struggle between rival state projects and of the symbolic role occupied by children in those projects. On the one hand, the **Cuban Revolution** constructed Cuban youth as embodiments and agents of the new national community under Socialism. On the other hand, US (and Cuban exile) middle-class values regarded children as an innocent constituency of potential individuals that required parental and state protection from "ideological abuse." Those divergent approaches to childhood have continued to influence rival forms of *Cubanidad* (Cubanness), as exemplified by the 1900/2000 Elián González custody struggle. Many Cuban Americans interpreted Elián's plight as analogous to the Pedro Pan generation, whereas the Cuban state responded by making Elián the symbolic representative of the revolutionary state. For Angeles Torres, the debates over Elián's rightful national location replayed the Pedro Pan debates, with all sides using the child as a means "to legitimize failed political choices."

Operation Wetback

Operation Wetback was the name for a large-scale clampdown in 1954 and 1955 on "**illegal aliens**" from Mexico. Ironically, the campaign coincided with the official **Bracero Program** (1942–1964), a binational government initiative to facilitate seasonal Mexican labor migration. Historians argue that the anti-Mexican campaign was initiated by the US government in a context of Cold War concerns about national border security, nativist anxieties about Mexican immigration, and union concerns that Mexicans were stealing local jobs. The operation involved law enforcement officers moving through border town **barrios** from California to Mexico looking for "aliens," the largest crackdown occurring in Texas. Many citizens of Mexican descent were apprehended in the round-ups and were repatriated to Mexico along with Mexicans, estimates of those returnees varying from 1 to 1.3 million. An unknown number of Mexican workers returned to Mexico in order to avoid the surveillance and harassment occurring throughout the US southwest (J.R. García 1980; Samora 1971). Not all Mexican Americans opposed the operation. The American GI Forum supported Operation Wetback by arguing that Mexican American jobs were threatened by undocumented Mexican workers who would work for less pay.

Oppositional Consciousness

Oppositional consciousness is an influential critical term, and praxis of political action, devised by Chicana feminist Chela Sandoval in the late 1980s and early 1990s and finding its most refined form in *Methodology of the Oppressed* (2000). Oppositional consciousness signals a theoretical and practical mode by which women of color, and other groups, might respond to, negotiate, and dismantle multiple structures of oppression. Those structures limit, or prevent, their political and subjective capacity to speak, enter modes of representation, and attain liberation and social justice. Sandoval's oppositional consciousness arises specifically from the aspirations of **Third World feminism**, and that movement's dispute with white First World feminists. Sandoval argues that US-based liberal, Marxist, radical, and socialist feminisms established distinct and exclusionary modes of political action that combine into a "four-phase hegemonic structure" in which the woman of color is rendered invisible, silenced, or marginalized. Rejecting this structure, oppositional or differential consciousness links gender domination to other histories of struggle against "race, class, and cultural hierarchies" (1991). Oppositional consciousness functions as a topography of political orientations neither determined by the "social order," nor imposed by various feminisms, on women of color in a neo-colonizing move. Oppositional topography has four possible modes, which nonetheless rework "hegemonic" feminist tactics into an interrelated whole. First, the equal rights mode underwriting liberal feminism and much identity politics demands recognition of subordinate people as equal and legitimate. Second, the revolutionary mode (Marxist feminism) asserts the right of subordinate groups to be different, arguing that social power must accommodate and legitimate that difference. Third, supremacism (radical feminism) argues that the difference of subordinate groups grants those groups a superior moral and ethical position from which to enact social change. Fourth, advocates of separatism (socialist feminism) eschew the offer of equal rights in a dominant order whose values and structures they reject (Sandoval 2000). Oppositional consciousness weaves between these feminist modes in the production of a fifth mode, one based on the recognition that differential political interests can, and should, find spaces of alignment (1991). Oppositional consciousness therefore responds to the changing sites and times in which identities are made and claimed, while acknowledging that the liberation of women of color may, at times, require pragmatic alliances or political affiliations with other social programs. Sandoval's theory thus has affinities with Pérez's *sitios y lenguas* and Anzaldúa's *nueva mestiza*, and its influence is evident in much Latino/a **cultural politics**.

P

P'acá y p'allá Dialectics

Coined by Lisa Sánchez González (2001), *p'acá y p'allá* dialectics designates the constantly shifting, transspatial, and **subaltern** coordinates of diasporic Puerto Rican cultural production, from literature to **salsa**. The phrase signifies "right here, over there, and everywhere in between," and implies the incessant crossing and transgression by Puerto Ricans of "places, communities, sounds, and genres." More than a diasporic aesthetic of a community subject to constant eviction, however, *p'acá y p'allá* dialectics also signifies a sense of the positive cultural connections enabled by movements between Puerto Rico and US cities, the sites of multiple homes impelled and enabled by Puerto Rico's colonial status. *P'acá y p'allá* dialectics thus has affinities with other Nuyorican critical terms that also gesture toward a mutable and multispatialized sense of Puerto Ricanness. See also **Charco, Guagua aérea, Vaivén**.

Pachuco/a

Pachuco/a, or *chuco/a*, was a name adopted by Mexican American youths, who may or may not have been part of local gangs, in Los Angeles and other urban centers in the US southwest in the 1940s. The origins of the *pachuco*, and associated cultural habitus and style (*pachuquismo*), have been traced to El Paso, Texas, in the 1920s and 1930s, and *Pachuco* or *Chuco* have had long historical currency as alternative names for the city. Another El Paso synonym for *pachuco* was *pasiente*. *Pachuquismo* and its migrating bearers moved west to California in those decades, and subsequently spread throughout the US southwest along other migratory routes. Among various theories of origin, *pachuco* may derive from the Mexican city of Pachuca, in the state of Hidalgo; a hand in poker with no value since the cards come from different suits (*pachuca*); or the **Náhuatl** word, *pachtli*, for a parasitic arboreal plant (R. Castro 2001). *Pachuco* was also a synonym for **Zoot Suiter**, an acknowledgment of the Zoot Suit style favored by many *pachucos*, and the term additionally designates the *pocho* dialect that developed in El Paso, and that has profoundly marked contemporary Chicano/a Spanish. As a result of their wide cultural influence, which is anchored in a conscious and defiant construction of an urban Mexican American youth identity outside the US and Mexican mainstreams, historians often regard *pachucos* as a significant precursor to the **Chicano Movement** of the 1960s. Sánchez-Tranquilino and Tagg (1992) argue that the *Pachucos* were not a subcultural group, in the sense that subculture implies a subordination to, and departure from, a preexisting cultural and national parent. Rather, the hybrid and remade zoot-suit style and accompanying cultural codes (*pocho* dialect, distinct fashion, favored music and dance steps, a street-level sensibility) announced an appropriation of North American cultural symbolism in **barrio** terms, hence the unease with which zoot suiters were regarded by many Mexican and Anglo-American outsiders. In 1950 the Mexican Octavio Paz (1999) famously wrote that the *pachuco* was an abject cultural orphan, irredeemably cut off from the traditions of both Mexico and the USA. Californian *pachucos* were perceived as an affront not only to US servicemen (good and loyal citizens), but also to contemporary understandings of the proper place of teenagers (Mazón 1984). The targeting of *pachucos* in the 1943 **Zoot Suit Riots** had a profound effect on Californian Mexican perceptions of their vulnerable, marginal, and disputed national place and collective identity. Traditional Mexican American family values were also affronted by *pachucos* and by the style and brash attitude of *pachucas*. By wearing tight short skirts, applying thick makeup, smoking, hanging out in public spaces, and speaking a slang that excluded parents and other outsiders, *pachucas* scandalized their families and challenged family conventions of dutiful femininity. With that disregard for parental authority and convention, *pachucas* and their male counterparts established an urban prototype for later *cholo/as* (R. Castro 2001).

Pan-Americanism

Pan-Americanism has been an important ideal of continental unity, and an equally influential cultural discourse, since the early 1800s. The two most significant architects of pan-Americanism were both involved in independence movements in the 1800s: Simón Bolivar, the "Liberator" and architect of independence in much of Latin America, and José Martí, the Cuban nationalist and a player in the Cuban independence struggle against Spain. Bolivar's pan-American vision arose in the context of the successful independence struggles against Spain in the first two decades of the nineteenth century. He envisaged a continental federation of states formed from the various parts of the Spanish empire. Martí's pan-Americanism was elaborated in his 1891 essay "Nuestra América" (Our America), in which he argued that Latin Americans needed to stop imitating foreign cultural and governmental models, whether emanating from Europe or the USA, and find their own local modes of development on economic and cultural lines (1999). The faith in continental solidarity evident here, and in Bolivar's confederation, was predicated on a discourse of shared historical legacies, cultural imaginaries and language, or **Hispanismo**. A sign of the enduring influence and resilience of these exponents of a united continent is provided by the Venezuelan President Hugo Chávez, who routinely evokes José Martí and Simón Bolivar in his speeches to underwrite his calls for continental unity in opposition to US hegemony. Notions of pan-American unity or "brotherhood" were particularly strong throughout the continent in the wake of the **Cuban Revolution**, and were also influential in the **Chicano Movement** and among Nuyorican civil rights activists such as the **Young Lords**. Some critical approaches to the discourse of **Latinidad** similarly propose that a US-based panethnic identification and imaginary has continent-wide affiliative potential.

Pinto, Pinto Art

Pinto (and its feminine form *pinta*) is a Chicano Spanish term for a prison, and also for a prison inmate or someone who has spent time in prison. Pinto art refers to the art practices of Chicano prison inmates, most of whom are not formally trained. Pinto artists tend chronicle prison and **gang** life, and incorporate into their work such imagery as la **Virgen de Guadalupe**, Jesus, **low riders**, scenes from the **barrio**, and symbols and text drawn from **graffiti** traditions. An important exhibition, *Mi Vida Loca/Mi Arte Loco: An Exhibition of Pinto Art*, was shown at the Galería de la Raza, San Francisco, in June 1999.

Pioneros

Pioneros (Pioneers) is the name for the first wave of Puerto Rican migrants to New York, beginning in the late 1800s, accelerating after the **Jones Act** of 1917, and ending with the close of World War II in 1945, after which the **Great Migration** began in earnest. The term *pionero* is thus applied to those Puerto Ricans who helped to pave the way for the mass migrations of Puerto Ricans from the 1940s through 1960s, most notably by finding housing in specific urban areas and establishing US-based Puerto Rican communities into which later arrivals could settle (Matos-Rodríguez and Hernández 2001). One of the first Puerto Rican narratives of migration, *Memorias de Bernardo Vega*, which was originally written in the late 1940s, provides an account of the *pionero* generation (1994). The Puerto Rican use of *pionero* is not to be confused with the term's use in Cuba, where it refers to members of the *Organización de Pioneros José Martí* (OPJM, Organization of José Martí Pioneers), named after the nineteenth-century independence advocate, José Martí. The OPJM is the national youth union for all Cuban elementary or primary school children, who join it on moving from the day-care system to the school system. Cuban *pioneros* wear the organization's distinctive white shirt and blue or red bandanna, depending on age. The OPJM conducts activities not only similar to the international Boy Scouts and Girl Guides organizations, but also has a pedagogic and ideological commitment to inculcate national revolutionary values in its young members.

Plan de Santa Barbara

Dating from 1969, the *Plan de Santa Barbara* is one of the important manifestos of the **Chicano Movement** and statement of **Chicanismo**, and was written and popularized by the student organization El Movimiento Estudiantil Chicano de Aztlán (MECha). Like *El **Plan Espiritual de Aztlán***, this *Plan* arose from a conference (held at the University of California, Santa Barbara), although its concerns differed from *El Plan Espiritual* by focusing on Chicano/a rights and representation in the education system. Aside from outlining and defining the organizational structures and aims of MECha, the *Plan* also regarded current Chicano/a activism as a necessary response to the historical oppression of Chicano/as, as exemplified by the call for self-determination and intervention into political processes to achieve that goal. Among the

Plan's educational demands were the development of Chicano/a studies programs in schools and universities, affirmative action programs for hiring Chicano/a faculty, student inputs into hiring decisions, university outreach programs in the **barrios** and local Chicano/a communities, and the employment of Chicano/a workers on campus building projects.

Plan espiritual de Aztlán

One of the most important documents of the **Chicano Movement**, *El Plan de Aztlán*, which is popularly known as *El Plan Espiritual de Aztlán* from the text's preamble, dates from the first Chicano National Conference held at Denver, Colorado, in March 1969 (Anaya and Lomelí 1989). Ostensibly a multi-pronged manifesto, program for self-determination, and call to action for Chicanos, the *Plan* was responsible for popularizing a number of central concepts in Movement discourse. *El Plan* has three parts: a manifesto-like text, seven concrete proposals for activism, and a section that focuses on how the Chicano Movement might achieve these aims. *El Plan* defined Chicanos as "La **Raza** de Bronce," a sign that Chicano ethnic and cultural identity was intimately tied to *mestizaje*. *El Plan* further defined the Chicano as the product of US imperialism and as the exploited labor resource on which the US economy in large part depends. Chicanos were an oppressed nation, and a people distinct from and opposed to the geopolitical structures of both the USA and Mexico. The Chicano nation, a "union of free pueblos," was identified with the southwest and called **Aztlán**. *El Plan*'s appeal to both Aztlán and *mestizaje* thus privileged the (**Aztec**) native over the European heritage in the construction of a Chicano collective fortified by, yet not assimilable into, Mexico. With its linking of Chicano identity to the land and to labor, its nationalistic calls for self-determination, and its ambition to establish autonomous cultural and political institutions, *El Plan* provided many Chicanos with a blueprint not only for resistance to **internal colonization**, but also for a politicized approach to cultural and artistic production. Emblematic of the overt link between activism and cultural work was *El Plan Espiritual de Aztlán*'s organizational call for cultural producers to be politically engaged as a means of upholding and defending the Chicano community against assimilationist imperatives. The language of *El Plan* was nonetheless cast in terms of a fraternally encoded androcentrism and an orthodox focus on family values, attitudes that also typified much of the literature associated with the Movimiento. See also **Chicano Renaissance**.

Plena,Bomba

Plena and *bomba*, which are often conjoined as *bombayplena*, are two important Afro-Puerto Rican music and dance forms that arose in the slave era, and that have influenced subsequent musical developments on the island. In the Dominican Republic an unrelated work-music style called *plena* also exists. Puerto Rico's *plena* is often dubbed the national music, and it has also been a significant music tradition in the Puerto Rican **diaspora**. Usually regarded as the direct precursor to the *plena*, the *bomba* arose on the island's eastern sugar plantations in the nineteenth century. The *bomba* was a highly percussive dance music performed with *barriles* (barrel-shaped drums) and hand-held percussion instruments, over which a vocalist would sing. The working-class *plena* evolved in Ponce, on the island's south coast, in the early 1900s. Incorporating African and European influences, the *plena*'s main percussion instruments are a small tambourine-like drum (*pandereta*) and the *güiro* (a notched scraper usually made from gourd), while the style's syncopated duple meter emerges from the interplay between a concertina (*sinfonía de mano*), guitar, and ensemble singers. The *plena*'s satirical lyrics recount daily events and matters of community concern, and often target authority figures or playfully mock locals who have come to public attention or achieved local notoriety. With those narrative capacities, the *plena* has functioned for its working-class audiences as an oral equivalent of the newspaper, much like the Mexican **corrido**. Juan Flores (2000) argues that the *plena* evolved through a number of phases. Between 1900 and 1926 the *plena* spread from Ponce; in 1926, the first *plena* songs were recorded, thus ensuring expansion of the genre's audiences; and in the 1950s and 1960s, a revival of interest in Puerto Rican cultural traditions and folklore saw the *plena* elevated to its status as a national music. Since the latter era in part coincided with **Operation Bootstrap**, which encouraged mass rural–urban migration, as well as the **Great Migration** of Puerto Ricans to New York City and other US destinations, the *plena* also became a cultural immigrant. Contemporary interest in maintaining cultural traditions in the US setting has seen the formation of such ensembles as Los Pleneros de la 21 (New York) and Los Pleneros de la 24 (San Francisco). These groups take advantage of the *plena*'s distinctive narrative qualities to elaborate on cultural links with the island and the rise of "diasporican" identifications. The documentary *Plena canto y trabajo/Plena is Song, Plena is Work* (1989, dir. Pedro Rivera and Susan Zeig) explores the genre's function in the construction of **Nuyorican** identities and the recording of immigrant experiences.

Pocho/a, Pochismo

For many decades in the twentieth century, the term *pocho/a* was a derogatory label from within Mexican communities directed at descendents of Mexican immigrants born or raised in the USA. *Pocho/a* remains a common term in Mexico for any Chicano/a or Americanized Mexican. Mexican nationals first coined the term *Pocho/a* to define second-generation Mexicans whose parents had fled across the US–Mexico border during the upheavals that followed the **Mexican Revolution** of 1910. *Pocho/as* were perceived to have been *agringado/as* or contaminated by *gringo* or ''American'' cultural values and the English language. *Pocho* may thus also refer to the hybrid Chicano-Spanish dialect, especially in southern Texas, while a *pochismo* refers to a Spanish language expression modulated by English spelling and pronunciation, or an Anglicism that has intruded into Chicano/a Spanish. These usages extended the quotidian meanings of *pocho*, which include discolored, faded, malnourished, pale, and rotten. Parallels of this disparagement also appeared in Octavio Paz's 1950 *El laberinto de la soledad* (1999), in which he dismissed the Mexican American **pachuco** as an abject orphan deculturated from home and host societies alike. The first Chicano novel to be published by a mainstream publishing house, José Antonio Villareal's *Pocho* (1970 [1959]), focuses on a *pocho* called Richard whose parents migrated to California during the Mexican revolutionary period. Coming of age during the 1930s and 1940s, and like many other children of Mexican immigrants at this time, Richard's identity is indelibly marked by the era in which *pocho* had widespread currency as an insult. Since the 1970s, many Chicano/a artists and writers have applied *pocho* ironically and parodically to themselves. For these cultural workers, *pocho* no longer connotes shame, a failed Mexicanness, or an abject in-betweenness derived from being lost in transition between Mexican and ''American'' cultures. Such cultural workers have remade *pocho* as the name for an ambivalent Chicano/a identity. A parodic, yet affectionate, embrace of the *pocho* term underwrites the video collaboration between Cuban American Coco Fusco and the performance group Chicano Secret Service, *Pochonovela* (1995). The video is presented as an episode from a fictive **telenovela** about a Chicano/a family thrown into crisis when Juan, the assimilated *pocho* son, brings his *gringa* girlfriend home to meet the family. Perhaps the most successful attempt to displace the negative valencies of *pocho* has been Esteban Zul and Lalo López's satirical magazine *Pocho* (www.pocho.com), and their film and video production company, Pocho Productions.

Premio Lo Nuestro

Organized by the Spanish-language TV network Univisión in February each year, Premio Lo Nuestro is the Spanish-speaking world's major music-prize award ceremony, and a rival in the US context to both the Grammy Awards and the Latin Grammy Awards, the latter inaugurated in 2000. Due to the penetration of Univisión in the US TV market, Premio Lo Nuestro has had an enormous influence on Latino/a musical consumption in that country since its beginnings in the late 1980s, and it has also played a key role in the national and international popularization of Latino/a singers and musical groups.

Prisons, Prison Industrial Complex

The USA has the dubious distinction of the highest rates of prison incarceration in the world. Texas, California, Florida, and New York account for just under a quarter of the total US prison population. More sobering, some 70 percent of the 2 million + prison population is non-white, the majority African American and Latino/a (Harrison and Beck 2005). For Angela Davis (1998) the prison industrial complex (PIC) designates the ways by which prisons form a specific industrial component of the broader US capitalist economy, and an institutionalized means of disciplining and controlling the poor and communities of color. The privatization of the prison system since the 1970s has made prisons less accountable in terms of respecting inmate rights, and seen the transformation of prisons into a source of captive labor power for national and multinational companies. Prisons in the USA, and increasingly throughout the world, no longer pretend to rehabilitate or reeducate prisoners. Rather, the PIC "disappears" people from racialized and class-specific communities as a means of socioeconomic and political control over those communities (Davis 1998). The PIC's inexorable expansion thus enables governments to ignore attacking the fundamental socioeconomic causes of crime: poverty, unemployment, or low-paying and insecure employment, lack of access to education, the drug economy that targets the poor and/or people of color, limited social welfare, lack of child-care provisions, and inadequate health care (Davis 1998). The PIC is predicated on, and justified by, widespread national discourses that regard certain populations as inherently "criminalized" and thus as a danger to the moral fabric of the nation, hence the need to survey, target, and preclude the mobility of those communities. The discursive and structural bases of the PIC align with the operations of American apartheid (Aponte-Parés 1998;

Massey and Denton 1993), an entrenched form of spatialized oppression that condemns communities of color to life in urban ghettos characterized by inadequate infrastructures, limited employment opportunities, underfunded education, bureaucratic inertia and disinterest, and an inordinate level of attention from the police and judicial systems.

Puerto Rican, *Puertorriqueño/a*

Puerto Rican (*Puertorriqueño/a*) is the name for a resident of Puerto Rico, and for a Puerto Rican resident of the USA. Puerto Rican is of note for being perhaps the only US minority identity term not conjoined routinely with "American" (see **Hyphenation**). A number of alternative terms distinguish USA from island residents: Amerícan, Diasporican, Florican, **Nuyorican**, Otherican, and Rican.

Q

Quinceañera

A *quinceañera* is the traditional birthday celebration—a ritual of liminality or rite of passage—held when a girl turns 15 in order to mark the passage to womanhood. *Quinceañera* celebrations combine religious and secular practices in a highly conventionalized and public performance of traditional gender and community values (Dávalos 2002). Customarily, girls wear white-, pink-, or pastel-colored dresses to symbolize purity and virginity, and a *diadema* (tiara). They carry a *ramo* (bunch of flowers), and wear jewelry given by their *padrinos* (godparents). During the *quinceañera* girls are given their last *muñeca* (doll) and surrender the childhood *libro y rosario* (prayer book and rosary) they received at first communion in exchange for adult versions. The *quinceañera* involves a girl's attendance at Catholic mass accompanied by her *damas y chambelanes* (page boys and girls) in what amounts to a ritual appropriation of Spanish courtly performances, which is witnessed by members of the girl's extended family and family friends, with a large fiesta afterward. The party is the setting for the *quinceañera*'s first adult dance, a choreographed waltz with the father or father figure. The *quinceañera* is often said to predate the arrival of the Spanish in Mexico and Central America, and its mixture of indigenous, Catholic, and Spanish courtly symbolism exemplifies the processes of **syncretism** that resulted from conquest. *Quinceañeras* are a highly popular family and community event. This is evident, for example, in Texas where *quinceañeras* are part of the Chicano/a community's performance of displaced *Mexicanidad* (Mexicanness), and featured prominently in the social section of local newspapers. Two contemporary appropriations and resemanticizations of the *quinceañera* ritual are of note for problematizing its traditional role in inculcating and maintaining conservative notions of dutiful Latina femininity. The first is the phenomenon in South Texas of the *cincuentañera* (fiftieth birthday celebration) to celebrate a Chicana's *cambio de vida* (menopause) (Cantú 2002). The second is the Chicano performance piece *Quinceañera* (Araiza et al. 2002), which celebrates a queer version of the *quinceañera* as a ritual of survival in the fifteenth anniversary of the **AIDS** era.

Quinto sol, Quinto Sol Generation

El Quinto sol (the Fifth Sun; in **Náhuatl**, *Ollin Tonatiuh*) is the name of a temporal cycle in the traditional **Aztec** calendar. According to Aztec myth and cosmography, the Earth's history is divided into solar cycles, the Fifth Sun being the current epoch whose end will be announced by massive earthquakes. Given that one of the hallmarks of the **Chicano Movement** was the adoption and appropriation of Aztec symbolism, El Quinto sol became a widespread marker of a politicized Chicano/a cultural habitus in the 1960s and 1970s. Indeed, the first publisher of Chicano literature was El Quinto Sol Publishers, founded in Berkeley, California, in the late 1960s. Martín-Rodríguez (2003) designates the writers who emerged in the late 1960s as the Quinto Sol Generation, by which he means the emergence of a new nationalist Chicano literary enterprise. Quinto sol is also the name of a music collective that formed in 1994 in East LA, which is notable for a post-Movimiento political ethos that translates East LA realities via a musical fusion of Latin American dance-music styles and reggae.

Quisqueya

Quisqueya (or *Kiskeya*) is the indigenous **Taíno** word for the island of **Hispaniola**, and is often used by Dominicans to signify the Dominican Republic, the Spanish-speaking state on the eastern part of the island it shares with Haiti. *Quisqueya* translates as Mother Earth, and functions as a term of endearment in the Dominican **diaspora** when referring to the homeland, as is clear from the film *Nueba Yol (A Funny Way to Say New York City)* (1995, dir. Angel Muñiz), a comedy about Dominican immigrants in New York that sends up the American Dream. A sense of the term's usage is captured in Junot Díaz's short story "Edison, New Jersey": "You can't go a block without passing a Quisqueya Bakery or a Quisqueya Supermercado or a Hotel Quisqueya" (1996).

R

Race, Racialization

Race (in Spanish *raza*) is a pivotal category of critical analysis and dispute in numerous disciplines. Popularly thought of as a meaningful identity essence — we all have a race — race is notoriously hard to define and verify, and is often used interchangeably with **ethnicity**. For some critics the challenge that race poses critical and political agendas is how to avoid appealing to an essentialist and fixed notion of race, or to that position's conceptual opposite, the idea that race is an illusion, and does not exist. Omi and Winant (1994) respond to that challenge by arguing that race remains an important concept because of the impossibility of fixing it or dispensing with it; that is, race has a fundamental role in "structuring and representing the social world." That role includes the discourses that permit some people to be identified, discriminated against, and even attacked on the basis of the ways in which their bodies are "read" and "interpreted," that is, as targets of racism. Omi and Winant further propose that critical attention to race needs to focus not on the truths inherent to race, but rather on the processes of racialization, or racial formation, by which the categories of race "are created, inhabited, transformed, and destroyed." As many Latino/a critics note, the processes of racial formation have a difficult time dealing with Latino/as, whose mixed-race or multiple race origins, ethnicization as "Hispanic" (implying European origins), and self and group identifications, generate a host of identity positions, imposed and claimed, in which "race" itself changes. A disjunction emerges between the US **CENSUS** use of Hispanic/Latino as ethnic categorizations, and the regular media reading of Hispanic as a racial category of the same order as black or white. Thus state apparatuses and media simultaneously create and dissolve "Hispanic" race. The self-conscious countercreation of race is demonstrated by the Chicano Movement's redefinition of Chicano/as as a **brown** or *mestizo* people, *la raza*. Recent Latino/a criticism on processes of racialization has drawn links between those processes and the trajectories of "colonial immigration" in the capitalist world economy (Grosfoguel et al. 2005). That is, the protocols of Latino/a racialization and ethnic profiling at work in the USA, for example, which derive from imperial takeovers of national territory (in the case of Chicano/as), colonial annexation (in the case of Puerto Ricans), or slavery (African Americans), are applied to new immigrant groups. These neocolonizing drives are evident in the Chicanoization of Central Americans in California, the Nuyoricanization of Dominicanos in New York, and the Africanamericanization of Haitians and Afro-Cubans in Miami. See **Critical Race Theory.**

Ranchera

Known in the early 1900s as the *canción mexicana* (Mexican song) or *canción vernácula* (vernacular song), *ranchera* is one of the most popular musical genres in Mexico and the Mexican diaspora, and a rival to the *corrido* with which it has affinities. *Ranchera* is a romantic song form, characterized by highly emotive or sentimental lyrics that deal with such pet themes as doomed love, the machinations of fate, uncomplicated life in the countryside, and masculine prowess. The genre's rhythmic and melodic structures draw on the waltz, polka, and Mexican **bolero.** The popularity of the *ranchera* as a national song form was secured after the **Mexican Revolution,** while the heyday of *rancheras* coincided with the Golden Age of the Mexican film industry in the 1930s and 1940s, when *rancheras* graced the soundtracks of numerous films, particularly the singing *vaquero* genre. The popularity of many acting-singing stars—Jorge Negrete, Pedro Infante, Lola Beltrán—was augmented by their recordings of *ranchera* and other romantic styles. The genre had its most prolific and influential exponent in José Alfredo Jiménez from the 1940s to the early 1970s. Many of his classic compositions were reinterpreted by Vicente Fernández, considered by aficionados to be the greatest *ranchera* singer. US-based *ranchera* singers also achieved popularity on both sides of the border, as exemplified by the long career of Lydia Mendoza, *La Alondra de Tejas*

(The Texan Skylark). Most Mexican *ranchera* singers tour the USA in order to target the lucrative Mexican-origin market. While women have been the genre's main fanbase, many critics note that *rancheras* represent women as the passive victims of romance and fate, and the macho lothario. In Denise Chávez's novel *Loving Pedro Infante* (2001), the Chicana protagonists fantasize in vain about finding a man like Pedro Infante (whose records they know by heart) who can fulfill the promise of love and romance encoded in his movie-idol looks and *ranchera* lyrics. The melodramatic *ranchera* and bolero genres are subject to a queer and a **kitsch** resemanticization in the film *Carmelita Tropicana: Your Kunst is Your Waffen* (1994, dir. Ela Troyano).

Rap and Hip-Hop

Rap and hip-hop (for many commentators, the terms are interchangeable) are popularly regarded as an all African American musical affair, and as one of the most dynamic, influential, and commercially successful forms of youth musical culture to have emanated from the USA in the twentieth century. However, Latino/a contributions to the evolution of these music forms, which are now practiced and consumed across the world, have also been crucial and reflect the complex and productive relations between Latino/as and African Americans in the USA's largest cities. At the same time, Nuyorican and other Latino/a hip-hop and rap artists, and the genre itself, played a significant role in the formation of new **latinidades** and panethnic symbioses (Raquel Rivera 2003). The origins of hip-hop and rap lie in 1970s New York City, and in such African American and Latino/a dominant inner-city areas as the Bronx, the Lower East Side, and Harlem. The direct forerunner of hip-hop and rap was the break dancing phenomenon, an athletic form of dancing performed in the street to music produced by DJs (Disc Jockeys), who would mix rhythms and sounds from vinyl records on turntables, and MCs (Masters of Ceremonies), the latter responsible for the spoken word rhyming accompaniments. Nuyorican rap artists and DJs, and associated **graffiti** artists, in New York City played leading roles in the evolution of breaking and MCing, their lyrics also notable for dealing with inner-city realities and issues in a mixture of Spanish and African American-modulated English. Rap and hip-hop continued to evolve and find new audiences in the late 1970s and 1980s, and by the 1990s the genre had become a big international business. Throughout that decade and into the new century the once working-class and inner-city credentials of the form were increasingly packaged and corporatized for mass consumption, a trend evident in the role played by video clips in disseminating and popularizing rap. Distinct regional rap and hip-hop styles also emerged on the East and West Coasts, and in cities such as Chicago, and subgeneric forms such as gangsta rap became highly popular in the 1990s. Rap and hip-hop have enjoyed a controversial reputation, with criticism directed at the lyrical obsession with violence, masculine sexual prowess, misogyny, homophobia, untrammeled consumption and the display of brand labels, and the celebration of gang life. Many rap artists, however, are highly political in terms of the issues they canvass: inner-city poverty, racism, police surveillance, US militarism, and media stereotyping of minorities. Paralleling the regional divergences in African American rap and hip-hop, Latino rap and hip-hop—or Latin(o) rap—has developed its own subcategories (Puerto Rican, Chicano, and Mexican) that also reflect east and west coast regional origins. Latino rap enjoyed a measure of commercial success in the early 1990s. As Juan Flores (2000) puts it, those years saw Spanish-language rap "break the language barrier" with mainstream crossover hits from Cuban American Mellow Man Ace ("Mentirosa" 1990), the Chicano Kid Frost ("La Raza" 1991), Ecuadorian American Gerardo ("Rico Suave" 1991), and Panamanian American El General. Due to the successes of these figures, other artists started to recognize the commercial possibilities of rap music that featured bilingual lyrics or **code switching**, or raps in English sprinkled with Spanish, about inner-city realities. Among the groups that achieved popular and commercial success in the 1990s were Latin Empire ("Puerto Rock" and "Krazy **Taíno**"), Latin Alliance, Lighter Shade of Brown, Cypress Hill, Proper Dos, Delinquent Habits, Thirstin' Howl III, Fat Joe, and ALT. Some Latino rappers, however, including the Nuyorican rap artist Big Pun, argued that the "Latino rap" category implied either Latino rappers' marginal status in the broader rap scene or their mere following of African American cultural styles. These regional and stylistic complexities are further modulated by the transnational influence of rap music on Latin American music forms such as *reggaetón*.

Rasquachismo

Rasquachismo (*rascuachismo*) is a particular Chicano/a popular cultural aesthetic or sensibility, most often but not exclusively related to theatrical and performance production. An appropriation from Mexican Spanish (*rasquache* is something that is provisional and poorly built), within Chicano/a discourse this aesthetic came to the fore in a range of cultural tendencies, notably theater, associated with the 1960s **Chicano Movement.** Ybarra-Frausto (1992) defines *rasquachismo* as a working-class "making-do" sensibility impelled by poverty; when adopted in performance, that making-do aesthetic also ensured that the construction of the performance work at the USA's geopolitical and socioeconomic edges was itself laid bare and prepared for debate. Perhaps the most significant manifestation of *rasquachismo* in action was the work of el **Teatro Campesino** (ETC). As Broyles-González argues, ETC extracted what she calls the "Rasquachi Aesthetic" from the stylistic and theatrical conventions of the Mexican *carpa* or tent-performance tradition (1994). ETC's *rasquachismo* entailed the intermixing of disparate performance styles, genres, and traditions: acrobatics, improvisation, mime and slapstick, poetry recitals, the use of Mexican puppetry and stock characters from Mexican folk theater traditions, live and prerecorded music, singing, and a Brechtian drawing attention to the constructedness of the performance that also dissolved the boundaries between audience and actors. The ensemble's defiant use of **bilingualism, code switching,** and **Spanglish** was intended to respect the linguistic realities of Chicano/a audiences (Broyles-González 1994; Ybarra-Frausto 1991). Gaspar de Alba (1998) combines Ybarra-Frausto's definition of *rasquachismo* with Olalquiaga's (1992) notion of the three degrees of Latino/a religious **kitsch** in her concept of Chicano/a **Alter-Native** culture. For Mesa-Bains (2003), *rasquachismo* informs domesticana, women's cultural practices in the **domestic** sphere. Ramón García (1998) regards the work of some Chicano/a cultural producers—the poet Alurista; the conceptual-art performance group ASCO— as camp rather than *rasquache.*

Raza, Raza cósmica

The Spanish term *la raza* signifies race and also connotes a people more generally. Throughout Latin America, and most commonly in the Andean regions, Central America, and Mexico, it also denotes *mestizos.* The term's first significant literary manifestation was the Bolivian writer Alcides Arguedas's novel *Raza de bronce* (1919), which established a new descriptor for *mestizos,* the bronze race. This descriptor was modified as *la raza cósmica,* or the cosmic race, by the Mexican José Vasconcelos in 1925 (1997). For Vasconcelos, *mestizaje* in the Americas had produced the world's first racial synthesis, which symbolized the mixed-racial and cultural future of all peoples. However, Vasconcelos's vision was also marked by a eugenicist logic that regarded some races (European, white) as more meritorious, cultured, and powerful than others (Asiatic peoples, American Indians). For Vasconcelos, the "transcendental mission" (conquest and colonization) of Europe's most vigorous peoples, the English and Spanish, ensured the breeding out of savagery and degeneracy from America's indigenous peoples. The Chicano Movement's redefinition of Chicanos as a **brown** race drew explicitly on Vasconcelos's cosmic vision, as did the Mexican national ideology of *mestizaje* (Pérez-Torres 2006). *El **Plan Espiritual de Aztlán*** defined Chicanos as "La raza de bronce." In her textual construction of a new Chicana consciousness, *la **nueva mestiza***, Anzaldúa (1987) reworked Vasconcelos's ideas by celebrating the Indian that he did not. For Spitta (1997), given that Vasconcelos's version of *mestizaje* involved white (Anglo-Saxon) with white (Spanish), later borrowings of the "cosmic race" thesis necessarily overlooked Vasconcelos's opinion that indigenous Americans were a degenerative "race" that would inevitably be bred away. Diana Taylor (2003) notes wryly that Vasconcelos's racial utopia does not appear to be under construction in the USA, despite the proximity of Anglo and "Hispanic" millions. Rather, Latino/as have become "la raza cosmética" (the cosmetic race), and thus cannot "merge" into the social landscape because discourses of racial difference categorize and disparage them, thus denying many millions access to "power, wealth, education and health care."

Reggaetón

Reggaetón (or Raggatón, Reguetón, or Requetón, with or without the accents) is a Puerto Rican dance music that draws on and synthesized influences from **salsa** (Nuyorican and Caribbean), **rap and hip-hop** (USA, Puerto Rican, and Panamanian), Jamaican dancehall reggae (which also had Panamanian practitioners) and ragga (ragamuffin reggae, a synthesis of dancehall reggae, dub music, and hip-hop), and Afro-Puerto Rican styles such as the *plena* and *bomba*. Aside from the Spanish-language rapping style and the DJ production of dub and sampling, *reggaetón* is characterized by a driving drum-machine beat, and an accompanying dance movement called *perreo* (grinding). Emerging in the early to mid-1990s as a working-**class** and underground youth music phenomenon that was ignored by local Puerto Rican record companies and radio stations, *reggaetón* has gone transnational. The style now has a mass following in such US cities as Miami and New York, throughout Latin America, and as far afield as Spain. *Reggaetón's* rapid evolution since the early 1990s has seen its practitioners shift from Spanish-language rap and lyric approaches that evoked US rap conventions (masculinist odes to guns, drugs, the conquest of women) to socially conscious comments on a range of issues (injustice, poverty, drug abuse, gender relations, racism, police corruption, the unresolved Puerto Rican national question). Most of the well-known *reggaetón* performers are male and include Tego Calderón, Don Cheriza, Daddy Yankee (whose 2005 "Gasolina" became an international hit), El Propheta, Don Omar, and Héctor y Tito. Ivy Queen is the best-known female practitioner.

Remittances

Remittances are the monies and funds sent by immigrants and cross-border workers to their countries of origin. Family members in migrant-source countries across the world are the traditional recipients of remittances. Such monies serve as a form of informal welfare and have arisen, in part, in response to the inability of particular states to guarantee basic living standards. Remittances may enable socioeconomic mobility, with incoming funds providing increased spending power. At times, remittances fund the emigration of other family members. Alongside family-directed remittances, migrants use remittances to invest in the home country, for example, by entering the housing market or contributing to community development and infrastructure programs, from church renovations to funding sport and social club construction and transport improvements. Such community-minded philanthropy is the subject of Alex Rivera's documentary *The Sixth Section* (2003) about Grupo Unión, a Mexican **Hometown Association**. At times, remittance flows resemble a form of community aid, for instance, following the impact of natural disasters such as hurricanes and earthquakes, or as a response to times of economic or fiscal crisis. In the case of large immigrant groups, the value of remittances can reach staggering proportions, with a concomitant influence on the receiving country's economy. The economies of states throughout the Caribbean, Central America, and South America are increasingly dependent on remitted funds. The dramatic growth in the amount of remittances sent back by Mexican workers and migrants in the USA now means that only the oil industry contributes more money to the Mexican economy. In 2002, for example, remittances sent to Mexico totaled some US$10 billion, or 15 percent of the world's total (Coronado 2004). Those amounts have risen steadily since 2002. Despite the long-standing US embargo on trade and other dealings with Cuba, remittances from the exile community to relatives on the island have become an integral feature of the Cuban economy. In many Caribbean and Central American countries, including the Dominican Republic and Honduras, remittances provide the largest source of foreign income and hard currency. The remittance economy, and the presence of innumerable money transfer businesses across the USA, provides a highly visible sign of new **transnational** communal and familial links across geopolitical borders.

Retablos

A *retablo* (from the Latin, *retro-tabula*, behind the altar) is a devotional image of thanks dedicated to a specific saint or the Virgin Mary, and usually painted in tempera on a rectangular wooded board or plate of tin, which is then placed in altars or recesses in churches or shrines. A dynamic folk art in Mexico and the USA, particularly in New Mexico, the *retablo* tradition is thought to have evolved from the centuries-old Catholic *ex-voto* tradition, by which worshippers commissioned or made a painting to record the vow they made to a particular saint (R. Castro 2001). That history survives in the way *retablos* are often called *retablos ex voto*, thus distinguishing them from *santos*, the Church-sanctioned images of the saints, the Virgin, or Christ produced until the early decades of the twentieth century. The Mexican *retablo* form appeared in the late 1700s. As gestures of gratitude for divine intercession in daily life, typical *retablo* images provide important insights into the daily lives and aspirations of their featured subjects. *Retablos* consist of a representation of a particular incident or event (an illness or hospitalization, a work or traffic accident, experience of crime, drunkenness, crossing the US–Mexico border, incarceration, an unmanageable donkey, crop failure, etc.), with a text in the lower part of the *retablo* that explains the scene and how the particular saint or Virgin intervened, and a representation of the saint or Virgin hovering in a cloud above the main action. Durand and Massey (1995) identify five characteristic formal features of the *retablo* genre, by which the three elements already noted (scene, saint or Virgin, and text) are executed: the use of bright, vivid colors; a self-conscious toying with spatial conventions to accentuate the drama; the collapse of time (for instance, with distinct stages in a particular event shown in the same image); use of elements drawn from the theater (a stage, curtains), again in order to heighten the drama; and, a more recent innovation, the use of collage techniques in order to incorporate photographs, documents, or mass-produced images of the Virgin. *Retablos* are normally commissioned from *retablo* painters (*retablistas*), who attract custom due to their reputations and the popularity of their stylistic approaches.

Rock en español

Literally meaning Spanish-language rock music, *Rock en español* (or *roc en español*) is an umbrella term for a set of diverse, and often unrelated, musical directions in the Spanish-speaking world that work with Anglophone pop and rock traditions while revising and mixing those traditions with Latin American alternative styles. *Rock en español* has multiple genealogies dating back to the 1950s, 1960s, and 1970s, the decades in which a number of US Latino/a musicians and outfits were hybridizing rock and Latino/a music genres, and in which rock styles and trajectories began to gain wider audiences in Latin America and Spain. Such forerunners include the 1950s hit "La Bamba" from the **Chicano** singer Ritchie Valens (Richard Valenzuela), Santana's version of the **salsa** classic "Oye Como Va," which appeared on the big-selling album from 1970 *Abraxas*, and the 1970s hits "Suavecito" (by Malo) and "Low Rider" (a **barrio**-rock classic by the LA group War). Many critics now recognize the seeds of *rock en español* in these breakthrough artists. Key influences in the evolution of *rock en español* were the debut from Argentina's Los Fabulosos Cadillacs, *Bares y fondas* (1986), and Paris-based group Mano Negra's 1989 *Puta's Fever*, the latter featuring songs in Spanish, French, English, and Arabic, and musical influences drawn from rock, reggae, and gypsy music. Los Fabulosos Cadillacs had perhaps the first *rock en español* hit in the USA in 1994 with their single "Matador." By the late 1980s *rock en español* was entrenched as a highly lucrative arm of the global music market, its popularity in the 1990s abetted by the expansion of the music video industry, in particular MTV Latin America, on cable television throughout the continent.

Rumba

Rumba (rhumba) is an Afro-Cuban dance style that, like many Cuban music genres, now enjoys international popularity. Its name derived from the verb "rumbear" (to get one's bearings, to go out on the town), rumba was a working-class urban dance style, with a highly percussive beat and a call-and-response vocal arrangement, that Afro-Cubans performed at parties. Rumba itself designates three specific subcategories: the *yambú* (where dancers pretend to have difficulty moving); the *guaguancó*, a faster paced and sexually charged form with the male dancer leading his partner; and the *columbia*, a highly acrobatic solo dance performed by men (Orovio 2004). The *guaguancó* style provides the basis for the standard *rumba* used in contemporary ballroom dancing.

S

Salsa

Salsa, literally sauce, is the name for a contemporary trans-American dance music, with audiences and practitioners across the globe. While salsa is popularly regarded as a Latin American music anchored in Afro-Cuban traditions, musicologists, and salsa musicians themselves, disagree over the origins of the genre, variously stressing its Cuban (Lemayrie 2002) or **Nuyorican** (Flores 2000) origins, or regarding salsa as a general cover-all for an array of Afro-Caribbean musical styles and traditions. Most salsa historians accept that the genre is the neocultural outcome of migration from the Caribbean to New York City, and that Nuyorican and Cuban musicians and singers were pivotal in the rise of salsa. Such musicians drew on Cuban (*son, mambo, guaracha, guaganco*) and Puerto Rican styles (*bomba* and **plena**), as well as rock, R'n'B, and jazz influences and instrumental conventions (Waxer 2002). The New York record label Fania, founded by Jerry Masucci and Johnny Pacheco, is normally accredited with developing and popularizing salsa in the 1970s. The label's catalogue featured a host of now legendary artists: Ray Baretto, Rubén Blades, Héctor Lavoé, Willie Colón, Celia Cruz, Larry Harlow, Eddie Palmieri, Johnny Pacheco, and the label's house orchestra, the Fania All Stars. The music produced by Fania records (the Fania movement) inspired imitators throughout the Spanish-speaking world. Juan Flores (2000) suggests that the rise of salsa was responsible for the decline of the 1960s Latino/a music style of boogaloo (*bugalú*), itself a fusion of **mambo, cha-cha-chá,** *son,* doo-wop, rock'n'roll, and soul music. Part of the "Latin Soul" movement that came to national prominence on such television shows as American Bandstand and on radio playlists, boogaloo was one of the first cultural signs of dynamic neo-cultural Nuyorican adaptations to the US host society, one that also provided a soundtrack to the Nuyorican civil rights movement of the late 1960s. Many Fania artists bridged the boogaloo and salsa eras, their work characterized by the elimination of English lyrics and R'n'B-musical influences (which typified Boogaloo) and a recovery of Afro-Caribbean musical traditions. Such reassessments of salsa's origins have nonetheless been critiqued for perpetuating a masculinist notion of salsa history, one that erases women's contributions. Aparicio (1998) argues that the Cuban exile singer Celia Cruz, "the Queen of Salsa," and La Lupe, "the Queen of Latin Soul," were key innovators in the genre's development whose achievements were not acknowledged in either the Fania-led marketing of salsa in the 1970s, or subsequent music scholarship. Similarly, critics have overlooked the contributions made in the 1990s by singers such as La India ("The Princess of Salsa"), Lisette Meléndez, and Brenda K. Starr, to new African American inflected salsa forms and notions of **Latinidad** (Aparicio 1998). Feminist critics have regarded salsa as a performative music and dance phenomenon characterized by gendered and heteronormative power hierarchies. Salsa has evolved into local forms and subcategories: *salsa gorda* or *salsa brava* (the percussive dance style popularized by Fania); *salsa romántica* (a stylized pop music characterized by emotive or melodramatic lyrics); and *timba*, or Cuban salsa, which developed in the 1980s and is influenced by **rap and hip-hop**, funk, and local music traditions. New York, Puerto Rico, Colombia, and Cuba remain the epicenters of salsa production. Salsa's complex origins, and morphing sites of production, exemplify Rowe's and Schelling's (1991) description of the globalization of local cultural forms. Anchored in the plantation and slave economy of Puerto Rico and Cuba, Afro-Caribbean music traditions evolved and relocated in line with the Caribbean's entry into an international capitalist system and its attendant rural–urban and Caribbean–New York migrations. By the 1970s, when New York musicians introduced salsa to international audiences, global capitalism's commodity and communication routes meant that salsa could not be tied to a single "nation" or cultural tradition. Salsa thus became a product and symptom of the globalization of culture itself. Challenges to received notions of what "Latin/o" culture signifies in a globalized epoch are posed by Japan's Orquesta de la Luz, which emerged in the 1990s to international acclaim with songs such as "Salsa no tiene fronteras" (Salsa Has No Borders), and Salsa Celtica, a Scottish Celtic and salsa fusion band formed in 1996, which combines bagpipes and flute with Afro-Caribbean percussion. The proliferation of salsa clubs and dancing studios in cities across the world may also indicate that the genre functions as a signifier of an exoticized and libidinized "Latin" culture to which non Latin Americans desire access.

Santería

Santería is the name for an Afro-Cuban religious and belief system with origins in the slave era. The survival of *santería* over many centuries required adherents to conduct their ceremonies and rituals away from the gaze of European slave owners and the Catholic Church. *Santería* also has many thousands of followers in the USA. Sometimes referred to as *la Regla de Ocha* (The Rule or Law of Ocha), *santería* represents a Cuban parallel to Haitian voudou(n) and Jamaican obeah, and is marked by the syncretic admixture of west African Yoruba and Catholic traditions in a complex cosmological and hierarchized system of some 400 *orishas* (deities), as well as saints, spirits, and ancestors. *Santería* ceremonies are led by priests and priestesses (*santero/as*), and may be characterized by ritual animal sacrifice (chickens, pigeons, goats, sheep), with percussive music and dance accompaniments. *Santería* has played a significant role in the Cuban American community, as exemplified by the references to santería throughout Cristina García's novel, *Dreaming in Cuban* (1992), and the *botánicas* in Miami and other US cities dedicated to selling products used in *santería* ceremonies, home altars, and healing rituals (De la Torre 2004). In the USA, however, the *santería* practice of animal sacrifice has been controversial. In June 1993, the US Supreme Court overturned a ruling by the Florida District Court that had outlawed animal sacrifice. The Supreme Court argued that practitioners of *santería* had been targeted by local laws passed by the City of Hialeah, in contradistinction to the constitutional "requirement that laws burdening religious practice must be of general applicability." During the 1999/2000 custody battle over Elián González, adherents of *santería* in Miami asserted that Elián had been chosen by the orisha Elegguá to overthrow Castro; others saw Elián as a child of Ochún, the sea deity regarded as the mother of all Cubans (De la Torre 2003).

Santos, Santeros

A *santo* is a carved and decorated or painted image of a Saint, Christ (*El santo niño*), the Virgin Mary, or an angel, the making of which has been a long-standing folk art practice across the US southwest since the first Spanish settlements and Catholic missions were founded in the eighteenth century. *Santero* (the maker or repairer of saints) refers to the artisan responsible for carving the *bultos* or painting the *santos* (on wood, animal hide, or tin). Both *bultos* and *santos* (also called *láminas*) were originally made for and displayed in the recesses or altars of a church or mission in the Spanish colonial era. *Santos* were also made for home altars. The *bulto* tradition remains a significant folk cultural practice in Mexican and Mexican American communities, particularly in New Mexico. Durand and Massey (1995) distinguish *santos* from **retablos** (a tradition of painting images on wood or tin in thanks for divine intervention) and claim that the *santo* tradition was a key feature of the evangelizing drives of the Catholic Church, intended to inculcate piety among parishioners, many of whom were illiterate. The tradition died out in the 1920s due to competition from cheaper mass-produced versions of saints, Christ, and the Virgin (Durand and Massey 1995). *Bultos* were traditionally carved from cottonwood tree roots, which were then covered with gesso and painted in bright colors. Contemporary *bulto* makers, many now visual artists, construct *bultos* from a range of media (other types of wood, clay, polymer resin, metal, found objects), and at times move away from the religious purview to construct images based on topical political issues and even celebrity figures. The New Mexican artist Nicholas Herrera, for example, bases his art practice on the *santo* tradition and its religious symbolism, but has transformed the *bulto* into a visual medium for sardonic commentary on such issues as the Gulf War, environmental degradation in the New Mexico desert, and the operations of the **Border Patrol**.

Sitios y lenguas

Sitios y lenguas (sites/spaces and tongues/languages) is Emma Pérez's (1991, 1994) conceptualization of the spatial and discursive limits and possibilities confronting Chicana lesbians. A *sitio y lengua* announces a strategic reclamation and decolonization of modes of speaking determined by Chicanas (1994). The plural ambit of *sitios y lenguas* implies that in the work of identity politics—the assertion of Chicana and Chicana lesbian identities, and the venues and texts in which they are elaborated—will be defined by, and change according to, specific historical exigencies. Using French feminist Luce Irigaray's notion of the female symbolic, a psycho-identificatory realm in which women may come to voice without patriarchal intervention, Pérez (1994) argues that *sitios y lenguas* signify a Chicana disruption to the historical links between the territorial colonization of the land and the Chicano/a body, and between the Chicana body and the body of the Chicana text. The inherent mutability and multiplicity of *sitios y lenguas* also helps Pérez address what she calls the "common enemy" fallacy that, at times, has prevented Chicana lesbians from taking advantage of political coalitions whose ostensible aims may run counter to Chicana lesbian political projects. The fallacy posits that the agendas of white feminists and heterosexual Chicano men have hindered or directly opposed the coming-to-voice of Chicana lesbians. *Sitios y lenguas*, on the other hand, indicate that at times white feminists and heterosexual Chicanos can become allies of the Chicana lesbian in the distinct but overlapping struggles against patriarchy and racism. See **Oppositional Consciousness, Third World Feminism.**

Situational Alliances

The concept of situational alliances was proposed by Felix Padilla (1985) to describe new panethnic identifications and political affiliations, Latinismo or Hispanismo. Situational alliances are intimately related to, and predicated on, a pragmatically adopted panethnic consciousness (**Latinidad**) without which there can be no strategic construction of an "ethnic principle of organization." Padilla identifies two drives in the evolution of Latinismo and the formation of situational alliances: Latino ethnic identity (a shared sense of identification anchored in Spanish language facility); and Latino ethnic mobilization (interaction between two or more Latino/a groups enabled by their sense of panethnic identity). Although distinct Latino/a groups may come together over a particular issue in the neighborhood or city they share, the often pragmatic panethnic Latinismo enabling that mobilization does not override or diminish quotidian identifications based on national-origin or cultural affiliation.

Slavery

Slavery is the name for a sociopolitical and economic system or mode of production by and in which human workers, and the labor power they represent, are owned and exploited by a **class** of slave owners. In the slave system, slaves function as commodities and private property, with limited or no rights of say in their own social place, the uses to which their labor is put, or their capacity to reproduce. In some historical periods and cultures (Greece, Rome, the Ottoman Empire, China) slaves could and did attain positions of authority and power. Most slave systems also had protocols by which slave owners could grant freedom to the slaves they owned. As this history suggests, slavery has taken distinct forms over historical time and place. The modern era was characterized by, and in many respects founded upon, the enslavement of African and many indigenous peoples, and slavery was a hallmark of all imperial, colonial, and most national enterprises in the Americas between the sixteenth and the late nineteenth centuries. The complex networks of the slave trade spanning Europe, Africa, and the Americas have been designated the Black Atlantic. In the Caribbean, USA, Brazil, and coastal regions throughout Latin America, African slavery was introduced in order to provide a controllable work force, notably in the agricultural and mining sectors, and as domestic labor. Afro-Caribbean slaves, like their US counterparts, often worked in the plantation economy, harvesting and processing such crops as sugar, coffee, and tobacco. Figures are disputed, but historians claim that between 11 and 15 million Africans were brought to the Americas in the three-century period before slavery was abolished (Thomas 1997). Preceding the introduction of African slaves, however, indigenous peoples were also compelled into slavery, particularly in the first decades after the Spanish and Portuguese conquests. The campaign against African slavery—which initially involved European powers banning their merchants from engaging in the slave trade, rather than outlawing slave ownership itself—began in Europe in the late 1700s, a reflection of changing European ideals about the "rights of men." The declaration by ex-slaves of the Haitian Republic in 1804 after years of struggle against the French was an important event in the history of nation building in the Americas, and a sign that the slave system always enjoyed a precarious hegemony. The issue of slavery was an underlying factor in the American Civil War in the 1860s, the conflict in part stemming from disagreement about the desired national balance between slave-owning and nonslave-owning states. The victory of the Union meant that abolition was achieved in 1865, three years after the Emancipation Proclamation. However, practices of racial segregation nonetheless continued to marginalize and discriminate against African Americans until the civil rights era; many commentators insist that the legacies of slavery continue today. Although most of the new Latin American states abolished slavery in the 1810s and 1820s, Spain abolished the practice in its two remaining colonies much later (1873 in Puerto Rico and 1886 in Cuba), and Brazil did not emancipate its slaves until 1888. As a result of slavery, the African inheritance has deeply marked an array of American cultural and religious traditions (such as **santería**), music, cuisine, and idiom. See **Afro-Latino**.

Sleepy Lagoon

Sleepy Lagoon was the name of a popular swimming hole located near the Los Angeles River in southeastern Los Angeles (possibly Maywood), frequented in the early 1940s by Mexican Americans who were denied access to the city's swimming pools because of segregationist policies. The lagoon's name may derive from a popular big-band instrumental by Harry James from 1942. Sleepy Lagoon hit national headlines in August 1942, after the body of José Díaz was found at the site. Despite the absence of clear evidence that Mexican Americans were implicated in Díaz's death, some 300 Mexican American males, many from local gangs, were arrested by police in one of the most publicized criminal and legal cases in the city's history. Many of those arrested were brutally beaten up by the police, and evidence was doctored to suit the police case. In the subsequent trial, 12 Mexican Americans were convicted of murder, while another five were successfully tried for assault. The overt racism of the police and the judge presiding over the case led to the formation of the Sleepy Lagoon Defense Committee at the urging of the political activist Josefina Fierro de Bright. Led by Carey McWilliams, the committee lobbied for a retrial and fair legal process for the 17 convicted men. The committee was ultimately successful, and in October 1944 the US District Court of Appeals quashed the Sleepy Lagoon murder trial convictions. The case, and its aftermath, did much to convince Mexican Californians that they were the targets of a biased and corrupt justice system and of a hostile media, all of which regarded Mexican Americans as a criminal "outsider" sector. See **Zoot Suits**, **Zoot Suit Riots**.

Son

A popular Cuban vocal dance music with origins in European and Afro-Cuban musical traditions in the nineteenth century, the *son* has provided one of the historical bases for the neocultural Latino/a musical form of **salsa**, and influenced numerous other musical styles in Cuba and Latin America. Orovio (2004) notes that the *son* emerged out of the Afro-Cuban dance form, *guaracha*, in the suburbs of Cuba's eastern cities and towns. Originally played by sextets and septets using the standard instrumental line up of guitar or *tres, marímbula* (an African origin hand piano, made from a strip of wood to which metal strips are added), *güiro* (a percussion instrument made from a hollowed-out gourd) and *bongó* drums, larger outfits developed in the twentieth century and added new instruments to the repertoire. The influence of the recording industry, and the proliferation of dance venues, ensured that the *son*'s popularity was cemented by the early 1930s, and attracting audiences outside the island. The term *son* now functions as a cover-all for a wide range of musical styles that draw on *son* structures.

Spanglish

Spanglish, Espanglés—or any of its synonyms, *casteyanqui, ingleñol, argot sajón, español bastardo, papiamento gringo,* **caló**, Tex-Mex, **pocho, pachuco**—designates the many Spanish-English dialects spoken by many millions of Latino/as. Linguists, however, do not necessarily agree on what Spanglish might mean in day-to-day practice. Some critics use Spanglish to refer only to Latino/a dialects marked profoundly by borrowings or interference from English. These borrowings can range from specific words to sentences, and may be detectable in changing word order conventions, and a tendency to literally translate English into Spanish, or to pronounce English words as speakers would Spanish. Dialects that have at times been designated Spanglish include *caló*, Tex-Mex, *pachuco*, and Nuyorican Spanish. Other critics regard **code switching** between English and Spanish as the key feature of Spanglish. There is some agreement that Spanglish exists on an interlingual spectrum, with speakers shifting between a Spanish-dominant grammatical and vocabulary extreme and an English-dominant alternative. Spanglish emerges from one end of the spectrum, *ingleñol* (*inglañol*) from the other. The difference between *ingleñol* and Spanglish would thus appear to reside in the primary linguistic base on which speakers rely when communicating. English grammatical structures and ordering principles dominate *Ingleñol*, while Spanish structures predominate in Spanglish. Levels of code switching also conform to that spectrum, which is, furthermore, characterized by its mutability and fluidity, depending on the socioeconomic status and degrees of familiarity of the speakers involved, and the social contexts in which interactions take place. Spanglish is a highly contested and emotive topic of debate, particularly among Spanish language purists who decry the rise of Spanglish in the USA. Yale academic González Echevaría, for example, has routinely made public pronouncements about the need to protect the language of Cervantes from adulteration by English. Other critics dispute the purist argument. Stavans (2003), the self-proclaimed champion of Spanglish, regards Spanglish as a new language in formation. Morales (2002) proposes Spanglish (an informal, hybrid code) as an alternative for both **Hispanic** and Latino/a. These debates often take place outside the sites in which Spanglish is spoken and lived. Anzaldúa (1987) famously wrote that her Chicana identity was, in part, a product of multiple Chicano/a linguistic realities, and regarded her use of Spanglish and code switching as an unequivocally resistant political act. Negrón-Muntaner (1997) emphasizes that Puerto Rican practitioners of Spanglish are widely dismissed as "*tartamudos* [stammerers]" who cannot communicate in either "parent" language. Such arguments provide useful correctives to the symbiotic romanticization and demonization of Spanglish. Many Spanglish speakers are fluent in both English and Spanish. However, for many Latino/as whose first and only language is a form of Spanglish, their linguistic world reflects their socioeconomic status: limited, marginalized, lacking mobility, and unlikely to be valued or heard beyond their immediate communities.

Spanish–American War

Fought in 1898, the Spanish–American War (*La Guerra Hispano-Estadounidense*) resulted in the end of Spain's empire in the Americas, and the transfer to US control of Cuba and Puerto Rico, and in the western Pacific, Guam and the Philippines. Of those territories, Guam and Puerto Rico remain US colonial possessions. Although historians disagree over the immediate causes of the war, the independence movement in Cuba, and support for it among many US politicians and business leaders, and by the Cuban political-exile community, provided a political and economic context in which armed force could be contemplated by the US administration under president McKinley. Another factor was US access to and involvement in the Cuban sugar industry, the latter in recession in the 1890s. That recession coincided with renewed efforts on the part of the Cuban independence movement. The US popular press, including Randall Hearst's *New York Journal*, fuelled anti-Spanish sentiment in this period. The pretext for war occurred on February 15, 1898, when the US ship, the USS Maine, was blown up in Havana harbor with great loss of life. Historians debate whether or not the explosion was orchestrated by the Spanish, or by prointerventionist advocates in the USA who wanted a pretext for military action. US calls to Spain to grant Cuba its independence were ignored, and after the USA recognized Cuban independence on April 20, Spain reacted by declaring war on the USA on April 24, with the latter following suit on April 25. The fighting in Cuba, in particular, was almost immediately accorded mythic status, largely on account of press coverage of the Rough Riders, a mounted cavalry troop commanded by Theodore Roosevelt. The war was a short but bloody conflict fought in four theaters, the Spanish suffering a string of military defeats until a ceasefire went into effect on August 21, 1898. The Treaty of Paris (December 10, 1898) obliged Spain to cede its last overseas colonies to the USA. In Spain, the war became known as *El Desastre* (The Disaster), and generated deep discussion in elite and intellectual circles about Spain's fall from imperial power. Criticisms of US militarism were also heard in the USA, as exemplified by the American Anti-Imperialist League (whose members included Mark Twain). In January 1899, nationalists in the Philippines declared independence; a brutal suppression of the independence movement by the USA ended with the movement's defeat in 1902.

Spic

In operation since the first decades of the twentieth century, spic (spick, spik) is one of the oldest racist terms in the USA to designate and **stereotype** Latino/as. Spic might derive from the phrase "I no spik English," as Pedro Juan Soto suggests in the prologue to the fourth edition of his short story collection *Spiks* (1974 [1956]), one of the first literary texts to deal with Puerto Rican migration to the US northeast. That possible origin is also alluded to in the title of Chicano Alurista's poetry collection, *Spik in Glyph?* (1981). Alternatively, spic might be an acronym of Spanish, Indian, and Colored, a contraction of Hispanic, or a variant of spig, an old New York City euphemism for an Italian. Recent variations of spic reflect popular, and often racist, reactions to panethnic or cross-racial **Latinidades**, especially in cities such as New York. Examples include spickaboo (mixed Mexican and African American heritage, from spic and jigaboo); spigger (Latino and African American heritage, from spic and nigger); spink (Latino/a and Chinese heritage, from spik and chink); Euro-spic (European and Latino/a heritage); and spizzician (possibly Nuyorican/Latino and Guatemalan mixed heritage). As indicated by John Leguizamo's off-broadway play, *Spic-O-Rama* (1992), spic has also been subject to parodic reclamations in the work of some cultural workers.

Stereotype

A stereotype is conventionally defined as any clichéd, reductive, negative, or demeaning representation of a group of people on the basis of that group's purported national origins, or ethnic, racial, class, gender, and sexual appearances or qualities. The media production and circulation of stock Latino/a or Hispanic types has a long history and has contributed to the widespread viewpoint that Latino/as comprise an alien sector. This viewpoint may encapsulate the fear that the USA is about to be swamped or taken over by "the brown tide rising" (Santa Ana 2002) or the Latino/a "sleeping giant" (Noriega 1993). The representations of Latino/as in films, media, literary texts, historical accounts, political and legal discourses, daily speeches, and the national imagination itself, has resulted in a stock set of Latino/a types: the overly sexualized Latino/a; the lazy greaser; the Mexican *campesino*, often shown in film sleeping under a brightly colored blanket against a cactus or saloon wall; the untrustworthy and unwashed bandit; the drug runner; the gang member; the "illegal alien"; and, the idea that Latino/as form a unitary constituency that can be targeted, exploited, and even researched. Such stock types reflect pervasive and long-standing attitudes toward Latin Americans, which may have historical roots in the **Black Legend**. The production and circulation of "Latin" types has been called **tropicalizations** (Aparicio and Chávez-Silverman 1997), savagism (A. Aldama 2001), the negative troping of Native Americans, Chicano/as, and Mexican immigrants alike, and Latinism (Berg 2002). Evoking the operations of Orientalism (Said 1978), Latinism denotes a discursive system anchored in US imperial constructions of Latin America as a territory to be conquered, exploited, or otherwise treated as worthy of intervention. Encapsulated in the doctrines of **Monroe Doctrine** and **Manifest Destiny**, Latinism does not permit Latin American peoples to contest the idea that the American hemisphere is a US sphere of influence. For Ramírez Berg, the US film apparatus based in Hollywood has, since its inception, endorsed this notion of the US-dominated Americas, and transferred and perpetuated it into the realm of popular visual culture in the twentieth century. Latinism underwrites many film genres: the **Western**; the border narrative that regards

Chicano/as as a marginal social problem; and science fiction, a rich source of narratives about "alien" invasion and threat that can be read as allegories of "Hispanic" immigration. Challenging the cultural production and perpetuation of such ideas has been a hallmark of much Latino/a cultural praxis. The pervasiveness of Latino/a stereotypes is also exemplified by the many offensive euphemisms for Latino/as circulating in colloquial speech: bean eater, beaner, bean burner, border bunny, border hopper, burrito head, coat (signifying that Latinos don perfume rather than bathe regularly), dry-waller (reflecting the view that all Latino/as are construction workers), fencehopper, fob (fresh off the boat, applied to Cubans, Haitians, and Asian Americans), fruit picker, gardener, gravel-belly (border crosser), **greaser**, latrino (Latino + latrine), nacho, orange picker, scratchback (border crosser), sexican (alluding to the Mexican-origin population's purportedly high birth rate), **spic**, taco bender, tomato picker, and wetback (**mojado**). This string of terms confirms the extent to which the US popular imagination reinforces a homogenizing conceptualization of Latino/as as a border-crossing, and therefore illegitimate, sector in national terms.

Subaltern, Subalternity, Subaltern Studies

Highly influential in postcolonial, Latin American, and Latino/a Studies since the 1980s, subaltern studies refers to a methodological and discursive practice that arose with the Indian Subaltern Studies collective in the 1970s and 1980s, and that inspired the formation of the Latin American Subaltern Studies Group (LASSG) in 1990 (disbanded 2000). The concept subaltern—originally a British military term for anyone of low rank—derives from Gramsci (1971), for whom it signified the general condition of sociopolitical subordination. In Gramsci's "Notes on Italian History," a series of essays written between 1929 and 1935 while he was in prison under the Italian Fascist regime, he argued that the question of subaltern agency and resistance was intimately connected to the operations of the geopolitical state, in his case Italy. Therefore, analysis of hegemonic political structures must attend to subaltern sectors' relations to modes of production and state political institutions in order to assess subaltern political agency and their contributions to the maintenance of the national order. Building from Gramsci's arguments, Guha (1988) defined the subaltern as any social player of low social status in India, and subalternity as a condition of subordination registered along lines of "class, caste, age, gender and office." Indian subaltern studies aimed to read against the grain of historiographical works, bureaucratic, legal, and government documents, print media, literary texts, and other records in order to register the subaltern's presence, function, and potential influence in, and resistance to, processes of domination and subordination. The issue of subaltern voice is crucial to this desired quest. Spivak (1988) argues that the subaltern per se is denied both agency and history, but the female subaltern is further silenced because of patriarchal ideology. Nonetheless, Spivak implies that once the subaltern speaks or her agency heeded, she is no longer a synonym for subordination, powerlessness, and absence. Spivak further argues that critics and intellectuals must recognize their role in the construction of subaltern powerlessness. Building on these approaches, the LASSG (1993) moved away from Gramsci's emphasis on the state and toward multiple racialized, gendered, and geospatial understandings of Latin American peoples not beholden to national organizations of continental space. The LASSG aimed to search for the subaltern agent in the fissures between states and state institutions where **globalization** influences local lives (LASSG 1993; I. Rodríguez 2001). The LASSG also regarded the literary text as an ideological form used to disseminate elite national ideals in Latin America. In Latino/a Studies, Aparicio and Chávez Silverman (1997) acknowledge LASSG reservations about the literary emphasis of standard transcultural discourse in their work on **tropicalizations**. José Saldívar (1997) defines the nineteenth-century Mexican American writer María Amparo Ruiz de Burton as a "subaltern mediator" and "insurgent critic" of Anglo-American historiography and capitalism in the decades after the US takeover of California. This reading, however, glosses over Ruiz de Burton's elite distance from the Mexican origin subjects who labored for and around her. Noting similar critical inconsistencies in the LASSG's project, Gareth Williams (2002) argues that the LASSG's project replicates the center (self-identity, knowledge) versus periphery (difference) logics of First World intellectual practice, while fetishizing the subaltern as an abstract and redemptive subject. Mallon (1994) points out that the focus on the problem of subaltern voicelessness glosses over the fact that subalterns are not invariably subordinate, and that subaltern relations to structures of domination are neither clearly graspable nor unchanging. Mignolo (2000) argues that the LASSG project remains imbricated in a tired disciplinary struggle within the US academy (for instance, between area, cultural, and historiographical studies), and thus fails to manage the epistemological shift to a genuinely "post-Occidental" or "post-traditional" criticism, or what Mignolo calls "border gnosis." Such criticism would heed subaltern "loci of enunciation" or speaking venues and **borderlands** knowledges emerging in the interstices of empires, globalizing imperatives, and academic disciplines.

Syncretism

A term that arose in comparative religious studies, and that has been taken up in anthropological discourse, as well as in performance and other branches of cultural studies, syncretism connotes the binding together and intermingling in new forms of distinct religious or cultural practices. Traditional approaches to syncretism tended to examine religious interactions in terms of fixed religious norms or conventions and the historical changes to those norms. The post-structuralist turn in many disciplines since the 1970s transformed critical approaches to religious change and cultural contamination, with the result that critics of syncretism began to attend to questions of power, mutual transformation, and the inevitable fluidity and transcultural worldliness and mutability of religious traditions. Syncretism in this guise thus parallels the notions of cultural **hybridity** and **creolization.** In the Americas, syncretism has been applied to the many popular forms of Catholicism that emerged in the wake of Spanish and Portuguese colonization. In Mexico, for example, pre-Columbian rituals, practices, and worldviews adapted to, and were incorporated in, a Catholic schema, two syncretic examples being the ritual celebrations of *El día de los muertos* (Day of the Dead) and the *quinceañera*.

T

Taíno

Taíno is the name for a group of Caribbean peoples, the first in the Americas to experience the arrival, and subsequent colonization, of the Spanish. Rouse (1992) distinguishes the Taínos from the Arawaks, and identifies Taínos as the predominant indigenous group in the Bahamas, all but the western section of Cuba (where the Guanahatabey resided), the Greater Antilles, and much of the Lesser Antilles. Rouse further differentiates the western Taínos (Bahamas, Cuba, Hispaniola, Jamaica, Puerto Rico) from the eastern Taínos (Lesser Antilles), the latter separated from the Arawaks to the south by the island Caribs. Taíno resistance to the Spanish was met by violent reprisals. European diseases killed many thousands, as did enslavement in goldmines and sugar cane plantations (introduced in 1515). Historical records nonetheless confirm that the Spanish assimilated Taíno women into the colonial system through intermarriage, and the practice continued after the introduction of African slaves, thus ensuring that many Caribbean people today can claim some indigenous ancestry. In the second half of the twentieth century a revival of interest in the Taíno inheritance occurred throughout the Caribbean, accompanied by the establishment of numerous organizations dedicated to reviving Taíno traditions, addressing the historical record to account for Taíno survival, and forging links with other indigenous peoples in the Americas. Cultural nationalist movements in Puerto Rico (**Borinquén**) and the Dominican Republic (**Quisqueya**) also resuscitated Taíno names for the islands as alternatives for the nation and people (Haslip-Viera 2001). Juan Flores (1993) points out that despite the recuperation of the Afro-Puerto Rican cultural base in such revisionist studies as José Luis González's 1980 *El país de cuatro pisos* (1989), that text neglected the Taíno foundational base in island culture. Dávila (1997) demonstrates that folkloric uses of the Taíno have occurred since the 1940s, as exemplified by the use of Taíno "princesses" and "chieftains" in island beauty pageants, fiestas, and historical celebrations. These popular appropriations serve what Dávila calls the project of "*haciendo patria*, or helping to forge and strengthen the nation" in opposition to US cultural pressures. This cultural drive nonetheless generates its own racialized hierarchy of cultural values, from white Hispanic down through brown Taíno to the least acceptable black African base. Popular cultural uses of the Taíno, moreover, may not address the historical material interrelationships between indigenous, African, and European peoples in terms of mutually affective transculturations that mean there can be no authentic Taíno at the heart of contemporary Puerto Rican culture (Dávila 1997). That said, popular cultural references to the Taínos and Arawaks reflect a widespread belief that those terms encode a sense of indigenous resilience and survival, and provide nominal alternatives for Puerto Rican. In the diaspora, too, that usage is commonplace. For example, Taíno (and Arawak) punctuate the lyrics of Nuyorican rap and hip-hop artists, and Carmen Rivera's 2002 play, "La gringa," grounds Nuyorican identity in the Taíno base.

Teatro Campesino

El Teatro Campesino (ETC, Farm Workers' Theater) was founded by the Chicano playwright Luis Valdez in 1965. As part of the United Farm Workers union that was based in Delano, California, from 1965 to 1968 ETC worked as a collective under Valdez's direction to raise awareness of and funds for the Delano Grape Strike. The ensemble's plays, part of a broader 1960s movement in "social protest theater" (Elam 1997), were delivered in fields and streets from the back of trucks, as well as in more formal settings in theaters and university campuses. The group also toured across the USA and Europe. In 1970 ETC established itself in San Juan Bautista, California, where it continues to produce plays, and, since 1980, films as well. ETC utilized a range of performative traditions, both popular and modernist, in order to mobilize audience members into political action. Broyles-González (1994) argues that ETC's stylistic approach to theatrical production was indebted to a range of Mexican oral and popular cultural traditions, thus emphasizing historical and cultural connections across the US–Mexico border. In its heyday from 1965 to 1980, ETC focused on producing improvised *actos*, or short one-act plays, derived from the *commedia dell'arte* (an Italian theatrical tradition based on improvization, parody, and satire, which was brought to the Americas by the Spanish), and influenced by the Mexican *carpa* (itinerant tent) tradition (Huerta 2000; Valdez 1971, 1990). ETC's *actos* were readily adaptable; with few props and resources they could be performed from the back of trucks or in the fields to workers, with the aim of exposing the structural exploitation of agricultural laborers and promoting union resistance to agricultural employers (Broyles-González 1994). Luis Valdez (1971) argued that ETC conjoined Mexican popular cultural sensibilities and a modernist notion of theatrical alienation derived from the German playwright Bertolt Brecht. Out of this mix ETC developed its own cultural political aesthetic, *rasquachismo*. This involved the intermixing and unexpected juxtaposition of acrobatics, improvisational and mime work, poetry, Mexican puppetry, folk theater, live and prerecorded music, singing, slapstick, chanting, and, at script level, **code switching** and **Spanglish** (Broyles-González 1994). Assessing ETC's theatrical influence, Broyles-González (1994) argues that the ensemble did not leave an enduring political aesthetic legacy due to the appropriation of ETC by Chicano patriarchal structures. ETC's contributions to Chicano/a civil rights struggles were reduced in the critical and popular imagination to the history of the group's founder, Luis Valdez. Women's contributions, and the ensemble emphasis on a democratic collectivity, have thus been discounted, disowned, or obscured. Nonetheless, it is arguable that ETC's performance aesthetic continues to shadow the work of such political performance groups as Chicano Secret Service (Los Angeles), Culture Clash (San Francisco), and the Taco Shop Poets (San Diego), and of performers such as Luis Alfaro, Nao Bustamante, and Monica Palacios.

Tejano/a, Tejano Music, Tex-Mex

Tejano/a is a Texan of Mexican background. The term, and its synonym Tex-Mex, may be used as a local identity marker, or a cover all for Texan Mexican language uses, cuisine, and cultural practices. *Tejano* also designates an array of music styles and genres that either emanated from, or became popular in, Texas in the 1980s and 1990s. *Tejano* represents a linguistic modulation of the Spanish *música tejana*, and encodes within it a sense of Texan American

cultural pride and aspiration, and a regional cultural habitus forged in contradistinction to Mexican, European American, and Chicano/a imaginaries. The
evolving Tejano or Tex-Mex sound has also been called *la Onda chicana* (the
Chicano wave), *la Onda tejana* (the Texan wave), and **brown** soul (Burr 1999).
Tejano fused traditional genres such as *corrido, ranchera,* and *conjunto,* with
pop and rock sounds and instruments, and Latin American genres (*cumbia,
salsa*). Tejano's rise to musical hegemony resulted from the increasing commercialization of the Mexican American music industry in centers such as San
Antonio in the mid-1980s (Mayer 2003; San Miguel 2002). That trend helped
groups and singers gain wider audiences, facilitated the distribution of recordings, and generated a star system. The commercialization of Tejano also coincided with what Manuel Peña calls the rise of a post-Chicano/a consumer
generation attuned to the logics of late US capitalism, detached from the
Chicano Movement's political drives and a sense of Mexican American history,
and sharing nontraditional musical and cultural tastes (1999b). While *Onda
chicana* groups such as El Grupo Mazz (formed in 1977) are credited with
being among the first ensembles to break from tradition by using synthesizers
and electronic instruments, La Mafia was the first *Tejano* outfit to gain international success, assisted by its use of pop-rock stage effects. The biggest selling and most popular *Tejano* star, however, was Selena, who had a string of hits
after the success of her first album, *Selena y los Dinos* in 1989. Selena's
celebrity status and her plans to cross over into the US pop market were curtailed when she was murdered on March 31, 1995, by the manager of the
Selena clothing chain. Her grave is now a site of memorialization and pilgrimage. Her life, and the corporate construction of Selena as the Tex-Mex
bombshell, provided the basis of *Selena* (1997, dir. Michael Nava), which
introduced Nuyorican actor Jennifer López to a wide audience.

Telenovela

Alongside music, the *telenovela* or soap opera is one of the most important
Latin American popular cultural forms, one that now attracts millions of viewers in the USA. The *telenovela,* or televised novel, is a hybrid genre, and it is
also a neocultural one. A descendant of early US television and radio soap
opera and the serial novel (*folletín*), the *telenovela* emerged in the mid-1960s
(from Mexico to Brazil), and now crosses back into the USA via Spanish-
language television stations. Unlike soap operas from the Anglophone world,

which can be screened for years without ending, *telenovelas* do end and rigorous conventions apply to fashioning *telenovela* plots in a finite number of episodes. Perhaps more overtly than the Anglophone soap opera, the *telenovela* deploys a stock-set of melodramatic narrative devices: financial and blood inheritances, transclass mobilities achieved through love affairs or marriage, doubtful paternities, identity secrets, crimes of the home and family, the operations of chance and fate, moral struggles between the forces of good and evil, and the reuniting of long-lost family members. The loyal spectatorship for *telenovelas* in the Americas has troubled some critics, who regard the genre as a mode produced by a capitalist media apparatus with the intention of providing the **subaltern** and working classes with a daily dose of televisual escape from quotidian despair, poverty, and powerlessness. Other critics argue that the *telenovela* affords the poor and the oppressed pleasurable insights into the unattainable world of money and power. That pleasure can also include delight at observing the suffering of the elite, *Los ricos también lloran* (The Rich Also Cry) being a typical example. Rowe and Schelling (1991) argue that over and beyond the pleasure afforded by the genre's melodramatic plots, the *telenovela* genre encodes within itself, and thus permits viewers to take a stand on, the **race**, **class**, and **gender** conflicts that animate the genre. Most *telenovelas* come from Mexico, Brazil, Venezuela, Argentina, and Colombia. The globalization of the *telenovela* industry thus means that *telenovelas* are shown across Latin America in each regional market, as well as in many other countries in translation (with subtitles or dubbing), in addition, the market reach of the Univisión and Telemundo networks ensures that *telenovelas* are shown throughout the USA. The industry's success in no small part derives from the convention of developing and selling stock formats and packages to distinct markets, and the generation of a superstar system of actors. At the same time, *telenovelas* continue to reflect local concerns, as is evident in Mexican *telenovelas*, in which the immigrant worker or the returned *mojado* are regular character types. A significant example is the character played by Erik Estrada of *CHIPS* fame in *Dos mujeres y un camino* (Two Women, One Road), from 1993. A recent trend is the rise of Miami as a site of *telenovela* production. At times, the success of *telenovelas* depends on the large US audience. For example, *Ramona*, which was produced by Televisa, was a failure in Mexico, but a huge success in the USA when aired on Univisión in early 2001. *Ramona* was an adaptation of Helen Hunt Jackson's 1884 novel of the same name. The Cuban intellectual and independence activist José Martí translated the novel into Spanish in 1887, describing it as "our novel" on account of its criticisms of US government policy toward Native Americans, and its laying bare of the racism that underpinned Anglo and Indian relations. *Ramona*'s televisual treatment of race relations resonated for Latino/as in ways that did not to audiences south of the border.

Testimonio, Testimonial

The *testimonio* (testimonial) is a Latin American narrative genre that emerged in the wake of the Cuban Revolution as a political medium for recording, presenting and circulating the life stories and experiences of **subaltern** or socially marginalized subjects. *Testimonios* have been written by Indian, working class, and peasant subjects, political prisoners, and torture victims. Most critics attribute the continental popularity of the genre to the decision by the Cuban Casa de las Américas to introduce the *testimonio* as a prize category in its annual literary contest for Latin American writing in 1970. The *testimonio* normally takes the form of a narrative that relays in the first person the life story of the protagonist or historical witness (Beverley 1993). The production of *testimonios* is often a collective process involving a second party who may record and transcribe a particular testimony and rearrange, modify, and mediate the result in the passage to publication. The testimonial genre is a broad categorization that may include, draw upon, or overlap with the concerns and conventions of many other genres, from the memoir and autobiography, to confession, oral history, and the nonfiction or "factual" novel. That generic complexity and fluidity, and the oral origins and mediated production of many *testimonios*, accords the genre an alternative literary status that defies definitional fixing and normalization by literary critics (Beverley 1993). The Guatemalan Rigoberta Menchú's *Me llamo Rigoberto Menchú y así me nació la conciencia* (1982) is the best known *testimonio*, and continues to center debates about the textual mediation of subaltern voices, the textual viability of subaltern resistances, and the victory of truth and authenticity over fiction and fabrication often attributed to the genre (Gugelberger 1996). In Latino/a literary production, the *testimonio* has also been an important genre. John Rechy's *The Sexual Outlaw: A Documentary* (1977) is considered by some critics to fall under the *testimonio* rubric, although the text was not mediated by a transcriber. For many Latinas, the *testimonio* genre has functioned as a mode by which women's neglected life stories and experiences could enter the realm of representation (Latina Feminist Group 2001; Moraga and Anzaldúa 1983). Moreover, as Rosaura Sánchez (1995) demonstrates, early testimonial-like texts written by Mexican Californians survive as a rich repository of responses to Anglo-American territorial consolidation, and to relations between Anglos, Mexicans, and Native Americans, after the **Mexican–American War.**

Texas Rangers, *Rinches*

Texas Rangers (*los rinches* or *los diablos tejanos,* or Texan devils) were a mounted militia formed in 1823 by Stephen Austin, a leader of Anglo-American settlement in Mexico's Texan province. With the declaration of Texan independence in March 1836, the Texas Rangers were deployed in the war with Mexico that followed. After 1836 the Rangers functioned as a quasipolice and **Border Patrol** militia (apprehending bandits and horse and cattle thieves, protecting ranch property), and were feared and despised by Mexicans and Native Americans for their violence and extralegal powers. Briefly disbanded after the American Civil War, the Rangers were re-formed in 1874 and in the following decades their reputation for violence was recorded in numerous *corridos,* which often rhyme *rinche* with *pinche* (damned). In the twentieth century, the Rangers enacted periodic clampdowns on local communities and undocumented immigrants, and at times attempted to stop Mexican Americans from holding political meetings, forming unions, or voting. Among Anglo-Texans, the Rangers have been mythologized as embodiments of heroic Texan values (Samora et al. 1979). The Rangers now serve as an elite detective agency in the Texan law enforcement apparatus (R. Castro 2001).

Third World Feminism, Women of Color Movement

The Third World Feminist or Women of Color Movement emerged as a significant US feminist enterprise in the 1970s and 1980s among women from diverse communities. Third World Feminism aimed to counteract a history of racial and ethnic marginalization and discrimination in a national historical setting, challenge male domination in their own communities (*carnalismo,* **machismo**), and dispute white and middle-class hegemony in feminist activism and theory. This tripartite concern reflected how various groups of women, marginalized or Third World-ized within the USA because of their race or ethnicity, regarded dominant feminist theories and movements, and specific civil rights drives, as having silenced women of color. In response, these women advocated the importance of speaking for and about themselves and their aspirations. The central motivation of Third World Feminism was a fundamental disagreement with the dominant feminist modes in the USA. Liberal feminism, the most widespread form, argued on an equal rights platform anchored in a humanist tradition for gender justice, and sexual equality in legal, educational, and other institutional structures. Marxist feminists linked women's oppression to class oppression, hence women's liberation would follow the overthrow of capitalism. Radical feminists argued that women's oppression has been the most fundamental form of oppression in history and in all cultures, hence the universal policing by men of reproduction and mothering, and the male control of women's sexuality and bodies. Those relations of reproduction thus need to be dismantled, a move to be achieved, some proponents argued, by removing women from male-dominated societies or eliminating the handicap of women's reproductive capacity. Socialist feminism proposed that patriarchy and capitalism intersect, producing the double oppression of women, hence the need for a bidirectional political struggle for women's liberation. For Chela Sandoval, these distinct feminist enterprises formed a totalized feminist system in which the woman of color was rendered invisible and silenced (1991, 2000). Third World feminists argued that such feminisms conceived of "woman" as implicitly Western, middle class, and white, in an uncanny parallel of the way that European "man" has functioned in Western societies as the model for the universal subject, a synonym for human. At the same time, feminists of color refused to become the teachers of white women, the ones who would show white women how their worldviews might be racist, and how to overcome this racism (Moraga and Anzaldúa 1983). One of the hallmarks of Third World Feminism was a commitment to publishing women's texts, critical and creative, outside mainstream and white feminist institutions. Such publishing ventures have contributed to the increased visibility of, and readership for, writings by women of color since the 1970s (Saldívar-Hull 2000). Third World Feminism altered the terrains of feminist debates by showing how feminisms are damaged by a failure to attend to racism and racializing protocols. Third World Feminism also showed that women of color had to come to terms with two patriarchies in a struggle against multiple levels of oppression: white, Anglo-American patriarchy and the patriarchal structures of their own communities. African American (Barbara Johnson, Audre Lorde, bell hooks) and Chicana strands (Gloria Anzaldúa, Cherríe Moraga, Norma Alarcón,

Chela Sandoval) were particularly influential in the identity debates of their own communities. Chela Sandoval's **oppositional consciousness** represents one of the most sophisticated theories of Third World feminism. In addition, Chicanas such as Moraga (1983), Anzaldúa (1987), and other writer-activists, impelled post-**Chicano Movement** debates to address the issues of gender and sexuality, in the process contributing to the rise of Chicano/a queer discourse.

Tortillera

The term *tortillera* is a euphemism, and at times an insult, for a lesbian in Mexican, Chicano/a, Caribbean, and other Hispanophone cultures. The word's metaphoric significance also shifts depending on the location and local Spanish idiom. For Chicano/as, Mexicans, and Central Americans, *tortillera* refers to the maker or kneader of *tortillas* (the flat cornflour patties eaten at most meals). In Cuba, a *tortillera* is the person who beats the eggs for a scrambled eggs dish. In Spain, a *tortillera* is the person who prepares the potato omelet. The term has been subject to a queer reclamation by Latina lesbian writers, performers, and artists (Torres and Pertusa 2003).

Transculturation

Transculturation is an influential Latin American critical discourse increasingly used to theorize Latino/a cultures. In Anglophone cultural and postcolonial criticism, however, transculturation has often been regarded simply as a synonym for cultural **hybridity** or *mestizaje*, and the discourse's evolution and divergent applications are not widely understood, perhaps due to the fact that some of the key transcultural texts have not been translated into English. Transculturation was first proposed by Fernando Ortiz in *Contrapunteo Cubana del tabaco y azúcar* (1940a, 1995) as a way of explaining the history of reciprocal cross-cultural adaptation between African and European peoples in Cuba. Unhappy with the unidirectional connotations of the term acculturation, Ortiz proposed a schema of three contrapuntal processes: *acculturation* or cultural acquisition; *deculturation*, or partial cultural destruction, uprooting, and loss; and *neoculturation* or the emergence of "new cultural phenomena." The tripartite processes of transculturation functioned according to a reproductive and heteronormative logic by which transcultural progeny retain traces of both parent cultures, in the Cuban case, European and African, while being assimilable into neither of them. Ortiz elaborated on these ideas (which appear in a short analytical "interruption" to his study) as and in a narrative mode, characterized by thick description, the contrapuntal interplay between the sugar (whiteness) and tobacco (blackness) metaphors, vivid historical contextualization, and a language marked by local Cuban idiom. The result was a work of theory done by narrative example, a new approach to anthropological, historical, and cultural analysis. Subsequent Cuban critics, such as Nancy Morejón (1982), built on Ortiz to argue that, however unequal and rent by power struggles, transcultural interactions involve processes of reciprocal influence in which no single element or group can fully supersede or overdetermine others: "Ninguno permanece inmutable" (none remain unchanged). After 1940, the discourse of transculturation attracted critics elsewhere in Latin America. The Uruguayan Angel Rama (1981, 1997) applied transculturation to literary texts associated with the Boom in Latin American writing. For Rama, transculturation explained why many Latin American writers had adopted a selective and inventive approach to European narrative genres and philosophical discourses, and language uses championed by national elites, in order to find new ways of representing, and coming to terms with, the processes that had shaped Latin American societies and cultures. Influenced as well by the Peruvian writer and ethnographer of Andean *mestizo* transculturation, José María Arguedas, Rama proposed transculturation as an analytical mode not beholden to "imposed," fixed, or unified literary, philosophical, and cultural ideals. Latin American writers were constructing local literary canons and modes that required transcultural reading practices. Mignolo (1995) describes Rama's approach as a "pluritopic hermeneutics," a radical reordering of the circuits of knowledge production based on the construction of multiple "loci of enunciation" or speaking positions. For many critics, Rama's transcultural discourse provided a radical bi- or multifocal model by which to deal with what Spitta (1995) calls the challenge posed by the intermixing of languages, cosmologies, epistemologies, cultural traditions, and signifying systems at messy work in the Americas as a result of conquest and colonialism. The first significant adaptation of transculturation to Anglophone terrains was Mary Pratt's *Imperial Eyes* (1992), in which she introduced the notion of the contact zone. Pratt drew on the use of contact in linguistics, where a contact language describes a hybrid, impromptu, and pragmatic idiom (a pidgin or creole) that develops along trading routes and in trade centers in order to enable people to surmount language barriers and facilitate economic and social transactions (Duranti 2001). Pratt conjoined this understanding of contact with transculturation in order to recognize in the contact zone "perspective" the ways by which "subjects are constituted in and by their relations to each other" in terms of mutually transformative, but hierarchized, historical encounters, intersections, and power struggles. Silvia Spitta approaches transcultural discourse from a feminist angle in order to overcome the gender limits of Ortiz's original formulation, and Rama's adaptations of it. Since transculturation in the Americas was inaugurated by the violation of indigenous women by European men, critical transculturation must recognize and confront the gendered vectors of power that pass unremarked in, and thus overburden, the cultural discourses of *mestizaje* and hybridity. The appearance of transcultural discourse in Latino/a studies has posed the challenge of how the discourse might adapt to Latino/a and US historical and sociocultural conditions. Spitta (1995) points out that some US deployments of transculturation have aimed to reconceive national (USA) and regional (Caribbean) imaginaries in broader continental frameworks. These adaptations include Benítez-Rojo's (1996) account of Caribbean transculturation as postmodernist disorder and chaos, and Pérez Firmat's (1989) approach to Cuban transculturation as an intralingual "translation sensibility," rather than a process of uneasy accommodation between African and Spanish peoples. Critical transculturations necessarily require contextual adjustments to account for the border and immigrant discourses that frame the national place and reception of Latino/as (Allatson 2002). Acknowledging those adjustments underwrites Aparicio and Chávez-Silverman's (1997) concept of **tropicalizations**. Sandoval-Sánchez and Saporta Sternbach (2001) return to the Cuban critic Nancy Morejón in theorizing a **cultural politics** of transcultural identity, location, and affinity. Morejón adjusted transcultural discourse in the 1970s and 1980s to account for the subject positions of Afro-Cuban women, hence her use of terms such as **subaltern** and *nueva sexualidad* (new sexuality), and her discussions of the mutability and fluidity of transcultural identities. Building on Morejón, Sandoval-Sánchez and Saporta Sternbach's "discursive transculturation" describes the performative variables and multiple historical and ideological contexts in which Latino/as negotiate discourses of ethnic, gender, and sexual identity. Transculturation has not been within its critics. Larsen (1990) cautions that critics such as Rama often assumed the cultural autonomy and agency of writers without acknowledging differential locations within modes of production and consumption regulated or tolerated by the state. Beverley (1999)

regards transculturation (and mestizaje, hybridity) as a fantasy of reconciliation between racial, gender, and class equals. However, that argument does not
credit Ortiz's recognition of the genocidal and violent forms that transculturation can take, exemplified by Ortiz's description of the fate of Cuba's native
people during the Spanish conquest as a "failed transculturation."

Transnationality, Translocalism, Transmigration

Transnationality is a term with wide currency in a number of disciplines: anthropology and ethnography, geography, political science, international studies,
globalization studies, **migration** studies, and Latino/a Studies. Transnationality
may refer to the international movement of people across state borders and
the migrant negotiation of a split time and place in which emerge new social
fields, networks, and cultural formations across geopolitical borders, and in
two or more languages. This understanding of transnationality is also at times
called translocalism or translocality, by which migrants establish tight local
communities—transnational or transmigrant communities—in the host society, with abiding links to home. Transnational migration may be regarded as
symptomatic of, or a response to, the forces of global capitalism and **globalization**. That is, in the current globalized epoch, migratory trajectories and
patterns of adaptation are not conforming to previous epochs. Allied to this
approach, the rise of nongovernment organizations or NGOs is often regarded
as a transnational phenomenon, as is sex tourism (Jeffreys 1999), and the
emergence, and increasing acceptance by states, of dual or multiple citizenship
(Kivisto 2001). Other critics regard the concept of transnationality as encoding a will to transcend unitary and limiting conceptions of either the **nation** or
the state (the postnational), or culture regarded in autochthonous (native or
home grown) and statist terms. Finally, transnationalism may be used simply
as a synonym for globalization itself. Complicating these approaches are debates
about whether or not transnational identities, communities, and processes are
impelled by external forces (from above), or arise in reaction to those forces
(from below). Some commentators question the newness of contemporary
migration patterns and investigate the extent to which those patterns conform
to and depart from previous epochs. Despite disagreement over what the term
signifies, transnationality designates a range of possible inter- and supranational
sociocultural, economic, and identity-forming phenomena, with varying degrees
of overlap and connection. Many critics assert that the rise of transnational

imaginaries among Latino/a communities has been a hallmark of Latin American immigration since the 1960s, while noting that the phenomenon has earlier precedents. Mexican transnational identifications were inaugurated by the US victory in the **Mexican–American War** (1846–1848), and the subsequent treaty acquisition by the USA of Mexico's northern half, which divided Mexican Americans from Mexico. Mexican American culture has since been marked by close relations and cultural interchange between communities on either side of the border (R. Saldívar 2006). Terms such as **Greater Mexico,** *México de Afuera, México lindo, México del Norte,* and *El otro México* reflect identifications that span geopolitical states. Similarly, Poyo (1989) has pointed out that a sense of *Cubanidad* marked by transnational emplacements emerged among Cuban nationalist **exiles** in the USA in the second half of the 1800s. Since the **Great Migration** of Puerto Ricans, the Puerto Rican diaspora has also conformed to the fluid logics and imaginaries of transnational connection and displacement. The increasing transnationalization of Latino/a communities since the 1980s has been identified in such phenomena as the **remittance** economy, **Hometown Associations** and *Comunidades satélites* (Satellite Communities), and *maras* (transnational **gangs**). For example, *Oaxacalifornia/n* is the name adopted by the Californian communities of Mixtecs, indigenous Mexicans from Oaxaca, that were established in the late twentieth century by the thousands of Mixtec seasonal laborers in the farming sector (J. Cohen 2001). While replicating the social structures of the migrants' home communities, these social formations also confirm the Mixtecs' creative adjustment to multidirectional familial and communal links, their adoption of new communication modes such as the internet, and their pragmatic adaptation to the US host society. Another example is the rise of Iony (from the popular car-sticker and tourism slogan, "I ♥ New York") in Ecuador since the late 1980s to designate migrants who returned after working in the USA, and who were regarded as having been "Americanized." The term is also applied to Ecuadorian residents of New York City. Transnational imaginaries may also derive from, or be influenced by, the increasing global traffic in commodities and cultural goods, as exemplified by the constant interactions and hybridizations of Latin American music forms. That traffic has meant that already transcultural styles (*bachata, corrido, reggaetón, rock en español,* salsa) quickly reach international audiences, find new practitioners, and evolve into new forms, assisted by the global mass media.

Treaty of Guadalupe Hidalgo

Officially called the "Treaty of Peace, Friendship, Limits, and Settlement between the United States of America and the United Mexican States," the Treaty of Guadalupe Hidalgo concluded the **Mexican–American War** of 1846–1848. Ratified by the administration of president Polk, and proclaimed on July 4, 1848, the treaty consisted of 23 articles, and was prefaced with a stated desire for Mexico and the USA to coexist as "good neighbours." Among the significant provisions was Article V, which established the Rio Grande as the boundary between Mexico and Texas, with the border extending westward from El Paso to San Diego on the Pacific coast. The new border transferred Mexico's northern half to US control. Article VIII gave the Mexican population of these territories the right to return to Mexico or remain as US citizens, with one year in which to make that decision. Some 80,000 Mexicans were affected by the treaty, but only 3,000 relocated to Mexico (Tatum 2001). Article IX granted to the Mexican nationals who stayed the same rights as enjoyed by extant US citizens. Article XI dealt with the problem posed by "savage tribes," with both governments agreeing to "forcibly restrain" incursions by Native peoples, and to assist in the apprehension and return of captive nationals. Article XII stated that the USA would pay the Mexican Republic US$15 million for the appropriated lands. Most of the remaining articles dealt with trade and tariff matters, while Article XXII set rules of conduct to be observed by both sides in the event of future conflict. Despite the treaty's recognition of Mexican property rights, the following decades saw widespread expropriation of Mexican-owned lands, and disregard of treaty articles, by Anglo-Americans. This situation was enabled by a number of factors: proof of land ownership under US law did not align with Mexican law; legal disputes were tested in English, thus putting most Mexican Americans at a linguistic disadvantage; and, corrupt banking, political and legal interests conspired to remove Mexican Americans from prime lands (Tatum 2001).

Tropicalizations

Aparicio and Chávez-Silverman's (1997) concept of "tropicalizations" (explicitly pluralized), or tropicalism, designates two related drives. First, the troping of Latino/as and Latin Americans by dominant cultures that "imbue a particular space, geography, group, or nation with a set of traits, images and values," and that appear in official documents of state, history, literary texts, and the media. Second, creative and critical responses to that troping. Borrowing from the title of Nuyorican Victor Hernández's poetry collection *Tropicalizations* (1976), Aparicio and Chávez-Silverman propose that tropicalizations signifies an American parallel to the operations of Orientalism identified and analyzed by the Palestinian critic Edward Said (1978), and a revision of the concept of **transculturation** developed by the Cuban Fernando Ortiz (1940a, 1995). However, by foregrounding **subaltern** agency and counter-troping, tropicalizations departs from Orientalism (a system by which Europe both colonizes and discursively produces the Orient or the East, with little acknowledgment of Eastern resistant engagement with that production), and transculturation (burdened in some applications by an emphasis on the intellectual agent and literary culture). Tropicalizations emerge in the dialectic between hegemonic tropicalizations of the Latin American south and Latino/as, and Latin American and Latino/a reworking of dominant cultural tropes into politicized and transformative representations. Applying this dialectic to the US context, Aparicio and Chávez-Silverman acknowledge the political limits to **Latinidad** identified by Román and Sandoval (1995). Those authors argue that the purported subversive or oppositional qualities attributed to Latinidad are constrained if the term's applications either exclude certain groups (women, queer Latinos) or replicate dominant cultural appropriating protocols, the latter responsible for the circulation of "tropicalized" stereotypes of Latino/as as aliens, peasants, criminals, terrorists, or an "exotic" constituency. Aparicio and Chávez-Silverman amend this argument; like tropicalizations, Latinidad needs to be pluralized (Latinidades) in order to recognize that ways of being, and being seen as, Latino/a emerge in a dialogic system of troping and countertroping. By implication, this dialectic does not, and cannot, preclude the production, circulation, and endorsement of tropicalized Latinidades by Latino/as themselves (self-tropicalizations). Exemplifying this trend is the ambivalent production of "Tropicalized Miami" from hegemonic Anglo-American troping (media and entertainment industry representations) and from the tropes favored by local Latino/a business interests, public relations approaches, and publicity machines, which gain marketing leverage by celebrating Miami-style "tropicality."

U

Undocumented Worker

An alternative to **illegal alien**, undocumented worker refers to any immigrant or resident worker who works and resides in the USA without the documents required to secure legal residency and/or a **green card**. In early 2006, media estimates put the US undocumented worker population at anywhere between 4 and 15 million, with most commentators settling for a figure of 11–12 million. The vast majority of these workers come from Mexico, with the next significant populations emanating from Central America. In March 2006 and subsequent months, unprecedented mass demonstrations by undocumented workers and their supporters erupted in many cities and towns across the USA, in opposition to the Republican-sponsored Sensenbrenner Bill that sought to felonize "illegal aliens" and to extend the border wall on the US side of the US–Mexico border by 1,000 miles.

United Farm Workers

The United Farm Workers of America (UFWA) was, and remains, one of the most important union organizations to emerge in the 1960s with the aim of safeguarding and ensuring the economic and civil rights of Mexican American and other farm workers. The UFWA grew from the National Farm Worker's Association (NFWA), which was formed in 1962 in Delano, California, under César Chávez, with a key founding and organizational role taken by Chicana activist Dolores Huerta. In 1966, the NFWA merged with the Filipino

American Agricultural Workers Organizing Committee (AWOC) in the new United Farm Workers (UFW) organization. In 1972 the UFW changed its name to the UFWA as a formally affiliated union. Among the significant activist struggles in which the NFWA participated was the Delano Grape Strike, a boycott of Californian wine grape companies that began in September 1965. Lasting some five years, the strike attracted national media attention and was supported by el **Teatro Campesino**, which delivered pro-union skits to farm laborers in the fields. Throughout the 1960s and 1970s, the UFW extended its strike and consumer-boycott strategies to other wine growers and to exploitative lettuce, citrus, strawberry growers, in California and other states. The UFW aimed to force agricultural concerns to permit the unionization of their work forces, and thus to allow unions to negotiate for better pay and work conditions. The UFW and the UFWA extended these tactics by establishing cooperative credit unions, pharmacies, medical clinics, and grocery stores, and by encouraging voter registration and support for pro-union candidates. Dolores Huerta was a major organizer of these initiatives in many states. In 1966, the UFW organized farm worker walkouts in the Rio Grande valley, an action that elicited brutal responses from the **Texas Rangers**. At times, some UFW members responded to police and company clampdowns with violence; in 1968 this situation caused César Chávez to embark on the first of a number of fasts in support of nonviolent protest. By the 1980s, UFWA campaigns were targeting the agricultural sector's use of pesticides and fertilizers. Since 1980 the UFWA has experienced a steady decline in membership, which has been attributed to the increasing urbanization of Mexican Americans and the changing sociopolitical and economic priorities of the community, factional, and personal disagreements within the UFWA, and a social backlash against unionism. César Chávez's presidency of the UFWA ended with his death in April 1993, after which the position was occupied by his son-in-law Arturo Rodríguez. The UFWA continues to fight for improved working conditions and better pay for farm workers, and to lobby for formalizing the legal status of **undocumented workers.**

Vaivén

El vaivén is a colloquial Spanish term used by Puerto Ricans to describe their constant journeying between the island and the US mainland. It thus joins many other metaphors—*brincar el **charco**, la **guagua aérea**, p'acá y p'allá*—used to describe the innate mutability and restless crossings of the Puerto Rican diaspora and its cultural habitus. According to Duany (2002), beyond its literal meaning of fluctuation, the term connotes the transience, constant change, uncertainty, and pragmatic dislocation of Puerto Rican migratory experiences. Duany utilizes the metaphor of the "nación en vaivén" (the nation on the move) to describe the mutable Puerto Rican island and diasporic identity. This metaphor allows him to recognize that, despite colonialism, the resilience of the Puerto Rican national imaginary challenges traditional conceptualizations of nationhood as requiring "a shared territory, language, economy, citizenship, or sovereignty."

Vaquero, Cowboy, Charro, Charreada

The cowboy (in Spanish *vaquero*) has long been romanticized as one of the quintessential icons of "Americanness." But the cowboy is a paradoxical national figure given that the archetype's culture (clothing, diet, music, language) continually reveal his origin in Mexico (Arteaga 1994b). Historians concur that the US cowboy tradition was marked by, and evolved from, the Mexican ranching tradition, a linguistic sign of that origin surviving in the English derivative from *vaquero*, buckaroo. In his study of cattle-raising and horse-riding cultures in the Americas, Slatta (1990) argues that the Mexican ranching tradition played a fundamental role in the agricultural domestication of the US southwest and midwest. Many ranches today employ Mexican and Chicano *vaqueros*, and this has always been the case. The cowboy's function as a national—and decidedly de-Mexicanized—masculine archetype evolved from the late 1800s in US literature, music, television, and film (notably the **Western**). Given that multiple cowboy traditions evolved in the Americas (for instance, the *gauchos* in Argentina), it is not surprising that the ranch culture of New Spain, and later Mexico and the USA, also developed tandem traditions. Mexican and Chicano/a cultures retain a distinct *vaquero* tradition based on the *charro* (horserider) and the *charreada* (a Mexican variant of the rodeo). Throughout the southwest, *charro* processions are often incorporated into local rodeos and fairdays. Nájera-Ramírez (2002; Chávez Candelaria et al. 2004) notes that the *charreada* diverges sharply from the Anglo rodeo tradition. The former emphasizes and rewards equestrian skills (grace, control, handling) but riding and rope-handling events are not timed. The Anglo rodeo is commercialized (with cash prizes), and winners are judged by time comparisons, for instance, length of stay on a bucking horse or bull, or time taken to rope a calf. Nájera-Ramírez also points out that Mexican *bronco* and bull-riding contests (*jaripeos*) have traditionally been separate from formal *charreada* demonstrations. Like the cowboy, the *charro* has been mythologized as an embodiment of national values. In Mexico, this mythologization occurred in the decades following the **Mexican Revolution** of 1910, and was linked to a cultural nationalism that sought symbols of *Mexicanidad* (Mexicanness) in rural and folkloric practices. This construction coincided with the naming of *mariachi* as the national music, the distinctive outfits worn by *mariachi* performers derived from the *charro* wardrobe. Mexican films from the 1940s through to the 1960s emphasized the link with the popular subgenre of singing *charro* "westerns" (R. Castro 2001).

Virgen de Guadalupe, de la Altagracia, de la Caridad del Cobre, de la Providencia

One of the ubiquitous religious symbols and cultural icons in Latin America is the Virgin Mary, who appears in numerous guises throughout the continent. The most important manifestation is La Virgen de Guadalupe (Nuestra Señora de Guadalupe), the patroness of Mexico (since 1737) and of the

Americas as a whole. The cult centered on Guadalupe (*guadalupismo*) represents a syncretic outcome of Aztec and Catholic myths, traditions, and symbolism. In popular lore, the Virgin is said to have appeared three times to an indigenous Mexican, Juan Diego, in 1531, at Tepeyac, which had been an Aztec site of pilgrimage for devotees of the mother earth deity, *Tonantzín*. In the third of her appearances, the Virgin, who addressed Juan Diego in Náhuatl, told him to climb the hill at Tepeyac, cut a bunch of flowers, and take them to the local Spanish bishop who had not believed Juan Diego's previous story of the Virgin's appearances. In the presence of the bishop, Juan Diego opened his cloak, whereupon the flowers (red roses, which should not have grown in winter) fell to the ground, revealing an image of the Virgin impressed on the cloak. The roses and the image convinced the bishop that the Virgin had indeed appeared, and a church in her honor was subsequently constructed at Tepayac (R. Castro 2001). Due to subsidence over the centuries, the old shrine was replaced in the 1970s by a new modernist Basilica, which remains a site of pilgrimage. Poole (1995) argues that the story of the Virgin's apparitions first appeared in print in 1648, and that the construction of the Virgin as a symbol of Mexican national identity, in contradistinction to Spanish cultural and political hegemony, occurred over the next 150 years. Over time Guadalupe came to be popularly regarded as the *mestiza* Virgin, a symbol of Mexico's, and Latin America's, mixed-racial culture. Images of Guadalupe are ubiquitous in Mexico, and among Chicano/as representations of the Virgin are found in home altars, restaurants, murals, tattoos, jewelry, clothing, lowrider art, and artistic and literary production, from el Teatro Campesino's play *La Virgen de Tepeyac* to the banners displayed by the United Farm Workers. The cult of Guadalupe or *guadalupismo* has been dubbed a Mexican variant of *marianismo*. Jeanette Rodríguez (1994) argues that rather than perpetuating gender conventions of dutiful and long-suffering femininity, the Virgin's iconic presence in daily life render her into a figure of gender empowerment and community resilience. Nonetheless, among Chicano/as the Virgen de Guadalupe has served as an admonitory example against which women's social conduct is judged (Rebolledo 1995). The challenge for Chicana feminists and cultural workers has thus been to manage a symbol that may resist a progressive politics. Artistic responses to that challenge have seen the Virgin of Guadalupe recast as a domestic or factory laborer (with cleaning materials or sewing machines), an icon of lesbian desire (two Virgins embracing), a political activist (giving the clenched fist salute), and an undocumented worker dodging the Border Patrol.

The patron saint of Cuba, La Virgen de la Caridad del Cobre (Our Lady of Charity of Cobre), is conventionally depicted hovering above a fishing boat containing three rowers. That image encapsulates the myth of her appearance in the early 1600s to two Indian men, Rodrigo and Juan de Hoyos, and Juan Moreno, a 10-year-old slave, who were out searching for salt. After sheltering from a storm, they encountered an object floating in the waves—a statue (with a name plaque) that was, miraculously, dry. It was the statue of the Virgin holding baby Jesus on her right arm and a gold cross in her left hand. The Virgin's Cuban name reflects her discovery by residents of El Cobre, the town in the province of Santiago. Her feast day, September 8, commemorates this event, and Cobre remains the home of the main shrine in her honor, La Ermita de la Caridad del Cobre. Tweed (1997) indicates that her evolution as a national symbol coincided with the nationalist movement of the 1800s. After the establishment of the Cuban Republic in 1902, Our Lady of Charity was entrenched as a national icon, the "patriot" and "rebel" Virgin. She was formally named Cuba's patron saint in May 1916. After the **Cuban Revolution** the cult of Our Lady of Charity was transferred to south Florida where she is evoked as Our Lady of Exile, with her own shrine, La Ermita de la Caridad, consecrated in December 1973 on Biscayne Bay, which hosts a replica of the original statue in Cobre. The replica, which had been displayed in a church in Havana, was smuggled out of the island and sent clandestinely to Miami on September 8, 1961, where she was revealed to exiles who had gathered in a football stadium to celebrate her feast day (Tweed 1997). For many Cuban Americans, Our Lady of Exile functions as a symbol of religious and political liberty, a rallying point for the anti-Castro struggle, and the spiritual force said to protect and watch over Cubans attempting to leave the island.

Nuestra Señora de la Divina Providencia (Our Lady of Divine Providence) is the patron saint of Puerto Rico, whose feast day is November 19, the day Columbus first saw the island in 1493. The origins of this Virgin reside in thirteenth-century Italy and her transportation to Catalonia in Spain (a church in Tarragona is consecrated in her honor), after which her image was brought to Puerto Rico. Declared the island's patron saint in 1969, she is depicted holding baby Jesus in her lap while she prays. Her image is found throughout the **barrios** and homes of the Puerto Rican diaspora. La Virgen de la Altagracia (Our Lady of High Grace), the patron saint of the Dominican Republic, is also known as the Protector and Queen of the Hearts of the Dominicans, and as Tatica from Higuey, the town in which the first portrait of the Virgin was brought from Spain around 1500. Her feast day is September 21, and Dominicans celebrate this day by holding festivals in order to thank the Virgin for watching over and protecting them. Representations of the Virgen de la Altagracia with her trademark crown and a halo of 12 stars grace most Dominican-run businesses and homes in such districts as New York's Washington Heights.

Voguing, Ballroom Scene

Thanks to the popularity of songs by Madonna ("Vogue") and Malcolm McLaren ("Waltz Darling") in 1989 and 1990, the term voguing entered the cultural lexicon of the 1990s to define a popular dance form that mimicked and reworked the highly stylized staccato moves and attitudes of fashion magazine and runway models: "Strike a pose!" However, voguing emerged originally in the 1980s among African American and Latino gay male and transvestite communities in the US northeast as one possible performative dance event among many organized by constructed queer "houses" or families in the larger Ballroom Scene. Such houses represented an alternative to the participants' real-world families; house mothers and fathers provided quasiparental role models for younger members as they learned about the queer community. McCarthy Brown's (2001) study of voguing in Newark, New Jersey, demonstrates that the Scene emerged in the context of entrenched racism and homophobia, exacerbated by poverty and the inroads of the **AIDS** epidemic. The Ballroom Scene thus attempted to construct safe spaces for gay men dealing with multiple forces of racial, ethnic and sexual discrimination, and violence, in the quotidian world outside. As McCarthy Brown describes them, the mostly gay-male Ballroom Scene consisted of competitive runway events organized by well-defined categories of entrants (Butch Queens, Butches, Femme Queens). The Scene evolved from earlier La-Cage-aux-Folles clubs, at which transvestites lip-synched to popular songs by female singers in competitions that rewarded the most convincing exponents of gender mimicry. To that tradition, various runway events of posing were eventually added, including voguing and physically challenging moves derived from the Brazilian martial art of *capoeira*. Voguing and other runway events represented a complex response to what McCarthy Brown calls "the normative white gaze" that marginalizes Latino and African American queers. Differing from critics who regard the Ballroom Scene as upholding gender essentialisms (hooks 1992), McCarthy Brown views the Scene as an ambivalent space in which participants at once toy with and parody gender mores, and presume that there is a gender truth to be found in the masquerade.

West, Western

The West is a longstanding geospatial conceptualization in US cultural and national discourse, "an idea that became a place" (Milner et al. 1994). The West also lends its name to the Western, a nineteenth-century literary and artistic genre that, in the twentieth century, moved into music, television, and film. Often regarded as analogous to the **frontier**, the West evokes an idea of state expansion and consolidation that conforms to an inexorable east–west movement until the country reaches its recognizably "American" form. That teleology builds on the idea that the USA's historical and cultural origins are anchored in Europe, from which wave after wave of immigrants crossed the Atlantic, the first move in the process of becoming "American." As the British colonies, and the USA that emerged from them, expanded into the continent, the West shifted into new terrains populated by indigenous peoples, many of whom resisted European American encroachments. The traditional idea of the West tends to regard Native Americans as an interruption or irritant to the West's inevitable evolution toward the Pacific Ocean. Similar irritations occur with the West's encroachment upon Mexican national territory in the 1830s and 1840s, the encounter confirming that north–south and south–north contact-zone emplacements were also at work in North America. From the Mexican vantage point, there was a north, but no west. The West thus designates a range of spatial, temporal, and critical entities. It is a shifting place, but one that became located west of the Mississippi and bounded to the south by Mexico. It is temporally finite, beginning with the first European colonies on the

East Coast and ending with the so-called closing of the frontier at the end of the nineteenth century. The West is an idea about a specific period in US history, most commonly restricted to the second half of the 1800s. It is a myth, a vast scenic space in which numerous authors have invested imaginative energies that perpetuate the myth, and yoked it to the national imaginary (Walker 2001). These versions of the West permeate the Western genre, a range of literary texts and films about the Western frontier in the 1700s and 1800s, with most films focusing on the zone west of the Mississippi between 1850 and 1900. Walker (2001) notes that the Western is an ambivalent genre of historical retrospection, given its toying with a historical record that is itself fragmented, allegorized, mythologized, exclusionary, and imbued with fantasy. Many Latino/a critics argue that Westerns have been ideologically primed to do representational damage to the genre's Mexican characters (Ramírez Berg 2002). At times, however, Westerns (not a unified or homogeneous genre) have provided nuanced depictions of Anglo-Mexican relations. The character of Helen Ramírez (Katy Jurado) in *High Noon* (1952, dir. Fred Zinnemann) is notable not simply because she is portrayed as a woman of strength and agency, but also because the script refrains from translating key moments of conversation in Spanish.

Young Lords

The Young Lords Organization, later the Young Lords Party, was a nationalist Puerto Rican organization that emerged among college students in New York City in 1969, its main influences being the African American Black Panther Movement, national liberation struggles across the globe, Marxist political currents, and the sociopolitical promise of the **Cuban Revolution.** The forerunner of the New York Young Lords was the Chicago Young Lords, a street gang founded in the 1950s that became a political force under Cha Cha Jiménez in the 1960s, and whose community activism influenced Nuyoricans to organize their own outfit. Like the Chicano **Brown Berets**, the New York Young Lords Organization was a pseudomilitary group (evident in the distinctive uniform worn by members) with an ethos of community autonomy. Although the links between the Chicago and New York Young Lords are debated, both groups were beset by factional differences over activist and organizational policy, which led to the disbanding of the Young Lords by 1976 (Melendez 2003; I. Morales 1998). The New York Young Lords' "13-Point Program and Platform" from October 1969 called for Puerto Rican independence, self-determination for all Latino/as and Latin Americans, and liberation for the Third World, thus emphasizing the Young Lords' leftist ethos of revolutionary nationalism, international solidarity, anticapitalism, and antiracism. The program advocated community control of **barrio** institutions, education programs about Puerto Rican history, and a need for dismantling **machismo.** It opposed the Vietnam War and US bases in Puerto Rico. In 1970, a revised version of the program adjusted its education demand to include Afro-Indio culture (Melendez 2003). Many female members were active in confronting their male counterparts over the marginalization of women in organizational structures, the persistence of machista attitudes, and the lack of attention to such issues as abortion, birth control, health care for women, and the enforced sterilization program in Puerto Rico. Their efforts resulted in ongoing revisions of Young Lords policies to include concrete strategies for dealing with women's concerns (Nelson 2003).

Z

Zoot Suiters, Zoot Suit Riots

The Californian Mexican or *pachuco* Zoot Suit youth culture was associated with the swing or hepcat jazz music scene from the late 1930s to the early 1950s. A Zoot Suit culture also emerged in Mexico in this period, with adherents called Tárzanes after the popular Tarzan films featuring Johnny Weismuller. Zoot suits consisted of jackets with wide padded shoulders, narrow waists, and a long drop to the knee, and high-braced baggy trousers that tapered in at the ankles. Eye-catching colors and fabrics added a dramatic effect. Zoot Suiters also wore broad-brimmed hats, thick-soled shoes, such accessories as a long watch or key chain and a brightly colored, wide necktie, and a hairstyle featuring the characteristic ducktail. Female Zoot Suiters also had a distinctive style: hair piled high in pompadour fashion and often decorated with razor blades, black short skirts or figure hugging slacks, black, flat-soled shoes, and striped tights or stockings (C.S. Ramírez 2002; Sánchez-Tranquilino and Tagg 1992). The Zoot Suit look has enjoyed a comeback among young urban Chicano/as since the early 1990s. Given the austerity measures that minimalized clothing fashion during the Great Depression and the war years of the 1940s, Zoot Suiters in LA from working-class Mexican American (and Asian, African, and Anglo-American) communities, positioned themselves and their public appearances against the sartorial grain of the era (Cosgrove 1984). In the national context of a country at war, and local targeting of Mexican Americans by the legal and juridical apparatuses, Zoot Suiters were regarded by outsiders with suspicion and hostility. Exemplifying that uneasy status, the Zoot Suit Riots followed such incidents as the **Sleepy Lagoon** case, and the heightened communal tensions that resulted from it. In June 1943, US sailors and soldiers on shore leave in Los Angeles began to assault Zoot Suiters, the attacks often accompanied by a violent, and semiotically telling, ritual declothing and cutting of the hair of *pachuco* targets. The attacks escalated, with non-*pachuco* Mexican Americans and non-Mexican American Zoot Suiters also being assaulted. Many critics regard the riots as a tacit declaration of war against Mexican American youth. Abetted by hysterical media coverage and the involvement of the Los Angeles Police Department on the side of servicemen, and eventually requiring Federal intervention, the riots left a legacy of resentment among working-class Mexican Americans. Historians often cite racism and anti-Mexican **nativism** as the underlying causes of the riots (Escobar 1999). However, Obregón Pagán (2003) argues that many Mexican Americans supported the police actions, many liberal Anglos campaigned on behalf of detained *pachucos*, and the Zoot Suiters reflected the complexities of working-class panethnic neighborhoods. The Zoot Suit Riots were not a Mexican only affair, nor were they attributable to the "anti-Mexican hysteria thesis." Obregón Pagán points out that attempts by *pachucos* to forge their own **barrio** cultural space were framed by specific structural pressures, for example, the reduction in urban space related to the need to house and provide training facilities for a massive military force, which resulted in Mexican displacement from their **barrios**. Notable representations of the riots include el **Teatro Campesino**'s play from the 1970s "Zoot Suit" (Valdez 1992), which was also made into a musical film (1981, dir. Luis Valdez), and Thomas Sánchez's novel *The Zoot-Suit Murders* (1991).

References

Abarca, Meredith. 2006. *Voices in the Kitchen: Views of Food and the World from Working-Class Mexican and Mexican American Women*. College Station: Texas A&M University Press.

Acevedo, Gregory. 2004. "Neither Here Nor There: Puerto Rican Circular Migration." *Journal of Immigrant and Refugee Services* 2.1–2: 69–85.

Acosta, Oscar "Zeta." 1972. *The Autobiography of a Brown Buffalo*. San Francisco, CA: Straight Arrow.

——. 1989. *The Revolt of the Cockroach People*. New York: Vintage.

Acosta-Belén, Edna. 1992. "Beyond Island Boundaries: Ethnicity, Gender, and Cultural Revitalization in Nuyorican Literature." *Callaloo* 15: 979–98.

Acuña, Rodolfo. 1996. *Anything But Mexican: Chicanos in Contemporary Los Angeles*. London: Verso.

——. 2000. *Occupied America: A History of Chicanos*. 4th edn. New York: Longman.

Alarcón, Daniel Cooper. 1997. *The Aztec Palimpsest: Mexico in the Modern Imagination*. Tucson: University of Arizona Press.

Alarcón, Norma. 1983. "Chicana's Feminist Literature: A Re-Vision Through Malintzin/Or Malintzin: Putting Flesh Back on the Object." In *This Bridge Called My Back: Writings By Radical Women of Color*. 2nd edn. Ed. C. Moraga and G. Anzaldúa. New York: Kitchen Table/Women of Color. 182–90.

——. 1990. "Chicana Feminism: In the Tracks of 'The' Native Woman." *Cultural Studies* 4.3 (October): 248–56.

——. 1991. "The Theoretical Subject(s) of *This Bridge Called My Back*." In *Criticism in the Borderlands: Studies in Chicano Literature, Culture and Ideology*. Ed. H. Calderón and J.D. Saldívar. Durham, NC: Duke University Press. 28–39.

Alcaraz, Lalo. 2004a. *La Cucaracha*. Kansas City: Andrews McMeel.

——. 2004b. *Migra Mouse: Political Cartoons on Immigration*. New York: RDV.

Aldama, Arturo, J. 2001. *Disrupting Savagism: Intersecting Chicano/a, Mexican Immigrant, and Native American Struggles for Self-Representation*. Durham, NC and London: Duke University Press.

Aldama, Arturo J. and Naomi H. Quiñónez, eds. 2002. *Decolonial Voices: Chicana and Chicano Cultural Studies in the 21st Century*. Bloomington and Indianapolis: Indiana University Press.

Aldama, Frederick Luis. 2003. *Postethnic Narrative Criticism: Magicorealism in Oscar "Zeta" Acosta, Ana Castillo, Julie Dash, Hanif Kureishi and Salman Rushdie*. Austin: University of Texas Press.

——. 2005. *Brown on Brown: Chicano/a Representations of Gender, Sexuality and Ethnicity*. Austin: University of Texas Press.

Alfaro, Luis. 1994. "Cuerpo Politizado." In *Uncontrollable Bodies: Testimonies of Art and Culture*. Ed. R. Sappington and T. Stallings. Seattle, WA: Bay. 216–41.

Algarín, Miguel. 1987. "Nuyorican Aesthetics." In *Images and Identities: The Puerto Rican in Two World Contexts*. Ed. A. Rodríguez de Laguna. New Brunswick, NJ: Transaction. 161–3.

Algarín, Miguel and Bob Holman, eds. 1994. *Aloud: Voices from the Nuyorican Poets Café*. New York: Henry Holt.

Algarín, Miguel and Miguel Piñero, eds. 1975. *Nuyorican Poetry: An Anthology of Puerto Rican Words and Feelings*. New York: William Morrow.

Alire Sáenz, Benjamin. 1994. "I Want to Write an American Poem." *Currents from the Dancing River: Contemporary Latino Fiction, Nonfiction, and Poetry*. Ed. R. Gonzalez. San Diego, CA: Harvest. 522–36.

——. 1995. *Carry Me Like Water*. New York: Hyperion.

——. 1997. "In the Borderlands of Chicano Identity, There Are Only Fragments." In *Border Theory: The Limits of Cultural Politics*. Ed. S. Michaelsen and D.E. Johnson. Minneapolis: University of Minnesota Press. 68–96.

Allatson, Paul. 2002. *Latino Dreams: Transcultural Traffic and the US National Imaginary*. Amsterdam and New York: Rodopi.

Almaguer, Tomás. 1991. "Chicano Men: A Cartography of Homosexual Identity and Behavior." *Differences* 3.2: 75–100.

Alonso, Ana María. 1997. *Thread of Blood: Colonialism, Revolution, and Gender on Mexico's Northern Frontier*. Tucson: University of Arizona Press.

Alonso, Ana María and María Teresa Koreck. 1993. "Silences: 'Hispanics,' AIDS, and Sexual Practices." In *The Lesbian and Gay Studies Reader*. Ed. H. Abelove, M.A. Barale, and D.M. Halperin. New York: Routledge. 110–26.

Alonso Pacheco, Manuel. 1974. *El gíbaro*. San Juan: Instituto de Cultura Puertorriqueña.

Alurista. 1981. *Spik in Glyph?* Houston, TX: Arte Público.

Alvarez Borland, Isabel. 1998. *Cuban American Literature of Exile: From Person to Persona*. Charlottesville: University Press of Virginia.

Alvarez, Julia. 1992. *How the García Girls Lost Their Accents*. New York: Plume.

Anaya, Rudolfo. 1984. *The Legend of La Llorona*. Berkeley, CA: Tonatiuh-Quinto Sol.

——. 1988 [1976]. *Heart of Aztlán*. Albuquerque: University of New Mexico Press.

Anaya, Rudolfo A. and Francisco A. Lomelí, eds. 1989. *Aztlán: Essays on the Chicano Homeland*. Albuquerque, NM: Academia/El Norte.

Anderson, Benedict. 1991. *Imagined Communities: Reflections on the Origin and Spread of Nationalism*. 2nd edn. London: Verso.

Andreas, Peter. 2000. *Border Games: Policing the US–Mexico Divide*. Ithaca, NJ and London: Cornell University Press.

Andrews, Emily L. 1997. "Active Marianismo: Women's Social and Political Action in Nicaraguan Christian Base Communities and the Sandinista Revolution." (August 20): http://web.grinnell.edu/LatinAmericanStudies/this.html

Angeles Torres, María de los. 1999. *In the Land of Mirrors: Cuban Exile Politics in the United States*. Ann Arbor: University of Michigan Press.

——. 2003. *The Lost Apple: Operation Pedro Pan, Cuban Children in the US, and the Promise of a Better Future*. Boston, MA: Beacon.

Anzaldúa, Gloria. 1987. *Borderlands/La Frontera: The New Mestiza*. San Francisco: Spinsters/Aunt Lute.

——.ed. 1990. *Making Face, Making Soul, Haciendo Caras: Creative and Critical Perspectives by Women of Color*. San Francisco: Aunt Lute.

——. 2000. *Interviews/Entrevistas*. Ed. AnaLouise Keating. New York and London: Routledge.

Aparicio, Frances R. 1998. *Listening to Salsa: Gender, Latin Popular Music, and Puerto Rican Cultures*. Hanover, NH: Wesleyan University Press.

——. 1999. "Reading the 'Latino' in Latino Studies: Toward Re-Imagining Our Academic Location." *Discourse* 21.3: 3–18.

Aparicio, Frances R. and Susana Chávez-Silverman, eds. 1997. *Tropicalizations: Transcultural Representations of Latinidad*. Hanover, NH: University Press of New England.

Aparicio, Frances R. and Cándida F. Jáquez, eds. 2003. *Musical Migrations: Transnationalism and Cultural Hybridity in Latin/o America*. Vol. 1. New York: Palgrave Macmillan.

Aponte-Parés, Luis. 1998. "What's Yellow and White and Has Land All Around It? Appropriating Place in Puerto Rican *Barrios*." In *The Latino Studies Reader: Culture, Economy, and Society*. Ed. A. Darder and R.D. Torres. Malden, MA: Blackwell. 271–80.

Araiza, Alberto Antonio, Paul Bonin-Rodríguez, Michael Marinez, and Danny Bolero Saldívar. 2002. "Quinceañera." In *The Color of Theater: Race, Culture, and Contemporary Performance*. Ed. R. Uno and L.M. San Pablo Burns. London and New York: Continuum. 260–301.

Aranda, Jr., José. 2003. *When We Arrive: A New Literary History of Mexican America*. Tucson: University of Arizona Press.

Aranda, Jr., José and Silvio Torres-Saillant, eds. 2002. *Recovering the US Hispanic Literary Heritage, Vol. 4*. Houston, TX: Arte Público.

Arenas, Reinaldo. 1992. *Antes que anochezca*. Barcelona: Tusquets.

——. 1993. *Before Night Falls*. Trans. D.M. Koch. New York: Viking.

Arguedas, Alcides. 1959 (1919). *Raza de bronce*. In *Obras completas*. Mexico City: Aguilar.

Arias, Arturo. 2003. "Central American-Americans: Invisibility, Power and Representation in the US Latino World." *Latino Studies* 1: 168–87.

Arias Jirasek, Rita and Carlos Tortolero. 2001. *Mexican Chicago*. Chicago, IL: Arcadia.

Arora, Shirley L. 1982. "A Critical Bibliography of Mexican American Proverbs." *Aztlán: International Journal of Chicano Studies Research* 13: 71–80.

Arredondo, Gabriela F., Aída Hurtado, Norma Klahn, Olga Nájera-Ramírez, and Patricia Zavella, eds. 2003. *Chicana Feminisms: A Critical Reader*. Durham, NC and London: Duke University Press.

Arreola, Daniel, ed. 2004. *Hispanic Spaces, Latino Places: Community and Cultural Diversity in Contemporary America*. Austin: University of Texas Press.

Arrizón, Alicia. 1999. *Latina Performance: Traversing the Stage*. Bloomington: Indiana University Press.

——. 2000a. "Introduction." In *Latinas on Stage*. Ed. A. Arrizón and L. Manzor. Berkeley, CA: Third Woman. 10–20.

——. 2000b. "Mythical Performativity: Relocating Aztlán in Chicana Feminist Cultural Productions." *Theatre Journal* 52.1 (March): 23–49.

Arrizón, Alicia and Lilian Manzor, eds. 2000. *Latinas on Stage*. Berkeley, CA: Third Woman.

Arteaga, Alfred, ed. 1994a. *An Other Tongue: Nation and Ethnicity in the Linguistic Borderlands*. Durham, NC: Duke University Press.

——. 1994b. "An Other Tongue." In *An Other Tongue: Nation and Ethnicity in the Linguistic Borderlands*. Ed. A. Arteaga. Durham, NC: Duke University Press. 8–33.

Arteaga, Alfred. 1997. *Chicano Poetics: Heterotexts and Hybridities*. Cambridge: Cambridge University Press.

Ashcroft, Bill, Gareth Griffiths, and Helen Tiffin. 1998. *Post-Colonial Studies: Key Concepts*. London and New York: Routledge.

Augenbraum, Harold and Margarite Fernández Olmos, eds. 2000. *U.S. Latino Literature: A Critical Guide for Students and Teachers*. Westport, CT: Greenwood.

Austerlitz, Paul. 1997. *Merengue: Dominican Music and Dominican Identity*. Philadelphia, PA: Temple University Press.

Avila, Eric. 2004. *Popular Culture in the Age of White Flight: Fear and Fantasy in Suburban Los Angeles*. Berkeley: University of California Press.

Baca Zinn, Maxine. 1982. "Chicano Men and Masculinity." *Journal of Ethnic Studies* 10.2: 29–44.

Barker, Francis, Peter Hulme, and Margaret Iversen, eds. 1998. *Cannibalism and the Colonial World*. Cambridge: Cambridge University Press.

Barrera, Mario, Carlos Muñoz, and Charles Ornelas. 1972. "The Barrio as an Internal Colony." In *People and Politics in Urban Society*. Ed. H. Hahn. Beverly Hills, CA: Sage. 465–98.

Barreto, Amilcar Antonio. 2001. *The Politics of Language in Puerto Rico*. Gainesville: University Press of Florida.

Barrio, Raymond. 1969. *The Plum Plum Pickers*. Guerneville, CA: Ventura.

Bary, Leslie, trans. 1991. "Oswald de Andrade's 'Cannibal Manifesto.' " *Latin American Literary Review* 19.38: 35–47.

Belnap, Jeffrey and Raúl Fernández, eds. 1998. *José Martí's "Our America": From National to Hemispheric Cultural Studies*. Durham, NC and London: Duke University Press.

Bencastro, Mario. 1999. *Odisea del norte*. Houston, TX: Arte Público.

Bender, Steven W. 2003. *Greasers and Gringos: Latinos, Law, and the American Imagination*. New York and London: New York University Press.

Benítez-Rojo, Antonio. 1996. *The Repeating Island: The Caribbean and the Postmodern Perspective*. Trans. J.E. Maraniss. 2nd edn. Durham, NC and London: Duke University Press.

Benjamín, Jules R. 1990. *The United States and the Origins of the Cuban Revolution: An Empire of Liberty in an Age of National Liberation*. Princeton, NJ: Princeton University Press.

Bennett, Tony, Lawrence Grossberg, and Meaghan Morris, eds. 2005. *New Keywords: A Revised Vocabulary of Culture and Society*. Malden, MA: Blackwell.

Bergmann, Emilie L. and Paul Julian Smith, eds. 1995. *¿Entiendes? Queer Readings, Hispanic Writings*. Durham, NC: Duke University Press.

Bertot, Lillian. 1995. *The Literary Imagination of the Mariel Imagination*. Washington, DC: Endowment for Cuban American Studies/Cuban American National Foundation.

Bettinger-López, Caroline. 2001. *Cuban-Jewish Journeys: Searching for Identity, Home and History in Miami*. Knoxville: University of Tennessee Press.

Beverley, John. 1993. *Against Literature*. Minneapolis and London: University of Minnesota Press.

——. 1999. *Subalternity and Representation: Arguments in Cultural Theory*. Durham, NC: Duke University Press.

Bhabha, Homi K. 1994. *The Location of Culture*. London: Routledge.

Boggs, Vernon W., ed. 1992. *Salsiology: Afro-Cuban Music and the Evolution of Salsa in New York City*. Westport, CT: Greenwood.

Bolton, Herbert E. 1921. *The Spanish Borderlands: A Chronicle of Old Florida and the Southwest*. New Haven, CT: Yale University Press.

Bonilla, Frank, Edwin Meléndez, Rebecca Morales, and María de los Angeles Torres, eds. 1998. *Borderless Borders: US Latinos, Latin Americans, and the Paradox of Interdependence*. Philadelphia, PA: Temple University Press.

Boone, Elizabeth H. 1996. *The Aztec World*. Washington, DC: Smithsonian Institution.

Bourgois, Philippe. 1996. *In Search of Respect: Selling Crack in the Barrio*. Cambridge: Cambridge University Press.

Bowers, Maggie Ann. 2004. *Magic(al) Realism*. London and New York: Routledge.

Brady, Mary Pratt. 2002. *Extinct Lands, Temporal Geographies: Chicana Literature and the Urgency of Space*. Durham, NC and London: Duke University Press.

Brotherton, David C. and Luis Barrios. 2004. *The Almighty Latin King and Queen Nation: Street Politics and the Transformation of a New York City Gang*. New York: Columbia University Press.

Brown, Karen McCarthy. 2001. "Mimesis in the Face of Fear: Femme Queens, Butch Queens, and Gender Play in the Houses of Greater Newark." In *Passing: Identity and Interpretation in Sexuality, Race, and Religion*. Ed. M.C. Sánchez and L. Schlossberg. New York: New York University Press. 208–27.

Brown, Monica. 2002. *Gang Nation: Delinquent Citizens in Puerto Rican, Chicano, and Chicana Narratives*. Minneapolis: University of Minnesota Press.

Broyles-González, Yolanda. 1994. *El Teatro Campesino: Theater in the Chicano Movement*. Austin: University of Texas Press.

Bruce-Novoa, [Juan]. 1982. *Chicano Poetry: A Response to Chaos*. Austin: University of Texas Press.

——. 1986. "Homosexuality and the Chicano Novel." *Confluencia* 2.1: 69–77.

——. 1990. *RetroSpace: Collected Essays on Chicano Literature, Theory and History*. Houston, TX: Arte Público.

Bruneau, Thomas C. 2005. "The Maras and National Security in Central America." *Strategic Insights* 4.5 (May): http://www.ccc.nps.navy.mil/si/2005/May/bruneauMay05.asp.

Burgos, Jr., Adrian. 2002. "Learning America's Other Game: Baseball, Race, and the Study of Latinos." In *Latino/a Popular Culture*. Ed. Michelle Habell-Pallán and Mary Romero. New York and London: New York University Press. 225–39.

Burr, Ramiro. 1999. *The Billboard Guide to Tejano and Regional Mexican Music*. New York: Billboard.

Bustos-Aguilar, Pedro. 1995. "Mister Don't Touch the Banana: Notes on the Popularity of the Ethnosexed Body South of the Border." *Critique of Anthropology* 15.2 (June): 149–70.

Calderón, Héctor. 2004. *Narratives of Greater Mexico: Essays on Chicano Literary History, Genre, and Borders*. Austin: University of Texas Press.

Calderón, Héctor and José David Saldívar, eds. 1991. *Criticism in the Borderlands: Studies in Chicano Literature, Culture and Ideology*. Durham, NC: Duke University Press.

Calinescu, Matei. 1987. *Five Faces of Modernity: Modernism, Avant-Garde, Decadence, Kitsch, Postmodernism*. Durham, NC: Duke University Press.

Calvo Ospina, Hernando. 1995. *¡Salsa! Havana Heat, Bronx Beat*. Trans. N. Caistor. London: Latin American Bureau.

Camarillo, Albert. 1979. *Chicanos in a Changing Society: From Mexican Pueblos to American Barrios in Santa Barbara and Southern California, 1848–1930*. Cambridge, MA: Harvard University Press.

Candelaria, Cordelia. 1986. *Chicano Poetry: A Critical Introduction*. Westport, CT: Greenwood.

Cantú, Norma E. 1986. "Women, Then and Now: An Analysis of the Adelita Image Versus the Chicana as Political Writer and Philosopher." In *Chicana Voices: Intersections of Class, Race, and Gender*. Ed. T. Córdova, N. Cantú, G. Cardenas, J. García, and C.M. Sierra. Austin, TX: Center for Mexican American Studies. 8–10.

——. 1995. *Canícula: Snapshots of a Girlhood en la Frontera*. Albuquerque: University of New Mexico Press.

——. 2002. "Chicana Life-Cycle Rituals." In *Chicana Traditions: Continuity and Change*. Ed. N. Cantú and O. Nájera-Ramírez. Urbana and Chicago: University of Illinois Press. 15–34.

Cantú, Norma E. and Olga Nájera-Ramírez, eds. 2002. *Chicana Traditions: Continuity and Change.* Urbana and Chicago: University of Illinois Press.

Carmichael, Stokely and Charles V. Hamilton. 1967. *Black Power.* New York: Random House.

Carrero, Jaime. 1964. *Jet Neorriqueño: NeoRican Jet Liner.* San Germán: Universidad Interamericana.

Carroll, Patrick James. 2003. *Felix Longoria's Wake: Bereavement, Racism, and the Rise of Mexican-American Activism.* Austin: University of Texas Press.

Castañeda Shular, Antonia, Tomás Ybarra-Frausto, and Joseph Sommers, eds. 1972. *Literatura Chicana: Texto y contexto/Chicano Literature: Text and Context.* Englewood Cliffs, NJ: Prentice-Hall.

Castillo, Ana. 1994. *Massacre of the Dreamers: Essays on Xicanisma.* Albuquerque: University of New Mexico Press.

Castillo, Debra A. 2005. *Redreaming America: Toward a Bilingual American Culture.* New York: State University of New York Press.

Castillo, Debra A. and María Socorro Tabuenca Córdoba. 2002. *Border Women: Writing from la frontera.* Minneapolis: University of Minnesota Press.

Castillo Guilbault, Rose. 2005. *Farmworker's Daughter: Growing Up Mexican in America.* Berkeley, CA: Heyday.

Castro, Max J. 1997. "The Politics of Language in Miami." In *Challenging Fronteras: Structuring Latina and Latino Lives in the US An Anthology of Readings.* Ed. M. Romero, P. Hondagneu-Sotelo, and V. Ortiz. New York: Routledge. 279–96.

Castro, Rafaela G. 2001. *Chicano Folklore: A Guide to the Folktales, Traditions, Rituals, and Religious Practices of Mexican-Americans.* Oxford: Oxford University Press.

Cervantes, Fred A. 2002. "Chicanos as a Postcolonial Minority: Some Questions Concerning the Adequacy of the Paradigm of Internal Colonialism." In *Latino/a Thought: Culture, Politics and Society.* Ed. F.H. Vázquez and R.D. Torres. Lanham, MD: Rowman & Littlefield. 330–42.

Cervantes, Lorna Dee. 1981. *Emplumada.* Pittsburgh, PA: University of Pittsburgh Press.

Chabram-Dernersesian, Angie. 1992. "'I Throw Punches for My Race, but I Don't Want to Be a Man': Writing Us—Chica-nos (Girl, Us)/Chicanas—into the Movement Script." In *Cultural Studies.* Ed. L. Grossberg, C. Nelson, and P. Treichler. New York and London: Routledge. 81–95.

Chabrán, Richard and Rafael Chabrán, eds. 1996. *The Latino Encyclopedia.* 6 vols. New York: Marshall Cavendish.

Chanady, Amaryll, ed. 1994. *Latin American Identity and Constructions of Difference.* Minneapolis: Minnesota University Press.

Chávez, Denise. 2001. *Loving Pedro Infante.* New York: Farrar, Strauss and Giroux.

Chávez, Ernesto. 2002. *Mi Raza Primero!: Nationalism, Identity, and Insurgency in the Chicano Movement in Los Angeles, 1966–1978.* Berkeley: University of California Press.

Chavez, John. 1984. *The Lost Land.* Albuquerque: University of New Mexico Press.

Chavez, Leo R. 2001. *Covering Immigration: Popular Images and the Politics of the Nation*. Berkeley: University of California Press.

Chavez, Linda. 1992. *Out of the Barrio: Toward a New Politics of Hispanic Assimilation*. New York: Basic.

Chávez Candelaria, Cordelia, Arturo J. Aldama, Peter J. García, and Alma Alvarez-Smith, eds. 2004. *Encyclopedia of Latino Popular Culture*. 2 vols. Westport, CT: Greenwood.

Chávez-Silverman, Susana. 2000. "'Chicanas in Love: Sandra Cisneros Talking Back and Alicia Gaspar de Alba 'Giving Back the Wor(l)d.'" In *Reading and Writing the Ambiente. Queer Sexualities in Latino, Latin American, and Spanish Culture*. Ed. S. Chávez-Silverman and L. Hernández. Madison: University of Wisconsin Press. 181–99.

——. 2004. *Killer Crónicas: Bilingual Memories*. Madison, TX: University of Wisconsin Press.

Chávez Silverman, Susana and Librada Hernández, eds. 2000. *Reading and Writing the Ambiente: Queer Sexualities in Latino, Latin American and Spanish Culture*. Madison: University of Wisconsin Press.

Christian, Karen. 1997. *Show and Tell: Identity as Performance in U.S. Latina/o Fiction*. Albuquerque: University of New Mexico Press.

Cisneros, Sandra. 1984. *The House on Mango Street*. Houston, TX: Arte Público.

——. 1991. *Woman Hollering Creek and Other Stories*. New York: Random House.

Cockcroft, Eva Sperling and Holly Barnet-Sanchez, eds. 1990. *Signs from the Heart: California Chicano Murals*. Venice, CA: Social and Public Art Resource Center.

Cohen, Jeffrey H. 2001. "Transnational Migration in Rural Oaxaca, Mexico: Dependency, Development, and the Household." *American Anthropologist* 103–4 (December): 954–67.

Cohen, Robin. 1997. *Global Diasporas: An Introduction*. Seattle: University of Washington Press.

Colectivo Nortec. 2003. *This is Tijuana!: El Paso de Nortec*. Mexico City: Trilce.

Colón, Jesús. 1961. *A Puerto Rican in New York and Other Sketches*. New York: Masses and Mainstream.

Conde, Yvonne M. 1999. *Operation Pedro Pan: The Untold Exodus of 14,048 Cuban Children*. New York and London: Routledge.

Conniff, Michael L. and T.J. Davis, eds. 1994. *Africans in the Americas: A History of the Black Diaspora*. New York: St. Martin's.

Coronado, Roberto. 2004. "Workers' Remittances to Mexico." *Business Frontier: Federal Reserve Bank of Dallas, El Paso Branch* 1: 1–5.

Cosgrove, Stuart. 1984. "The Zoot-Suit and Style Warfare." *History Workshop Journal* 18 (Autumn): 77–91.

Crawford, James. 1992. *Hold Your Tongue: Bilingualism and the Politics of "English Only."* Reading, MA: Addison-Wesley.

Crenshaw, Kimberlé Neil Gotanda, Gary Peller, and Kendall Thomas, eds. 1995. *Critical Race Theory: The Key Writings that Formed the Movement*. New York: New Press.

Cruz, Migdalia. 1996. "The Have-Little." In *Contemporary Plays by Women of Color*. Ed. K. Perkins and R. Uno. New York: Routledge. 106–26.

Cuadros, Gil. 1994. *City of God*. San Francisco, CA: City Lights.

Cull, Nicholas J. and Davíd Carrasco, eds. 2004. *Alambrista and the US–Mexico Border: Film, Music, and Stories of Undocumented Immigrants*. Albuquerque: University of New Mexico Press.

Cypress, Sandra Messinger. 1991. *La Malinche in Mexican Literature: From History to Myth*. Austin: University of Texas Press.

Darder, Antonia, ed. 1995. *Culture and Difference: Critical Perspectives on the Bicultural Experience in the United States*. Westport, CT: Bergin and Harvey.

Darder, Antonia and Rodolfo D. Torres, eds. 1998. *The Latino Studies Reader: Culture, Economy, and Society*. Malden, MA: Blackwell.

——. 2003. "Mapping Latino Studies: Critical Reflections on Class and Social Theory." *Latino Studies* 1: 303–24.

Dávalos, Karen Mary. 2002. "*La Quinceañera*: Making Gender and Ethnic Identities." In *Velvet Barrios: Popular Culture and Chicano/a Sexualities*. Ed. A. Gaspar de Alba. Basingstoke and New York: Palgrave Macmillan. 141–62.

Dávila, Arlene M. 1997. *Sponsored Identities: Cultural Politics in Puerto Rico*. Philadelphia, PA: Temple University Press.

——. 2000. *Latinos, Inc.: The Marketing and Making of a People*. Berkeley: University of California Press.

——. 2004. *Barrio Dreams: Puerto Ricans, Latinos and the Neoliberal City*. Berkeley: University of California Press.

Davis, Angela Y. 1998. "Masked Racism: Reflections on the Prison Industrial Complex." *ColorLines* (Fall): http://home.ican.net/~edtoth/lawprisonrace.html

Davis, Marilyn P. 1990. *Mexican Voices/American Dreams: An Oral History of Mexican Immigration to the United States*. New York: Henry Holt.

Davis, Mike. 2000. *Magical Urbanism: Latinos Reinventing the U.S. Big City*. London and New York: Verso.

De Genova, Nicholas and Ana Y. Ramos-Zayas. 2003. *Latino Crossings: Mexicans, Puerto Ricans, and the Politics of Race and Citizenship*. New York and London: Routledge.

DeGuzmán, María. 2005. *Spain's Long Shadow: The Black Legend, Off-Whiteness, and Anglo-American Empire*. Minneapolis: University of Minnesota Press.

de la Campa, Román. 2000. *Cuba on My Mind: Journeys to a Second Nation*. London and New York: Verso.

De la Garza, Rodolfo O., Z. Anthony Kruszewski, and Tomás A. Arciniega. 1973. *Chicanos and Native Americans: The Territorial Minorities*. Englewood Cliffs, NJ: Prentice-Hall.

de las Casas, Bartolomé. 1999. *Brevísima relación de la destrucción de las Indias: Primera edición crítica* (1522). Ed. I. Pérez Fernández. Madrid: Punto.

De La Torre, Miguel A. 2003. *La Lucha for Cuba: Religion and Politics on the Streets of Miami*. Berkeley: University of California Press.

——. 2004. *Santería: The Beliefs and Rituals of a Growing Religion in America*. Grand Rapids, MI: Wm B. Eerdmans.

Del Castillo, Adelaida R. 1977. "Malintzin Tenepal: A Preliminary Look into a New Perspective." In *Essays on La Mujer*. Ed. R. Sánchez and R. Martínez Cruz. Los Angeles: Chicano Studies Center Publications, University of California. 2–27.

Delgado, Celeste Fraser and José Esteban Muñoz, eds. 1997. *Everynight Life: Culture and Dance in Latin/o America*. Durham, NC and London: Duke University Press.

Delgado, Richard, ed. 1995. *Critical Race Theory: The Cutting Edge*. Philadelphia, PA: Temple University Press.

Delgado, Richard and Jean Stefancic, eds. 1997. *Critical White Studies: Looking Behind the Mirror*. Philadelphia, PA: Temple University Press.

——. eds. 1998. *The Latino/a Condition: A Critical Reader*. New York: New York University Press.

——. 2001. *Critical Race Theory: An Introduction*. New York and London: New York University Press.

Del Sarto, Ana, Alicia Rios, and Abril Trigo, eds. 2004. *The Latin American Cultural Studies Reader*. Durham, NC and London: Duke University Press.

Díaz, Junot. 1996. *Drown*. New York: Riverhead.

Diaz, Rafael M. 1998. *Latino Gay Men and HIV: Culture, Sexuality, and Risk Behavior*. New York and London: Routledge.

Díaz del Castillo, Bernal. 1963. *The Conquest of New Spain*. Trans. J.M. Cohen. New York: Penguin.

Dorfles, Gillo, ed. 1968. *Kitsch: The World of Bad Taste*. New York: Universe.

Dorfman, Ariel and Armand Mattelart. 1971. *Para leer al Pato Donald*. Valparaíso: Ediciones Universitarías de Valparaíso.

——. 1975. *How to Read Donald Duck: Imperialist Ideology in the Disney Comic*. New York: International General.

Dorsey, Margaret E. 2005. "The Best of the Texas *Tornados*, Partners, and ¡*Viva Luckenbach!*" *Latin American Music Review* 26.1: 23–56.

Duany, Jorge. 2002. *The Puerto Rican Nation on the Move: Identities on the Island and in the United States*. Chapel Hill and London: University of North Carolina Press.

Dundes, Alan, ed. 1994. *The Cockfight: A Casebook*. Madison: University of Wisconsin Press.

Dunn, Timothy J. 1996. *The Militarization of the US–Mexico Border, 1978–1992: Low Intensity Conflict Doctrine Comes Home*. Austin: Center of Mexican American Studies, University of Texas at Austin.

Durán West, Alan, ed. 2004. *Latino and Latina Writers*. 2 vols. New York: Charles Scribner's/Thomson Gale.

Durand, Jorge and Douglas S. Massey. 1995. *Miracles on the Border: Retablos of Mexican Migrants to the United States*. Tucson: University of Arizona Press.

Duranti, Alessandro, ed. 2001. *Key Terms in Language and Culture*. Malden, MA and Oxford: Blackwell.

Dussel, Enrique. 1995. *The Invention of the Americas: Eclipse of "the Other" and the Myth of Modernity*. Trans. M.D. Barber. New York: Continuum.

Dzidzienyo, Anani and Suzanne Oboler, eds. 2005. *Neither Enemies Nor Friends: Latinos, Blacks, Afro-Latinos*. New York: Palgrave Macmillan.

Edberg, Mark Cameron. 2004. *El Narcotraficante: Narcocorridos and the Construction of a Cultural Persona on the U.S.–Mexico Border*. Austin: University of Texas Press.

Edgar, Andrew and Peter Sedgwick, eds. 2002. *Cultural Theory: The Key Concepts*. London and New York: Routledge.

Ehlers, Tracy Bachrach. 1991. "Debunking Marianismo: Economic Vulnerability and Survival Strategies among Guatemalan Wives." *Ethnology* 30.1: 1–16.

Ehrenrich, Barbara. 2004. *Global Woman: Nannies, Maids, and Sex Workers in the New Economy*. New York: Owl.

Elam, Jr., Harry J. 1997. *Taking It to the Streets: The Social Protest Theater of Luis Valdez and Amiri Baraka*. Ann Arbor: University of Michigan Press.

Ellis, Robert Richmond. 2000. "Introduction." In *Reading and Writing the Ambiente. Queer Sexualities in Latino, Latin American, and Spanish Culture*. Ed. S. Chávez-Silverman and L. Hernández. Madison: University of Wisconsin Press. 3–18.

Escobar, Edward J. 1999. *Race, Police, and the Making of a Political Identity: Mexican Americans and the Los Angeles Police Department, 1900–1945*. Berkeley: University of California Press.

Esparza, Laura. 2000. "I DisMember the Alamo: A Long Poem for Performance." In *Latinas on Stage*. Ed. A. Arrizón and L. Manzor. Berkeley, CA: Third Woman Press. 70–89.

Espinosa, Gastón, Virgilio Elizondo, and Jesse Miranda. 2005. *Latino Religions and Civic Activism in the United States*. New York and Oxford: Oxford University Press.

Esteves, Sandra María. 1990. *Bluestown Mockingbird Mambo*. Houston, TX: Arte Público.

Evans, Graham and Jeffrey Newnham. 1998. *Penguin Dictionary of International Relations*. London: Penguin.

Fernández, Damián J. 2000. *Cuba and the Politics of Passion*. Austin: University of Texas Press.

Fernández, Ronald, Serafín Méndez Méndez, and Gail Cueto. 1998. *Puerto Rico Past and Present: An Encyclopedia*. Westport, CT and London: Greenwood.

Fernández Retamar, Roberto. 1979. *Calibán y otros ensayos: nuestra américa y el mundo*. Havana: Arte y Literatura.

Flores, Juan. 1993. *Divided Borders: Essays on Puerto Rican Identity*. Houston, TX: Arte Público.

——. 2000. *From Bomba to Hip-Hop: Puerto Rican Culture and Latino Identity*. New York: Columbia University Press. 115–39.

——. 2001. "Life off the Hyphen: Latino Literature and Nuyorican Traditions." In *Mambo Montage: The Latinization of New York*. Ed. A. Laó-Montes and A. Dávila. New York: Columbia University Press. 185–206.

Flores, Richard R. 2002. *Remembering the Alamo: Memory, Modernity, and the Master Symbol*. Austin: University of Texas Press.

Flores, William F. and Rina Benmayor, eds. 1997. *Latino Cultural Citizenship: Claiming Identity, Space, and Rights*. Boston, MA: Beacon.

Fornés, María Irene. 1986. *María Irene Fornés: Plays*. New York: PAJ.

Foster, David William, ed. 1999. *Chicano/Latino Homoerotic Identities*. New York: Garland.

Fought, Carmen. 2002. *Chicano English in Context*. New York: Palgrave Macmillan.

Fox, Claire F. 1999. *The Fence and the River: Culture and Politics at the US–Mexico Border*. Minneapolis: University of Minnesota Press.

Fox, Geoffrey. 1996. *Hispanic Nation: Culture, Politics, and the Construction of Identity*. Tucson: University of Arizona Press.

Fregoso, Rosa Linda, ed. 1989. *The Bronze Screen: Chicana and Chicano Film*. Minneapolis: University of Minnesota Press.

——. 2001. *Lourdes Portillo: "The Devil Never Sleeps" and Other Films*. Austin: University of Texas Press.

——. 2003. *MeXicana Encounters: The Making of Social Identities on the Borderlands*. Berkeley: University of California Press.

Fusco, Coco. 1995. *English is Broken Here: Notes on Cultural Fusion in the Americas*. New York: New.

——. ed. 2001. *The Bodies that Were Not Ours and Other Writings*. London and New York: Routledge.

Fusco, Coco and Nao Bustamante. 2000. "Stuff." In *Out of the Fringe: Contemporary Latina/Latino Theater and Performance*. Ed. C. Svich and M.T. Marrero. New York: Theatre Communications Group. 43–68.

Galarza, Ernesto. 1971. *Barrio Boy: The Story of a Boy's Acculturation*. Notre Dame, IN and London: University of Notre Dame Press.

Galindo, D. Letticia and María Dolores Gonzales, eds. 1999. *Speaking Chicana: Voice, Power, and Identity*. Tucson: University of Arizona Press.

García, Alma M, ed. 1997. *Chicana Feminist Thought: The Basic Historical Writings*. New York: Routledge.

García, Cristina. 1992. *Dreaming in Cuban*. New York: Alfred A. Knopf.

García, Eugene E., Francisco A. Lomelí, and Isidro D. Ortiz, eds. 1984. *Chicano Studies: A Multidisciplinary Approach*. New York: Teachers College.

García, Ignacio M. 1997. *Chicanismo: The Forging of a Militant Ethos among Mexican Americans*. Tucson: University of Arizona Press.

García, Jerry. 2004. "The Measure of a Cock: Mexican Cockfighting, Culture and Masculinity." In *I am Aztlán: The Personal Essay in Chicano Studies*. Ed. Chon A. Noriega. Los Angeles: UCLA Chicano Studies Research Center Press. 109–38.

García, Juan Ramón. 1980. *Operation Wetback: The Mass Deportation of Mexican Undocumented Workers in 1954*. Westport, CT: Greenwood.

García, María Cristina. 1997. *Havana USA: Cuban Exiles and Cuban Americans in South Florida, 1959–1994*. Berkeley: University of California Press.

García, Ramón. 1998. "Against *Rasquache*: Chicano Identity and the Politics of Popular Culture in Los Angeles." *Critica: A Journal of Critical Essays* (Spring): 1–26.

García Canclini, Néstor. 1990. *Culturas híbridas: estrategias para entrar y salir de la modernidad*. Mexico City: Grijalbo.

——. 1993. "The Hybrid." *The Postmodernism Debate in Latin America*. Ed. John Beverley and José Oviedo. *Boundary 2* 20.3 (Fall): 77–92.

——. 1995. *Hybrid Cultures: Strategies for Entering and Leaving Modernity.* Trans. C. Chiappari and S. López. Minneapolis: University of Minnesota Press.

——. 2001. *Consumers and Citizens: Globalization and Multicultural Conflicts.* Trans. George Yúdice. Minneapolis and London: University of Minnesota Press.

——. 2002. *Latinoamericanos buscando lugar en este siglo.* Buenos Aires: Piados.

García Márquez, Gabriel. 1967. *Cien años de soledad.* Buenos Aires: Sudamericana.

Garza-Falcón, Leticia M. 1998. *Gente Decente: A Borderlands Response to the Rhetoric of Dominance.* Austin: University of Texas Press.

Gaspar de Alba, Alicia. 1998. *Chicano Art Inside/Outside the Master's House: Cultural Politics and the Cara Exhibition.* Austin: University of Texas Press.

——. ed. 2002. *Velvet Barrios: Popular Culture and Chicano/a Sexualities.* Basingstoke, England, and New York: Palgrave Macmillan.

Georges, Eugenia. 1990. *The Making of a Transnational Community: Migration, Development and Cultural Change in the Dominican Republic.* New York: Columbia University Press.

Gibson, Charles, ed. 1963. *The Black Legend: Anti-Spanish Attitudes in the Old World and the New.* New York: McGraw Hill.

Gifford, Gloria. 1992. *Mexican Folk Retablos.* Albuquerque: University of New Mexico Press.

Gilb, Dagoberto. 2003. *Gritos: Essays.* New York: Grove.

Giménez, Martha E., Fred A. López, III, and Carlos Muñoz, Jr., eds. 1992. Special ed.: The Politics of Ethnic Construction: Hispanic, Chicano, Latino? *Latin American Perspectives* 19.4.

Glantz, Margo, ed. 2001. *La Malinche, sus padres y sus hijos.* Mexico City: Taurus.

Glasser, Ruth. 1995. *My Music Is My Flag: Puerto Rican Musicians and Their New York Communities.* Berkeley: University of California Press.

Glazer, Nathan and Daniel Patrick Moynihan. 1963. *Beyond the Melting Pot.* Cambridge, MA: MIT.

Gómez-Peña, Guillermo. 1993. *Warrior for Gringostroika: Essays, Performance Texts and Poetry.* Paul, MN: Graywolf.

——. 1996. *The New World Border: Prophecies, Poems and Loqueras for the End of the Century.* San Francisco, CA: City Lights.

——. 2000. *Dangerous Border Crossers: The Artist Talks Back.* New York and London: Routledge.

Gómez-Quiñones, Juan. 1990. *Chicano Politics: Reality and Promise, 1940–1990.* Albuquerque: University of New Mexico Press.

Gonzales, Rodolfo "Corky." 2001. *Message to Aztlán: Selected Writings.* Houston, TX: Arte Público.

Gonzales-Berry, Erlinda and Chuck Tatum, eds. 1996. *Recovering the US Hispanic Literary Heritage, Vol. 2.* Houston, TX: Arte Público.

González, Gilbert G. 2004. *Culture of Empire: American Writers, Mexico, and Mexican Immigrants, 1880–1930.* Austin: University of Texas Press.

González, José Luis. 1989. *El país de cuatro pisos y otros ensayos.* 7a ed. Río Piedras, PR: Huracán.

Gonzalez, Juan. 2000. *Harvest of Empire: A History of Latinos in America.* New York: Penguin.

González, Ray, ed. 1996. *Muy Macho: Latino Men Confront Their Manhood*. New York: Anchor.

González Echevarría, Roberto. 1999. *The Pride of Havana: A History of Cuban Baseball*. Oxford: Oxford University Press.

Gordon, Milton M. 1964. *Assimilation in American Life*. New York: Oxford University Press.

Gramsci, Antonio. 1971. "Notes on Italian History." In *Selections from the Prison Notebooks*. Ed. Q. Hoare and G.N. Smith. New York: International. 44–120.

Grasmuck, Sherri and Patricia Pessar. 1991. *Between Two Islands: Dominican International Migration*. Berkeley: University of California Press.

Greenhill, Kelly M. 2002. "Engineered Migration and the Use of Refugees as Political Weapons: A Case Study of the 1994 Cuban *Balsero* Crisis." *International Migration* 40.4: 39–74.

Grieco, Elizabeth M. and Rachel C. Cassidy. 2001. "Overview of Race and Hispanic Origin: Census 2000 Brief." US Census Bureau, Washington, March: 1–11.

Grosfoguel, Ramón. 2003. *Colonial Subjects: Puerto Ricans in a Global Perspective*. Berkeley: University of California Press.

Grosfoguel, Ramón, Nelson Maldonado-Torres, and José David Saldívar, eds. 2005. *Latin@s in the World-System: Decolonization Struggles in the Twenty-First Century*. Boulder, CO: Paradigm.

Gruesz, Kirsten Silva. 2001. *Ambassadors of Culture: The Transamerican Origins of Latino Writing*. Princeton, NJ: Princeton University Press.

Guarnizo, Luis Eduardo and Michael Peter Smith, eds. 1998. *Transnationalism from Below*. New Brunswick, NJ: Transaction.

Gugelberger, Georg M., ed. 1996. *The Real Thing: Testimonial Discourse and Latin America*. Durham, NC and London: Duke University Press.

Guha, Ranajit. 1988. "Preface." In *Selected Subaltern Studies*. Ed. R. Guha and G.C. Spivak. New York: Oxford University Press. 35–6.

Guillory, John. 1993. *Cultural Capital: The Problem of Literary Canon Formation*. Chicago, IL and London: University of Chicago Press.

Gutiérrez, David G. 1995. *Walls and Mirrors: Mexican Americans, Mexican Immigrants, and the Politics of Ethnicity*. Berkeley: University of California Press.

——. ed. 2004. *The Columbia History of Latinos in the United States since 1960*. New York: Columbia University Press.

Gutiérrez, Laura G. 2006. "Gender Parody, Political Satire, and Postmodern *Rancheras*: Astrid Hadad's *Heavy Nopal*." Unpublished paper.

Gutiérrez, Ramón and Genaro Padilla, eds. 1993. *Recovering the US Hispanic Literary Heritage, Vol. 1*. Houston, TX: Arte Público.

Gutiérrez-Jones, Carl. 1995. *Rethinking the Borderlands: Between Chicano Discourse and Legal Discourse*. Berkeley: University of California Press.

Gutmann, Matthew C. 1996. *The Meanings of Macho: Being a Man in Mexico City*. Los Angeles: University of California Press.

——. ed. 2003. *Changing Men and Masculinities in Latin America*. Durham, NC and London: Duke University Press.

Guzmán, Manuel. 1997. "'Pa' la escuelita con mucho cuida'o y por la orillita': A Journey Through the Contested Terrains of Nation and Sexual Orientation." In *Puerto Rican Jam: Essays on Culture and Politics*. Ed. F. Negrón-Muntaner and R. Grosfoguel. Minneapolis: University of Minnesota Press. 209–28.

Habell-Pallán, Michelle. 2005. *Loca Motion: The Travels of Chicana and Latina Popular Culture*. New York and London: New York University Press.

Habell-Pallán, Michelle and Mary Romero, eds. 2002. *Latino/a Popular Culture*. New York and London: New York University Press.

Hamamoto, Darrell Y. and Rodolfo D. Torres, eds. 1997. *New American Destinies: A Reader in Contemporary Asian and Latino Immigration*. New York and London: Routledge.

Hansen, Todd, ed. 2003. *The Alamo Reader: A Study in History*. Mechanicsburg, PA: Stackpole.

Harrison, Paige M. and Allen J. Beck. 2005. "Bureau of Justice Statistics: Prison and Jail Inmates at Midyear 2004." Washington: US Dept. of Justice, April.

Haslip-Viera, Gabriel, ed. 2001. *The Taino Revival: Critical Perspectives on Puerto Rican Identity and Cultural Politics*. Princeton, NJ: Markus Wiener.

Hayes-Bautista, David E. and Jorge Chapa. 1987. "Latino Terminology: Conceptual Bases for Standard Terminology." *American Journal of Public Health*, 68.1 (January): 61–8.

Henken, Ted. 2005. "*Balseros, Boteros,* and *El Bombo*: Post-1994 Cuban Immigration to the United States and the Persistence of Special Treatment." *Latino Studies* 3.3 (November): 393–416.

Hennessy, Alistair. 1978. *The Frontier in Latin American History*. London: Edward Arnold.

Hernández, Deborah Pacini. 1995. *Bachata: A Social History of a Dominican Popular Music*. Philadelphia, PA: Temple University Press.

Hernández, Deborah Pacini, Héctor Fernández L'Hoeste, and Eric Zolov, eds. 2004. *Rockin' Las Americas: The Global Politics of Rock in Latin/o America*. Pittsburgh, PA: University of Pittsburgh Press.

Hernández-Cruz, Victor. 1976. *Tropicalization*. New York: Reed, Cannon and Johnson.

Hernández-Gutiérrez, Manuel de Jesús. 1994. *El colonialismo interno en la narrativa chicana: El barrio, el anti-barrio y el exterior*. Tempe, AZ: Bilingual P/Editorial Bilingüe.

Herrera-Sobek, María. 1979. *The Bracero Program: Elitelore versus Folklore*. Los Angeles: University of California Press.

——. ed. 1985. *Beyond Stereotypes: The Critical Analysis of Chicana Literature*. Binghamton, NY: Bilingual Press/Editorial Bilingüe.

——. 1990. *The Mexican Corrido: A Feminist Analysis*. Bloomington: Indiana University Press.

Herrera-Sobek, María and Helena María Viramontes, eds. 1996. *Chicana Creativity and Criticism: New Frontiers in American Literature*. 2nd edn. Albuquerque: University of New Mexico Press.

Herrera-Sobek, María and Virginia Sánchez Korrol, eds. 1998. *Recovering the US Hispanic Literary Heritage, Vol. 3*. Houston, TX: Arte Público.

Heyck, Denis Lynn Daly, ed. 1994. *Barrios and Borderlands: Cultures of Latinos and Latinas in the United States*. New York and London: Routledge.

Hijuelos, Oscar. 1983. *Our House in the Last World*. New York: Persea.

——. 1989. *The Mambo Kings Play Songs of Love*. New York: Farrar, Straus and Giroux.

——. 1999. *Empress of the Splendid Season*. New York: Harper Flamingo.

Hillgarth, J.N. 2000. *The Mirror of Spain, 1500–1700: The Formation of a Myth*. Ann Arbor: University of Michigan Press.

Hinojosa, Rolando. 1981. *Querido Rafa*. Houston, TX: Arte Público.

Holden, Robert H. and Eric Zolov, eds. 2000. *Latin America and the United States: A Documentary History*. New York and London: Oxford University Press.

Hondagneu-Sotelo, Pierrette. 2001. *Doméstica: Immigrant Workers Cleaning and Caring in the Shadows of Affluence*. Berkeley: University of California Press.

hooks, bell. 1992. *Black Looks: Race and Representation*. Boston, MA: South End.

Horno-Delgado, Asunción, Eliana Ortega, Nina M. Scott, and Nancy Saporta Sternbach, eds. 1989. *Breaking Boundaries: Latina Writing and Critical Readings*. Amherst: University of Massachusetts Press.

Huerta, Jorge A. 2000. *Chicano Drama: Performance, Society and Myth*. Cambridge: Cambridge University Press.

Hulme, Peter. 1992. *Colonial Encounters: Europe and the Native Caribbean, 1492–1797*. London and New York: Routledge.

Iorio Sandín, Lyn Di. 2004. *Killing Spanish: Literary Essays on Ambivalent US Latino/a Identity*. New York: Palgrave Macmillan.

Itzigsohn, José, Carlos Dore Cabral, Esther Hernández Medina, and Obed Vázquez. 1999. "Mapping Dominican Transnationalism: Narrow and Broad Transnational Practices." *Ethnic and Racial Studies* 22.2 (March): 316–38.

Jameson, Fredric. 1986. "On Magic Realism in Film." *Critical Inquiry* 12.2: 301–25.

Jeffreys, Sheila. 1999. "Globalizing Sexual Exploitation: Sex Tourism and the Traffic in Women." *Leisure Studies* 18.3 (July): 179–86.

Jiménez, Alfredo, ed. 1994. *Handbook of Hispanic Cultures in the United States: History*. Houston, TX: Arte Público.

Johnson, Allan G. 2000. *The Blackwell Dictionary of Sociology*. 2nd edn. Malden, MA: Blackwell.

Joseph, Gilbert M., Catherine C. Legrand, and Ricardo D. Salvatore, eds. 1998. *Close Encounters of Empire: Writing the Cultural History of US–Latin American Relations*. Durham, NC: Duke University Press.

Juderías y Loyot, Julián. 1974 [1914]. *La leyenda negra: Estudios acerca del concepto de España en el extranjero*. Madrid: Editora Nacional.

Kafka, Phillipa. 2000. *"Saddling La Gringa": Gatekeeping in Literature by Contemporary Latina Writers*. Westport, CT: Greenwood.

Kaminsky, Amy. 1999. *After Exile: Writing the Latin American Diaspora*. Minneapolis: University of Minnesota Press.

Kanellos, Nicolás, ed. 1984. *Hispanic Theater in the United States*. Houston, TX: Arte Público.

——. 1990. *History of Hispanic Theatre in the United States: Origins to 1940*. Austin: University of Texas Press.

——. ed. 1996. *The Hispanic Literary Companion*. Detroit, MI: Visible Ink.

Kaplan, Amy. 1993. " 'Left Alone With America': The Absence of Empire in the Study of American Culture." In *Cultures of United States Imperialism*. Ed. A. Kaplan and D.E. Pease. Durham, NC: Duke University Press. 3–21.

——. 2002. *The Anarchy of Empire in the Making of US Culture*. Cambridge, MA, and London: Harvard University Press.

Kaplan, Amy and Donald E. Pease, eds. 1993. *Cultures of United States Imperialism*. Durham, NC: Duke University Press.

Kay, Cristóbal. 1989. *Latin American Theories of Development and Underdevelopment*. London and New York: Routledge.

Kivisto, Peter. 2001. "Theorizing Transnational Immigration: A Critical Review of Current Efforts." *Ethnic and Racial Studies* 24.4 (July): 549–77.

Klor de Alva, J. Jorge. 1997. "The Invention of Ethnic Origins and the Negotiation of Latino Identity, 1969–1981." In *Challenging Fronteras: Structuring Latina and Latino Lives in the US An Anthology of Readings*. Ed. M. Romero, P. Hondagneu-Sotelo, and V. Ortiz. New York: Routledge. 55–79.

——. 1998 [1989]. "Aztlán, Borinquen, and Hispanic Nationalism in the United States." In *The Latino Studies Reader: Culture, Economy, and Society*. Ed. A. Darder and R.D. Torres. Malden, MA: Blackwell. 63–82.

Lancaster, Roger N. 1992. *Life Is Hard: Machismo, Danger and the Intimacy of Power in Nicaragua*. Los Angeles: University of California Press.

Lao-Montes, Agustín and Arlene Dávila, eds. 2001. *Mambo Montage: The Latinization of New York*. New York: Columbia University Press.

Larsen, Neil. 1990. *Modernism and Hegemony: A Materialist Critique of Aesthetic Agencies*. Minneapolis: University of Minnesota Press.

Larzelere, Alex. 1988. *The 1980 Cuban Boatlift*. Washington, DC: National Defense University Press.

LatCrit: Latinas/os and the Law, A Joint Symposium. 1997/1998. Special joint issue of the *California Law Review* 85.5 (October 1997), and *La Raza Law Journal* 10.1 (1998).

Latina Feminist Group. 2001. *Telling to Live: Latina Feminist Testimonios*. Durham, NC and London: Duke University Press.

Latin American Subaltern Studies Group. 1993. "Founding Statement." In *The Postmodernism Debate in Latin America*. Ed. John Beverley and José Oviedo. *Boundary 2* 20.3: 110–21.

Laviera, Tato. 1985. *AmeRícan*. Houston, TX: Arte Público.

Lazo, Rodrigo. 2005. *Writing to Cuba: Filibustering and Cuban Exiles in the United States*. Chapel Hill, NC and London: University of North Carolina Press.

León-Portilla, Miguel. 1962. *The Broken Spears: The Aztec Account of the Conquest of Mexico*. Boston, MA: Beacon.

Levi, Heather. 2001. "Masked Media: The Adventures of *Lucha Libre* on the Small Screen." In *Fragments of a Golden Age: The Politics of Culture in Mexico Since*

1940. Ed. G.M. Joseph, A. Rubenstein, and E. Zolov. Durham, NC and London: Duke University Press. 330–72.

Lewis, Oscar. 1959. *Five Families: Mexican Case Studies in the Culture of Poverty.* New York: Basic.

——. 1964. "The Culture of Poverty." In *Explosive Forces in Latin America.* Ed. J.J. TePaske and S.N. Fischer. Columbus: Ohio State University Press. 149–73.

——. 1965. *La Vida: A Puerto Rican Family in the Culture of Poverty—San Juan and New York.* New York: Random House.

Leymarie, Isabelle. 2002. *Cuban Fire: The Story of Salsa and Latin Jazz.* Boston, MA: Continuum Publishing.

Limón, José E. 1992. *Mexican Ballads, Chicano Poems: History and Influence in Mexican-American Social Poetry.* Berkeley: University of California Press.

——. 1994. *Dancing with the Devil: Society and Cultural Poetics in Mexican American South Texas.* Madison: University of Wisconsin Press.

——. 1998. *American Encounters: Greater Mexico, the United States, and the Erotics of Culture.* Boston, MA: Beacon.

Lomas Garza, Carmen. 1987. *Lo real maravilloso: The Marvelous, the Real.* San Francisco, CA: Mexican Museum.

Lomelí, Francisco A., ed. 1993. *Handbook of Hispanic Cultures in the United States: Literature and Art.* Houston, TX: Arte Público.

Lomelí, Francisco A. and Donaldo W. Urioste. 1976. *Chicano Perspectives in Literature: A Critical and Annotated Bibliography.* Albuquerque, NM: Pajarito.

Lomnitz, Claudio. 2005. *Death and the Idea of Mexico.* New York: Zone.

López, Ana M. 1996. "Greater Cuba." In *The Ethnic Eye: Latino Media Arts.* Ed. C. Noriega and A. López. Minneapolis: University of Minnesota Press. 38–58.

López, Ian F. Haney. 2003. *Racism on Trial: The Chicano Fight for Justice.* Cambridge, MA and London: Belknap.

Luis, William. 1997. *Dance Between Two Cultures: Latino Caribbean Literature Written in the United States.* Nashville, TN: Vanderbilt University Press.

Maciel, David R. and María Herrera-Sobek, eds and intro. 1998. *Culture Across Borders: Mexican Immigration and Popular Culture.* Tucson: University of Arizona Press.

Maciel, David R., Isidro D. Ortiz, and María Herrera-Sobek, eds. 2000. *Chicano Renaissance: Contemporary Cultural Trends.* Tucson: University of Arizona Press.

Magaña, Lisa. 2003. *Straddling the Border: Immigration Policy and the INS.* Austin: University of Texas Press.

Maldonado, A.W. 1997. *Teodoro Moscoso and Puerto Rico's Operation Bootstrap.* Gainesville: University Press of Florida.

Mallon, Florencia. 1994. "The Promise and Dilemma of Subaltern Studies: Perspectives from Latin American History." *American Historical Review* 99.5 (December): 1491–515.

Maltby, William S. 1971. *The Black Legend in England: The Development of Anti-Spanish Sentiment, 1558–1660.* Durham, NC: Duke University Press.

Mañach, Jorge. 1940. *Indignación del choteo*. 2a edn. Havana: La Verónica.

Manzor-Coats, Liliana. 1994. "Introduction." In *Latin American Writers on Gay and Lesbian Themes: A Bio-Critical Sourcebook*. Ed. D.W. Foster. Westport, CT: Greenwood. xv–xxxvi.

Mariscal, George. 2005. *Brown-Eyed Children of the Sun: Lessons from the Chicano Movement, 1965–1975*. Albuquerque: University of New Mexico Press.

Marqués, René. 1966. "El puertorriqueño dócil (Literatura y realidad psicológica)." *Ensayos 1953–1966*. Barcelona: Antillana. 147–209.

Márquez, Antonio. 1989. "Literatura Chicanesca: The View From Without." In *Dictionary of Literary Biography. Vol. 82. Chicano Writers: First Series*. Ed. F. Lomelí and C.R. Shirley. Detroit, MI: Gale. 309–15.

Martí, José. 1997. *Versos sencillos/Simple Verses*. Trans. M.A. Tellechea. Houston, TX: Arte Público.

——. 1999. *José Martí Reader: Writings on the Americas*. Ed. D. Shnookal and M. Muñiz. Melbourne: Ocean.

Martínez, Elizabeth. 1998. *De Colores Means All of Us: Latina Views for a Multi-Colored Century*. Albuquerque, NM: West End.

Martínez, Manuel Luis. 2003. *Countering the Counterculture: Rereading Postwar American Dissent from Jack Kerouac to Tomás Rivera*. Madison: University of Wisconsin Press.

Massey, Douglas S. and Nancy A. Denton. 1993. *American Apartheid: Segregation and the Making of the Underclass*. Cambridge, MA: Harvard University Press.

Masud-Piloto, Felix R. 1995. *From Welcomed Exiles to Illegal Immigrants: Cuban Migration to the US, 1959–1995*. Oxford: Rowman & Littlefield.

Matos-Rodríguez, Félix V. and Pedro Juan Hernández. 2001. *Pioneros: Puerto Ricans in New York City, 1896–1948*. Charleston, SC: Arcadia.

Mayer, Vicki. 2003. *Producing Dreams, Consuming Youth: Mexican Americans and Mass Media*. New Brunswick, NJ: Rutgers University Press.

Mazón, Mauricio. 1984. *The Zoot-Suit Riots: The Psychology of Symbolic Annihilation*. Austin: University of Texas Press.

McCloud, Scott. 1993. *Understanding Comics: The Invisible Art*. Northampton, MA: Kitchen Sink.

McCracken, Ellen. 1999. *New Latina Narrative: The Feminine Space of Postmodern Ethnicity*. Tucson: University of Arizona Press.

McKenna, Teresa. 1997. *Migrant Song: Politics and Process in Contemporary Chicano Literature*. Austin: University of Texas Press.

Meier, Matt S. and Margo Gutiérrez, eds. 2000. *Encyclopedia of the Mexican American Civil Rights Movement*. Westport, CT: Greenwood.

Melendez, Miguel "Mickey." 2003. *We Took the Streets: Fighting for Latino Rights with the Young Lords*. New York: St Martin's.

Menchú, Rigoberta. 1982. *Me llamo Rigoberta Menchú y así me nació la conciencia*. Barcelona: Seix Barral.

Mesa-Bains, Amalia. 2003. "Domesticana: The Sensibility of Chicana Rasquachismo." In *Chicana Feminisms: A Critical Reader*. Ed. G.F. Arredondo, A. Hurtado, N. Klahn,

O. Nájera-Ramírez, and P. Zavella. Durham, NC and London: Duke University Press. 298–315.

Michaelsen, Scott and David E. Johnson, eds. 1997. *Border Theory: The Limits of Cultural Politics*. Minneapolis: University of Minnesota Press.

Mignolo, Walter D. 1995. *The Darker Side of the Renaissance: Literacy, Territoriality, and Colonization*. Ann Arbor: University of Michigan Press.

——. 2000. *Local Histories/Global Designs: Coloniality, Subaltern Knowledges, and Border Thinking*. Princeton, NJ: Princeton University Press.

——. 2005. *The Idea of Latin America*. Malden, MA: Blackwell.

Miller, Tom, ed. 2003. *Writing on the Edge: A Borderlands Reader*. Tucson: University of Arizona Press.

Milner, Andrew and Jeff Browitt. 2002. *Contemporary Cultural Theory*. 3rd edn. London and New York: Routledge.

Milner, Clyde A. II, Carol A O'Connor, and Martha A. Sandweiss. 1994. *The Oxford History of the American West*. New York and Oxford: Oxford University Press.

Mirandé, Alfredo. 1997. *Hombres y Machos: Masculinity and Latino Culture*. Boulder, CO: Westview.

Mohr, Eugene V. 1982. *The Nuyorican Experience: Literature of the Puerto Rican Minority*. Westport, CT: Greenwood.

Montague, Trevor. 2004. *A to Z of Sport: The Compendium of Sporting Knowledge*. London: Little, Brown.

Montejano, David. 1987. *Anglos and Mexicans in the Making of Texas, 1836–1986*. Austin: University of Texas Press.

Mora, Pat. 1993. *Nepantla: Essays from the Land in the Middle*. Albuquerque: University of New Mexico Press.

Moraga, Cherríe. 1983. *Loving in the War Years: Lo que nunca pasó por sus labios*. Boston, MA: South End.

——. 1993. *The Last Generation: Prose and Poetry*. Boston, MA: South End.

——. 2000. "Mexican Medea: La Llorona Retold." In *Latinas on Stage*. Ed. A. Arrizón and L. Manzor. Berkeley, CA: Third Woman. 158–61.

Moraga, Cherríe and Gloria Anzaldúa, eds. 1983. *This Bridge Called My Back: Writings by Radical Women of Color*. 2nd edn. New York: Kitchen Table/Women of Color.

Morales, Alejandro. 1988. *The Brick People*. Houston, TX: Arte Público.

Morales, Ed. 2002. *Living in Spanglish: The Search for Latino Identity in America*. New York: St Martin's.

Morales, Iris. 1998. "¡Palante, Siempre Palante!" In *The Puerto Rican Movement: Voices from the Diaspora*. Ed. A. Torres and José E. Velázquez. Philadelphia, PA: Temple University Press. 210–27.

Moreiras, Alberto. 2001. *The Exhaustion of Difference: The Politics of Latin American Cultural Studies*. Durham, NC and London: Duke University Press.

Morejón, Nancy. 1982. *Nación y mestizaje en Nicolás Guillén*. Havana: Rodríguez Feo.

——. 1988. *Fundación de la imagen*. Havana: Letras Cubanas.

Muñoz Jr., Carlos. 1989. *Youth, Identity, Power: The Chicano Movement*. New York and London: Verso.

Muñoz, José Esteban. 1995. "No es fácil: Notes on the Negotiation of Cubanidad and Exilic Memory in Carmelita Tropicana's *Milk of Amnesia*." *Drama Review* 39.3: 76–82.

——. 1999. *Disidentifications: Queers of Color and the Performance of Politics*. Minneapolis: University of Minnesota Press.

Murray, Yxta Maya. 1999. *What it Takes to Get to Vegas*. New York: Grove.

Nájera-Ramírez, Olga. 2002. "*Haciendo patria*: The *charreada* and the Formation of a Mexican Transnational Community." In *Transnational Latina/o Communities: Politics, Processes, and Cultures*. Ed. C.G. Vélez-Ibáñez and A. Sampaio. Lanham, MD: Rowman & Littlefield. 167–80.

Negrón-Muntaner, Frances. 1997. "English Only Jamás but Spanish Only Cuidado: Language and Nationalism in Contemporary Puerto Rico." In *Puerto-Rican Jam: Essays on Culture and Politics*. Ed. F. Negrón-Muntaner and R. Grosfoguel. Minneapolis: University of Minnesota Press. 257–85.

——. 2004. *Boricua Pop: Puerto Ricans and American Culture from West Side Story to Jennifer Lopez*. New York: New York University Press.

Negrón-Muntaner, Frances and Ramón Grosfoguel, eds. 1997. *Puerto-Rican Jam: Essays on Culture and Politics*. Minneapolis: University of Minnesota Press.

Nelson, Candace and Marta Tienda. 1997. "The Structuring of Hispanic Ethnicity: Historical and Contemporary Perspectives." In *Challenging Fronteras: Structuring Latina and Latino Lives in the US An Anthology of Readings*. Ed. M. Romero, P. Hondagneu-Sotelo, and V. Ortiz. New York: Routledge. 7–29.

Nelson, Jennifer. 2003. *Women of Color and the Reproductive Rights Movement*. New York: New York University Press.

Nevin, Jeff. 2002. *Virtuoso Mariachi*. Lanham, MD: University Press of America.

Nevins, Joseph. 2002. *Operation Gatekeeper: The Rise of the "Illegal Alien" and the Making of the US–Mexico Boundary*. New York and London: Routledge.

Niggli, Josephine. 1938. *Mexican Folk Plays*. Chapel Hill, NC: University of California Press.

Noriega, Chon, ed. 1992. *Chicanos and Film: Representation and Resistance*. Minneapolis: University of Minnesota Press.

——. 1993. "*El hilo latino*: Representation, Identity and National Culture," *Jump Cut* 38: 45–50.

——. 2000. *Shot in America: Television, the State, and the Rise of Chicano Cinema*. Minneapolis: University of Minnesota Press.

Noriega, Chon A., Eric A. Avila, Karen Mary Davalos, Chela Sandoval, and Rafael Pérez-Torres., eds. 2001. *The Chicano Studies Reader: An Anthology of Aztlán, 1970–2000*. Los Angeles, CA: UCLA Chicano Studies Research Center.

Noriega, Chon A. and Wendy L. Belcher, eds. 2004. *I Am Aztlán: The Personal Essay in Chicano Studies*. Los Angeles, CA: UCLA Chicano Studies Research Center.

Noriega, Chon A. and Ana M. López, eds. 1996. *The Ethnic Eye: Latino Media Arts*. Minneapolis: University of Minnesota Press.

Oboler, Suzanne. 1995. *Ethnic Labels, Latino Lives: Identity and the Politics of (Re)Presentation in the United States*. Minneapolis: University of Minnesota Press.

——. 1999. "Anecdotes of Citizens' Dishonor in the Age of Cultural Racism: Toward a (Trans)national Approach to Latino Studies." *Discourse* 21.3: 19–41.

Oboler, Suzanne and Deena J. González, eds. 2005. *The Oxford Encyclopedia of Latinos and Latinas in the United States*. 4 vol. New York and Oxford: Oxford University Press.

Obregón Pagán, Eduardo. 2003. *Murder at the Sleepy Lagoon: Zoot Suits, Race, and Riot in Wartime LA*. Chapel Hill and London: University of North Carolina Press.

O'Gorman, Edmundo. 1984. *La invención de America: Investigación acerca de la estructura histórica del Nuevo Mundo y del sentido de su devenir*. 3rd edn. Mexico City: Fondo de Cultura Económica.

Olalquiaga, Celeste. 1992. *Megalopolis: Contemporary Cultural Sensibilities*. Minneapolis: University of Minnesota Press.

——. 2002. *The Artificial Kingdom: On the Kitsch Experience*. Minneapolis: University of Minnesota Press.

Omi, Michael and Howard Winant. 1994. *Racial Formations in the United States: From the 1960s to the 1990s*. 2nd edn. New York and London: Routledge.

Orme, William A., Jr., 1996. *Understanding NAFTA: Mexico, Free Trade, and the New North America*. Austin: University of Texas Press.

Oropeza, Lorena. 2005. *¡Raza Si! ¡Guerra No!: Chicano Protest and Patriotism during the Vietnam War Era*. Berkeley: University of California Press.

Orovio, Helio. 2004. *Cuban Music from A to Z*. Durham, NC and London: Duke University Press.

Ortega, Eliana. 1989. "Poetic Discourse of the Puerto Rican Woman in the US: New Voices of Anacaonian Liberation." In *Breaking Boundaries: Latina Writing and Critical Readings*. Ed. A. Horno-Delgado, E. Ortega, N.M. Scott, and N. Saporta Sternbach. Amherst: University of Massachusetts Press. 122–35.

Ortiz, Fernando. 1924. *Glosario de Afronegrismo*. Havana: El Siglo XX.

——. 1940a. *Contrapunteo Cubano del tabaco y azúcar*. Havana: J. Montero.

——. 1940b. "Los factores humanos de la cubanidad." *Revista Bimestre Cubana* 45.2: 161–86.

——. 1995. *Cuban Counterpoint: Tobacco and Sugar*. Trans. H. de Onís. Durham, NC: Duke University Press.

Ortíz-González, Victor M. 2004. *El Paso: Local Frontiers at a Global Crossroads*. Minneapolis: University of Minnesota Press.

O'Sullivan, John. 1839. "The Great Nation of Futurity." *United States Democratic Review* 6.23: 426–30.

——. 1845. "Annexation." *United States Democratic Review* 17.1: 5–10.

Pacini Hernandez, Deborah. 1995. *Bachata: A Social History of a Dominican Popular Music*. Philadelphia, PA: Temple University Press.

Padilla, Felix. 1985. *Latino Ethnic Consciousness: The Case of Mexican Americans and Puerto Ricans in Chicago*. Notre Dame, IN: University of Notre Dame Press.

Padilla, Genaro M. 1993. *My History, Not Yours: The Formation of Mexican American Autobiography*. Madison: University of Wisconsin Press.

Paredes Américo, ed. 1970. *The Folktales of Mexico*. Chicago, IL: University of Chicago Press.

Paredes, Américo. 1976. *A Texas Mexican Cancionero: Folksongs of the Lower Border*. Urbana: University of Illinois Press.

——. 1979. "The Folk Base of Chicano Literature." In *Modern Chicano Writers: A Collection of Critical Essays*. Ed. J. Sommers and T. Ybarra-Frausto. Englewood Cliffs, NJ: Prentice-Hall. 4–17.

——. 1986 [1958]. *"With His Pistol in His Hand": A Border Ballad and Its Hero*. Austin: University of Texas Press.

——. 1993a. *Folklore and Culture on the Texas–Mexican Border*. Austin: University of Texas Press.

——. 1993b. *Uncle Remus con chile*. Houston, TX: Arte Público.

Paredes, Américo and Richard Bauman, eds. 1972. *Toward New Perspectives in Folklore*. Austin: University of Texas Press.

Paredes, Américo and Raymund Paredes, eds. 1972. *Mexican American Authors*. Boston: Houghton Mifflin.

Parsons, Jack, Carmela, Pardilla, and Juan Estevan Arellano. 1999. *Low 'n Slow: Lowriding in New Mexico*. Santa Fe, NM: Museum of New Mexico.

Paz, Octavio. 1999. *El laberinto de la soledad. Postdata. Vuelta a El laberinto de la soledad*. 3rd edn. Mexico City: Fondo de Cultura Económica.

Pease, Donald A. and Robyn Wiegman, eds. 2002. *The Futures of American Studies*. Durham, NC and London: Duke University Press.

Pedreira, Antonio S. 1992 [1934]. *Insularismo: Ensayos de interpretación puertorriqueña*. Río Piedras, PR: Edil.

Peña, Devon G. 1997. *The Terror of the Machine: Technology, Work, Gender, and Ecology on the US–Mexico Border*. Austin: University of Texas Press.

Peña, Manuel. 1985. *The Texas–Mexican Conjunto: History of a Working-Class Music*. Austin: University of Texas Press.

——. 1992–1996. *"Música fronteriza*/Border Music." *Aztlán: A Journal of Chicano Studies* 21.1–2: 191–225.

——. 1999a. *The Mexican American Orquesta: Music, Culture, and the Dialectic of Conflict*. Austin: University of Texas Press.

——. 1999b. *Música Tejana: The Cultural Economy of Artistic Transformation*. College Station: Texas A&M University Press.

Perera, Juan F., ed. 1997a. *Immigrants Out!: The New Nativism and the Anti-Immigrant Impulse in the United States*. New York: New York University Press.

——. 1997b. "The Black/White Binary Paradigm of Race: The 'Normal Science' of American Racial Thought." *California Law Review* 85.5: 1213–58.

Pérez, Emma. 1991. "Sexuality and Discourse: Notes from a Chicana Survivor." In *Chicana Lesbians: The Girls Our Mothers Warned Us About*. Ed. C. Trujillo. Berkeley, CA: Third Woman. 159–84.

Pérez, Emma. 1994. "Irigaray's Female Symbolic in the Making of Chicana Lesbian *Sitios y Lenguas (Sites and Discourses)*." In *The Lesbian Postmodern*. Ed. L. Doan. New York: Columbia University Press. 104–17.

——. 1999. *The Decolonial Imaginary: Writing Chicanas into History*. Bloomington and Indianapolis: Indiana University Press.

Pérez Jr., Louis A. 1998. *The War of 1898: The US and Cuba in History and Historiography*. Chapel Hill: University of North Carolina Press.

——. 1999. *On Becoming Cuban: Identity, Nationality, and Culture*. Chapel Hill: University of North Carolina Press.

Pérez, Ramón "Tianguis." 1991. *Diary of an Undocumented Immigrant*. Trans. D.J. Reavis. Houston, TX: Arte Público.

Pérez Firmat, Gustavo. 1989. *The Cuban Condition: Translation and Identity in Modern Cuban Literature*. Cambridge: Cambridge University Press.

——. 1994. *Life on the Hyphen: The Cuban-American Way*. Austin: University of Texas Press.

——. 2003. *Tongue Ties: Logo-Eroticism in Anglo-Hispanic Literature*. New York: Palgrave Macmillan.

Pérez-Reverte, Arturo. 2002. *La reina del sur*. Madrid: Alfaguara.

Pérez-Torres, Rafael. 1995a. "Chicano Culture Reclaiming Our America: Coyotes at the Border." *American Literature* 67: 815–24.

——. 1995b. *Movements in Chicano Poetry: Against Myths, Against Margins*. Cambridge: Cambridge University Press.

——. 2006. *Mestizaje: Critical Uses of Race in Chicano Culture*. Minneapolis and London: University of Minnesota Press.

Pessar, Patricia R. 1995. *A Visa for a Dream: Dominicans in the United States*. Boston, MA: Allyn & Bacon.

——. 1997. *Caribbean Circuits: New Directions in the Study of Caribbean Migration*. New York: Center for Migration Studies.

Phillips, Susan A. 1999. *Wallbangin': Graffiti and Gangs in LA*. Chicago IL, and London: University of Chicago Press.

Piñero, Miguel. 1974. *Short Eyes*. New York: Hill & Wang.

Plan Espiritual de Aztlán, El. 1989. In *Aztlán: Essays on the Chicano Homeland*. Ed. R.A. Anaya and F.A. Lomelí. Albuquerque, NM: Academia/El Norte. 1–5.

Plascencia, Luis F.B. 1983. "Low Riding in the Southwest: Cultural Symbols in the Mexican Community." In *History, Culture and Society: Chicano Studies in the 1980s*. Ed. M.T. García et al. Ypsilanti, MI: Bilingual Review. 141–75.

Poblete, Juan, ed. and intro. 2003. *Critical Latin American and Latino Studies*. Minneapolis: University of Minnesota Press.

Poole, Stafford. 1995. *Our Lady of Guadalupe: The Origins and Sources of a Mexican National Symbol, 1531–1797*. Tucson: University of Arizona Press.

Portes, Alejandro, Luis E. Guarnizo, and Patricia Landolt. 1999. "The Study of Transnationalism: Pitfalls and Promise of an Emergent Research Field." *Ethnic and Racial Studies* 22.2 (March): 217–37.

Portillo Trambley, Estela. 1983. *Sor Juana and Other Plays*. Ypsilanti, MI: Bilingual Press/Editorial Bilingüe.

Powell, Philip Wayne. 1971. *Tree of Hate: Propaganda and Prejudices Affecting United States Relations with the Hispanic World*. New York: Basic.

Poyo, Gerald E. 1989. *With All, and For the Good of All: The Emergence of Popular Nationalism in the Cuban Communities of the United States, 1848–1898*. Durham, NC and London: Duke University Press.

Pratt, Mary Louise. 1992. *Imperial Eyes: Travel Writing and Transculturation*. London and New York: Routledge.

Prieur, Annick. 1998. *Mama's House, Mexico City: On Transvestites, Queens and Machos*. Chicago, IL and London: Chicago University Press.

Quiñonez, Sam. 2001. *True Tales from Another Mexico: The Lynch Mob, the Popsicle Kings, Chalino, and the Bronx*. Albuquerque: University of New Mexico Press.

Quintana, Alvina E., ed. 2003. *Reading US Latina Writers: Remapping American Literature*. New York: Palgrave Macmillan.

Quintera Rivera, Angel. 1987. *Music, Social Classes, and the National Question in Puerto Rico*. Rio Piedras, PR: University of Puerto Rico.

——. 1998. *Salsa, sabor y control: Sociología de la música tropical*. Mexico City: Siglo Veintiuno.

Quiroga, José. 2000. *Tropics of Desire: Queer Interventions in Latino America*. New York: New York University Press.

——. 2005. *Cuban Palimpsests*. Minneapolis and London: University of Minnesota Press.

Rafael Sánchez, Luis. 1987. "The Flying Bus." In *Images and Identities: The Puerto Rican in Two World Contexts*. Ed. A. Rodríguez de Laguna. New Brunswick, NJ: Transaction. 17–25.

——. 1994. *La guagua aérea*. Rio Piedras, PR: Cultural.

Rama, Angel. 1982. *Transculturación narrativa en América Latina*. 2nd edn. Mexico City: Siglo Veintiuno.

——. 1996. *The Lettered City*. Trans. J.C. Chasteen. Durham, NC: Duke University Press.

——. 1997. "Processes of Transculturation in Latin American Narrative." Trans. M. Moore. *Journal of Latin American Cultural Studies* 6.2: 155–71.

Ramírez, Catherine S. 2002. "Crimes of Fashion: The Pachuca and Chicana Style Politics." *Meridians* 2.2 (Spring): 1–35.

Ramírez, Elizabeth C. 2000. *Chicanas/Latinas in American Theatre: A History of Performance*. Bloomington and Indianapolis: Indiana University Press.

Ramírez, Rafael L. 1999. *What It Means to Be a Man: Reflections on Puerto Rican Masculinity*. Trans. R.E. Casper. New Brunswick, NJ: Rutgers University Press.

Ramírez Berg, Charles. 2002. *Latino Images in Film: Stereotypes, Subversion, and Resistance*. Austin: University of Texas Press.

Ramos-García, Luis A., ed. 2002. *The State of Latino Theater in the US: Hybridity, Transculturation, and Identity*. New York and London: Routledge.

Rebolledo, Tey Diana. 1995. *Women Singing in the Snow: A Cultural Analysis of Chicana Literature*. Tucson: University of Arizona Press.

Rebolledo, Tey Diana. 1996. "The Politics of Poetics: Or, What am I, a Critic, Doing in this Text Anyhow?" In *Chicana Creativity and Criticism: New Frontiers in American Literature*. Ed. M. Herrera-Sobek and H.M. Viramontes. 2nd edn. Albuquerque: University of New Mexico Press. 203–12.

——. 2005. *The Chronicles of Panchita Villa and Other Guerrilleras: Essays on Chicana/Latinoa Literature and Criticism*. Austin: University of Texas Press.

Rechy, John. 1963. *City of Night*. New York: Grove.

——. 1977. *The Sexual Outlaw: A Documentary. A Non-Fiction Account with Commentary, of Three Days and Nights in the Sexual Underground*. New York: Grove.

——. 1991. *The Miraculous Day of Amalia Gómez*. New York: Arcade.

Reesman, Jeanne Campbell, ed. 2001. *Trickster Lives: Culture and Myth in American Fiction*. Athens, GA, and London: University of Georgia Press.

Regalado, Samuel O. 1988. *Viva Baseball!: Latin Major Leaguers and Their Special Hunger*. Urbana: University of Illinois Press.

Rendón, Armando B. 1971. *Chicano Manifesto: The History and Aspirations of the Second Largest Minority in America*. New York: Macmillan.

Reyes, David and Tom Waldman. 1998. *Land of a Thousand Dances: Chicano Rock 'n' Roll from Southern California*. Albuquerque: University of New Mexico Press.

Richardson, Chad. 1999. *Batos, Bollillos, Pochos, and Pelados: Class and Culture on the South Texas Border*. Austin: University of Texas Press.

Ricourt, Milagros and Ruby Danta. 2003. *Hispanas de Queens: Latino Panethnicity in a New York City Neighborhood*. Ithaca, NY and London: Cornell University Press.

Ridway, Jan. 1998. "What's in a Name?" In *Close Encounters of Empire: Writing the Cultural History of US–Latin American Relations*. Ed. G.M. Joseph, C.C. Legrand, and R.D. Salvatore. Durham, NC and London: Duke University Press. 45–75.

Rius. 1965. *Cuba para principiantes*. Mexico City: Grijalbo.

——. 1973. *The Chicanos*. Berkeley, CA: NACLA.

——. 1976. *Marx para principiantes*. Mexico City: Grijalbo.

Rivas-Rodríguez, Maggie, ed. 2005. *Mexican Americans and World War II*. Austin: University of Texas Press.

Rivera, Raquel Z. 2003. *New York Ricans from the Hip Hop Zone*. New York: Palgrave Macmillan.

Rivera, Tomás. 1971. *... y no se lo tragó la tierra/And the Earth Did Not Devour Him*. Berkeley, CA: Quinto Sol.

Rivero, Eliana. 1989. "From Immigrants to Ethnics: Cuban Women Writers in the US" In *Breaking Boundaries: Latina Writing and Critical Readings*. Ed. A. Horno-Delgado, E. Ortega, N.M. Scott, and N. Saporta Sternbach. Amherst: University of Massachusetts Press. 189–200.

Roberts, John Storm. 1999. *The Latin Tinge: The Impact of Latin American Music on the United States*. 2nd edn. Oxford: Oxford University Press.

Robertson, Roland. 1992. *Globalization: Social Theory and Global Culture*. London: Sage.

Rodgers, Dennis. 1999. "Youth Gangs and Violence in Latin America and the Caribbean: A Literature Survey." LCR Sustainable Development Working Paper No. 4, Urban Peace Program Series. Washington, DC: World Bank.

Rodó, José Enrique. 1988 [1900]. *Ariel*. Trans. M. Sayers Peden. Austin: University of Texas Press.

Rodriguez, Jr., Abraham. 1993. *Spidertown*. New York: Hyperion.

Rodríguez, Clara E., ed. 1997. *Latin Looks: Images of Latinas and Latinos in the US Media*. Boulder, CO: Westview.

——. 2000. *Changing Race: Latinos, the Census, and the History of Ethnicity in the United States*. New York: New York University Press.

——. 2004. *Heroes, Lovers and Others: The Story of Latinos in Hollywood*. Washington, DC: Smithsonian.

Rodríguez, Gregory. 2002. "Boxing and Masculinity: The History and (Her)story of Oscar de la Hoya." In *Latino/a Popular Culture*. Ed. M. Habell-Pallán and M. Romero. New York and London: New York University Press. 252–68.

Rodríguez, Ileana, ed. 2001. *The Latin American Subaltern Studies Reader*. Durham, NC and London: Duke University Press.

Rodríguez, Jeanette. 1994. *Our Lady of Guadalupe: Faith and Empowerment among Mexican American Women*. Austin: University of Texas Press.

Rodríguez, Juana María. 2003. *Queer Latinidad: Identity Practices, Discursive Spaces*. New York and London: New York University Press.

Rodriguez, Luis. 1993. *Always Running. La Vida Loca: Gang Days in LA*. Willimantic, CT: Curbstone.

Rodríguez, Ralph E. 2005. *Brown Gumshoes: Detective Fiction and the Search for Chicano/a Identity*. Austin: University of Texas Press.

Rodriguez, Richard. 1983. *Hunger of Memory: The Education of Richard Rodriguez, An Autobiography*. New York: Bantam.

——. 2002. *Brown: The Last Discovery of America*. New York: Viking.

Rodríguez de Laguna, Asela, ed. 1987. *Images and Identities: The Puerto Rican in Two World Contexts*. New Brunswick, NJ: Transaction.

Román, David. 1997. "Tropical Fruit." In *Tropicalizations: Transcultural Representations of Latinidad*. Ed. F. Aparicio and S. Chávez-Silverman. Hanover, NH: University Press of New England. 119–35.

——. 1998. *Acts of Intervention: Performance, Gay Culture, and AIDS*. Bloomington: Indiana University Press.

——. 2005. *Performance in America: Contemporary US Culture and the Performing Arts*. Durham, NC and London: Duke University Press.

Román, David and Alberto Sandoval. 1995. "Caught in the Web: Latinidad, AIDS, and Allegory in *Kiss of the Spider Woman*, the Musical." *American Literature* 67: 553–85.

Romero, Mary. 2002. *Maid in the USA: 10th Anniversary Edition*. New York and London: Routledge.

Romero, Mary, Pierette Hondagneu-Sotelo, and Vilma Ortiz, eds. 1997. *Challenging Fronteras: Structuring Latina and Latino Lives in the US An Anthology of Readings*. New York: Routledge.

Rosaldo, Renato. 1989. *Culture and Truth: The Remaking of Social Analysis*. New York: Beacon.

Rosaldo, Renato. 1997. "Cultural Citizenship, Inequality, and Multiculturalism." In *Latino Cultural Citizenship: Claiming Identity, Space, and Rights*. Ed. W. Flores and R. Benmayor. Boston, MA: Beacon. 27–38.

Rosales, F. Arturo. 1996. *Chicano! The History of the Mexican American Civil Rights Movement*. Houston, TX: Arte Público.

——. 1999. *Pobre Raza! Violence, Justice, and Mobilization among México Lindo Immigrants, 1900–1936*. Austin: University of Texas Press.

——. 2000. *Testimonio: A Documentary History of the Mexican American Struggle for Civil Rights*. Houston, TX: Arte Público.

Rosen, Martin D. and James Fisher. 2001. "Chicano Park and the Chicano Park Murals: Barrio Logan, City of San Diego, California." *Public Historian* 23.4 (Fall): 91–111.

Rouse, Irving. 1992. *The Tainos: Rise and Decline of the People Who Greeted Columbus*. New Haven, CT and London: Yale University Press.

Rowe, John Carlos, ed. 2000. *Post-Nationalist American Studies*. Berkeley: University of California Press.

——. 2002. *The New American Studies*. Minneapolis and London: University of Minnesota Press.

Rowe, William and Vivian Schelling. 1991. *Memory and Modernity: Popular Culture in Latin America*. London: Verso.

Ruck, Bob. 1999. *The Tropic of Baseball: Baseball in the Dominican Republic*. Lincoln, NE, and London: University of Nebraska Press, Bison.

Rumbaut, Rubén G. 1991. "The Agony of Exile: A Study of the Migration and Adaptation of Indochinese Refugee Adults and Children." In *Refugee Children: Theory, Research, and Services*. Ed. F.L. Ahearn and J.L. Athey. Baltimore, MD: Johns Hopkins University Press. 53–91.

Said, Edward. 1978. *Orientalism*. London: Routledge & Kegan Paul.

Salas, Elizabeth. 1990. *Soldaderas in the Mexican Military: Myth and History*. Austin: University of Texas Press.

Salas, Floyd. 1967. *Tattoo the Wicked Cross*. New York: Grove.

——. 1992. *Buffalo Nickel: A Memoir*. Houston, TX: Arte Público.

Salazar, Max. 2002. *Mambo Kingdom: Latin Music in New York*. New York: Omnibus.

Saldívar, José David. 1991. *The Dialectics of Our America: Genealogy, Cultural Critique, and Literary Theory*. Durham, NC: Duke University Press.

——. 1997. *Border Matters: Remapping American Cultural Studies*. Berkeley: University of California Press.

Saldívar, Ramón. 1990. *Chicano Narrative: The Dialectics of Difference*. Madison: University of Wisconsin Press.

——. 2006. *The Borderlands of Culture: Américo Paredes and the Transnational Imaginary*. Durham, NC and London: Duke University Press.

Saldívar-Hull, Sonia. 2000. *Feminism on the Border: Chicana Gender Politics and Literature*. Berkeley: University of California Press.

Samora, Julian. 1971. *Los Mojados: The Wetback Story*. Notre Dame, NC: University of Notre Dame Press.

Samora, Julian, Joe Bernal, and Albert Peña. 1979. *Gunpowder Justice: A Reassessment of the Texas Rangers*. Notre Dame, IN: University of Notre Dame Press.

Sánchez, David. 1978. *Expedition through Aztlán*. La Puente, CA: Perspective.

Sánchez, George J. 1993. *Becoming Mexican American: Ethnicity, Culture and Identity in Chicano Los Angeles, 1900–1945*. New York and Oxford: Oxford University Press.

Sánchez, Marta E. 2005. *"Shakin' Up" Race and Gender: Intercultural Connections in Puerto Rican, African American, and Chicano Narratives and Culture (1965–1995)*. Austin: University of Texas Press.

Sánchez, Rosaura. 1995. *Telling Identities: The California Testimonios*. Minneapolis and London: University of Minnesota Press.

Sánchez, Thomas. 1991. *Zoot-Suit Murders*. New York: Vintage.

Sánchez González, Lisa. 2001. *Boricua Literature: A Literary History of the Puerto Rican Diaspora*. New York and London: New York University Press.

Sánchez Korrol, Virginia E. 1994. *From Colonia to Community: The History of Puerto Ricans in New York City*. Berkeley: University of California Press.

Sánchez-Tranquilino, Marcos and John Tagg. 1992. "The Pachuco's Flayed Hide: Mobility, Identity, and *Buenas Garras*." In *Cultural Studies*. Ed. L. Grossberg, C. Nelson, and P. Treichler. New York: Routledge. 556–70.

Sandoval, Chela. 1991. "US Third World Feminism: The Theory and Method of Oppositional Consciousness in the Postmodern World." *Genders* 10 (Spring): 1–23.

——. 2000. *Methodology of the Oppressed*. Minneapolis: University of Minnesota Press.

Sandoval, Moises. 1991. *A History of the Hispanic Church in the United States*. Maryknoll, NY: Orbis.

Sandoval-Sánchez, Alberto. 1997. "Puerto Rican Identity Up in the Air: Air Migration, Its Cultural Representations, and Me 'Cruzando el Charco.' " In *Puerto-Rican Jam: Essays on Culture and Politics*. Ed. F. Negrón-Muntaner and R. Grosfoguel. Minneapolis: University of Minnesota Press. 189–208.

——. 1999. *José, Can You See?: Latinos on and off Broadway*. Madison: University of Wisconsin Press.

——. 2005. "Politicizing Abjection: In the Manner of a Prologue for the Articulation of AIDS Latino Queer Identities." *American Literary History* 17.3 (Fall): 542–9.

Sandoval-Sánchez, Alberto and Nancy Saporta Sternbach, eds. 1999. *Puro Teatro: A Latina Anthology*. Tucson: University of Arizona Press.

——. 2001. *Stages of Life: Transcultural Performance and Identity in US Latina Theater*. Tucson: University of Arizona Press.

Sands, Kathleen Mullen. 1993. *Charrería Mexicana: An Equestrian Folk Tradition*. Tucson and London: University of Arizona Press.

San Miguel, Jr., Guadalupe. 2002. *Tejano Proud: Tex-Mex Music in the Twentieth Century*. College Station: Texas A&M University Press.

Santa Ana, Otto. 2002. *Brown Tide Rising: Metaphors of Latinos in Contemporary American Public Discourse*. Austin: University of Texas Press.

Santiago, Danny. 1983. *Famous All Over Town*. New York: Plume.

Santiago, Esmeralda. 1993. *When I Was Puerto Rican*. New York: Random House.

——. 1996. *América's Dream*. New York: HarperCollins.

Santos-Febres, Mayra. 2000. *Sirena Selena vestida de pena*. Barcelona: Mondadori.

Shakespeare, William. 1968. *The Tempest*. Harmondsworth: Penguin.

Sheehy, Daniel. 2005. *Mariachi Music in America: Experiencing Music, Expressing Culture*. New York: Oxford University Press.

Shinn, Christopher A. 2002. "Fútbol Nation: US Latinos and the Goal of a Homeland." In *Latino/a Popular Culture*. Ed. M. Habell-Pallán and M. Romero. New York and London: New York University Press. 240–51.

Simonett, Helena. 2001. *Banda: Mexican Musical Life across Border*. Middletown, CT: Wesleyan University Press.

Sinclair, John. 1999. *Latin American Television: A Global View*. Oxford: Oxford University Press.

Slatta, Richard W. 1990. *Cowboys of the Americas*. New Haven, CT and London: Yale University Press.

Smith, Marian L. 1998. "Overview of INS History." In *A Historical Guide to the US Government*. Ed. G.T. Kurian. New York: Oxford University Press. 305–8.

Sommers, Joseph and Tomás Ybarra-Frausto, eds. 1979. *Modern Chicano Writers: A Collection of Critical Essays*. Englewood Cliffs, NJ: Prentice-Hall.

Sontag, Susan. 1994. "Notes on 'Camp.'" *Against Interpretation*. London: Vintage. 275–92.

Soto, Pedro Juan. 1974. *Spiks*. 4th edn. Rio Piedras, PR: Cultural.

Spitta, Silvia. 1995. *Between Two Waters: Narratives of Transculturation in Latin America*. Houston, TX: Rice University Press.

——. 1997. "De lo có(s)mico: José Vasconcelos en México y Aztlán." In *Formaciones sociales e identidades culturales en la literatyra hispanoamericana. Ensayos en honor de Juan Armando Epple*. Ed. R.S. Benavides. Valdivia, Chile: Barba de Palo. 194–201.

Spivak, Gayatri Chakravorty. 1988. "Can the Subaltern Speak?" In *Marxism and the Interpretation of Culture*. Ed. C. Nelson and L. Grossberg. London: Macmillan. 271–313.

Stavans, Ilan. 1994. *The Hispanic Condition: Reflections on Culture and Identity in America*. New York: Harper.

——. 2000. *Latino USA: A Cartoon History*. New York: Basic Books.

——. 2003. *Spanglish: The Making of a New American Language*. New York: Rayo.

Steele, Thomas J. 1994. *Santos and Saints: The Religious Folk Art of Hispanic New Mexico*. Santa Fe, NM: Ancient City.

Steinberg, Stephen, ed. 1999. *Race and Ethnicity in the United States: Issues and Debates*. Malden, MA and Oxford: Blackwell.

Stephens, Thomas M. 1989. *Dictionary of Latin American Racial and Ethnic Terminology*. Gainesville: University of Florida Press.

Stevens, Evelyn P. 1973a. "Machismo and Marianismo." *Society* 10: 57–63.

——. 1973b. "Marianismo: The Other Face of Machismo in Latin America." In *Female and Male in Latin America: Essays*. Ed. A. Pescatello. Pittsburgh, PA: University of Pittsburgh Press. 89–101.

Stone, Michael C. 1990. "Bajito y suavecito: Low Riding and the Class of Class." *Studies in Latin American Popular Culture* 9: 85–126.

Suárez-Orozco, Marcelo M. 2000. "Everything You Ever Wanted to Know about Assimilation but Were Afraid to Ask." *Daedalus* 129.4 (Fall): 1–30.

Suárez-Orozco, Marcelo M. and Mariela M. Páez, eds. 2002. *Latinos: Remaking America*. Berkeley: University of California Press.

Suro, Roberto. 1998. *Strangers among Us: How Latino Immigration Is Transforming America*. New York: Knopf.

Svich, Caridad and María Teresa Marrero, eds. 2000. *Out of the Fringe: Contemporary Latina/Latino Theater and Performance*. New York: Theatre Communications Group.

Taco Shop Poets and Stephanie de la Torre, eds. 2000. *Chorizo Tonguefire*: *The Taco Shop Poets Anthology*. Intro. G. Lipsitz. San Diego, CA: Chorizo Tonguefire.

Tatum, Charles M. 2001. *Chicano Popular Culture: que hable el pueblo*. Tucson: University of Arizona Press.

Taylor, Diana. 2003. *The Archive and the Repertoire: Performing Cultural Memory in the Americas*. Durham, NC and London: Duke University Press.

Taylor, Diana and Juan Villegas, eds. 1994. *Negotiating Performance: Gender, Sexuality, and Theatricality in Latin/o America*. Durham, NC and London: Duke University Press.

Thomas, Hugh. 1997. *The Slave Trade: The History of the Atlantic Slave Trade, 1440–1870*. New York: Simon & Schuster.

Thomas, Piri. 1967. *Down These Mean Streets*. New York: Knopf.

Thompson, Peter. 2000. *Cassell's Dictionary of American History*. London: Cassell.

Tomlinson, John. 1991. *Cultural Imperialism*. Baltimore, MD: Johns Hopkins University Press.

Torres, Andrés and José E. Velázquez, eds. 1998. *The Puerto Rican Movement: Voices from the Diaspora*. Philadelphia, PA: Temple University Press.

Torres, Edén E. 2003. *Chicana without Apology: The New Chicana Cultural Studies*. New York: Routledge.

Torres, Edwin. 1975. *Carlito's Way*. New York: Dutton.

Torres, Lourdes and Inmaculada Pertusa, eds. 2003. *Tortilleras: Hispanic and US Latina Lesbian Expression*. Philadelphia, PA: Temple University Press.

Torres, Rodolfo D. and George Katsiaficas, eds. 1999. *Latino Social Movements: Historical and Theoretical Perspectives*. New York: Routledge.

Triay, Victor Andres. 1998. *Fleeing Castro: Operation Pedro Pan and the Cuban Children's Program*. Gainesville: University Press of Florida.

Troyano, Alina. 2000. "Chicas 2000." *I, Carmelita Tropicana: Performing Between Cultures*. Boston, MA: Beacon. 72–122.

Truett, Samuel and Elliott Young, eds. 2004. *Continental Crossroads: Remapping US–Mexico Borderlands History*. Durham, NC and London: Duke University Press.

Trujillo, Carla, ed. 1997. *Living Chicana Theory*. Berkeley, CA: Third Woman.

Turner, Frederick Jackson. 1994. *Rereading Frederick Jackson Turner: "The Significance of the Frontier in American History" and Other Essays*. New York: Holt.

Tweed, Thomas A. 1997. *Our Lady of the Exile: Diasporic Religion at a Cuban Catholic Shrine in Miami*. Oxford: Oxford University Press.

Urciuoli, Bonnie. 1996. *Exposing Prejudice: Puerto Rican Experiences of Language, Race, and Class*. Boulder, CO: Westview.

Vaca, Nicolás C. 2004. *The Presumed Alliance: The Unspoken Conflict between Latinos and Blacks and What It Means for America*. New York: Rayo.

Valdes, Francisco. 1997. "Foreword: Under Construction—LatCrit Consciousness, Community, and Theory." *California Law Review* 85.5: 1087–142.

Valdez, Luis. 1971. *Actos*. Fresno, CA: Cucaracha Press.

——. 1990. *Early Works*. Houston, TX: Arte Público Press.

——. 1992. *Zoot Suit and Other Plays*. Houston, TX: Arte Público Press.

Valdivia, Angharad N. 2000. *A Latina in the Land of Hollywood and Other Essays on Media Culture*. Tucson: University of Arizona Press.

Valis, Noel. 2002. *Culture of Cursilería: Bad Taste, Kitsch, and Class in Modern Spain*. Durham, NC and London: Duke University Press.

Valle, Victor M. and Rodolfo D. Torres. 2000. *Latino Metropolis*. Minneapolis: University of Minnesota Press.

Vasconcelos, José. 1997. *The Cosmic Race/La raza cósmica: A Bilingual Edition*. Trans. D.T. Jaén. Baltimore, MD: Johns Hopkins University Press.

Vázquez, Francisco H. and Rodolfo D. Torres, eds. 2002. *Latino/a Thought: Culture, Politics and Society*. Lanham, MD: Rowman & Littlefield.

Vega, Bernardo. 1994. *Memorias de Bernardo Vega: Contribución a la historia de la comunidad puertorriqueña en Nueva York*. 5th edn. Rio Piedras, PR: Huracán.

Vélez-Ibáñez, Carlos G. 1996. *Border Visions: Mexican Cultures of the Southwest United States*. Tucson: University of Arizona Press.

Vélez-Ibáñez, Carlos G. and Anna Sampaio, eds. 2002. *Transnational Latina/o Communities: Politics, Processes, and Cultures*. Lanham, MD: Rowman & Littlefield.

Vigil, James Diego. 1988. *Barrio Gangs: Street Life and Identity in Southern California*. Austin: University of Texas Press.

——. 2002. *A Rainbow of Gangs: Street Cultures in the Mega-City*. Austin: University of Texas Press.

Vila, Pablo. 2000. *Crossing Borders: Social Categories, Metaphors, and Narrative Identities on the US–Mexico Frontier*. Austin: University of Texas Press.

——. 2005. *Border Identifications: Narratives of Religion, Gender, and Class on the US–Mexico Border*. Austin: University of Texas Press.

Villa, Raúl Homero. 2000. *Barrio Logos: Space and Place in Urban Chicano Literature and Culture*. Austin: University of Texas Press.

Villareal, José Antonio. 1970. *Pocho*. New York: Anchor Books.

Villaseñor, Victor. 1973. *Macho!* New York: Bantam.

Wald, Elijah. 2001. *Narcocorrido: A Journey into the Music of Drugs, Guns, and Guerrillas*. New York: Rayo.

Walker, Janet, ed. 2001. *Westerns: Films through History*. New York and London: Routledge.

Waxer, Lisa, ed. 2002. *Situating Salsa: Global Markets and Local Meaning in Latin Popular Culture*. New York and London: Routledge.

Weaver, Thomas, ed. 1994. *Handbook of Hispanic Cultures in the United States: Anthropology.* Houston, TX: Arte Público.

Webb, Walter Prescott. 1931. *The Great Plains.* New York: Ginn.

——. 1935. *The Texas Rangers.* Cambridge, MA: Houghton Mifflin.

Weber, David J. and Jane M. Rausch, eds. 1994. *Where Cultures Meet: Frontiers in Latin American History.* Wilmington, DE: Scholarly Resources.

Werbner, Pnina and Tariq Modood, eds. 1997. *Debating Cultural Hybridity: Multi-Cultural Identities and the Politics of Anti-Racism.* London: Zed.

Whalen, Carmen Teresa and Víctor Vázquez-Hernández, eds. 2005. *The Puerto Rican Diaspora: Historical Perspectives.* Philadelphia, PA: Temple University Press.

Williams, Gareth. 2002. *The Other Side of the Popular: Neoliberalism and Subalternity in Latin America.* Durham, NC and London: Duke University Press.

Williams, Raymond. 1988. *Keywords: A Vocabulary of Culture and Society.* London: Fontana.

Wilson, Colwick M. and Leon C. Wilson. 2000. "Domestic Work in the United States of America: Past Perspectives and Future Directions." *African-American Research Perspectives* 6.1 (Winter): 1–8.

Xóchitl, Bada. 2003. "Mexican Hometown Associations." *Citizen Action in the Americas* 5 (March): http://americas.irc-online.org/citizen-action/series/05-hta_body.html.

Yarbro-Bejarano, Yvonne. 2001. *The Wounded Heart: Writing on Cherríe Moraga.* Austin: University of Texas Press.

Ybarra-Frausto, Tomás. 1991. "Rasquachismo: An Aesthetic Sensibility." In *Chicano Art, Resistance and Affirmation: An Interpretative Exhibition of the Chicano Art Movement, 1965–1985.* Ed. R. Griswold de Castillo, T. McKenna, and Y. Yarbro-Bejerano. Los Angeles, CA: Wright Art Gallery, UCLA. 155–62.

——. 1992. "Interview." In *On Edge: The Crisis of Contemporary Latin American Culture.* Ed. G. Yúdice, J. Franco, and J. Flores. Minneapolis: University of Minnesota Press. 207–15.

Young, Robert C. 1995. *Colonial Desire: Hybridity in Theory, Culture and Race.* London: Routledge.

Yúdice, George. 2003. *The Expediency of Culture: Uses of Culture in the Global Era.* Durham, NC and London: Duke University Press.

Zamora, Lois Parkinson and Wendy B. Faris, eds. 1995. *Magical Realism: Theory, History, Community.* Durham, NC: Duke University Press.

Zangwill, Israel. 1933 [1909]. *The Melting Pot.* New York: Macmillan.

Zimmerman, Marc. 1992. *US Latino Literature: An Essay and Annotated Bibliography.* Chicago, IL: March/Abrazo.

34243820R00166

Made in the USA
Middletown, DE
24 January 2019